G-5857

# TEACHING
# BAND & ORCHESTRA
## methods and materials

## LYNN G. COOPER

**GIA Publications, Inc.**
**Chicago**

ISBN: 1-57999-275-7

Copyright © 2004 GIA Publications, Inc.,
7404 S. Mason Ave., Chicago, IL 60638.
www.giamusic.com

Manufactured in United States of America.

# Table of Contents

# Introduction

College music educators are well aware that it is impossible to prepare students for every situation they may encounter as a teacher. Typically, methods course teachers compile lists of the skills, understandings, and knowledge we consider essential for new teachers—and then we consider the reality of the semester schedule and decide what must be left out. Those are difficult decisions. We just hope we cover enough information and give enough reference materials to enable our college students to begin their teaching career with success.

I have included a great deal of material in this book that I believe is essential for all instrumental music teachers. My decisions about what to include (and what to leave out) were based on extensive research, 19 years experience as an instrumental music educator in the public schools, and almost that many years as a college teacher of instrumental music education methods courses. Part of the preparation for this book came from my dissertation research, which included lengthy questionnaires to school music teachers and college methods teachers designed to identify the topics they believe are essential (and those that are unessential) for the college instrumental music methods course. The contents of this book include that broad spectrum of tools and information necessary for instrumental music education majors to be successful in the schools. This information is valuable as both a text for study in methods courses and as an accessible reference throughout the teaching career.

# Acknowledgements

As with any large project, this book is the result of the input and effort of many people. First, I want to thank the thousands of students who have helped me become a better teacher. Thanks are also due to Asbury College for providing the sabbatical leave that allowed me to complete much of the research for this book.

I am indebted to a number of friends who served as content readers for this book: Michael Kaufman (Director of Bands at Grand Ledge High School in Grand Ledge, Michigan); Jack Walker (retired band director in the Laurel County Schools in London, Kentucky); Nan Moore (Director of Bands at Male High School in Louisville, Kentucky); Glen Flanigan (Jazz Ensemble Director at Asbury College, Wilmore, Kentucky); Dr. Susan Creasap (Assistant Director of Bands at Morehead State University in Morehead, Kentucky); Dr. Larry Blocher (Assistant Director of Bands and Director of Music Education at Wichita State University in Wichita, Kansas); Prof. John Whitwell (Director Bands at Michigan State University in East Lansing, Michigan); Dr. Peter LaRue (Director Bands at Georgetown College in Georgetown, Kentucky); and James Curnow (Composer-in-Residence at Asbury College in Wilmore, Kentucky). I especially acknowledge two great friends who read every word of the manuscript and gave insightful, honest, and knowledgeable comments: Kenneth L. Bowman (retired Director of Bands at Lincoln High School in Ypsilanti, Michigan) and Russell Reed (retired Orchestra Conductor at Eastern Michigan University in Ypsilanti, Michigan). This book greatly benefited from the comments and suggestions of all these readers.

I want to thank my gifted and patient wife, Rosie, for her insightful editing of the manuscript—it improved the book immeasurably and made it decidedly more readable. And I note my appreciation to Denise Wheatley and Justyn Harkin at GIA Publications, Inc., for their excellent editing, and to my friend Dr. Darrel Walters (Temple University), who did the final editing of the manuscript.

I would like to publicly thank Mr. Alan Townsend—my high school band director—for modeling all the attributes desirable in a school band director. I also want to thank Mr. Harold Goodsman—who was the very best administrator I ever worked with during my teaching career.

I thank my parents—James Robert and Anita Cooper—for their gifts of love and unfailing encouragement through the years. And, finally, I thank my family (my wife, Rosie; son, Matt; daughter, Julie; son-in-law, Rob; and grandsons, Wesley and Josiah) for their love and for their continuing support and encouragement of my work.

*Soli Deo Gloria!*

# TEACHING
# BAND
# &
# ORCHESTRA

# *Part I:*
# The Beginning Program

Chapter One

# LAYING THE FOUNDATION

## Roles and Goals

Systematic instrumental music instruction in the public schools is uniquely American. The excellent work of many fine teachers in prior years has led to broad public support for beginning instrumental music classes in elementary and middle schools. This public trust deserves to be answered by dedicated and skillful teaching.

To guide your decision-making and curriculum building, you will do well to adopt a list of goals for the beginning instrumental music program, which then can be developed into a philosophy of instrumental music education. Goals and philosophy are important, particularly for the beginning program because of its foundational nature. What you do at the beginning level affects your instrumental music program for the next six or more years as those students move through the schools. More important, the beginning class experience will help determine whether instrumental music will become a lifetime activity for your students. This foundational work is not only a matter of teaching correct embouchures, hand positions, posture, etc., but also a matter of transmitting to the students a love, respect, and appreciation for music; and, indeed, for all the arts. This is a trust and responsibility that should not be taken lightly. As an instrumental music educator, you will be responsible for consciously planning to teach—and model—exceptional skills and attitudes in the beginning instrumental class.

Emil Holz and Roger Jacobi (1966) wrote *Teaching Band Instruments to Beginners*, one of the finest books written on this topic. Their goal

*The true test of a good leader is that they aren't needed.*

for music instruction still serves us well today: "The goal of music instruction in the public school is to provide for every child an opportunity to learn to love and to understand music" (p. 22). The writing of a broad philosophical goal (such as this example), or a more specific statement of skill or attitude goals, will help the teacher develop a comprehensive philosophy of instrumental music education. Holz and Jacobi also provide a useful example of a statement of philosophy:

> Music has become an integral part of the life of the American child—in school, at home, and in the community. Great philosophers and educators of all time have recognized its importance in education, but most eras and most parts of the world have made it available only to children from families of favorable economic status. It remained for the American public to demand music for all children. Out of this demand has come increasing attention to the study of music as a fundamental part of the school curriculum. The primary purpose of all music education is the development of a love and appreciation of music.
>
> Music can contribute to the physical, intellectual, social, and spiritual growth of the child. Through varied experiences such as singing, rhythmic movement, creative activities, listening, and playing on instruments, each child can discover and develop his own ability and interest in music. The pleasure of making music not only affords a means of self-expression, but it also helps the child adjust more effectively to the society in which he lives. Our basic philosophy is that such opportunity should be provided for every child in our school system. Music is a universal language, and it is the fervent hope of this school system that all children will understand, enjoy, and use this language. (p. 16)

*Learning about yourself is a spiritual experience*

This fine example from Holz and Jacobi provides direction for the development of a personal philosophy statement. Another worthy example of a philosophy and goals statement comes from the Michigan School Band and Orchestra Association:

> The fine arts are a vital part of the educational process. In a civilization stressing scientific achievement, material wealth and specialization, the fine arts contribute greatly

toward the maintenance of a proper cultural balance. As one of the areas of the fine arts, instrumental music has as its primary purpose, the improvement of the quality of life of the individual. This is accomplished by helping students acquire the skills of musical communication, thereby providing yet another means of sharing ideas with others. For many students, music is the most feasible and enjoyable means of communication available to them. As an expressive art, instrumental music requires growth in physical, intellectual, emotional and aesthetic areas. The integration of the various fine arts is necessary for a comprehensive arts education.

The primary goal of a comprehensive music education is to lead the student to a life style of musical independence. The initial objective of the school instrumental music program is to provide worthwhile experiences to all children who demonstrate aptitude and interest. Achieving ability with an instrument should be the result of a positive beginning process. The product would be an individual capable of becoming a knowledgeable consumer of music.

From *Instrumental Music for Michigan Schools* (1980)

Recent publications by the Music Educators National Conference (MENC) concerning the National Standards in music will stimulate additional reflection about goals and philosophy. Several of these publications are listed at the end of this chapter, but *National Standards for Arts Education—What Every Young American Should Know and Be Able to Do in the Arts* will be particularly helpful.

It is important to develop goals and objectives for yourself and your students. Decisions, large and small, need to be made every day in the classroom. A statement of goals and objectives, which serves as a kind of "reference point" in your teaching, helps ensure that those daily decisions will be made based on reasoned and thoughtful educational positions. Goals and objectives give you standards by which to measure your success and the success of your students.

**Goals** usually refer to long-term, general, or "big picture" items or ideas, with **objectives** being the short-term or more specific items that support or accomplish goals. There are many ways to state goals and objectives. Some will be very brief and concise, while others are more complex and thorough. Figure 1-1 is an example of a goal and objectives statement for a beginning instrumental music class.

*Figure 1-1. Rhythm Goal and Objectives*

**Goal:**
By the end of the first year of study, students will play rhythmic notation that includes sixteenth notes and simple rhythmic combinations involving subdivisions of the whole note, as measured by an objective-referenced test.

**Objectives:**
1. To accomplish the Rhythm Goal, apply this instructional sequence.
Play rhythmic notations that include the following patterns collectively:
   a. Whole, half, and quarter notes, and rests of the same value, in base-4 meters
   b. Dotted half notes in base-4 meters
   c. Eighth notes in base-4 and cut-time meters
   d. Dotted quarter notes in base-4 meters; dotted-half notes in cut time
   d. Three subdivisions on a single beat
   e. All the above rhythm units that are appropriate in base-8 meters
   f. All the above and sixteenth notes in base-4 and base-8 meters

2. Students should be able to define and describe the function of each meter signature in terms of number of beats per measure and the type of note that gets each beat.

Another type of goal and objective statement is found in Figure 1-2.

*Figure 1-2. 5th Grade Minimum Goals and Objectives*

By the end of the school year, students should:
1. Play with proper regard for characteristic tone quality, pitch, tempo, phrasing, and articulation.
2. Demonstrate correct assembly of instruments; correct instrument, body, and hand positions; and the appropriate maintenance procedures for their instrument.

3. Perform simple melodies individually and in unison; two- and three-part songs, and simple harmony in small groups or the full class.

4. Have a range of approximately one to one and one-half octaves, including enharmonic tones, depending on the instrument.

5. Be able to play the following rhythms: whole notes; half notes; quarter notes; eighth notes; dotted half notes; the equivalent rests; and various combinations of those notes and rest values listed.

6. Be able to verbalize an understanding of the following: clef signs; time or meter signatures of 2/4, 3/4, and 4/4; all forms of repeat signs; and basic dynamic and tempo change indications ( *f*, *p*, ritard, crescendo, diminuendo).

7. Be able to play in the following key signatures: concert F, Bb, Eb, Ab, C, and G and their relative minor scales.

The National Standards for Music Education, developed by the Music Educators National Conference (MENC), list "content standards" applicable for all grade levels and then "achievement standards" to specify desired competencies for PreK-grade 4, grades 5-8, and grades 9-12. The nine content and achievement standards developed by MENC for grades 5-8 (Figure 1-3) are found in the *National Standards for Arts Education* (pp. 42-45). These nine standards are a useful guide in developing your own objectives or standards, and in developing the curriculum for your students.

**Fig. 1-3. MENC National Standards, grades 5-8**

1. **Content Standard**: Singing, alone and with others, a varied repertoire of music
**Achievement Standard:**
Students
a. Sing accurately and with good breath control throughout their singing ranges, alone and in small and large ensembles
b. Sing with expression and technical accuracy a repertoire of vocal literature with a level of difficulty of 2, on a

scale of 1 to 6, including some songs performed from memory

c. Sing music representing diverse genres and cultures, with expression appropriate for the work being performed

d. Sing music written in two and three parts

Students who participate in a choral ensemble

e. Sing with expression and technical accuracy a varied repertoire of vocal literature with a level of difficulty of 3, on a scale of 1 to 6, including some songs performed from memory

2. **Content Standard**: Performing on instruments, alone and with others, a varied repertoire of music
   **Achievement Standard:**
   Students

   a. Perform on at least one instrument accurately and independently, alone and in small and large ensembles, with good posture, good playing position, and good breath, bow, or stick control

   b. Perform with expression and technical accuracy on at least one string, wind, percussion, or classroom instrument a repertoire of instrumental literature with a level of difficulty of 2, on a scale of 1 to 6

   c. Perform music representing diverse genres and cultures, with expression appropriate for the work being performed

   d. Play by ear simple melodies on a melodic instrument and simple accompaniments on a harmonic instrument

   Student who participate in an instrumental ensemble or class

   e. Perform with expression and technical accuracy a varied repertoire of instrumental literature with a level of difficulty of 3, on a scale of 1 to 6, including some solos performed from memory

3. **Content Standard**: Improvising melodies, variations, and accompaniments
   **Achievement Standard:**
   Students

a. Improvise simple harmonic accompaniments

b. Improvise melodic embellishments and simple rhythmic and melodic variations on given pentatonic melodies and melodies in major keys

c. Improvise short melodies, unaccompanied and over given rhythmic accompaniments, each in a consistent style, meter, and tonality

4. **Content Standard**: Composing and arranging music within specified guidelines
**Achievement Standard:**
Students

a. Compose short pieces with specified guidelines, demonstrating how the elements of music are used to achieve unity and variety, tension and release, and balance

b. Arrange simple pieces for voices or instruments other than those for which the pieces are written

c. Use a variety of traditional and nontraditional sound sources and electronic media when composing and arranging

5. **Content Standard**: Reading and notating music
**Achievement Standard:**
Students

a. Read whole, half, quarter, and eighth, sixteenth, and dotted notes and rests in 2/4, 3/4, and 4/4, 6/8, 3/8, and alla breve meter signatures

b. Read at sight simple melodies in both the treble and bass clefs

c. Identify and define standard notation symbols for pitch, rhythm, dynamics, tempo, articulation, and expression

d. Use standard notation to record their musical ideas and the musical ideas of others

Students who participate in a choral or instrumental ensemble or class

e. Sight-read, accurately and expressively, music with a level of difficulty of 2, on a scale of 1 to 6

6. **Content Standard**: Listening to, analyzing, and describing music

**Achievement Standard:**

Students

a. Describe specific music events in a given aural example, using appropriate terminology

b. Analyze the uses of elements of music in aural examples representing diverse genres and cultures

c. Demonstrate knowledge of the basic principles of meter, rhythm, tonality, intervals, chords, and harmonic progressions in their analyses of music

7. **Content Standard**: Evaluating music and music performances

**Achievement Standard:**

Students

a. Develop criteria for evaluating the quality and effectiveness of music performances and compositions and apply the criteria in their personal listening and performing

b. Evaluate the quality and effectiveness of their own and others' performances, compositions, arrangements, and improvisations by applying specific criteria appropriate for the style of the music and offer constructive suggestions for improvement

8. **Content Standard**: Understanding relationships between music, the other arts, and disciplines outside the arts

**Achievement Standard:**

Students

a. Compare in two or more arts how the characteristic materials of each art can be used to transform similar events, scenes, emotions, or ideas into works of art

b. Describe ways in which the principles and subject matter of other disciplines taught in the school are interrelated with those of music

9. **Content Standard**: Understanding music in relation to history and culture

**Achievement Standard:**

Students

a. Describe distinguishing characteristics of representative music genres and styles from a variety of cultures
b. Classify by genre and style (and, if applicable, by historical period, composer, and title) a varied body of exemplary (that is, high-quality and characteristic) musical works and explain the characteristics that cause each work to be considered exemplary
c. Compare, in several cultures of the world, functions music serves, roles of musicians, and conditions under which music is typically performed

MENC has developed a number of publications to help music educators include the National Standards in their curriculum. Among them are *Performance Standards for Music—Grades PreK-12*; *The School Music Program—A New Vision*; and *Opportunity-to-Learn Standards for Music Instruction—Grades PreK-12*.

A thoughtful statement of goals and objectives, or standards, for each level of the instrumental music program is an important ingredient in developing a successful band or orchestra program. In Chapters 12 and 14 you will find a more comprehensive discussion of goals and objectives, along with advice for developing a personal philosophy of music education.

## Five Principles

Holz and Jacobi developed five principles of beginning instrumental music instruction rooted in the work of the American educator, psychologist, and philosopher John Dewey (1859-1952) and noted Swiss educator Johann Heinrich Pestalozzi (1746-1827). These principles are important for teachers of beginning instrumentalists.

**Principle I** *Enjoyment needs to start early!*
Underlying all instruction, in music as well as in other subjects, is the principle that learning is often most effective when *experience precedes theory*, or in Pestalozzian terms, the thing before the sign. . . .

*Suzuki Method* →

**Principle II**
Obviously, not all students have had the same experiences, nor have they all been equally successful in understanding

11

their experiences. Therefore, the teacher must organize instruction in such a way as to proceed *from the known to the unknown*. . . .

### Principle III

The learning process proceeds most effectively when it is organized in such a way that the specific is related to the general and the general to the specific—in other words, *from the whole to the parts and back again*. . . .

### Principle IV

Throughout the educational process, the teacher must realize that the important activity in the classroom is not teaching but learning, and that *learning depends upon the desire to learn*. . . .

### Principle V

If learning depends on wanting to learn, then *teaching is the art of making students want to learn*. . . .

(Holz and Jacobi, pp. 47-50)

Following these principles, you should do a lot of demonstrating and teaching by sound, not sight—without notation (Principle I). You should plan instruction so that students can find success in their playing before continuing sequentially to more difficult skills (Principle II). Because students learn at varying rates and have different levels of musical experience, you should meet the individual needs of students by supplying missing information or providing additional opportunities for musical enrichment. Principle III is a reminder to teach with the "big picture" in mind. For a beginner, this could simply be playing a single half-note well while reviewing all those small actions needed to sound that note; or for an older student it could mean playing through a complete etude, song, or band arrangement while still taking time to drill the details of the music so that success with the "big picture" is possible.

Because *real* learning takes place only when the learner has a desire to learn (Principle IV), plan instruction that will make students interested and active learners. Choose attractive and interesting literature, offer appropriate positive reinforcement, maintain an appropriate pace to the class lessons, and be sure to demonstrate your own enjoyment, personal satisfaction, and pleasure in teaching (especially in teaching the beginner).

Principle V is a succinct and useful definition of teaching: ". . . teaching is the art of making students want to learn" (p. 50). Holz and Jacobi continue with an important reminder of what teaching in a beginning class is really about. "In the beginning instrumental music class, then, teaching is *not* conducting, *not* lecturing, *not* judging. Teaching *is* motivation, explaining, demonstrating, encouraging, suggesting, organizing, and evaluating" (p. 50). You will find that *leading* students to musical discoveries and enjoyment is a great privilege and high responsibility. In summary, Principles I-III will help teachers plan effective instruction, and Principles IV and V will guide the effective delivery of that instruction.

## Instructional Groupings

A fundamental decision to be made with beginning classes is how to organize the classes: private lessons; like-instruments only; separate woodwind, brass, percussion, and string classes; all strings, and all winds and percussion; or a true heterogeneous class with all band and orchestra instruments together. In many communities that decision was made years ago and you will have little chance to alter the established procedure. However, in an era of restructuring, reform, and realignment of grade groupings, you may have an opportunity to make changes to improve the effectiveness of an existing program.

While the private lesson setting might seem to provide the optimal learning experience, most research, and years of informed practice, indicate that group instruction—taught by fine teachers—is actually the most effective method of teaching beginners (Grunow and Gamble, 1989, p. 194). Group lessons are more cost effective for a school system, and you may find that students in classes will help teach and encourage each other in their cooperative effort to learn to play a musical instrument. You might find that a combination of some of the class alignments listed above are most beneficial for the beginning instrumental class. The very early stages of instruction are best taught in like-instrument groups or in separate woodwind, brass, percussion, and string classes. The skills and techniques for each of these instrument groups are unique, so a few weeks of separate instruction should lead to a higher level of competence. After the initial weeks of like-instrument or "section" classes, you will find that more comprehensive groupings of instruments may be more productive. The most typical groupings would be woodwinds, brass, and percussion (the "beginning band" or the band class), and all strings (the "beginning orchestra" or the string class).

One key to success in these comprehensive groupings is to maintain a reasonable student-teacher ratio. The widely accepted 20-1 ratio is probably the maximum, which will allow you to be effective in this special classroom setting. Obviously, the greater the variety of instruments in the same class, the more complex the problem of teaching the new skills, techniques, and information for each instrument. Many school districts find that team-teaching (several teachers working together in one or more classroom) is a good solution to maintaining a reasonable student-teacher ratio. Team-teaching also makes it possible for all band or string students to be taken out of the regular classroom at the same time. That causes less conflict with the already-busy regular classroom schedule. Even less conflict with the classroom schedule occurs when the string and band classes are held at the same time.

I believe the "ideal" time to start woodwind, brass, and percussion students is the 5th grade. Fifth grade students are physically capable of playing the instruments, they may not yet be involved in a host of available after-school activities, and they are often very eager to begin this exciting new experience. A program that begins with the 5th grade will typically be housed in a K-5 or K-6 school and will be a "pull-out" program, i.e., a program which takes students out of scheduled classroom activities. The recommended total weekly instructional time in this situation would be 90 minutes—three days a week for 30 minutes each day, or two days a week for 45 minutes each day. Teaching a 45-minute beginning class will require excellent pacing and a variety of teaching strategies, because of 1) the relatively short attention span of students of this age, and 2) the physical demands of learning an instrument.

School districts that use a K-5, 6-8, 9-12, or a K-4, 5-8, 9-12 alignment commonly start the beginning instrumental program in the 6th or even 7th grade. The disadvantages are obvious—fewer years to develop essential performance skills, musicianship, and attitudes; and the likelihood that many students will already have become involved in several other after-school activities and will be less likely to elect an additional activity. The primary *advantage* of a middle school beginning class is that it will probably be scheduled as a regular, five days per week class. More material can be covered with greater continuity of instruction.

Another option that is sometimes successful is to start the beginning instrumental music program during the summer before the 5th or 6th grade year. The advantage with this plan is that classes may be scheduled every day for a six or eight week period, leading to greater continuity of instruction and more frequent opportunities to reinforce correct skills, techniques, and understandings. The obvious disadvantage of the summer beginning program is that many families take vacations during that time.

I recommend, if the local school budget allows, starting string classes one year earlier than winds and percussion. The primary reasons for an earlier start for strings are that students are physically capable of playing strings before they are ready for a wind instrument (and small-size string instruments are readily available), and a one year "head-start" will help string recruitment.

## Instrumentation

Most beginning class teachers find that offering instruction for only a basic core of band and orchestra instruments allows the teacher to provide more thorough instruction, and allows the class to move faster. A good basic core of instruments for the beginning band class is flute, clarinet, alto saxophone (possibly tenor saxophone), cornet/trumpet, trombone, possibly euphonium, and percussion. A beginning string class might consist of violin, viola, and cello. While limiting the number of different instruments taught in the beginning classes may be ideal, some teachers find success starting a broader range of instruments. In addition, a highly motivated and gifted student who wants to play another instrument—for example, oboe or French horn—will often be successful on that instrument in the beginning class.

Transfers to other instruments not taught in the beginning class may be made after a few years of instruction. By waiting to transfer students to other instruments, you have time to evaluate students and determine who might find greater success on another instrument. Another advantage in delaying instruction on what are sometimes called the "color" or "background" instruments is that any problems of dropout and balance will be more apparent. Plan ahead for instrument transfers. That is, if you start a large number of cornet and trumpet players, for example, there will be enough students to transfer to euphonium, French horn, and tuba at the appropriate time.

You will find that instrument transfers work well any time after the first year of instruction, but should certainly be done by the 8th or 9th grade to allow these players time to develop adequate performance skills. I believe that 7th grade—the second or third year of instruction—is the ideal time for such transfers. The following is a list of "color" instruments and some possible sources for transfer students:

- Oboe and bassoon: from saxophone, flute, or clarinet
- Bass clarinet: from clarinet
- Tenor and baritone saxophone: from alto saxophone, clarinet, or flute
- French horn: from cornet or trumpet, or flute *(size of the aperture)*
- Euphonium and tuba: from cornet or trumpet, or trombone
- Viola, cello, or string bass: from violin

While these suggested transfers are the most typical, other transfers can work, depending on the attitude and enthusiasm of the student. I once had a 9th grade bass clarinet player talk me into letting her transfer to French horn. This is not a transfer I would normally approve, but she was very enthusiastic and hard-working. This student was so successful that she eventually majored in music in college with French horn as her principal instrument. Attitude does matter!

An obvious source of viola, cello, and string bass players for middle and high school orchestras is young violinists willing to transfer. Still, some teachers have found good success in recruiting students for these instruments who play piano, guitar, or electric bass. These students already have an interest in music and read music (hopefully!), and guitar and bass players have some familiarity with basic string concepts.

## *For Discussion or Assignment*

1. How would you convince an elementary school principal that instrumental music should be offered at his/her school?

2. Develop two goals—with two objectives for each goal—for your beginning instrumental music class.

3. Discuss the pros and cons of limiting the instruments taught in the beginning class.

4. Write a personal Philosophy of the Beginning Instrumental Music Program. This should be no longer than one double-spaced page.

# *For Reference and Further Reading*

*The Crane Symposium: Toward an Understanding of the Teaching and Learning of Music Performance* (1988). Potsdam: Crane School of Music, State University of New York.

Elliott, David J. (1995). *Music Matters: A New Philosophy of Music Education*. New York: Oxford University Press.

Froseth, James O. (1974). *NABIM Recruiting Manual*. Chicago: G.I.A. Publications.

Froseth, James O. (1974). *Teacher's Guide to the Individualized Instructor*. Chicago: G.I.A. Publications.

Froseth, James O. (1976). *Introducing the Instruments—Preliminary Book* (Text and Picture Full Score). Chicago: G.I.A. Publications.

Froseth, James O. (1998). *Do It! Play in Band*. Chicago: GIA Publications, Inc.

Gardner, Howard (1993). *Multiple Intelligences: The Theory in Practice*. New York: Basic Books.

Gordon, Edwin (1988). *Learning Sequences in Music*. Chicago: G.I.A. Publications.

Gordon, Edwin (1971). *The Psychology of Music Teaching*. Englewood Cliffs, NJ: Prentice-Hall, Inc.

Grunow, Richard F. and Gamble, Denise K. (1989). Music learning sequence techniques in beginning instrumental music. In *Reading in Music Learning Theory*. Chicago: G.I.A. Publications.

Grunow, Richard F. and Gordon, Edwin E. (1989). *Jump Right In: The Instrumental Series Teacher's Guide*. Chicago: G.I.A. Publications.

Holz, Emil A., and Jacobi, Roger E. (1966). *Teaching Band Instruments to Beginners*. Englewood Cliffs, NJ: Prentice-Hall, Inc.

Instrumental Music for Michigan Schools (1980). Ann Arbor, MI: Michigan School Band and Orchestra Association.

Leonhard, Charles, and House, Robert W. (1972). *Foundations and Principles of Music Education (2nd ed.)*. New York: McGraw-Hill.

*National Standards for Arts Education—What Every Young American Should Know and Be Able to Do in the Arts* (1994). Reston, VA: Music Educators National Conference.

*Opportunity-to-Learn Standards for Music Instruction—Grades PreK-12* (1994). Reston, VA: Music Educators National Conference.

*The School Music Program—A New Vision* (1994). Reston, VA: Music Educators National Conference.

# Chapter Two

# RECRUITING AND RETAINING BEGINNING STUDENTS

## Recruitment Strategies

The goal of a recruiting program for beginning instrumental music classes should be to gather adequate and accurate information about each child's aptitude for music, and to use that information to counsel the child and parents concerning the child's potential for success in instrumental music (Taggart, 1989; Gordon, 1971; Gardner, 1993). The information gathered is used only to provide a professional evaluation of the opportunity for success in music—it is never used to eliminate students from the instrumental music program. In a democratic society, with schools supported by taxes from *all* the people in the community, *every* child has the right to participate in the beginning instrumental music program (Franks, 1996, p. 20). Some may not find success, or may lose interest and drop out of the program, but all children should have equal access to the beginning instrumental music program (Gordon, 1988, p. 291; Holz and Jacobi, 1966, p. 21). Special-needs children (those with physical, mental, or emotional concerns) must also be allowed to participate in the instrumental music program as their individual conditions allow. This may require specially trained personnel in the beginning instrumental music classroom to help students with special needs.

Recruiting students for beginning instrument music classes is extremely important for the long-term success of all school instrumental music programs. Some school districts give a music store the responsibility of recruiting students for the beginning instrumental

19

music program, and many do it very successfully. While that may seem to be a great time-saver, you must remember that you are the professional hired by the local school district to provide instruction and administer the music program. You have the responsibility to meet the musical needs of students in a professional and thorough manner. Delegating a major portion of those responsibilities—recruiting beginning students—to someone principally interested in selling instruments could lead to inappropriate instrument selections and discouraged students who drop out of the program after a short time.

## Communication

As with all human endeavors, communication is a key to successful recruiting, and indeed to a successful total instrumental music education program. The building principal, classroom teachers, and parents must be well informed about all aspects of the recruiting program. The building principal has responsibility for the total educational program in the school and determines scheduling, budget, and administrative support for the instrumental music program. It is crucial that the building principal be "on your team" and kept well informed of all aspects of the program prior to your giving information to classroom teachers or parents.

Classroom teachers have an important impact on the instrumental music program, because their attitude toward you and the program will affect the attitudes of their students. Keep classroom teachers well informed in order to earn their support. The daily schedule in an elementary school classroom is getting more and more complex. Be sensitive to the problems that "extra" or "pull-out" programs can cause to a classroom teacher. Once your class schedule is established, adhere closely to the assigned time. Do not encroach into classroom teachers' time or ask for alterations in the schedule, except for the most serious reasons. You might use a memo like the one found in Figure 2-1 to inform and involve the classroom teacher.

Unfortunately, teachers seldom have a good understanding of the problems faced by teachers of other subjects or grade levels. Since the elementary classroom teacher has the students all day, you may think that the classroom teacher should be flexible and willing to accommodate the instrumental music class. At the same time, the classroom teacher may feel that you have more control over your teaching schedule and should be able, and willing, to change. Obviously, both views are mistaken! Still, it would be wise to seek compromises that help the classroom teachers and maintain their support.

**Figure 2-1. Memo to Classroom Teachers**

**Memorandum**

To:        Mr. Townsend [building principal]

             Mr. Kenton [5th grade teacher]

             Mrs. Brown [5th grade teacher]

From:     George Allen [beginning band teacher] and

             Roger Smith [beginning string teacher]

Date:      September 6

RE:        Schedule for the Smithville Elementary School band and string program

We are very pleased that 5th grade band and string classes at Smithville Elementary School will begin soon! As per our usual schedule and our discussions with each of you, the following is our schedule for the next four weeks. All classes meet from 11:00 a.m. to 11:30 a.m.—except on Sept 17, 20, and 22, when classes meet until 12:00 noon for testing.

Sept. 13 - A film about band & strings will be shown.

Sept. 15 - A timbre preference test will be given.

Sept. 17 - Part One of a music aptitude test will be administered.

Sept. 20 - Part Two of a music aptitude test will be administered.

Sept. 22 - Part Three of a music aptitude test will be administered.

Sept. 24 - We will demonstrate the instruments to both classes.

Sept. 27 - Individual conferences with students to counsel them about their instrument choices. We will meet with students in the hall by each room, causing a minimal interference with your class plans. We will meet with Mr. Kenton's class today.

Sept. 29 - Individual student conferences with Mrs.Brown's class today.

Oct. 1 - Individual conferences with students absent on their regular day.

Oct. 4, 6, 8 - We will meet all 5th graders for Music Fundamentals classes.

Oct. 11 - 5th grade Band and String Classes begin!

We will meet with all parents on September 30th at 7:30 p.m. in the gym to explain the instrumental music program and answer questions. You are invited to attend this parents meeting. Your support of our instrumental music program and these students would be greatly appreciated. Students will receive a letter to take home on September 17th.

If you have any questions about our program please let us know. We want to work with you to make sure the instrumental music program is smoothly integrated into the school curriculum with minimal interference to your class plans.

The most influential people in the life of elementary school students are usually their parents. Parents who are knowledgeable and involved in the instrumental music program will probably be supportive of that program. For the benefit of everyone involved, keep parents thoroughly informed. All communications with parents, classroom teachers, and principals must be carefully and clearly written. These communications must be factually accurate, free of spelling or grammatical errors, positive in character, and concise. After your recruiting schedule and program has been approved by the principal and communicated to the classroom teachers, a letter should be sent home to parents announcing the start of the beginning instrumental music program. If possible, this letter should be mailed home to ensure that all parents receive the letter in a timely fashion. See Figure 2-2 for an example of a letter to parents.

The instrumental music program should begin with the start of the school year. Too many busy high school marching band directors delay starting the beginning program until marching season is well under way. This may be of immediate help to the band director's schedule, but fails to take advantage of the excitement of starting a new school year. Recruiting preparation—such as grading aptitude tests and gathering other data—may require several weeks to complete and should be started as soon as possible. In fact, delaying the start of the beginning program may result in students becoming involved in other activities that prevent them from joining the instrumental music program.

Colleen Conway (1997) suggests that teachers of beginning classes start regular class meetings right away and use that time to teach musical concepts and skills—such as learning to sing the song material to be used later with their instruments, teaching movement activities, doing tonal and rhythmic echoes, teaching correct posture, and learning conducting patterns. This is also a good time to teach classroom rules and procedures, tuning procedures, instrumental care, etc. Having several classes that focus on important musical and behavioral skills, without the additional technical concerns presented by the instruments, can pay rich dividends in the beginning instrumental class. Starting the beginning class during the first week of classes helps establish that time—for students and classroom teachers—as the band or orchestra period. It says: "I have a lot of things to teach my students and I need, and will use, all of my allotted time." In addition, this is an outstanding recruiting tool. By the time parents are asked to decide about having their child join the program, students have already bonded with the teacher and begun to feel part of the group. For parents to decide against having their child join the program becomes a

*Figure 2-2. First Letter to Parents*

---

### Smithville Elementary School

(Date)

Dear Parents:

The Smithville Elementary School is pleased to announce that beginning classes in band and orchestra instruments will begin soon! Our instrumental music teachers are now meeting with all students to explain the program, complete a music aptitude test, and demonstrate the instruments. We hope that you will encourage your child to become involved in this exciting experience! Instrumental music will further enrich your child's basic educational and cultural understandings and provide a very positive peer group for your child.

Students involved in music are at the top in academic performance, and score significantly higher on national tests such as the SAT than those students not in music. These students become leaders in their schools and as adults. Wouldn't you like to have your child involved in instrumental music?

Parent involvement in the instrumental music program is very important. We invite you and your child to attend a brief meeting on Thursday, September 30, at 7:30 p.m. The meeting will be held in the Smithville Elementary School gym, and we will try to answer all of your questions about this important educational opportunity for your child. We hope you will plan to attend!

Please complete the form below and have your child return it to his or her classroom teacher tomorrow. We hope to see you at 7:30 p.m. on September 30th!

Sincerely yours,

George Allen  Roger Smith
Band Teacher  String Teacher

---

**Instrumental Music Instruction
Is Scheduled to Begin Soon!**

(Please detach and return to your classroom teacher tomorrow!)

Name of student _____ Grade _____

Classroom Teacher _____

Name of parent(s) _____

Phone _____

Address _____


_____ I will attend the meeting on Thursday, Sept. 30th!

_____ I am interested but I cannot attend the meeting. (Please call me to schedule an appointment.)

_____ I am not interested.

decision to *withdraw* them from the class. This is a decision most parents and children will not be eager to make.

## Data Gathering

A recruiting program should consist of two parts: data gathering (aptitude, academic achievement, and timbre preference) and recruitment activities. Gathered data provides the instrumental music teacher with valuable information to counsel parents and students about possible participation in the beginning instrumental music program. James Froseth (1974) stated that a relationship might exist between academic achievement test scores and success in instrumental music. While academic achievement test scores can indicate a good work ethic, motivation, good study habits, etc., these scores should be used only as a part of the recruiting process, and not as the primary data for predicting musical success. The results of a reliable and valid music aptitude test may be the most valuable data in the recruiting program. A discussion about aptitude tests will be found in this chapter. If time and budget allow, the *Instrument Timbre Preference Test* (ITPT) by Edwin Gordon should be used to help identify the instrument tone qualities the student prefers. Students who play an instrument that has a sound they like are less likely to drop out of the program (Grunow and Gordon, 1989, p. 13). ITPT results, along with a music aptitude test such as the *Musical Aptitude Profile* (MAP), can help predict the potential for success of the student in instrumental music. Some students with high test results may not express interest—but if they can be encouraged to try the beginning instrumental music program, they are highly likely to find success and become more enthusiastic because of that success.

Again, it must be emphasized that this data is to be used to help instrumental music teachers counsel parents and students about involvement in the beginning program. It should never be used to exclude students from the program. All who want to play should be encouraged to play. A positive attitude and enthusiasm on the part of the student and teacher will help overcome any reported deficiency in music aptitude.

## *Activities and Resources*

The demonstration of instruments may be the most crucial part of the entire recruitment program (Holz and Jacobi, p. 23). The enthusiasm and interest of students may be at an all-time high at the demonstration, so plan carefully and take advantage of this situation. Completing an Instrumentation Analysis (see Figure 2-3) regularly will help you anticipate imbalances in sections of the band or orchestra, and will be a guide in planning the demonstration of instruments to prospective students. Planning for instrumentation balance is important for both the short term and the long term. A beginning band class with 2 flutes, 1 clarinet, 10 alto saxophones, 8 trumpets, no trombones, and 8 percussionists is usually not a pleasant musical experience! Likewise, a high school orchestra with 20 violins, 2 violas, 1 cello, and no basses will probably not be a very musical experience. While a creative teacher may be able to minimize the potentially negative musical result of poorly balanced ensembles, a better musical experience is likely to occur when an ensemble has good instrumentation balance.

*Figure 2-3. Instrumentation Analysis Chart*

## INSTRUMENTATION ANALYSIS BY GRADE

School _____ Teacher _____

| Instrument | 5 | 6 | 7 | 8 | 9 | 10 | 11 | 12 |
|---|---|---|---|---|---|---|---|---|
| Flute | | | | | | | | |
| Oboe | | | | | | | | |
| Bassoon | | | | | | | | |
| B♭ Clarinet | | | | | | | | |
| Alto Clarinet | | | | | | | | |
| Bass Clarinet | | | | | | | | |
| Contra Clarinet | | | | | | | | |
| Alto Saxophone | | | | | | | | |
| Tenor Saxophone | | | | | | | | |
| Baritone Saxophone | | | | | | | | |
| French Horn | | | | | | | | |
| Cornet/Trumpet | | | | | | | | |
| Trombone | | | | | | | | |
| Euphonium | | | | | | | | |
| Tuba | | | | | | | | |
| Percussion | | | | | | | | |
| Violin | | | | | | | | |
| Viola | | | | | | | | |
| Cello/Bass | | | | | | | | |
| TOTALS | | | | | | | | |
| | | | | | | | | |

During the demonstration of instruments, ask students to make a list of three instruments they might like to play. When students consider more than a single choice, you will be able to guide them to the best instrument based on a combination of their stated instrument preference, and any physical characteristics that could affect instrumental performance, timbre preference, and the need for balanced instrumentation. You may decide not to demonstrate instruments (such as percussion) that have traditionally been over-selected by students.

Plan instrument demonstrations carefully and thoughtfully. Just a few sentences about the instrument followed by a brief melody or a scale is all that is necessary. However, it is vital that the tone quality demonstrated be characteristic for each instrument. You may want to perform on many of the instruments yourself—if you can do it with a beautiful tone and confident technique—or you may want to use outstanding students from the next grade level for the demonstration. Using students who are close in age to those you are trying to recruit can be beneficial because the students being recruited can see and hear an accurate representation of what they could sound like in just one year. This approach is more honest than having your All-State 12th grade trumpet player demonstrate!

A brief conference with each student will allow you to assess the physical characteristics of the student and determine if certain instrument choices would be better than others. Obviously, you must have a solid grasp on the demands of this task! A form like Figure 2-4 will help. Many students have been successful learning to play an instrument in spite of physical characteristics that indicated a potential problem, but students will usually find greater success playing instruments with which they are physically compatible. Many teachers find it beneficial to have prospective students actually try to produce a tone on the instrument(s) of choice. Although this can be time consuming and expensive (mouthpieces must be sterilized and reeds replaced), trying to produce a tone on an instrument gives valuable information and direction to the student and the teacher. The student conference is the time to guide students toward an appropriate instrument selection based on their preferences (do they have that list of three instruments that they like?), their physical characteristics, the results of the ITPT (if given), and consideration for instrumentation balance. If it is necessary for you to recommend another instrument, clearly explain the reasons for the recommendation; but if at all possible, allow students to play the instrument of their choosing.

An optional recruiting activity is a concert for your potential recruits by the ensemble of second year players at the school. Again, this is an honest and realistic performance of what the beginning class could sound like in just one year. Many teachers find good student and parent response when they show one of the recruiting videotapes or movies available from an instrument manufacturer. Schedule these early (through your local dealer or directly through the manufacturer) to ensure their availability.

Another essential part of the recruiting process is a meeting with parents. I suggest that the first letter to parents (Figure 2-2) be sent 2

27

*Figure 2-4. Physical Characteristics Checklist*

## Physical Characteristics Checklist

Student_____Date_____

Use this checklist for each of the instruments selected by the student. Use this evaluation to counsel the student and parents about an appropriate instrument selection.

| *Desirable Characteristics* | *Undesirable Characteristics* |
|---|---|
| **Flute:** | |
| __ Average size lips | __ Thick, thin, or teardrop (bud) lips |
| __ Straight teeth | __ Underbite |
| __ Average size hands | __ Small hands |
| __ Average size fingers | __ Thin pads, short or stubby fingers |
| | |
| **Oboe:** | |
| __ Average size lips | __ Thick or thin lips |
| __ Straight teeth | __ Overbite and underbite |
| __ Large hands | __ Small hands |
| __ Long fingers | __ Thick, short or stubby fingers |
| | |
| **Bassoon:** | |
| __ Average size lips | __ Thick or thin lips |
| __ Straight or overbite teeth | __ Underbite, protruding lower jaw |
| __ Large hands | __ Small hands |
| __ Long or average fingers | __ Thick, short or stubby fingers |
| __ Average to large overall physique | __ Small overall physique |
| | |
| **Clarinet:** | |
| __ Average lips | __ Small hands |
| __ Straight teeth | __ Thick, thin pads, short or stubby |
| __ Average hands | fingers |
| __ Average fingers | |
| | |
| **Saxophone:** | |
| __ Average lips | __ Small hands |
| __ Straight teeth | __ Short or stubby fingers |
| __ Average to large hands | |
| __ Average to long fingers | |
| | |
| **Horn:** | |
| __ Average to thin lips | __ Thick lips |
| __ Straight teeth | __ Braces, extreme overbite or under- |
| | bite, unusual front teeth |
| **Cornet/Trumpet:** | |
| __ Average lips | __ Thick, teardrop lips |
| __ Straight teeth | __ Braces, extreme overbite or underbite |
| __ Average hand size | __ Small hands |
| __ Average finger size | __ Stubby fingers |

Things to be Aware Of

| Desirable Characteristics | Undesirable Characteristics |
|---|---|
| **Trombone & Euphonium:** | |
| __ Average lips | __ Short arms |
| __ Straight teeth | __ Small overall physique |
| __ Average to long arms | |
| __ Large enough overall physique to handle instrument | |
| **Tuba:** | |
| __ Average to large hands | __ Small hands |
| __ Large enough overall physique to handle instrument | __ Small overall physique |
| **Percussion:** | |
| __ Full range of wrist motion | __ No wrist motion |
| __ Average ability to grip with hands | __ No grip ability |
| **Violin/Viola:** | |
| __ Strong fingers | __ Thick or stubby fingers |
| __ Adequate hand size | __ Small hands |
| __ Full range of motion in right elbow | __ No elbow motion |
| **Cello:** | |
| __ Physically able to reach around instrument (average to large overall physique) | __ Small overall physique |
| | __ Thick or stubby fingers |
| __ Strong fingers | __ Small hands |
| __ Adequate hand size | __ Lack of right arm motion |
| __ Full range of motion in right arm | |
| **String Bass:** | |
| __ Physically around to reach around instrument | __ Small/short overall physique |
| | __ Thick or stubby fingers |
| __ Large/tall overall physique | __ Small hands |
| __ Strong fingers | __ Lack of right arm motion |
| __ Adequate hand size | |
| __ Full range of motion in right arm | |

Recommendations for parents and students:

Used by permission of Emily Adkison and Catherine Hilgers

29

or 3 weeks prior to the meeting. A brief reminder might be sent one week before the meeting, and a simple announcement (see Figure 2-5) should be sent home with students on the day of the meeting.

*Figure 2-5. Reminder to Parents*

---

### THIS IS IT!

(date)

Dear Parents:

This is a reminder of the important meeting tonight concerning our beginning instrumental music program. The program will begin soon and we want you to know all of the details!

We urge you to attend this brief meeting about an important educational opportunity for your child. The meeting will begin at 7:30 p.m. in the Smithville Elementary School gym.

Please come and find out how your child can become involved in instrumental music!

Sincerely yours,

George Allen          Roger Smith
Band Teacher          String Teacher

---

Ask the building principal to begin the meeting with a welcome to the parents and an introduction of the instrumental music teachers. Your presentation should include:

- An expression of thanks to the principal for the introduction and for support of the program
- An introduction of any classroom teachers or other administrator, with an expression of appreciation for their presence
- A brief statement about the goals and philosophy of the beginning instrumental music program
- Brief comments about recent studies identifying the many positive benefits of instrumental music study

- A discussion of the recruiting activities already held for students
- The starting date for instruction and major events planned for the year
- A list of the options for securing instruments in your community
- A request that students who already have an instrument bring it in to be checked for playing condition
- A list of the method books students will need to purchase and where they are available
- An opportunity for questions from parents
- A demonstration of the instruments for parents, along with showing any recruiting film you used with students
- An invitation to schedule an individual appointment if needed
- A thank you to everyone for attending the meeting!

Specific questions about each child are handled best in a private conversation with parents. This can be done at the end of the meeting, or you may want to schedule these extra parent conferences for later in the week. Having a sign-up form listing your available times will speed up this scheduling process.

You should talk to parents about their role as encourager. Ask parents to give positive comments about their child's progress, and to attend their child's performances. Also, advise parents of the importance of providing a folding music stand for home practice, arranging a quiet space for regular practice, and encouraging their children to handle their instrument carefully and to maintain it properly. Most musicians (beginners and professionals) reach a plateau (or even a valley) in their playing. Parent support and encouragement will help the beginner (and even the professional!) get past that plateau.

The selection of a quality instrument for beginners is extremely important. While first instruments are often referred to as "beginner instruments," they are often played by the student throughout their musical careers. Instruments should be of the best quality parents can afford. Better quality instruments are easier to play, produce a better tone, and are often more durable than less expensive instruments. Instruments that are difficult to play can discourage students and lead to their dropping out of the program. Music stores will work with teachers to supply quality instruments for the beginning instrumental music program.

Parents will appreciate a handout with the basic information presented at the meeting (see Figure 2-6). Those who do not attend the meeting or have not responded within a few days should receive a telephone call from you to encourage them to enroll their child in the program. Be sure to call the parents of students who scored well on the music aptitude test—they may be some of your most outstanding instrumentalists. A follow-up letter to the parents of all prospective students should include a brief review of points discussed at the parents meeting and a reminder about the important role of parents in the success of their child in the instrumental music program.

*Figure 2-6. Elementary Instrumental Music Program Information*

---

**Smithville Elementary School**
**Elementary Instrumental Music Program Information**

I. Instruments taught
    A. Band: flute, clarinet, alto saxophone, cornet or trumpet, trombone, and percussion (we start with a bell kit, which can be exchanged for a drum kit after 4-6 months)
    B. Strings: violin, viola, and cello

II. Sources for instruments:
    A. Local music dealers (rental/purchase plans available)
    1. Joe's Music Store
       100 Main St.
       (phone: 888-8888)
    2. Sam's Musical Emporium
       30000 Short St.
       (phone: 888-1111)

    B. Used instrument from newspaper ads or bulletin board notices.
Music teachers often know of used instruments available. Music teachers and music stores will usually evaluate a used instrument for you.

III. Music book:
    *Do It! Play In Band,* by James Froseth

IV. 5th grade Band and String Classes start on October 11!

Please call Mr. Allen (band) or Mr. Smith (strings) at Smithville Elementary School (888-1234) if you have more questions or would like to schedule an appointment to talk about the opportunities for your child in instrumental music.

Tim Lautzenheiser (1993) writes that "Recruitment is the most critical part of any program. Period. It is to a band what a foundation is to a building" (p. 11). Recruiting must be thorough and well planned. Using a recruiting program similar to the one discussed above will produce an excellent enrollment in beginning instrumental music classes. Recruiting a high percentage of each elementary class is important, because it exposes more students to the benefits of the instrumental music experience. In addition, programs with high enrollment positively influence school administrators and school boards.

Important additional resources for the recruiting program are in the *NABIM Recruiting Manual* by James O. Froseth (published by the National Association of Band Instrument Manufacturers, Inc.) and *Director's Communication Kit for All Band Programs* by Tim Lautzenheiser (published by the Hal Leonard Corp.). Many of the recruiting activities discussed above come from these two valuable resources. Although the *NABIM Recruiting Manual* is now out of print, copies may be found at some local music stores or in libraries. Local libraries can help you find a copy of this comprehensive booklet through the Inter-Library Loan program. The information in the *NABIM Recruiting Manual* is certainly worth this extra effort.

## Aptitude Testing

First, some definitions. **Music aptitude** tests measure the potential a student may possess to achieve in music. **Music achievement** tests measure the skills and understandings that a student has achieved in music as a result of their aptitude (or potential) and experience in music—it is a measure of their current musical status (Grunow and Gordon, 1989, p. 10-11). Both types of tests are of benefit for you, the student, and parents. Results of these types of tests will enable you to do three things:

- Plan instruction (based on identified strengths and weaknesses)
- Counsel the student and parents about musical involvement

33

- Evaluate your own instructional program and teaching methods

A teacher who knows the musical strengths and weaknesses of each student can plan appropriate instruction—remedial or enrichment—to meet the individual needs of students. (Gardner, 1993, p. 11 and Taggart, 1989, p. 50)

You should design your own music achievement tests because you know the students, the method of instruction used, and the actual material covered in the particular unit being tested. But music aptitude tests must have a high degree of validity and reliability, which can be established only through controlled field testing over a period of time and in a variety of conditions. Most teachers do not have the expertise to design aptitude tests, or the time to do the field testing necessary to establish their validity and reliability.

Three of the many music aptitude tests designed, tested, and used over the years are the *Seashore Measures of Musical Talent* (the first standardized music aptitude test, published in 1919 and revised in 1939, 1956, and 1960), the *Drake Musical Aptitude Tests* (1954 and 1957), and the *Musical Aptitude Profile* by Edwin Gordon (published in 1965). While all of these tests, and others published during this time, have proved useful to teachers, the *Musical Aptitude Profile* (MAP) may be the most useful standardized music aptitude test available today.

Practical issues in deciding which test should be used include cost, ease of administration and correction, time required to administer the test, logic of test layout, and understandability of directions. However, the primary criterion in deciding which music aptitude test to use is whether it is **valid** (does it really measure what it says it is going to measure) and **reliable** (is it consistent over time in measuring what it says it is going to measure). The MAP—which needs three test periods of 50 minutes each to complete—has a long history of proven validity and reliability. Some teachers and researchers now feel that the third test, Musical Sensitivity, may have lost some of its validity over the years. For that reason, and because the time demands of three tests are so great, some teachers are giving only the *Tonal Imagery* and *Rhythm Imagery* test. The results of these tests seem to give a broad view of the most critical elements of music aptitude.

The *Intermediate Measures of Music Audiation* (IMMA) by Edwin Gordon is designed for students through eleven years of age. Grunow and Gamble (1989, p. 12) suggest using the IMMA and two of the sub-tests of the MAP (*Melody* and *Meter*) when you do not have time for the full MAP, and the *Instrument Timbre Preference Test* (ITPT) to identify student preferences of instrument tone qualities. "With the exception of music aptitude, timbre preference is the most important factor in predicting students' success in beginning instrumental music" (p. 13).

Several instrument manufacturing companies produce "music aptitude tests" that are available at little or no charge through local music dealers. While some of these tests may be marginally helpful in predicting musical potential or interest, most have not had long-term field trials to determine validity and reliability. Such tests may have some usefulness if administrators, students, and parents understand that you are using them primarily to create interest in the instrumental music program, but you should not rely on them for meaningful diagnostic information.

A strong word of caution about the use of music aptitude tests: **these tests should never be used to exclude students from the beginning instrumental music program**. Grunow and Gamble (1989) write that "Just as there is no student without intelligence, so there is no student without music aptitude. Because every student in a school is capable of music achievement to some extent, *no student should be denied music instruction on the basis of his or her level of music aptitude*" (p. 11).

## Student Retention

Ideally, music teachers would like every student who starts in beginning band or orchestra to continue playing in school ensembles until high school graduation and beyond. Unfortunately, that does not happen! Teachers who follow an honest and forthright recruiting program, such as the one described above, will find that their retention rate is high because student expectations are realistic. Every program will experience some dropout throughout the school years. It is not the end of the world—either for the student, or for the band or orchestra program. Choices are a natural and necessary part of life. Some students will discover that their personal interests have changed—either because of new activities, their own low level of achievement in music, a conflict with a teacher, a conflict with the schedule, the influence of new friends, difficult circumstances at home, or myriad other possible reasons.

Choices *are* a part of life, but you should try to control those issues over which you have influence. Try to minimize conflicts. Instrumental music classes should not meet during recess, gym class, general music class, lunch—or any other "fun" activity or class. This is unfair to students because it forces them to make choices they should not have to make. Also, make sure that you treat all students alike and that everyone has confidence in your "fairness." Students are quick to notice "favorites" in a class.

You also need to control your own attitude and behavior. Be sure you honestly enjoy teaching *this* class, at *this* school, at *this* time! Students can easily sense the attitude of their teacher; make sure yours is positive, supportive, and full of honest enthusiasm for your job and your students. Sometimes you will need to *decide* to have a good attitude. We all have good days and bad days, but when the bad outnumber the good, it is probably time to reevaluate your current position or your choice of profession. Children deserve to be taught by teachers who love to teach and love their subject.

The role of parents in a student's decision about whether to remain in the beginning instrumental music program is significant. Help parents realize that their patient, consistent encouragement is crucial, since most children will go through brief periods of discouragement in the beginning. We all need to be reminded that any worthwhile endeavor takes work to develop understanding and skill.

Two other factors are important in retaining students: the beginning class must inspire a sense of progress and value, and it must be enjoyable. Students who are challenged appropriately, and who sense that they are learning and becoming more skilled on their instruments, will develop a sense of enjoyment about instrumental music. Beginning band or orchestra students should have fun making music. It should be an enjoyable, exciting, stress-free experience. As students mature, teachers should help them understand that "enjoyment" is more than the simple term "fun." Enjoyment certainly can be "fun," but it also means achieving a sense of fulfillment or accomplishment after working hard on something believed to be worthwhile. In addition, enjoyment can be doing something *well* for the "fun" of it.

In the insightful book *Talented Teenagers: The Roots of Success and Failure*, Mihaly Csikszentmihalyi (1993) discussed why teenagers choose to continue a certain course of study or activity. The main reason they do what they do is that they enjoy it (p. 8). Such a simple, but profound statement. Teenagers do, and continue to do, what they enjoy. The same is certainly true for those in our beginning instrumental music programs who are *almost* teenagers. It is our job as educators to make sure that we make our activities "enjoyable." Csikszentmihalyi also wrote that "Whether a teenager will want to devote a great deal of time to studying chemistry or music depends also on the quality of the experience he or she derives from working in the lab or practicing an instrument" (p. 7-8). How is "the quality of the experience" in your classroom?

## For Discussion or Assignment

1. Discuss the positive and negative arguments for having a music store in charge of the recruiting activities for the beginning instrumental music class.

2. What would you do if a beginning student insisted on playing an instrument that the student—because of certain physical characteristics—is not suited to play?

3. What are some of the factors in your community that negatively affect the recruiting of beginning instrumental music students? How would you deal with those factors?

4. Develop a timetable of recruiting activities to be used in your beginning band or orchestra program.

5. Prepare a thorough but concise checklist of desirable and/or undesirable physical characteristics for your major instrument. Share your checklist with the other class members. (Your instrument checklist and the Physical Characteristics Checklist found in Figure 2-4 will be valuable aids as you guide students to appropriate instrument choices.)

6. Why are music aptitude tests a useful tool for the instrumental music educator? How can you justify the expense of these tests to your administrator?

## For Reference and Further Reading

### Books and Articles

Conway, Colleen M. (1997). Why wait to start beginning band rehearsals? *Teaching Music*, 5, 1, 36 & 45.

Csikszentmihalyi, Mihaly, et al. (1993). *Talented Teenagers: The Roots of Success and Failure.* New York: Cambridge University Press.

Elliott, David J. (1992). Rethinking music teacher education. *Journal of Music Teacher Education.* (Fall, pp. 6-15).

Franks, Earl (1996). Without wasting words or time: An interview with John M. Long. *The Instrumentalist.* February, pp. 18-22.

Froseth, James O. (1971). Using MAP scores in the instruction of beginning students in instrumental music. *Journal of Research in Music Education.* 19/1, 98-105.

Froseth, James O. (1974). *NABIM Recruiting Manual.* Chicago: GIA Publications, Inc.

Froseth, James O. (1974). *Teacher's Guide to the Individualized Instructor.* Chicago: GIA Publications, Inc.

Froseth, James O. (1976). *Introducing The Instruments—Preliminary Book (Text and Picture Full Score).* Chicago: GIA Publications, Inc.

Froseth, James O. (1998). *Do It! Play in Band.* Chicago: GIA Publications, Inc.

Gardner, Howard (1993). *Multiple Intelligences: The Theory in Practice.* New York: Basic Books.

Gordon, Edwin (1967). *A Three-Year Longitudinal Predictive Validity Study of the Musical Aptitude Profile.* Iowa City, IA: University of Iowa Press.

Gordon, Edwin (1971). *The Psychology of Music Teaching.* Englewood Cliffs, NJ: Prentice-Hall, Inc.

Gordon, Edwin (1988). *Learning Sequences in Music.* Chicago: GIA Publications, Inc.

Grunow, Richard F. and Gamble, Denise K. (1989). Music learning sequence techniques in beginning instrumental music. In *Readings in Music Learning Theory.* Chicago: GIA Pub.

Grunow, Richard F. and Gordon, Edwin E. (1989). *Jump Right In: The Instrumental Series Teacher's Guide.* Chicago: GIA Publications, Inc.

Holz, Emil A., and Jacobi, Roger E. (1966). *Teaching Band Instruments to Beginners.* Englewood Cliffs, NJ: Prentice-Hall, Inc.

Lautzenheiser, Tim (1993). *Director's Communication Kit for All Band Programs.* Milwaukee: Hal Leonard Corp.

Leonhard, Charles, and House, Robert W. (1972). *Foundations and Principles of Music Education (2nd ed.).* New York: McGraw-Hill.

Schleuter Stanley L. (1997). *A Sound Approach to Teaching Instrumentalist (2nd ed.).* New York: Schirmer Books.

Taggart, Cynthia Crump (1989). The measurement and evaluation of music aptitudes and achievement, from *Readings in Music Learning Theory.* Chicago: GIA Pub.

Walters, Darrel L. and Taggart, Cynthia C. (1989). *Readings in Music Learning Theory.* Chicago: GIA Publications, Inc.

Young, William T. (1971). The role of musical aptitude, intelligence, and academic achievement in predicting the musical attainment of elementary instrumental students. *Journal of Research in Music Education.* 19/4, 385-398.

## Music Aptitude Tests

Drake, Raleigh M. (1954, 1957). *Drake Musical Aptitude Test.* Sarasota, FL: Raleigh M. Drake. (mailing address: 711 Beach Road, Sarasota, FL 33581)

Gordon, Edwin (1989). *Advanced Measures of Music Audiation.* Chicago: GIA Publications, Inc.

Gordon, Edwin (1984). *Instrument Timbre Preference Test.* Chicago: GIA Publications, Inc.

Gordon, Edwin (1982). *Intermediate Measures of Music Audiation.* Chicago: GIA Publications, Inc.

Gordon, Edwin (1965). *Musical Aptitude Profile.* Chicago: GIA Publications, Inc.

Gordon, Edwin (1979). *Primary Measures of Music Audiation.* Chicago: GIA Publications, Inc.

Seashore, Carl E. (1919, 1939, 1956, 1960). *Seashore Measures of Musical Talent.* New York: The Psychological Corporation.

Chapter Three

# PLANNING FOR SUCCESS

## Materials

The teacher of beginning instrumental music classes must undertake a thoughtful search for the best method book series to use in class. *The Universal Teacher*, written by Joseph E. Maddy and Thaddeus P. Giddings in 1923, was the first published heterogeneous class method. Since that time, hundreds of beginning instrumental music class method books—from a variety of pedagogical schools and with varying effectiveness—have been published. While it may be true that a great teacher can use any method book and still be an effective teacher, a well designed and pedagogically sound book will make the learning process easier for both the teacher and student.

The evaluation of a new class method book should include consideration of some of the following questions:

- What is the educational philosophy that guides this series?
- Are the choices of first pitches and note values appropriate?
- Does the text use the real tune and not a "simplified" version (which actually makes the learning process more difficult, because the students may already know the real tune)?
- Are the words for all song material included to encourage the use of singing?
- Does the material include both major and minor songs, and material in other modes?

- Does the text include rounds, duets, trios, etc. to develop ensemble playing?
- Can your students relate to the pictures, or are they dated?
- Are the fingering charts visually clear, and easy to read and understand?
- Are musical signs, symbols, and terms explained clearly, and are they found in a musical glossary so that students can look them up themselves?
- Is the sequence of instruction pedagogically sound?
- Are allowances made for the individualization of instruction?
- Is the teacher's book easy to use, and does it include piano accompaniments, helpful hints for the teacher, or other teaching aids?
- Is the book part of a complete series covering several grade levels, and with a variety of supplementary books?
- Does the series help the teacher teach musical concepts such as phrasing, tone quality, dynamics, styles of articulation, and expressive playing?
- Does it teach special problems well—such as going over the clarinet break, use of the third valve slide on trumpets, tuning procedures, care of the instruments, practicing techniques, and playing by ear?
- Is the general format and layout of the book attractive? In other words, is it visually pleasing as far as cover design, use of graphics, use of color, and general format of the text?

The lengthy list above covers many concerns about class method books that veteran teachers consider when searching for a new series. You may want to add additional items to this list as you evaluate a new class method book. The selection of a method book series is one of the most important tasks of the band and orchestra teacher. Following is a list of some of the most popular of the many class method book series on the market:

**Band Class Books**
*Accent on Achievement*, John O'Reilly and Mark Williams—Alfred Publishing Co., Inc.
*Band Today*, James D. Ployhar—Belwin-Mills Publishing Corp.
*Belwin 21st Century Band Method*, Jack Bullock and Anthony Maiello—Warner Bros. Publications
*Best in Class*, Bruce Pearson—Kjos West Publishers
*The Comprehensive Music Instructor*, James Froseth—GIA Publications

*Division of Beat*, Harry H. Haines and J.R. McEntyre—Southern Music Co.

*Do It! Play in Band*, James Froseth—GIA Publications

*Ed Sueta Band Method*—Ed Sueta Music Publications

*Essential Elements*, Tom C. Rhodes, Donald Bierschenk, and Tim Lautzenheiser—Hal Leonard Corp.

*The Individualized Instructor*, James Froseth—GIA Publications

*Jump Right In*, Richard F. Grunow, Edwin E. Gordon and Christopher D. Azzara—GIA Publications

*Sounds Spectacular Band Course*, Andrew Balent—Carl Fischer Music

*Standard of Excellence*, Bruce Pearson—Kjos Music Co.

*Yamaha Band Student*, Sandy Feldstein and John O'Reilly—Alfred Publishing

**String Class Books**

*All for Strings*, Gerald E. Anderson and Robert S. Frost—Kjos Music Co.

*Essential Elements for Strings*, Michael Allen, Robert Gillespie, and Pamela Tellejohn Hayes—Hal Leonard Corp.

*Essentials for Strings*, Gerald Anderson—Kjos Music Co.

*Spotlight on Strings*, Doris Gazda and Albert Stoutamire—Kjos Music Co.

*Strictly Strings*, Jacquelyn Dillon, James Kjelland, and John O'Reilly—Alfred Publishing Co., Inc.

*String Builder*, Samuel Applebaum—Belwin-Mills Publishing Co.

# The First Lessons

The importance of the first few lessons cannot be overemphasized, as they can greatly affect the future musical endeavors of students. Students are never more receptive to teaching and learning than at this time, so your very best effort should go into preparation for these crucial lessons. Correct attitudes, musical excitement, and the desire to be musical should be implanted and reinforced during the first days. Meeting all students at the appointed music class time prior to recruitment will give you a head start on this mission. Do not allow any other responsibilities to detract from your very important work in the beginning class.

An effective teacher will establish an atmosphere of successful and enjoyable learning in class. Part of this atmosphere will stem from an orderly room (set up for each class before the students enter) and a teacher who is friendly with students without feeling the need to be a "buddy." The primary interest of the teacher should be in successful teaching and learning, not in becoming friends with each student. A friendly and appropriate relationship will develop between you and the students when learning is taking place in the classroom.

At least in the initial few lessons, chairs should be in straight rows with adequate space between them to permit the teacher to move easily from student to student. Having the room in order and the instrument cases closed will help create a more structured and calm class. Be sure to remind students how to identify the top of the case to avoid dropping and damaging the instrument: a piece of tape placed on the case lid is helpful.

Because students have so many new—and sometimes difficult—things to learn and do, the emphasis of the first few lessons should be on rote learning. Many songs can be played with just three or four notes. To introduce songs, you might present short melodic patterns from the selected tunes (two or four measures long)—first vocally and then instrumentally—and have the students imitate. This process is often called "echoes" or "do what I do," and is very effective in presenting new melodic material. As you notice which patterns are difficult for the class, you can use repetition to achieve greater student success. Having the class sing echoes before playing them is a major factor in developing musicality and pitch consciousness. Using the actual song text is highly recommended because it helps students remember the tune and it teaches correct musical style.

The use of echoes will improve the student's musical ear, and can be used to introduce or reinforce musical concepts related to style, articulation, dynamics, etc. This technique—and other types of modeling (live and recorded)—is usually more effective than verbal explanations for students of all ages (Anderson, 1981; Crane Symposium, 1988; Sang, 1987; Delzell, 1989). Elliott (1992) notes that

> Practical concepts are too complex to be fully translated into verbal statements. This is the reason that modeling plays such an important role in the development of musicianship (p. 10).

All teachers of beginning band and orchestra classes should develop a systematic written plan of instruction for each instrument—including embouchure formation, hand and body position, posture, breath support, instrument assembly and care, etc. *Do It! Play in Band— Teacher's Resource Edition* by James O. Froseth is an important source of sequential instruction outlines for each band instrument. The information from the Froseth text should serve as the basis for your personal teaching guides. These written guides, which should be sequential and concise, will be indispensable for the young teacher.

Students are eager to *play* their instruments; they want to make as much progress toward that goal as possible in the first class meeting. To accomplish that, avoid talking about your program or expectations, etc. Also, prepare nametags for each student so that you can address them by name. (Prepare them before class and place them on students' chairs.) Students appreciate a teacher who tries to learn and use their names. Another effective technique—when music stands are being used—is to write the student's name on half of a folded piece of 8.5-by-11-inch paper and drape it over the top of the stand so that the name is visible. Assigning student seats also will help you memorize names.

I highly recommend that you teach the first several lessons in like-instrument classes. This may require a series of shorter classes for separate sections during the regular class time, or a temporary schedule of before-school or after-school classes. Whenever possible, arrange at least one like-instrument class for everyone before combining into a heterogeneous group.

If you must teach the first lessons in a heterogeneous class, you will find that lessons are difficult to structure: there is a great volume of information to be taught at one time to six or more instruments. To maintain classroom discipline, you must keep everyone as occupied as possible while working with each section or type of instrument in order. Figure 3-1 is a suggestion for the first class meeting of a heterogeneous band class. The size of the class, experience of the teacher, and effectiveness of classroom discipline will determine the amount of time needed for each item. When you have separate classes for woodwinds, brass, and percussion, the appropriate items from this general outline should be extracted for each group.

*Figure 3-1. The First Beginning Band Class*

---

### LESSON NUMBER 1

- Entire group: Get students into their assigned seats. All cases are on the floor (closed).

- Entire group: Discuss correct posture and breath support (include percussionists in this discussion).

- Clarinets and Saxophones: Discuss handling of the reed and have students moisten the reed. Have them get the

---

45

mouthpiece and cap, ligature, and barrel out of the case (all others silently review and practice good posture).

• Cornets, Trombones, Euphoniums: Teach the embouchure and mouthpiece placement. Buzz (*without*, then *with* the mouthpiece) and make "siren" sounds (ascending and descending glissandi) while buzzing (clarinets & saxophones continue to moisten reeds).

• Flutes: Teach the embouchure and allow them to play on the headjoint (brass, review embouchure formation and mouthpiece placement—do not play audibly).

• Percussion: Teach correct hand and body position, followed by the first rudimentary strokes (flutes, review embouchure and headjoint placement—do not play).

• Clarinets and Saxophones: Teach mounting the reed. Teach the correct embouchure and have them play a sound on the mouthpiece and barrel or neck. Teach instrument assembly. Teach correct hand & body positions. Have students play the first note (remainder of class quietly practices breath support exercises).

• Flute: Teach instrument assembly, then hand and body positions. Together, play the first note.

• Cornets, Trombones, and Euphoniums: Teach instrument assembly then hand and body positions. All play the first note.

• Percussion: Set up the instrument (bell kit, drum pad, or snare drum) and play a brief pattern by rote (echo).

• If time permits, teach the second note and do two-note echoes (rote snare drum pattern to accompany), or all play first note together.

• Teach instrument disassembly and give important care reminders.

• Give assignment: Practice good posture and good breath support. Check embouchure formation, and hand and body positions in a mirror. Play with your best tone.

Pace instruction so that all students can keep up with and thoroughly understand the lesson. Everyone needs to feel, and be, successful in the beginning instrumental music class. Teachers perform a "pedagogical balancing act" to avoid moving too fast for the slower students, but fast enough to challenge the more gifted students. The use of material designed for individualized instruction will facilitate this "balancing act." James Froseth (1974) reminds us that "A wide variety and range of differences exist *between* students in any given class and also *within* individual students" (p. 4). For some students, the entire music making experience is easy—but most students find that *some* aspects of music performance (characteristic tone, articulation, technique, rhythmic reading, etc.) are easy to master and others are difficult. The successful teacher will be sensitive to those differences and find a way to meet the educational needs of each student.

## Lesson Plans

Discipline problems in the beginning instrumental class sometimes can be traced to the teacher being unprepared for class or not having established a basic routine for students to follow each day. No teacher ever feels *overly* prepared for class! The use of a routine to begin each class will create a quieter and more productive classroom. For example, you might have students take instruments out of the cases only *after* you give the instruction to do so, you might use a consistent group warm-up, and you might install a policy about extraneous playing or talking.

Thorough preparation and planning will pave the way for a class that flows smoothly from activity to activity, and in which active learning is taking place. Lesson plans are essential for every teacher—including the instrumental music teacher. Those who teach a beginning instrumental class will usually have four to 10 or more different instruments in each class, with several students on each of those instruments. Keeping track of student progress and developing a well-reasoned plan of instruction that meets the individual needs of each student will take time and effort; but isn't that what effective teaching is all about?

Successful veteran teachers use a wide variety of lesson planning strategies. In some school districts a specific format may be required of all teachers. Other teachers simply use a listing of the music to be covered in class, the specific problems to be worked on in each piece, and the length of time to be devoted to each. In the past, many instrumental music teachers seemed to believe that "the music is the lesson plan." They would simply determine an order of music for each class

47

and then teach until some error occurred that needed to be corrected. That is not efficient use of valuable class time, and is not a professional approach to instrumental music education.

Lesson plans must be *written* plans. Do not rely on memory. Good lesson plans provide a means to evaluate your effectiveness. At the end of the day, try to spend a few moments reflecting on the success of the lesson plan, noting any necessary deviations from the plan. What worked; what did not work; what could be done to make the lesson more effective, the learning more thorough? Teachers are human and will make mistakes. The effective teacher will learn from those mistakes.

Many school districts require teachers to complete lesson plans and indicate how the lesson meets any state or national standards or objectives that have been adopted by the school district. This type of detailed planning almost forces the teacher to consider thoroughly how a single lesson plan, or an entire curriculum, meets the objectives or standards mandated by the school system or the state department of education. An excellent example of such a lesson plan is found in Figure 3-2. This actual lesson plan was designed by a student teacher to comply with the Learner Goals and Expectations and the Learner Core Concepts adopted by the Kentucky Department of Education as a result of the Kentucky Education Reform Act (KERA). Part one of the plan (Lesson Preparation) indicates which Learner Goals and Expectations, and Core Concepts, are encompassed by the lesson. It states the teacher's instructional objectives and materials needed, and includes both references and resources. The second part of the plan (Lesson Procedural Outline) lists the actual procedures used to teach the class, including a Concept Map (an overhead to reinforce concepts visually) and a handout (sometimes called a quiz!) to measure student comprehension. A scoring rubric is included for the handout. The third part of the lesson (Lesson Closure) describes review and closure of the lesson.

*Figure 3-2. 6th grade Lesson Plan addressing Kentucky Learner Core Concepts and Learner Goals and Expectations*

## 6TH GRADE LESSON PLAN

**I. Lesson Preparation**
   A.  Learner Goals and Expectations

    1.4  Students make sense of the various messages to which they listen

    2.23 Students analyze their and others' artistic products and performances using accepted standards

    5.4  Students use decision-making process to develop or change their understanding of a concept

    6.3  Students expand their understanding of existing knowledge by making connections with new knowledge, skills, and experiences

B. Learner Core Concepts
    #26  Elements of Music: Form
          Music can be expressed in various forms (designs)

C. Subject:   Band
   Topic:     Solo, Soli, and Tutti form
   Grade:    Sixth

D. Instructional Objective:
        Given instruction on solo, soli, and tutti playing, each student will correctly identify 10 such sections in a listening example.

E. Materials Needed:
        Instrument
        Paper and pencil
        "Standard of Excellence" - Book 1
        CD and player

F. Cited References and Resources
    "Standard of Excellence" - Book 1
    KERA Core Concept Cards

## II. Lesson Procedural Outline
### (Procedural Task Analysis)
### Step One: Lesson Initiation
A. Advance Organizer:
    Date:           November 20
    Course News:   Christmas Concert, December 15
    Today's Exercise: "Good King Wenceslas" - #26
    For Next Class:  Practice F concert scale and #26

B. Beginning Review (Warm-up):

Breathing Exercises (on mouthpiece):

    In for one, out for four; eight; 12; 16

    Whole note; two half notes; four quarter notes; (mix)

Assemble Instruments:

    "Down By the Station" - #18

        Correct posture, breathing, instrument carriage

        Make notable difference between half note and quarter note, quarter rest

    "Easy Street"" - #19

        Play Eb Concert with good tone

    "Gettin' It Together" - #21

        Play F Concert with good tone

C. Establish Lesson Purpose:

    We will be performing "Good King Wenceslas" for the Christmas Concert, possibly in solo-soli-tutti format. It is important to understand the difference in these terms both when performing (so as not to play at the wrong time) and when listening.

**Step Two: Learning Experience**

A. Identify target concept and give definition:

| | |
|---|---|
| Solo | - one line of music, perhaps a melody, is played by one person |
| Soli | - one line of music, perhaps a melody, is played by a small group of instruments |
| Tutti | - everyone plays the same line of music all together |

B. Concept Map:

    See attached

C. Guided Application:

    Ask one person to play #26 - "Solo, soli, or tutti?"

    Ask the clarinets to play #26 - "Solo, soli, or tutti?"

Ask the entire band to play #26 - "Solo, soli, or tutti?"

Ask one person from each section to play # 26 together - "Solo, soli, or tutti?"

D. Independent Application

Complete the handout that asks for examples of solo, soli, and tutti playing and has students identify them within a listening example.

**Step Three: Lesson Closure**

A. Ending Review:

Perform "Good King Wenceslas" using various combinations in solo and soli sections. Ask students for ideas of different combinations (i.e. "everyone wearing red").

**III. Rubric for Scoring Handout:**

A. Distinguished (A) - Student correctly identifies examples of solo, soli, and tutti sections in both the writing exercise and the listening examples. Written examples display creativity (not just examples given in class.

B. Proficient (B) - Student correctly identifies eight or more exercises. Writing examples are adequate.

C. Apprentice (C) - Student misses more than three examples in the listening portion and/or fails to provide three adequate examples for the written sections

## SOLO, SOLI, & TUTTI

**Concept Map**

Solo: One person plays a musical line

Soli: A section or a small group of players plays a musical line

Tutti: The entire ensemble plays a musical line together

## SOLO, SOLI, & TUTTI?

Name _____ Class _____

**Section One: Listening (to be completed in class)**
Directions: Listen to the musical examples to be played by the teacher. Using the definitions you have just been given, determine if the selection is an example of solo, soli, or tutti playing. Fully write out the word "solo," "soli," or "tutti" following the number of the musical selection. The first one has been done for you.

1. Solo

2.

3.

4.

5.

6.

7.

8.

9.

10.

**Section Two: Writing (to be completed at home)**
Directions: You have now been informed of the definitions of solo, soli, and tutti playing, and you have listened to and performed examples. Now I want you to think of examples you may have heard in a performance or even in the music you listen to at home. List below at least one example of each of these types of playing. Do not limit yourself to those we discussed in class. Be creative! Use the back of this page if you need more room.

Solo:

Soli:

Tutti:

Used by permission of Joseph Stone

Another sample lesson plan is found in Figure 3-3. This type of lesson plan is primarily for the more experienced teacher and for those who do not have to satisfy any adopted objectives or standards. Teachers in their first few years of teaching will need greater detail. As teachers gain experience, more and more lesson plan material becomes second nature, causing lesson plans to go through many phases from Figure 3-2 to 3-3, and eventually on to a relatively simple sketch.

Although lesson planning can be a time consuming task, especially early in your teaching career, keep reminding yourself that it is time well spent and that it will lead to better teaching and better learning in

*Figure 3-3. Sample Basic Lesson Plan—5th Grade Band*

## Lesson Plan for Timbuktu Elementary School–5th Grade Band–October 30

| Time | Activity | Emphasis or Objective |
|------|----------|----------------------|
| | | At all times emphasize good posture and positions, and correct breathing techniques |
| 10:00am | Warm-up: Echos (concert F, Eb, D) (half & quarter notes; vocal and instru.) Use legato and staccato articulations | Emphasize tone quality<br><br>Check articulation in saxes |
| 10:08am | Project 18 ("Twinkle"): Remind class about the D.C. and Fine. Introduce "ABA" form. Sing first. | Continue to work with trumpets to get first interval. Are flutes playing at least a 2-meas. phrase? |
| 10:13 am | Project 19 (Round I): "What is a round?" 2 groups: brass and woodwind (w/perc.). Note the repeat. | True independence? Check clar. Only in two groups. Also check trombones? |
| 10:18am | Rhythm reading exercise (p. 8): Unison reading, by section, and a few volunteers. | Is Jim reading better today? Does everyone participate confidently? |
| 10:25am | Project 20 (At Pierrot's Door): Legato style of articulation (sing first). Check flutes on both octaves. | Do we sing in legato style? Do we play in legato style? Are all the flutes getting each octave? (review technique) |
| 10:34am | Assignment: Review Project 18-20 and begin Project 21 and 22. (no new notes or rhythms) | Remind all to practice 20 minutes each day! Note any special progress! |

the classroom. A basic lesson format that many teachers find useful includes a brief warm-up, a review of previous material and remedial work, an introduction of new material, a final line of music or an activity the class can do well, and an assignment. The assignment must be stated clearly and concisely so that all students fully understand their responsibility.

If assignments are to be effective, you will need to teach students how to practice. For a student to work on one project in the lesson book incorrectly for 45 minutes is not helpful! Students need to be taught a practice routine, and will need instruction on how to listen objectively to their own playing so they can detect and correct errors in performance. Singing lesson material during the instrumental music class will help students internalize a model that can serve as a reference for home practice.

## Student Assessment

Some formal student assessment or evaluation should be available for parents and students. Both the assessment process and the form of communication are important. Lack of adequate communication between parents and teachers is a common cause of student failure in instrumental music.

Many school districts continue to use a single letter grade for each subject, including instrumental music, on report cards. A single grade is inadequate to provide a diagnosis of progress and potential, a measure of student attitude, and other information helpful to parents, students, and teachers. Figure 3-4 is an example of an assessment format that provides specific information about progress in instrumental music. Periodic formal testing of students on the material assigned in class, along with informal daily class observations, will provide you with the information you need to assess student progress for completion of the form. Taking a few moments after each class to write brief notes in your grade book about each student, based on your observations during class, gives you reference material and prevents you from having to rely on your memory.

A copy of the formal evaluation form should go into a permanent instrumental music student file (see Chapter 9) that follows students as they move through the school system. These permanent files are a valuable resource for diagnosing student performance, advising parents and students, and evaluating the quality of instruction given to students.

**Figure 3-4. Beginning Band Assessment Form**

## Beginning Band Assessment Form

Name _____ Date _____

School_____

Name of Classroom Teacher _____

Grade _____ Instrument _____

The following information is provided to students and parents as an evaluation of student progress in our Beginning Band. This information helps all of us—student, parent, and teacher—evaluate progress and suggest any future action that may be needed.

|  | Poor | Fair | Average | Good | Superior |
|---|---|---|---|---|---|
| General Progress to Date | 1 | 2 | 3 | 4 | 5 |
| Tone Quality | 1 | 2 | 3 | 4 | 5 |
| Breath Control | 1 | 2 | 3 | 4 | 5 |
| Positions (hand, body, instrument) | 1 | 2 | 3 | 4 | 5 |
| Music Reading | 1 | 2 | 3 | 4 | 5 |
| Knowledge of Fingerings | 1 | 2 | 3 | 4 | 5 |
| Sense of Rhythm | 1 | 2 | 3 | 4 | 5 |
| Sense of Pitch | 1 | 2 | 3 | 4 | 5 |
| Prepared for Class Lessons | 1 | 2 | 3 | 4 | 5 |
| Attention during Class | 1 | 2 | 3 | 4 | 5 |
| Care of Instrument | 1 | 2 | 3 | 4 | 5 |
| Behavior (cooperation, courtesy) | 1 | 2 | 3 | 4 | 5 |
| Attendance with instrument & music | 1 | 2 | 3 | 4 | 5 |

Additional Comments:

Please call me if you have any questions about this report.

Instrumental Music Teacher:_____

Phone:_____

Parents appreciate a teacher who can help them guide the educational needs of their child by providing an honest evaluation of the performance and potential of that child. Whatever form of evaluation is used, it should be mailed home to parents or distributed at Parent-Teacher Conferences to ensure delivery.

# Teacher Self-Evaluation

The results of student achievement tests can help teachers evaluate their own teaching effectiveness. Teachers will find that they also need to develop other forms of self-evaluation to identify their shortcomings. Most school systems require school administrators to evaluate teachers once or twice each year. These administrator evaluations generally are limited to teaching style, discipline, classroom management, etc. They rarely evaluate lesson content, appropriateness of content, knowledge of subject matter, and other subject-specific topics.

In addition to considering administrator evaluations, young teachers should invite an experienced music teacher colleague to observe classes and give suggestions for improvement. Some states, and some individual school districts, have an established mentoring program for new teachers. A mentor can be an excellent source of help for the new teacher. Another useful technique is to videotape yourself while teaching and then evaluate your performance as objectively as possible, either alone or with the help of an experienced teacher. Self-evaluation of videotaped teaching should be done on a regular basis for best results. As education professionals, we have the responsibility to improve our teaching—both in content and in delivery of that content. Student learning improves when teaching improves.

## *For Discussion or Assignment*

1. Using the criteria discussed in this chapter, evaluate two instrumental music class methods series currently available. Share this evaluation with other class members.

2. Using an appropriate format, prepare a 30-minute lesson plan for a beginning instrumental music class. Include an estimate of time to be used for each item.

3. Design a student progress evaluation form or procedure to use with a beginning instrumental music class.

4. Interview a beginning instrumental music teacher and observe at least one beginning instrumental class. Write a brief paper describing the type of program you observed. List materials used, scheduling of classes, instructional techniques, student responses, etc.

## *For Reference and Further Reading*

Anderson, J. N. (1981). Effects of tape-recorded aural models on sight-reading and performance skills. *Journal of Research in Music Education*, 29, pp. 23-30.

Conway, Colleen M. (1997). Why wait to start beginning band rehearsals? *Teaching Music*, 5/1, pp. 36 & 45.

*The Crane Symposium: Toward an Understanding of the Teaching and Learning of Music Performance*. (1988). Potsdam: Crane School of Music, State University of New York.

Delzell, Judith K. (1989). The effects of musical discrimination training in beginning instrumental music classes. *Journal of Research in Music Education*, 37/1, pp. 21-31.

Elliott, David J. (1992). Rethinking music teacher education. *Journal of Music Teacher Education*. Fall, pp. 6-15.

Elliott, David J. (1995). Music Matters: *A New Philosophy of Music Education*. New York: Oxford University Press.

Franks, Earl (1996). Without wasting words or time: An interview with John M. Long. *The Instrumentalist*. February, pp. 18-22.

Froseth, James O. (1971). Using MAP scores in the instruction of beginning students in instrumental music. *Journal of Research in Music Education*. 19/1, pp. 98-105.

Froseth, James O. (1974). *Teacher's Guide to the Individualized Instructor*. Chicago: GIA Publications, Inc.

Froseth, James O. (1976). *Introducing the Instruments—Preliminary Book* (Text and Picture Full Score). Chicago: GIA Publications, Inc.

Froseth, James O. (1998). *Do It! Play in Band*. Chicago: GIA Publications, Inc.

Gordon, Edwin (1988). *Learning Sequences in Music*. Chicago: GIA Publications, Inc.

Gordon, Edwin (1971). *The Psychology of Music Teaching*. Englewood Cliffs, NJ: Prentice-Hall, Inc.

Grunow, Richard F. and Gordon, Edwin E. (1989). *Jump Right In: The Instrumental Series Teacher's Guide*. Chicago: GIA Publications, Inc.

Grunow, Richard F. and Gamble, Denise K. (1989). Music learning sequence techniques in beginning instrumental music. In *Readings in Music Learning Theory*. Chicago: GIA Publications, Inc.

Holz, Emil A., and Jacobi, Roger E. (1966). *Teaching Band Instruments to Beginners*. Englewood Cliffs, NJ: Prentice-Hall, Inc.

**58**

Lautzenheiser, Tim (1993). *Director's Communication Kit for All Band Programs*. Milwaukee: Hal Leonard Corp.

Leonhard, Charles, and House, Robert W. (1972). *Foundations and Principles of Music Education (2nd ed.)*. New York: McGraw-Hill.

Maddy, Joseph and Giddings, Thaddeus (1923, 1928). *The Universal Teacher*. Elkhart, IN: C.G. Conn Co., Cincinnati, OH: The Willis Music Co.

Mursell, James L. (1943, 1953). *Music in American Schools*. New York: Silver Burdett Co.

*National Standards for Arts Education: What Every Young American Should Know and Be Able to Do in the Arts* (1994). Reston, VA: Music Educators National Conference.

*Performance Standards for Music: Grades PreK-12* (1996). Reston, VA: Music Educators National Conference.

Sang, R. (1987). A study of the relationship between instrumental music teachers' modeling skills and pupil performance behaviors. *Bulletin of the Council for Research in Music Education*, 91, pp. 155-159.

Schleuter Stanley L. (1997). *A Sound Approach to Teaching Instrumentalist* (2nd ed.). New York: Schirmer Books.

*The School Music Program: A New Vision* (1994). Reston, VA: Music Educators National Conference.

Walters, Darrel L. and Taggart, Cynthia C. (1989). *Readings in Music Learning Theory*. Chicago: GIA Publications, Inc.

# Part II:
## The Secondary Program

Chapter Four

# BUILDING A CURRICULUM

## Program Balance

### The Instrumental Program

The instrumental music program should offer a range of musical activities and ensembles to meet the musical needs of the students and the performance responsibilities of the program. At the center of those various ensembles should be the concert band and the orchestra.

James Curnow (see Moss, 1995) stated that:

> At all times the emphasis should be on the concert band. The great programs around the country, those with 20 and 30 years of strong reputations, maintain a high standard because the primary focus is on the concert band; the other ensembles come out of that program. . . . The concert band acts as a foundation for other ensembles and is the place to develop tone quality, intonation, and musicality (14).

A fine instrumental music program is like an old wooden wagon wheel. In a band program the rim of the wheel represents the total, comprehensive program; the spokes represent the marching band, the jazz ensemble, chamber ensembles, solo program, private lessons, pep band, etc.; and the hub of the wheel is the concert band. A wheel *must* have a strong, stable hub if it is to work at all—and the more spokes in the wheel, the stronger the wheel. The same is true of a band or orchestra program—a high quality program must have a strong "hub," but it is even stronger with many strong "spokes."

**Figure 4-1**

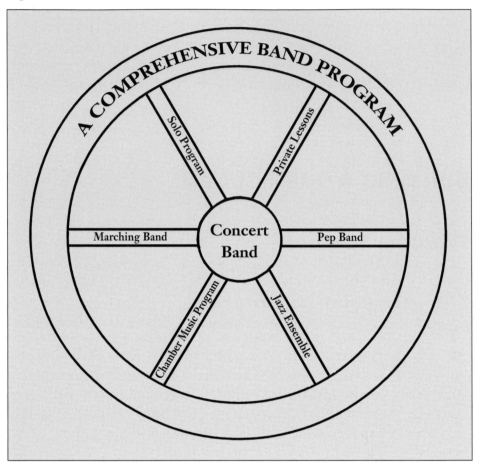

The large concert ensembles provide teaching and learning opportunities not possible in other ensembles. The concert ensemble experience should focus on playing with a characteristic tone on each instrument, improving pitch consciousness, developing individual and ensemble technique, playing with appropriate musical phrasing, playing with rhythmic accuracy, developing personal and ensemble sight-reading skills, learning to play in balance, learning to match tone qualities and pitch, etc. Developing these performance skills should be part of every ensemble experience, but they are most efficiently and economically taught in the large concert ensemble. While many of these skills are taught well—even best—in chamber ensemble experiences, most schools cannot schedule all band or orchestra students into a chamber experience on a regular basis.

Membership in the other ensembles (marching band, jazz ensemble, etc.) should, in most cases, be available only to those students already in the primary concert ensemble. The other ensembles are very important for the total music education of students, and should be encouraged, but they should always be considered as additions to the primary instrumental performing ensembles. A band program that offers a jazz ensemble and various woodwind, brass, and percussion chamber ensembles; or an orchestra program that includes chamber group experience, strolling strings or "fiddling" groups, will be stronger programs. These programs are stronger—assuming that the offerings are of top-quality—because of the richness of program diversity and a higher level of student involvement in the instrumental program. Further discussion about these "special groups" is found later in this chapter.

There are sometimes extenuating circumstances that prevent a student from enrolling in the primary concert ensemble. In rare cases it might be best to allow a student to participate in one of the other ensembles as a means of continuing his or her participation in the instrumental music program. Use caution in such decisions to prevent a landslide of students with "extenuating circumstances" wanting to participate only in the popular and showy groups.

## The Total Secondary Music Program

For the sake of our art, and the complete music education of students, it is important that instrumental music teachers support the development of a strong choral music program in the middle and high schools. Not every child will be involved in instrumental music, but all music educators should be concerned about providing musical opportunities for every student in a school. This would include instrumental and choral performing groups, but it should also include classes for those students who are not interested in performing groups. Will Schmid (1996), former president of the Music Educators National Conference, reminded us that:

> The number one goal of middle and high school music teachers should be to add meaningful music experiences (not just listening courses) for the general students not now enrolled in band, choir, or orchestra. Growth in this area will ensure wider public support and will strengthen the concept of music as a basic subject. (pp. 4-5)

It is important that music teachers attempt to determine the most appropriate courses to offer at their school. Bruce Boston (1995) wrote that "There is a serious need to match instruction in music with the interests of today's students, particularly in terms of drawing on the musical environment and culture outside schools, where music is such a large part of student life" (p. 20).

# What to Teach

## Non-Performance Courses

Whenever possible, high schools should offer courses in music theory and composition and in music history. While this is particularly important for students considering a career in music, many other students may be interested in these courses. In smaller schools that cannot offer such courses during the school day, it might be possible to teach them to interested students using one of the several programmed texts designed for this use. Several suggested texts are listed at the end of this chapter. Other non-performance courses that might be offered include classes in guitar and piano. Some schools may find an interest in what used to be called "general music" or "music appreciation" classes. These are primarily designed to help students learn about and listen to fine music.

## Concert Ensembles

When enrollment reaches 100 or more, the middle or high school band or orchestra should be divided into two ensembles. It is very difficult in a large ensemble to keep track of individual student performance problems, and it becomes almost impossible to individualize instruction. The question of how to divide students into two or more ensembles has no easy answers. When dividing into two bands or orchestras, the obvious solution is to divide strictly by ability. This can work well but will require much effort and planning on your part to avoid the "second best syndrome." The "second" band or orchestra experience must—as closely as possible—equal the experience of students in the "first" band or orchestra. It is vital that the second ensemble students have very successful and musically fulfilling experiences. In some schools, students are divided equally between two ensembles in an effort to avoid the second band or orchestra problem. A little healthy competition may even develop, bringing the skill level higher in both groups. Work closely with the administration to achieve a successful change to two ensembles. Also, try to gain the support of the upper-class students in the ensembles. Their enthusiasm and support will attract the support of younger students and parents.

Some directors find that dividing students by grade level works well in their school system. This is often done in middle schools, where it is developmentally appropriate to keep students in a 6th Grade Band, 7th Grade Band, and an 8th Grade Band. Dividing a high school program by grade level is not usually possible except in large schools with high instrumental music enrollment. High schools with enough students for two bands or orchestras will commonly divide by ability, but some find success grouping grade levels together—such as 9th and 10th grade students in one ensemble, and 11th and 12th in another ensemble.

If you are part of a large high school instrumental music programs (enough students for three or more ensembles), you might consider keeping all 9th grade students together in a Freshman Band or Freshman Orchestra, and dividing all upper-class students into ensembles by ability. This arrangement allows you to focus on the fundamental skills and understandings you believe to be important. The range of musical ability level of 9th grade students is quite wide, but many directors find that 9th grade "stars" benefit from being "big fish in a little pond," and that they develop musical leadership skills they may not otherwise acquire as "little freshmen" in a top band. In addition, the outstanding players will be models for the rest of the band and will help raise the performance level expectation of that band.

After you decide how to divide your bands, the next big problem is to decide what to call them. There is much creativity in the naming of school bands today. Band names run the gamut from Smalltown High School Band in a small school with one band, to Bigtown High School Wind Symphony in a large school with multiple bands. The name selected for your bands is important. A band named "Second Band" would have some real self-image problems!

A few suggestions for band names:
- Symphony Band (usually used for the top band in a multi-band program)
- Symphonic Band (also used for the top band)
- Concert Band (could be used for the top band at a one-band school or for the second band in a multi-band program)
- Varsity Band (could be a second or third band in a multi-band program)

- Freshman Band (seems obvious, doesn't it?)
- Wind Ensemble (often used for the top band in a multi-band program. While the name implies a wind ensemble concept [primarily one-to-a-part], it is sometimes used just to indicate a "small band.")
- Symphonic Wind Ensemble (same use as Wind Ensemble)
- Wind Symphony (same use as Wind Ensemble)
- Concert Winds (same use as Wind Ensemble)
- Wind Band (same use as Wind Ensemble)
- Chamber Winds (same use as Wind Ensemble)

There are many different names used for bands in schools and colleges around the country. Find the one that is appropriate—and not overly pretentious—for your band.

Middle and high school orchestras have similar problems in finding just the right name to use for their ensembles. Some suggestions for orchestras:

- Symphony Orchestra (usually used for the top orchestra in a multi-orchestra program)
- Symphonic Orchestra (same use as Symphony Orchestra)
- Philharmonic Orchestra (same use as Symphony Orchestra)
- Concert Orchestra (usually used for the second orchestra in a multi-orchestra program)
- Orchestra (often used at a small, one-orchestra, program)
- Chamber Orchestra (used to indicate a smaller orchestra)
- String Orchestra (often used in middle schools or high schools when winds and percussion are not added for performances)

## Other Ensembles

With a diversity of ensembles and activities (in addition to your program's primary concert ensembles), teaching instrumental music is a wonderfully multi-faceted enterprise. The additional ensembles not only enrich the music education of your students, they also add great strength to your program because of the unique skills, musical understanding, musical maturity, and variety of literature required in various ensembles. In addition, students who participate in numerous ensembles and activities naturally have more of a connection with the total program and become more committed ensemble members.

For band directors, the extra ensembles could include marching band, pep band, and jazz ensemble. Orchestra directors may find student interest in developing a strolling strings group or a fiddling group. In addition, band and orchestra directors will find that an extensive chamber music program will be of great benefit to student musicians in developing independent musicianship skills, sight-reading skills, and more mature balance and intonation skills.

## Marching Band

Marching band is a vital part of any band program. Typically, the marching band will be seen and heard by more people in one major parade than the concert band in all its performances during a school year. Some in a community will evaluate the quality of the entire program by the quality of a single marching band performance. While this might not be fair, it is a fact; and a wise band director will ensure that the band is always well prepared to give a top-notch marching performance.

Because the work of the marching band is so visible and thought to be so important, every future high school band director should take a complete course in marching band techniques—in fact, most colleges make it a degree requirement. It is beyond the scope of this text to cover even the basic information needed to successfully implement and sustain a quality marching band program. As you thoughtfully consider the possibilities of running a high school marching band program, be sure to keep in mind your own music education philosophy. You may also want to read the helpful book *The Marching Band Program* by Bentley Shellahamer, James Swearingen, and Jon Woods. This book is not a "how to" book, but a "why to" book, and it will provoke a thoughtful analysis of your involvement in marching band.

At most high schools, the concert band becomes the marching band during the fall by requiring all concert band members to be in the marching band. This policy ensures full participation and more cohesiveness in the band program, and may be essential in smaller band programs. Some large band programs offer marching band as an optional after-school activity, which allows the concert bands to work on concert music all year. This procedure allows students who do not like marching band to opt out of that part of the band program without penalty.

In many schools, marching band seems to dominate the time and resources of the total band program. This situation may cause a band program to become out of balance and lacking in musical depth. While marching band does attract a lot of attention from the public, parents, and administrators, it is a support that is often not based on musical principles, but on public relations, visibility, and trophies won at contests. A word of caution: Positive public reaction to the marching band can easily lead to more and more emphasis on that ensemble. Be careful to keep all aspects of the band program in balance, with the primary focus remaining on concert band. Also, because of the many performances available for marching band—football games, marching contests, parades, grand openings (!), etc.—directors sometimes begin to make unreasonable time demands on students, both for extra rehearsals and all those performances. Keep it in balance! One of the major contributors to student and band director burnout is a "hyperactive" marching band.

## Jazz Ensemble

Many public schools offer jazz ensemble as a credit course during the regular school day, but some schools have found great success scheduling their jazz ensemble as an after school—no credit—ensemble. Whichever way works best at your school, this original American art form should be available to instrumental music education students. When interest and ability allow, offer a second jazz ensemble or jazz combos either during the school day or after school. As with the marching band, the jazz ensemble requires much specific skill and knowledge. We will cover only some of the basic issues in this section.

Members of the jazz ensemble should come from the concert band. You may need to allow occasional exceptions to this policy—such as for guitar, bass, and piano players—but even these rhythm section players can usually be found in the concert band. Requiring membership in concert band helps establish the centrality of that ensemble, which in turn keeps a perspective on the small ensembles as family units rather than as independent, elite groups.

When you first start a jazz ensemble, you may need to offer it as a volunteer group instead of a for-credit class. Find the time that is best for the majority of the interested students—before or after school, evenings, or lunch hour. Offering jazz ensemble as a no-credit course can be an advantage because more of the best students may be able to participate if they do not have to give up a regular class. Obviously, it is best to eventually offer jazz ensemble as part of the school curriculum, because rehearsals every day provide time to develop improvisation skills and to learn more literature.

The instrumentation of a contemporary jazz ensemble (or "big band") has become standardized, with four trumpets, four trombones, five saxes (two altos, two tenors, and a baritone), and a rhythm section (piano, drums, bass, and guitar). Sometimes a fifth trumpet is used to allow alternating on the first part if endurance is a concern, and a fifth trombone could be used to double the third part. It is helpful if some of the saxophones can double on clarinet or flute, but this is not essential with most music written for high school jazz ensemble. The piano, bass, and drums are the critical members of the rhythm section. The guitar is a good addition (especially in rock-oriented pieces), and you may want to use two piano players and two drummers to give more people a chance to play—and to give experience to younger players who may be your leaders in future years. Also, having a second drummer allows you to add vibes, congas, etc., as desired.

Figure 4-2 illustrates one of the traditional set-ups for a jazz ensemble. Note that this set-up puts the "leads" (first alto saxophone, first trombone, and first trumpet) almost in a line. This is desirable because these three players set the style for their sections, and, obviously, it is helpful if the three of them can hear each other and agree on style! This set-up also puts the traditional soloists—first alto saxophone, first tenor saxophone, second trombone, and second trumpet—near the rhythm section. Notice that the guitar player is by the piano (which, among other things, allows them to easily decide who should "comp" during solos), and the bass player is by the drummer (which encourages better rhythmic and tempo precision). Another advantage to this set-up is that all e-flat saxophones, and the b-flat saxophones, are together and can easily share a chord chart for soloing.

*Figure 4-2. A Traditional Jazz Ensemble Set-up*

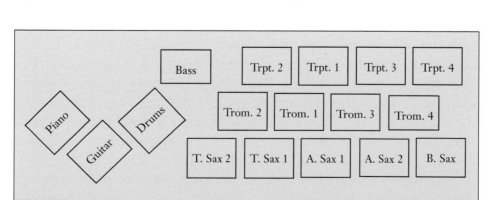

Some general suggestions:
- Auditions (which may not be necessary when you begin your jazz ensemble) should include something prepared (jazz standards or popular songs), plenty of sight-reading in a variety of jazz styles, and perhaps some improvisation.
- Insist on good tone! A bad tone is a bad tone whether it is playing Beethoven's *Symphony No. 1* or Nestico's *Basie Straight-Ahead.*
- When playing jazz, some saxophonists like to use a jazz mouthpiece that permits them to get a little more fullness and edge to the sound. Many saxophonists also change to a reed cut for jazz. A caution: insist on a good tone, no matter the mouthpiece or reed!
- Articulations are often different in jazz styles. The use of "scat" singing and jazz syllables are great aids in teaching correct jazz style.
- Just like your players in the concert band, jazz musicians need to hear outstanding models. In fact, since jazz is such an aural art, it is important that you develop a fine listening library for your musicians so they can hear the models you want them to emulate.
- Go to many "how-to" clinics if you are not a jazz musician. There is a lot of help available—make good use of it!

Improvisation—sometimes called "instant composition"—is essential for any complete jazz musician. Some people seem to have a natural gift or ability in improvisation, but *all* students can be taught some level of improvisation skill. It may not be "inspired," but it can be acceptable and "listenable." The aural tradition is vitally important in jazz, and much understanding and inspiration in improvisation will happen when your students listen to outstanding models. There are many tools available to help guide young musicians to develop improvisation skills. The widely used Jamey Aebersold series of books and CDs is a very complete series that uses scales and patterns to build a musical "vocabulary" to use in developing improvisations. The strength of the series may be that it helps students become familiar with the process of making their note choices fit into the sounding chords, which gets students used to hearing—and anticipating—chord changes. The Aebersold video *Anyone Can Improvise* is a very good general introduction to improvisation.

*Improvise!* by James Froseth and Al Blazer is an excellent introduction to improvisation through a primarily aural approach. Froseth's compact disk series—titled *Do It! Improvise*—with Blazer (Volume I) and with David Froseth (Volume II) uses a wide range of popular music styles in a variety of keys and modes. Recommended articles on directing a school jazz ensemble and teaching improvisation are found at the end of this chapter—the articles by Alphonso M. Young, Jr. (1999) and John Kuzmich, Jr. (1998) are particularly helpful. There are many books, articles, and clinics available to help a band director who does not have a jazz background. It is worth the time investment to develop your own understanding of this great American art form, and to be able to help your students discover jazz.

## *Pep Band*

Organizing a pep band to help support various athletic and other school events is a common expectation for a high school band director. In a sense, there is a kind of civic responsibility related to pep bands in high schools. As a part of the larger school community, the band can make an important contribution to school spirit and morale. While this can be an important activity for the band, it also must be kept in balance and should never detract from the important music education function of the concert bands. Band students are usually *busy* students, so keep their time commitment to pep band under control. You might consider dividing the concert band in half, or even in thirds with a larger band, and have the two or three pep bands alternate playing at games. Also, you might have the pep band play only at Friday or Saturday games so that your students do not have to be at a game on a weeknight. Many creative things can be done to keep pep band from becoming a monster.

If you do have a pep band, try to make it a first-rate group by choosing well-arranged music, rehearsing the music thoroughly (usually after school or just before games), and insisting on high performance standards. This group represents the entire band program—make sure they always give a *quality* impression. They should play well, dress and act appropriately, and support the athletic team.

A pep band can also provide a good opportunity to develop student musical leadership. Choose responsible older students to be student conductors and allow them to do a lot of the conducting during pep band performances. This is a particularly valuable experience for students thinking about majoring in instrumental music education.

## *Chamber Ensembles*

Many outstanding school band and orchestra programs include a well-organized chamber music program that involves a majority of their members. Students who participate in a fine chamber music program learn valuable musical skills and understandings that are difficult to teach in large ensemble rehearsals. They also learn to make mature musical decisions about performance, and become more independent, self-sufficient musicians. Performing in chamber ensembles opens up a whole new realm of musical possibilities to students and gives them valuable options for adult musical involvement. The musical growth experienced by students in chamber ensembles leads to mature and confident players who have a positive impact on the large concert ensembles in their schools.

Many band and orchestra teachers encourage their students to be involved in annual solo and ensemble festivals sponsored by district or state music organizations. You might even consider assigning all members of the large ensembles to a chamber ensemble that rehearses most of the school year. For example, in a high school band you might have a basic core of ensembles such as a woodwind quintet, brass quintet, saxophone quartet, and percussion ensemble. In addition, you could have a flute choir and clarinet choir, or a woodwind choir. You might also have a trumpet choir, horn quartet, trombone choir, tuba and euphonium ensemble, or a large brass choir. You might want to have several small ensembles (duet, trios, and quartets). An orchestra might have a number of duets, trios, and quartets. The important thing is to have *every* student involved so that they all reap the significant benefits of the chamber music experience.

You should coach these ensembles, but a mature student in the ensemble should lead them. In the initial stages of establishing a chamber ensemble program, you will need to give up large ensemble time for chamber rehearsals. Find a place for each ensemble to practice (practice rooms, the choir room, the stage, the instrument storage room, the hall, etc.) and then go around to each chamber group to monitor progress and offer musical suggestions. This will be time well spent! Having each chamber ensemble perform for the rest of the band or orchestra (or in a more formal recital) is a good motivator. One fortunate by-product of a regular chamber music program is that you will always have student ensembles ready to perform for local civic clubs and organizations—and you could use their chamber ensemble performance as part of grading period assessment to determine course grades.

## String Ensembles

String ensembles, such as strolling strings and fiddling groups, introduce different styles of music to students and broaden their musical knowledge. In addition, these ensembles may reach a different audience than the school orchestra, and can help develop a more broad-based community support for the string program. Many orchestra students greatly enjoy participating in such groups.

## Community Bands and Orchestras

Although not a part of their school responsibilities, many school band or orchestra directors also conduct a community band or orchestra. It is very rewarding to work with adult musicians who are in an ensemble just because they love music and music-making. Many music educators are concerned that so many who played an instrument in high school or college do not play as adults. One of the reasons they do not play may be that there are not enough ensemble opportunities available. That is where you come in! Think of the community band or orchestra as a kind of extension of the school music program. In addition, the members of a community band or orchestra are built-in supporters of the school music program. It is a "win-win" situation!

*The Community Band—A Manual of Organization and Operation*, published by the Northshore Concert Band in the Chicago area, is a great help for organizing a community band or orchestra. It gives valuable advice on programming, budgets, organizational structure, etc. The address for requesting a copy of this booklet is:

Northshore Concert Band
422 E. Oakwood Dr.
Barrington, IL 60010
847-487-7036
www.northshoreband.org

It may be best to allow only those past high school age to be in the community ensemble. Younger players, who are playing every day, can intimidate an older player who plays once or twice a week—especially one who has not played in several years. The older players will usually regain much of their technical skills after a while, and they will play with a maturity that more than offsets most technical deficiencies. If there is no community band or orchestra established in your area, and you can make time in your busy schedule, be a part of organizing such a worthy community group. Perhaps this is something you and your spouse can enjoy together.

## Course Descriptions

It is important to develop the ability to write concise but thorough course descriptions. Published course descriptions are considered legally binding documents, and so must be accurate and complete. Any prerequisites and special course requirements or expectations—such as required attendance at all performances—must be clearly stated in the course description. Any major issues that are important to the director and promote the smooth running of the ensemble should be included in the course description.

Figure 4-3 is an example of a course description for a high school band. Note the requirement of an audition for admission, that all students are also members of the marching band, that occasional after school rehearsals are required, and that all performances are required. Also, at this school, performing in band fulfills the one-semester physical education requirement. This policy seems logical because of the physical activity required for marching band. In addition, the physical education waiver is an excellent incentive to continue enrollment in band!

*Figure 4-3. High School Band Course Description.*

| Number | Course Name | Grade Level | Course Length | Credit |
|--------|-------------|-------------|---------------|--------|
| 536 | SYMPHONY BAND | 10 11 12 | Full Year | 1.00 |

PREREQUISITE: PERMISSION OF INSTRUCTOR
The Symphony Band is open to those students who have demonstrated an adequately high level of performance on their instrument in an audition. The finest in band literature will be studied in preparation for concerts, band festivals, solo and ensemble festivals, football games, parades, school and community events, and tours. All members of the Symphony Band also participate in the Marching Band. The band director may schedule occasional after school rehearsals. Students must show reasonable musical progress on their instrument to maintain membership in the Symphony Band. Attendance at all performances is required. This class will fulfill the Physical Education course requirement.

Figure 4-4 is an example of a high school jazz ensemble course description. Again, note the performance requirement and a prerequisite of "permission of instructor." Figure 4-5 is for a high school orchestra.

*Figure 4-4. High School Jazz Ensemble Course Description.*

| Number | Course Name | Grade Level | Course Length | Credit |
|---|---|---|---|---|
| 539 | JAZZ ENSEMBLE | 10 11 12 | Full Year | 1.00 |

PREREQUISITE: PERMISSION OF INSTRUCTOR

The Jazz Ensemble rehearses and performs a wide range of popular music. Much time is spent developing improvisatory skills. Attendance at all performances is required. Jazz Ensemble members must also be enrolled in a school band or orchestra.

*Figure 4-5. Course Description for a High School Orchestra.*

| Number | Course Name | Grade Level | Course Length | Credit |
|---|---|---|---|---|
| 526 | SYMPHONY ORCHESTRA | 10 11 12 | Full Year | 1.00 |

PREREQUISITE: PERMISSION OF INSTRUCTOR

The Symphony Orchestra is open to all string players who can demonstrate a high level of proficiency on their instrument through an audition. The wind and percussion players will be selected by the orchestra and band conductors from among the top Symphony Band members. The Symphony Orchestra will explore the range of orchestral music from pre-classical to contemporary. They will perform concerts, participate in festivals, and make occasional tours. The string members of the orchestra meet every day and the full orchestra rehearses once per week. Occasional after school rehearsals may be scheduled and attendance is required. Attendance at all performances is required.

Schools that offer a music theory and composition or a music history course may find the description of a Comprehensive Musicianship course (Figure 4-6) to be helpful. This course, designed for junior or senior students who are in the music program or have advanced skills through private study, is a one-semester survey course combining music theory, music history, and music literature.

*Figure 4-6. Course Description for Comprehensive Musicianship.*

Number    Course Name                    Grade Level  Course Length  Credit
542 COMPREHENSIVE MUSICIANSHIP  11 12    One Semester   .50

PREREQUISITE: TWO YEARS OF HIGH SCHOOL MUSIC EXPERIENCE AND PERMISSION OF INSTRUCTOR

This elective course is available to students with a minimum of two years experience in a high school music ensemble. Students with extensive private study on instruments such as piano may enroll with permission of the instructor. This course is designed to offer students basic instruction in music theory and composition, and in music history and literature. This course is recommended for students considering a college music major, and for others who desire a more full understanding of the structure of music and of the great masterworks of music literature.

Course descriptions provide students and parents with information about the content of courses and basic requirements. They also help administrators, counselors, and other teachers gain a better understanding of various courses, and help in advising students as they select courses. A well-stated course description can also be a valuable way for the teacher to set parameters for classes, outline course standards, and monitor course enrollment.

## Sequential Instruction

Teachers have always recognized the importance of determining the appropriate sequence of instruction. The sequence of content is vitally important if students are to learn most effectively and efficiently. In 1943, James Mursell stated his belief that, "The really essential thing is the sequence of the program" (p. 71). Almost 50 years later, Darrel Walters (1992) wrote that "Good teachers think about more than what to teach and how to teach; they think about when and when not to teach particular lessons" (p. 535). Elizabeth Green (1966) produced a valuable resource for string teachers in her *Orchestral Bowings and Routines* with a sequential program for teaching string bowings in the school orchestra rehearsal. This program would be a helpful model as you develop sequential instruction in your courses and ensembles.

In some areas of study, such as history, teachers find the content and sequence of instruction is decided, for the most part, by the authors of their textbook. In bands and orchestras, the director chooses the curriculum through selection of literature, and will plan the sequential development of skills, techniques, and musical understandings in students.

One factor to consider when choosing literature for ensembles is how that literature will contribute to the sequential development of your student musicians. For example, after you decide when multiple tonguing on brass instruments should be introduced, you will want to select some literature that requires multiple tonguing. Sequential development of musical skills, techniques, and understandings must not be left to chance. You should decide when such things as multiple tonguing, vibrato, advanced bowings, extended range fingerings, alternate fingerings, etc., should be taught to students, and then develop a plan to introduce those skills, techniques, and understandings. Too often students learn these things only through observation or through the suggestions of other students.

## Scheduling Issues

The issue of when courses are scheduled during the school day is a significant one for the band or orchestra director. Do you get "prime" or "left-over" time? If single-section courses—especially the so-called "college prep" courses—are scheduled at the same time as band or orchestra, you will lose students. These students will often be juniors and seniors who are the leaders in your ensembles. It is essential to talk with all people involved in developing the master schedule at your school, and clearly explain the *needs of your students*. Administrators should be shown that these issues concern the needs of your *students*— not your needs or the needs of your program. Administrators are usually interested in meeting student needs; and most will see the value in enabling students to participate in courses and experiences in which they have already invested much time, effort, and money.

When discussing scheduling concerns with administrators, be prepared with suggestions for correcting any current problems. Also, realize that administrators are dealing with many issues about which you may be unaware, and they may not always be able to solve your problem immediately. Be patient—and politely persistent! You may not solve your scheduling problems right away, but establishing collegial relationships with administrators (and other teachers) will have long-term beneficial results. I once had an administrator suggest, without my prompting, that we put all the sophomores from our "second band" in the same English class and schedule it the same period as our "first band." By scheduling the English teacher's planning period during the period for second band, we were able to have that entire class (which was more than half of the second band) come to first band during the marching season and then go back to their regular class time during concert season. This unique and effective solution to a real problem grew out of a respectful collegial relationship established over several years.

Finding the *right* period for the ensemble is not easy. It is usually best to avoid times around the lunch period—students are hungry just before lunch and sleepy just after lunch! Some directors like to have band at the very end of the day so students can change for marching rehearsals, and also so that the rehearsal can flow right into any scheduled after-school rehearsal. The major downside of having band last period is that students are mentally tired at the end of the day and there are often many interruptions—pep assemblies, students leaving early for athletic events, lengthy end-of-the-day public address system announcements, etc. The advantage to scheduling band early in the day is that students are more mentally fresh and there seem to be fewer interruptions—except for morning announcements. However, some teachers find it difficult to sustain a high level of concentration early in the morning.

In the past 25 years there have been many experiments with class schedule design in secondary schools. What are often termed "conventional" or "traditional" schedules (usually six to eight class periods of 45-50 minutes length) have given way to many new ideas in schedule design. Modular schedules typically divide the school day into 20- or 30-minute modules, or "mods," and classes can be assigned a different number of mods depending on their needs. For instance, a science class might have only one mod on Tuesday and Thursday (when lectures are planned) but might need three or four mods when lab work is scheduled on Monday, Wednesday, and Friday. Orchestra might be scheduled for four mods, but only on Monday, Wednesday, and Friday. While the flexibility of such a schedule may initially seem attractive, it will take much time to design (with many turf battles); and it is difficult for students *and* faculty to keep track of their schedules. In addition, it is difficult for teachers who teach in several buildings—like music teachers—to align such a schedule with a traditional schedule being used in another building.

Another class schedule design that is meant to allow more flexibility in the school day is the rotating schedule. One example of this design is to offer six courses on a five-period day by using a Six-Day Schedule. On this plan classes A, B, C, D, and E are scheduled on Day One; classes B, C, D, E, and F on Day Two; classes A, C, D, E, and F on Day Three; and so forth through Day Six. Again, the difficulty for teachers who teach in other buildings is aligning their schedules.

Many schools around the country now use some type of block scheduling. The basic "4x4" schedule offers four 90-minute blocks each semester. Under this plan, a course that would have been a full-year course on a traditional schedule now meets for only one semester. Some schools offer courses that would have been one-semester courses under a traditional plan as nine-week (1/2 semester) courses. These are usually clustered with other nine-week courses for ease of scheduling. One "modified block" plan offers some courses that meet on alternate days for the full year in addition to the core of classes that are on a full block plan.

A variation on the basic block schedule is the "A/B Block." The A/B Block schedules two groups of four classes on alternating days so that classes are, again, full-year classes. Another variation is to have three or four large blocks (90-minutes each) and one small block (45-minutes) for classes such as music, art, drama, Advanced Placement classes, etc. There are many variations of block scheduling being used around the country. Some are more favorable to music than others, and it is vitally important that you get involved in the process of changing a school class schedule. A caution: block scheduling is not, in the opinion of most educators, appropriate for use in middle schools. High school students have difficulty maintaining concentration for a 90-minute period—middle school students have a notoriously shorter attention span.

While having 90-minute rehearsals five days a week may seem desirable, many directors find that few students are able to commit 25-percent of their high school schedule to band or orchestra for all four years. Typically, upper-class students decide they need to fulfill a language requirement, take an Advanced Placement course, or take some other course to prepare them for college or technical school. Many schools have experienced a significant decrease in the number of students able to take music courses under the block schedule plan. Another factor—especially in schools with a large music program—is that with only four periods to offer music, finding rehearsal space is often a significant problem. There are many documented cases of the potential detrimental effect of block scheduling on the music program

(Blocher and Miles, 1995). If your school is considering a change to block scheduling, be sure you are knowledgeable about current studies on the topic, and stay involved in the study and decision-making process. Keep students and parents fully informed of the progress at each phase, since their influence may become a critical part of the outcome.

A six, seven, or eight period class schedule gives students more opportunities to take "extra" classes such as music, art, shop, foreign language, etc. Having more class options, even if that means classes of only 40 or 45 minutes, will allow more students to continue their participation in music. A larger number of class periods also means that courses such as jazz ensemble or chamber ensembles could be offered for credit at your school. The music program benefits when there are more periods in the class schedule.

## For Discussion or Assignment

1. Identify intermediate and advanced skills on your major instrument. Determine at what grade level those skills should be introduced and discuss how it should be done. Share your work with your class colleagues.

2. Do you think high school bands and orchestras should be divided by ability or by grade level? Why?

3. Write a course description for an 8th grade band or orchestra at a grades 6-8 middle school.

4. Discuss your beliefs about the position of the marching band in the total band program.

## For Reference and Further Reading

Boston, Bruce (1995). *With One Voice: A Report from the 1994 Summit on Music Education.* Reston, VA: Music Educators National Conference.

Brown, Michael R. (1998). Chamber music for better bands. *Teaching Music,* 5/5 (April), 38-39, 72.

Choksy, Lois, et al. (1986). *Teaching Music in the Twentieth Century.* Englewood Cliffs, NJ: Prentice-Hall.

Colwell, Richard (1970). *The Evaluation of Music Teaching and Learning.* Englewood Cliffs, NJ: Prentice-Hall, Inc.

The Community Band—A Manual of Organization and Operation (1977). Barrington, IL: The Northshore Concert Band.

Gordon, Edwin (1988). *Learning Sequences in Music*. Chicago: G.I.A. Publications.

Green, Elizabeth A.H. (1966). *Orchestral Bowings and Routines*. Ann Arbor: Campus Publishers.

Green, Elizabeth A. H. (1966). *Teaching Stringed Instruments in Classes*. Englewood Cliffs, NJ: Prentice-Hall, Inc.

Hopper, Dale F. (1977). *Corps Style Marching*. Oskaloosa, IA: C.L. Barnhouse Co.

Moss, Bruce. (1995). Curnow on composing. *The Instrumentalist*, April, 11-15.

Murphy, John (1993). What's In? What's Out? American education in the nineties. *Phi Delta Kappan*, 74/8, 641-646.

Mursell, James L. (1943, 1953). *Music in American Schools*. New York: Silver Burdett Co.

Pautz, Mary (1989). Musical Thinking in the Teacher Education Classroom. *In Dimensions of Musical Thinking*, ed. by Eunice Boardman. Reston, VA: Music Educators National Conference.

Raxdale, Bill (1981). *Contemporary Show Design Manual*. New Berlin, WI: Jenson Publications, Inc.

Shellahamer, Bentley; Swearingen, James; and Woods, Jon (1986). *The Marching Band Program*. Oskaloosa, IA: C.L. Barnhouse Co.

Schmid, Will (1996). Parting shots. *Teaching Music*, 3/6, 4-5.

Snoeck, Kenneth M. (1981). *Contemporary Drill Design*. Oskaloosa, IA: C.L. Barnhouse Co.

Thomson, John (1995). Teaching with goals, not answers: an interview with John Whitwell. *The Instrumentalist*, December, 11-15.

Walters, Darrel L. (1992). Sequencing for efficient learning. In *Handbook of Research on Music Teaching and Learning*, ed. by Richard Colwell. New York: Schirmer Books.

Walters, Darrel L. and Taggart, Cynthia C. (1989). *Readings in Music Learning Theory*. Chicago: G.I.A. Publications.

## Jazz Ensemble

Aebersold, Jamey. *JAZZ: Anyone Can Improvise* (video). New Albany, IN: Jazz Aids.

Bash, Lee, and Kuzmich, John (1992). *Complete Guide to Improvisation Instruction: Techniques for Developing a Successful School Jazz Program*. Miami: CPP/Belwin, Inc.

Berg, Shelton (1990). Jazz improvisation. *BD Guide*, November/December, 7-9.

Berg, Shelton (1989). The rhythm section—piano. *BD Guide*, November/December, 14 & 16.

Blaser, Albert and Froseth James O. (1979). *Improvise!* (recording). Chicago: G.I.A. Publications, Inc.

Dunscomb, Dick (1989). The director—listen here! *BD Guide*, November/December, 22-23.

Fedchock, John and Schneider, Maria (1991). The big band—a creative and unique musical experience. *BD Guide*, November/December, 5-8.

Froseth, James O. and Blaser, Albert (1994). *Do It! Improvise*. Chicago: G.I.A. Publications, Inc.

Froseth, James O. and Froseth, David (1995). *Do It! Improvise II*. Chicago: G.I.A. Publications, Inc.

Garcia, Antonio J. (1991). Fine-tuning your ensemble's jazz style. *Music Educators Journal*, February, 30-35.

Gridley, Mark C. (1992). *Concise Guide to Jazz*. Englewood Cliffs, NJ: Prentice Hall.

Jarvis, Jeff (1998). The top ten mistakes in jazz performances. *The Instrumentalist*, April, 17-20.

Kidwell, Kent (1991). Jazz band rehearsal techniques. *BD Guide*, November/December, 16 & 18.

Kuzmich, John, Jr. (1998). Teaching improv in a big-band setting. *School Band and Orchestra*, December, 53-56.

Leach, Joel (1989). The rhythm section—an adjudicator's look at drummer. *BD Guide*, November/December, 20-21.

Mack, Kyle (1998). Simplifying jazz improvisation. *The Instrumentalist*, October, 10-13.

Mantooth, Frank (1996). *Patterns for Improvisation—From the Beginning* (book with compact disk). Milwaukee: Hal Leonard Corporation.

Mason, Thom (1987). Teaching improvisation in your rehearsal. *BD Guide*, November/December, 3-5.

Mason, Thom (1989). The saxophone section. *BD Guide*, November/December, 6-10.

Matteson, Rich (1989). The brass section. *BD Guide*, November/December, 11-12.

Osland, Miles (1998). Jazz improvisation—how to "shed." *Selmer Woodwind Notes*, Spring, 4-5.

Petersen, Jack (1989). The rhythm section—guitar. *BD Guide*, November/December, 19.

Reid, Rufus (1989). The rhythm section—acoustic bass. *BD Guide*, November/December, 12-13.

Warrick, James (1992). Sound reinforcement and your jazz ensemble. *BD Guide*, November/December, 39-50.

Wiskirchen, George (1987). Rehearsing the jazz band. *BD Guide*, November/December, 10-14.

Young, Alphonso M., Jr. (1999). Easy in's and out's to improvisation. *NBA Journal*, 39/ 3, 21-23.

## Scheduling The School Day and Year

Anderson, Julia (1994). Alternative approaches to organizing the school day and year. *School Administrator*, 51/3, 8-11 & 15.

Blocher, Larry, and Miles, Richard (1999). *Scheduling and Teaching Music*. Chicago: GIA Publications, Inc.

Blocher, Larry R. and Miles, Richard B. (1995). *High School Restructuring-Block Scheduling: Implications for Music Educators.*. Prepared for the Kentucky Coalition for Music Education. Morehead, KY: Morehead State University.

Campbell, Alice (1996). Better and better. *Director*, 3/2-16, 9-10.

Canady, Robert L., and Rettig, Michael D. (1993). Unlocking the lockstep high school schedule. *Phi Delta Kappan*, December, 310-314.

Carroll, Joseph M. (1994). The Copernican plan evaluated: the evolution of a revolution. *Phi Delta Kappan*, 76/2, 104-110 & 112-113.

Hamann, Mary (1996). Building blocks: making music fit into block schedules. *Director*, 3/1-16, 3-6.

Milleman, Jon (1996). Do what is right for your school. *Director*, 3/3-16, 9-11.

Miles, Richard B., and Blocher, Larry R. (1996). *Block Scheduling: Implications for Music Education*. Chicago: GIA Publications.

Miles, Richard B., and Blocher, Larry R. (1998). Research on block scheduling. *The Instrumentalist*, November, 84-89.

O'Neil, I. Riley, and Adamson, David R. (1993). When less is more. *American School Board Journal*, 180/4, 39-41.

Patterson, Glenn W. (1997). Modifying block schedules to salvage music programs. *The Instrumentalist*, January, 17-20.

Trimis, Edward (1990). Can year-round scheduling work for your program? *Music Educators Journal*, 77/1, 50-52.

Trimis, Edward (1997). Year-round music—a pattern for success. *Music Educators Journal*, 83/4 (January), 17-21.

White, William D. (1992). Year-round no more. *American School Board Journal*, 178/7, 27-28 & 30.

## Music Theory Texts

Harder, Paul O. and Steinke, Greg A. (1991). *Basic Materials in Music Theory: A Programmed Course, 8th ed*. Needham Heights, MA: Allyn and Bacon.

Nelson, Robert and Christensen, Carl J. (1997). *Foundations Of Music: A Computer-Assisted Introduction, 3rd ed*. Belmont, CA: Wadsworth Publishing Company.

Ottman, Robert W. and Mainous, Frank D. (1994). *Programmed Rudiments of Music, 2nd ed*. Englewood Cliffs, NJ: Prentice-Hall, Inc.

Spencer, Peter (1996). *Music Theory for Non-Music Majors*. Upper Saddle River, NJ: Prentice-Hall, Inc.

# Chapter Five

## SELECTING LITERATURE AND ORGANIZING THE MUSIC LIBRARY

### "Good" Music

Selection of appropriate materials to use in middle school and high school bands and orchestras is one of the primary responsibilities of instrumental music teachers. You will devote many hours of study and research to this important task.

In a discussion of quality literature for band and orchestra, the term "quality literature," or "good music," must be defined. I believe that good music has the qualities of excellent construction and genuine expressiveness. In addition, good music may have stood the test of time, but much new music will also possess these qualities.

James Neilson, in "What Is Quality in Music?" identified several factors that he believed are present in "quality" music.

- Rhythmic Vitality
- Genuine Originality → *Robert J. Smith, all his places sound the same*
- Melody that has the qualities of economy, logic and inspiration
- Harmony that is consistent with and is suitable to the style
- Craftsmanship
- A Sense of Values (meaning that everything is in balance and proportion and that there is a sense of continuity)
- Emotion Justified (". . .'good' music ennobles the soul and enlightens both mind and spirit.")
- Quality and Personal Taste

• The Test of Time

You may find this list useful when you evaluate and select music for use in your ensembles.

Using only a subjective process to make decisions may lead you nowhere. For example, most people agree that the operas of Richard Wagner are masterpieces of good music, but they might not agree about whether they like them. Likewise, some would say that many melodies written by the Beatles in the 1960s fit our definition of good music, but others do not like that music. What considerations are most important?

## A Good Match

You will spend many hours searching for the right literature each year. A dispassionate evaluation of your ensembles, noting strengths and weaknesses, will help you choose music that features strengths and diminishes weaknesses. To evaluate your ensemble in a systematic way, use a form like the Ensemble Evaluation Form (Fig. 5-1).

Most of the literature you select should be sight-readable. This will allow you to spend less rehearsal time overcoming technical problems and more time developing tone, intonation, balance, phrasing, and musical expression. Choose challenging pieces also, but be careful not to over-estimate your ensemble's potential for growth. You will only frustrate yourself and your students if you burden the ensemble with unreasonable musical and technical demands. It is good to remember the admonition of Bennett Reimer (1970): "Music of high quality need not be music of high complexity" (p. 133).

## The Search

Instrumental music teachers are inundated with recordings of new music publications, so you will need to use a "sifting" process to find the few "grains of wheat." New music reviews in professional journals can be helpful. Compare your evaluation of several new pieces with the published reviews to make sure you and the reviewers are using similar standards.

Several publications identify good band music. I recommend, as excellent sources of quality music, *Best Music for Beginning Band*, *Best Music for Young Bands*, and *Best Music for High School Bands* by Thomas L. Dvorak, *et al* (edited by Bob Margolis), and *Music for Concert Band* by Joseph Kreines. *Teaching Music Through Performance in Band* (Vol. 1,

*Be subjective, just don't be always subjective.*

**Figure 5-1. Ensemble Evaluation Form**

## Ypsilanti High School — Ensemble Evaluation Form

| | Tone | Intonation | Technique | Articulation | Staccato | Legato | Musicality | Range | Endurance | Soloists | Maturity | Overall |
|---|---|---|---|---|---|---|---|---|---|---|---|---|
| Flute/Piccolo | | | | | | | | | | | | |
| Oboe/English Horn | | | | | | | | | | | | |
| Bassoon | | | | | | | | | | | | |
| Clarinet | | | | | | | | | | | | |
| Lower Clarinet | | | | | | | | | | | | |
| Saxophone | | | | | | | | | | | | |
| French Horn | | | | | | | | | | | | |
| Cornet/Trumpet | | | | | | | | | | | | |
| Trombone | | | | | | | | | | | | |
| Euphonium | | | | | | | | | | | | |
| Tuba | | | | | | | | | | | | |
| Percussion | | | | | | | | | | | | |
| Violin | | | | | | | | | | | | |
| Viola | | | | | | | | | | | | |
| Cello | | | | | | | | | | | | |
| Bass | | | | | | | | | | | | |
| Total Ensemble | | | | | | | | | | | | |

Major Strengths:

Major Weaknesses:

Suggestions for Improvement:

Goals:

Possible Literature:

+ = above average
x = average
- = below average
o = not applicable

89

2, 3 and for Beginning Band) by Richard Miles, *et al*, is a valuable list of outstanding band literature at various grade levels that includes information about each piece, along with a recording. In addition, the "Young Band Repertoire Project" is a series of recordings of fine literature for the middle school and high school band. This series is produced by the Institute for Music Research at The University of Texas at San Antonio (http://imr.utsa.edu/). Included with each recording is a booklet that contains information about each piece.

A number of state band and orchestra associations publish lists of recommended or approved music, and the National Band Association regularly publishes a "Selective Music List for Bands." These can be valuable resources to help select appropriate music for your ensembles. Programs from conventions and state band and orchestra festivals will identify what is being played by other ensembles; however, they may be the least reliable resource, because much music being played across the country does not meet the definition of "good music" used in this chapter.

Students do respond to quality literature. Directors do not have to provide only what students *think* they want. That is not to say that our ensembles should play only heavier, "serious" music all the time. Some lighter music is of excellent construction and has genuine expressiveness. I suggest you avoid what might be called "pop fluff"—light, poorly arranged popular music that inadequately represents the original version and maintains little musical integrity. Even many new concert pieces published recently have that same pop quality. There is so little time to rehearse and perform music with our students—let's use our limited time working on music of *lasting value*.

## The Selection

Many issues in addition to those already mentioned will influence choices of literature for your ensembles. The following checklist may be helpful as you choose music for your ensembles.

- Does it have musical integrity based on the attributes given by James Neilson in his booklet "What Is Quality in Music?"
- Will this piece cause my ensemble members to grow musically?
- Are there opportunities for expressive playing?
- Does this piece have good melodies, harmonies, and textures?

- Does this piece contain a variety of keys, styles, meters, and technical complexity?
- How does this piece relate to the strengths and weaknesses identified in the Ensemble Evaluation Form? In other words: Does it "fit" the group?
- Is there a good full score to allow for thorough score study?
- Can we play this piece without making major substitutions for solos or other rewriting of important parts?
- Can we cover all the percussion parts?
- Are the ranges and technical demands of this piece developmentally appropriate for my ensemble?
- Is the percussion writing in this piece musical and logical?
- Does this piece fulfill a particular programming need (patriotic program, "pops" concert, Christmas concert, etc.)?
- Will my students enjoy and/or benefit from working on this piece? Will our audience enjoy and/or benefit from hearing this piece? Will I enjoy and/or benefit from studying, rehearsing, and conducting this piece?
- Would the maturity level of this music balance well with other music selected for study or programming at this time?
- Do all of the pieces selected for this program provide a variety of styles; lengths; technical, dynamic, and rhythmic demands; meters; tempi; musical forms; solo versus tutti sections; emotions; tonal centers; etc.?
- Will this piece help develop solo skills in my ensemble members?
- Does this piece represent one of the finest examples of its type in the repertoire?
- Do we have adequate time to learn this piece?

You may want to add other items to this list, and some of the items may not be appropriate for all the music being considered, but this should get you started through a thoughtful process of selecting the very best literature for your student ensembles. Because the literature played by your ensembles is the core of the curriculum, wise selection will also help you achieve your goal of offering a well-reasoned and high quality curriculum. In sum, you will select literature that enables students to enjoy outstanding musical performance and learn about music (music theory, music history, listening skills, etc.).

# A Core Repertoire

I recommend that school band and orchestra directors establish a core repertoire of the best literature available for their particular ensemble. A rotation schedule of this core over a three or four year period will allow all ensemble members the opportunity to rehearse and perform that literature during their school career. You will then add literature (marches, exceptional music—both new and old, solos with ensemble accompaniment, good lighter music, etc.) to the core repertoire to develop all of the programs needed during a school year.

Figure 5-2 is an example of a Core Repertoire for band that uses the commonly found six-grade, or level, scale. Figure 5-3 is a recommended Core Repertoire for orchestra. Grade One is typically used for first-year players; Grade Two for second-year players; Grade Three for middle school or junior high and less experienced high school players; Grade Four for most high school ensembles; Grade Five for advanced high school ensembles and college or university ensembles; and Grade Six for advanced college, military, and professional ensembles.

Assigning a grade level designation to a musical work is certainly not an exact science. The technical demands of a piece are usually the principal consideration in assigning a grade level. However, other factors, such as the musical maturity of a piece, transparent scoring, or unusual solo demands should also be considered. There is much quality literature at all grade levels, and directors should become familiar with a wide range of fine literature. Selecting literature that balances grade levels and type or style of composition exposes students to a greater quantity of fine literature. Too many concerts are marred by poor performances of overly difficult music. Many students and directors proudly tell everyone that their band "plays only Grade Six music." However, the students in those ensembles might have a richer and broader musical experience if the band or orchestra played at least a few pieces more easily within their reach. Reducing the technical demands of the music allows time to rehearse and perform a greater body of literature, to understand more about each composition, and to learn more about music (theory, history, composition, improvisation, etc.).

**Figure 5-2. Examples of Core Repertories for Band (title - composer/arranger-publisher)**

### Grade One
**Year One**
Sugar Creek Saga - James Curnow - CMP
Rondo Royale - Frank Erickson - Summitt

**Year Two**
English Hunting Song - John Kinyon - Alfred
Prelude and March - Bob Margolis - Manhattan Beach

**Year Three**
A Londonderry Air - John Kinyon - Alfred
Minuet and Country Dance - Mozart/Philip Gordon - Presser

### Grade Two
**Year One**
Balladair - Frank Erickson - Bourne
Two Moods - Clare Grundman - B&H
Musette and March - J.S. Bach/John Kinyon - Studio PR/CPP
Three Songs of Colonial America - Leroy Jackson - Warner Bros.
Jefferson County Overture - John O'Reilly - Alfred

**Year Two**
Firebrook Prelude - James Curnow - CMP
Early English Suite - Duncombe/Finlayson - B&H
Air for Band - Frank Erickson - Bourne
Crusaders Hymn - James Ployhar - Belwin/CPP
Bist Du Bei Mir - J.S. Bach/Anne McGinty - Queenwood

**Year Three**
Dorian Festival - Frank Erickson - Belwin/CPP
Ukranian Bell Carol - James Ployhar - Carl Fischer
Bristol Bay Legend - Robert Sheldon - Barnhouse
Courtly Festival - H. Purcell/Philip Gordon - Belwin/CPP
From an 18th Century Album - Theldon Meyers - TRN

## Grade Three

**Year One**

Fanfare, Ode and Festival - Bob Margolis - Manhattan Beach
Festivo - Vaclav Nelhybel - Belwin
Kentucky 1800 - Clare Grundman - Boosey & Hawkes
Variants on an Early American Hymn Tune - James Curnow
    - Jenson
Variation Overture - Clifton Williams - Ludwig

**Year Two**

Chant and Jubilo - W. Francis McBeth - Southern
Court Festival - William Latham - Summy-Birchard
Polly Oliver - Thomas Root - Kjos
Royal Coronation Dances - Bob Margolis - Manhattan Beach
Two Gaelic Folk Songs - Thomas Tyra - Barnhouse

**Year Three**

Overture for Winds - Charles Carter - Bourne
Hebrides Suite - Clare Grundman - Boosey & Hawkes
Nathan Hale Trilogy - James Curnow - Hal Leonard
Prospect - Pierre LaPlante - Bourne
Three Ayres from Gloucester - Hugh Stuart - Shawnee

## Grade Four

**Year One**

A Festival Prelude - Alfred Reed - Marks/Belwin
Blessed Are They - Johannes Brahms/Barbara Buehlman -
    Ludwig
Emperata Overture - Claude T. Smith - Wingert-Jones
First Suite in E-flat for Military Band - Gustav Holst -
    Boosey & Hawkes
Salvation is Created - Pavel Tschesnokoff/Bruce House-
    knecht - Kjos

**Year Two**

Variations on a Korean Folk Song - John Barnes Chance -
    Boosey & Hawkes
An Original Suite - Gordon Jacob - Boosey & Hawkes
Chorale and Shaker Dance - John Zdechlik - Kjos

Irish Tune From County Derry - Percy A. Grainger - C. Fischer or Southern

Masque - W. Francis McBeth - Southern

### Year Three

Cajun Folk Songs - Frank Ticheli - Manhattan Beach

Elsa's Procession to the Cathedral - Richard Wagner/Lucien Cailliet - Warner

English Folk Song Suite - Ralph Vaughan Williams - Boosey & Hawkes

On a Hymnsong of Philip Bliss - David Holsinger - TRN

Pageant - Vincent Persichetti - C. Fischer

## Grade Five

### Year One

Armenian Dances, Part I - Alfred Reed - Fox

Candide, Overture to - Leonard Bernstein/Walter Beeler - Schirmer

Festive Overture - Dmitri Shostakovich/Donald Hunsberger - MCA

Overture for Band - Felix Mendelssohn - Schirmer

Suite Francaise - Darius Milhaud - MCA

### Year Two

After A Gentle Rain - Anthony Iannaccone - Shawnee

Chester Overture - William Schuman - Presser

Scenes from the Louvre - Norman Dello Joio - Marks

Second Suite in F for Military Band - Gustav Holst - Boosey & Hawkes

Where Never Lark or Eagle Flew - James Curnow - Hal Leonard

### Year Three

Of Sailors and Whales - W. Francis McBeth - Southern

Rejouissance - James Curnow - Jenson

Russian Christmas Music - Alfred Reed - Sam Fox

Sketches on A Tudor Psalm - Fischer Tull - Boosey & Hawkes

William Byrd Suite - Gordon Jacob - Boosey & Hawkes

**Grade Six**

**Year One**

Lincolnshire Posy - Percy Aldridge Grainger - Schott or Ludwig

Symphony No. 2 - John Barnes Chance - Boosey & Hawkes

Symphony in Bb - Paul Hindemith - Schott

Theme and Variations, Op. 43a - Arnold Schoenberg - G. Schirmer

**Year Two**

Lochinvar - James Curnow - CMP

Symphony for Band - Vincent Persichetti - Elkan-Vogel

Symphony for Band - Jerry Bilik - RBC Publications

Variants on a Mediaeval Tune - Norman Dello Joio - Marks

**Year Three**

Colonial Song - Percy Aldridge Grainger - Fischer or Southern

Mutanza - James Curnow - Jenson

Symphony No. 1 ("Lord of the Rings") - Johan de Meij - Amstel

Symphony No. 3 - Vittorio Giannini - Belwin

A much more extensive list of recommended literature for band will be found in Appendix A and for orchestra in Appendix B.

**Figure 5-3. Examples of Core Repertories for Orchestra**
**(title - composer/arranger - publisher)**

**Grade One**
**(Note: all in this grade level for strings only)**

**Year One**

Two by Two - Fred Hubbell - Highland/Etling

St. Anthony's Chorale - Haydn/Dackow - Ludwig

**Year Two**

Wexford Circle - Elliott DelBorgo - Kendor

Variations on A Ground - Shapiro - Kjos

**Year Three**
Dona Nobis Pacem - Elliott DelBorgo - Belwin-Mills
Sinfonietta for Strings - Spinosa/Rusch - Kjos

## Grade Two
### (Note: all in this grade level for strings only)

**Year One**
Air and Dance - Daniels - Kjos
Musette and Minuet - J.S. Bach/Siennicki - Ludwig

**Year Two**
Symphony No. 14 (1st mvt.) - F. J. Haydn/P. Gordon - Kendor
Belvedere Suite - Isaac - Highland/Etling

**Year Three**
Handel Suite - Kreichbaum - Kjos
Two Moods - Philip Gordon - Elkan-Vogel

## Grade Three
### (for full orchestra)

**Year One**
March and Sonatina - W.A. Mozart/Isaac - Highland/Etling
Prelude and Polka - Arthur Frankenpohl - Shawnee Press
Sinfonia - Scarlatti/Errante - Highland/Etling

**Year Two**
An English Suite - H. Purcell/Scarmolin - Ludwig
Exultate Jubilate-Alleluia - W. A. Mozart/Isaac - Highland/Etling
Rhosymedre - R. Vaughan Williams/Foster - Galaxy Music

**Year Three**
Slavonic Dance No. 8 - Antonin Dvorak/Isaac - Highland/Etling
Kamarinskaya - Glinka/Barnes - Tempo
Sleigh Ride - W.A. Mozart/Stone - Boosey & Hawkes

## Grade Four
### (for full orchestra unless otherwise noted)
**Year One**
Academic Festival Overture - J. Brahms/Mueller - Kjos
La Pinta Giardiniera - W. A. Mozart - Carl Fischer
Sheep May Safely Graze - J.S. Bach/L. Cailliet - Boosey & Hawkes
Short Overture for Strings - Berger - G. Schirmer

**Year Two**
Fidelio Overture - Beethoven/Isaac - Wynn
Sinfonia in Bb - J.S. Bach/Muller - Kjos
Suite from Tannhauser - R. Wagner/Isaac - Highland/Etling
Vocalise, Op. 34 - Rachmaninoff/Gearhart - Shawnee Press

**Year Three**
Il Re Pastore - W.A. Mozart/Mueller - Kjos
March to the Scaffold - H. Berlioz/Carter - Oxford
Russian Sailors Dance - Gliere/Isaac - Carl Fischer
Symphony in D Major - Sammartini/Scarmolin - Ludwig

## Grade Five
### (for full orchestra)
**Year One**
Egmont Overture - Beethoven - Kalmus
Alceste Overture - Gluck - Kalmus
Dance Rhythms, Op. 58 - Riegger - Associated
Rosamunde Overture - Schubert/Roberts - Carl Fischer

**Year Two**
Hungarian Dances - Brahms - Bourne
Variations on a Shaker Melody - Copland - Boosey & Hawkes
Marche Militaire Francaise - Saint-Saens/Isaac - Carl Fischer
Catskill Legend Overture - Whear - Ludwig

**Year Three**
A Moorside Suite - Holst - Boosey & Hawkes
Titus Overture - Mozart - Highland-Etling
The Good Daughter Overture - Piccini/Scarmolin

St. Lawrence Overture - Washburn - Boosey & Hawkes

**Grade Six**
**(for full orchestra)**
**Year One**
Fidelio Overture - Beethoven - Kalmus
Outdoor Overture - Copland - Boosey & Hawkes
Russlan and Ludmilla Overture - Glinka - Bourne
Colas Breugnon Overture - Kabalevsky - Kalmus
Capriccio Italien - Tschaikowsky - Kalmus

**Year Two**
Overture to Candide - Bernstein - G. Schirmer
Symphony No. 94 - Haydn - Boosey & Hawkes
Les Preludes - Liszt - Kalmus
Donna Diana Overture - Reznicek - Kalmus
Semiramide Overture - Rossini - Kalmus

**Year Three**
Academic Festival Overture, Op. 80 - Brahms - Kalmus
Soirees Musicales - Britten - Boosey & Hawkes
Roumanian Rhapsody No. 1 - Enesco - Kalmus
American Salute - Gould - Belwin/CPP
The Impressario Overture - Mozart - Kalmus

# The Band and Orchestra Library

## *Music Purchases*

Ordering music from a local music dealer is becoming easier all the time. Phone orders, mail orders, and on-line orders are possible with most major music retailers. Make sure that you understand and follow the process required by your local school district to place an order. Many districts require that an actual Purchase Order (P.O.) be processed before the order may be sent to a music dealer. This policy allows the school district to maintain control of both the ordering and the expenditure of budgeted funds. The "business" portion of this process is very important. You should follow the established school district policy strictly and keep your own ledger of all budget expenditures (including all postage and handling charges) so that you can remain within your budget allocation. Obviously, being required to submit a P.O. prior to placing an order will require careful advance planning to ensure that music is received when needed for rehearsal.

A very helpful service provided by many music retailers is the "on approval" service. This service allows a director to place a tentative order for music with the understanding that 50-percent or more of the order will be retained and a P.O. processed. This service is particularly helpful with newly published music because it allows the director to study the score and parts, or have the ensemble sight-read the music. Typically, you are given about 30 days to make a decision about the music.

The "on approval" service usually applies only to music that the music dealer already has in stock. You may have to contact several retailers to locate all of the music you would like to review. I have found it helpful to locate several reliable music retailers and use them on a rotating basis. A few music retailers still give a discount on all school orders and/or if the school bill is paid within a certain number of days. This certainly helps stretch the music budget, but the importance of any discount should always be balanced against timely, courteous, and helpful service.

If you place music orders by telephone or on the Internet, keep a complete record of the order and submit a request for a purchase order as quickly as possible. That request should include the name and address of the music retailer, a complete list of all music ordered, and the statement "As Per Telephone Order" or "For Confirmation Only" to ensure that the retailer understands that the P.O. is simply confirmation of an earlier telephone order. Examples of a Requisition for a P.O. and an actual P.O. form are found in Figure 5-4 and Figure 5-5.

When deciding how to spend your music budget, consider both the immediate literature needs of your ensembles and the need to build a quality band or orchestra library. Make a list of the major band or orchestra works that are appropriate for your ensembles and then order a few of those each year to add to the library. The same process works well for establishing a comprehensive library of solo and ensemble literature for the band and orchestra program.

You should establish your own private collection of scores for the major works you perform. Start this collection while you are a college student by purchasing scores of the pieces being rehearsed and performed by your college ensembles. The study of these scores and the thoughtful analysis of the rehearsal techniques and strategies used

*Figure 5-4. Requisition for a Purchase Order*

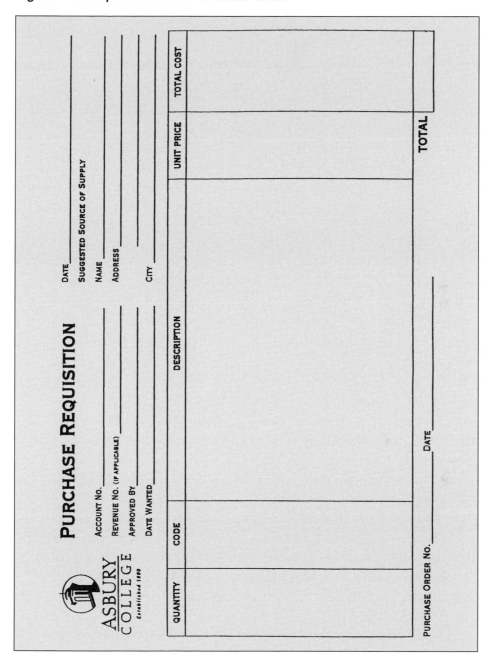

by your college director can be a rich source of learning. Maintaining a notebook of rehearsal techniques and strategies is a good habit to begin as a college student, and one you should continue throughout your teaching career as you observe guest conductors, clinic band conductors, and colleagues, or read articles in books and journals.

***Figure 5-5. Purchase Order form***

PURCHASE ORDER NO.

NO.

SHOW THIS NUMBER ON ALL PACKAGES, INVOICES, CORRESPONDENCE AND BILLS OF LADING

ASBURY COLLEGE

PURCHASE ORDER

**ASBURY COLLEGE**

WILMORE, KENTUCKY
606 858-3511
SALES USE-TAX PERMIT NUMBER F-248

PLEASE SHIP & CHARGE TO:

ASBURY COLLEGE
1 MACKLEM DRIVE
WILMORE, KENTUCKY 40390

ATTN:

DATE REQUIRED

FOR OFFICE USE ONLY

| QUANTITY | CODE | DESCRIPTION | UNIT PRICE | TOTAL |
|---|---|---|---|---|
| | | | | |

IF ORDER CANNOT BE FILLED PROMPTLY PLEASE ADVISE US.

TOTAL

RECEIVED BY

DATE

PLEASE SEND DUPLICATE INVOICE

I believe that school districts should purchase an extra full score of the *major* works being rehearsed and performed by school ensembles to be used and retained by the ensemble directors. This would be much like a desk copy of the textbooks being given to classroom teachers for personal marking and preparation for use in classes. Full scores of major works are the "textbooks" for our ensembles. It is unreasonable to expect a director to spend many hours preparing and marking a score, and then ask the director to leave that prepared score in the school music library. You should discuss this issue with your building administrator to make sure that the administrator supports this position. Whether through your own purchases or as supplied by the school district, however, it is important to establish a collection of major scores. In addition, you will want to establish your own library of fine recordings, including outstanding performances of the pieces from your core repertoire, examples of excellent solo instrumental performers, and examples of other exemplary performances outside your primary area of interest and expertise.

## Music Library Organization

You will want to establish a systematic method of cataloging music so you will know the complete contents of the ensemble library and be able to locate that music. An accurate listing of all the pieces owned by the school will prevent duplicate purchases and will allow you to knowledgeably plan your music purchases. There are many types of filing systems—each with its degrees of efficiency and logic. Music can be filed alphabetically by title (which requires frequent moving of music in the files), by size of music (full size, octavo, march size, etc.), or by type of music (concert band, marching band, orchestra, jazz ensemble, solo and ensemble, etc.). Two additional options are 1) a continuous number system, or 2) a letter to identify music type, followed by a catalog number. Variations are limited only by your own creativity.

Most directors find that, assuming even a modest organizational structure, some type of filing system will be in place before they arrive on the job. It is wise to work with that system a while before instituting major changes. Whatever system you use for cataloging music, use it consistently. There are several useful books available to help you develop a cataloging system for the school music library, including "A Practical Guide to the Music Library" by Frank P. Byrne (published by Ludwig Music Co.), and the booklet "A Better Way to File and Find Music" (published by J.W. Pepper & Son, Inc.).

## Large Ensemble Music

Typically, when new music arrives you begin the cataloging process by assigning the music a catalog number and stamping each individual sheet of music with the school name and assigned number. A new concert band piece might be stamped **CB-601** to identify it as the six hundred first piece in the **C**oncert **B**and music file. Other identifiers used in cataloging large ensemble music could include **OR** for Orchestra, **JE** for Jazz Ensemble, or **MB** for Marching Band. Some directors also put all the parts in score order and then number every part consecutively. This system allows librarians to return music to correct score order quickly and identifies missing parts easily. An accurate list of the number of parts per instrument in each set of music is important. This may be done on the card files, in the computer file, on the filing envelope, or on a separate sheet of paper placed in each set of music.

Rubber stamps, made to your exact specifications, are available from sources in most local communities and will save an enormous amount of work for you and your student workers. A word of caution: make sure the stamps are small enough so that they do not obscure any of the printing on the music! In some cases it is better to place the stamp image on the back of a piece of music rather than obscure any part of the printed information. An "all-in-one" stamp with the school name and changeable numbers and letters (for the catalog number) is the most efficient choice for the music library. Using a stamp pad ink color other than black will help your stamp information stand out on the printed music page.

*Figure 5-6. Music Library Cards*

**TITLE CARD**

Name of Composition _____    Composer _____

Publisher _____    Publisher No. _____    Classification _____

| **Band/Orchestra** | ___ Bb Contra Cl. | ___ 3rd Horn | ___ 1st Violin | ___ 3rd Trumpet |
|---|---|---|---|---|
| ___ Full Score | ___ 1st Bassoon | ___ 4th Horn | ___ 2nd Violin | ___ 4th Trumpet |
| ___ Cond. Score | ___ 2nd Bassoon | ___ 1st Trombone | ___ 3rd Violin | ___ 5th Trumpet |
| ___ Piccolo | ___ Con. Bassoon | ___ 2nd Trombone | ___ Viola | ___ 1st Trombone |
| ___ 1st Flute | ___ Bb Sop. Sax | ___ 3rd Trombone | ___ Cello | ___ 2nd Trombone |
| ___ 2nd Flute | ___ 1st Eb A. Sax | ___ Euph. B.C. | ___ Contrabass | ___ 3rd Trombone |
| ___ 3rd Flute | ___ 2nd Eb A.Sax | ___ Euph. T.C. | ___ Piano | ___ 4th Trombone |
| ___ 1st Oboe | ___ Bb Tenor Sax | ___ String Bass | ___ Harp | ___ 5th Trombone |
| ___ 2nd Oboe | ___ Eb Bari. Sax | ___ Tuba/Basses | | ___ Piano |
| ___ English Horn | ___ 1st Cornet | ___ Tympani | **Jazz Ensemble** | ___ Drums |
| ___ Eb Sop. Clar. | ___ 2nd Cornet | ___ 1st Percussion | ___ Conductor | ___ Guitar |
| ___ 1st Bb Clar. | ___ 3rd Cornet | ___ 2nd Perc. | ___ 1st Alto Sax | ___ Bass |
| ___ 2nd Bb Clar. | ___ 4th Cornet | ___ 3rd Perc. | ___ 2nd Alto Sax | ___ Aux. Percussion |
| ___ 3rd Bb Clar. | ___ 1st Trumpet | ___ 4th Perc. | ___ 1st Tenor Sax | ___ _____ |
| ___ 4th Bb Clar. | ___ 2nd Trumpet | ___ _____ | ___ 2nd Tenor Sax | ___ _____ |
| ___ Eb Alto Clar. | ___ 3rd Trumpet | ___ _____ | ___ Baritone Sax | ___ _____ |
| ___ Bb Bass Clar. | ___ 1st Horn | ___ _____ | ___ 1st Trumpet | |
| ___ Eb Contra Cl. | ___ 2nd Horn | | ___ 2nd Trumpet | LGC 2000 |

Grade _____    Performance Time _____    Library No. _____

## COMPOSER CARD

Name of Composition _____    Composer _____

Publisher _____    Publisher No. _____    Classification _____

| **Band/Orchestra** | ___ Bb Contra Cl. | ___ 3rd Horn | ___ 1st Violin | ___ 3rd Trumpet |
|---|---|---|---|---|
| ___ Full Score | ___ 1st Bassoon | ___ 4th Horn | ___ 2nd Violin | ___ 4th Trumpet |
| ___ Cond. Score | ___ 2nd Bassoon | ___ 1st Trombone | ___ 3rd Violin | ___ 5th Trumpet |
| ___ Piccolo | ___ Con. Bassoon | ___ 2nd Trombone | ___ Viola | ___ 1st Trombone |
| ___ 1st Flute | ___ Bb Sop. Sax | ___ 3rd Trombone | ___ Cello | ___ 2nd Trombone |
| ___ 2nd Flute | ___ 1st Eb A. Sax | ___ Euph. B.C. | ___ Contrabass | ___ 3rd Trombone |
| ___ 3rd Flute | ___ 2nd Eb A.Sax | ___ Euph. T.C. | ___ Piano | ___ 4th Trombone |
| ___ 1st Oboe | ___ Bb Tenor Sax | ___ String Bass | ___ Harp | ___ 5th Trombone |
| ___ 2nd Oboe | ___ Eb Bari. Sax | ___ Tuba/Basses | | ___ Piano |
| ___ English Horn | ___ 1st Cornet | ___ Tympani | **Jazz Ensemble** | ___ Drums |
| ___ Eb Sop. Clar. | ___ 2nd Cornet | ___ 1st Percussion | ___ Conductor | ___ Guitar |
| ___ 1st Bb Clar. | ___ 3rd Cornet | ___ 2nd Perc. | ___ 1st Alto Sax | ___ Bass |
| ___ 2nd Bb Clar. | ___ 4th Cornet | ___ 3rd Perc. | ___ 2nd Alto Sax | ___ Aux. Percussion |
| ___ 3rd Bb Clar. | ___ 1st Trumpet | ___ 4th Perc. | ___ 1st Tenor Sax | ___ _____ |
| ___ 4th Bb Clar. | ___ 2nd Trumpet | ___ _____ | ___ 2nd Tenor Sax | ___ _____ |
| ___ Eb Alto Clar. | ___ 3rd Trumpet | ___ _____ | ___ Baritone Sax | ___ _____ |
| ___ Bb Bass Clar. | ___ 1st Horn | ___ _____ | ___ 1st Trumpet | |
| ___ Eb Contra Cl. | ___ 2nd Horn | ___ _____ | ___ 2nd Trumpet | LGC 2000 |

Grade _____    Performance Time _____    Library No. _____

## CATALOG NUMBER CARD

Name of Composition _____    Composer _____

Publisher _____    Publisher No. _____    Classification _____

| **Band/Orchestra** | ___ Bb Contra Cl. | ___ 3rd Horn | ___ 1st Violin | ___ 3rd Trumpet |
|---|---|---|---|---|
| ___ Full Score | ___ 1st Bassoon | ___ 4th Horn | ___ 2nd Violin | ___ 4th Trumpet |
| ___ Cond. Score | ___ 2nd Bassoon | ___ 1st Trombone | ___ 3rd Violin | ___ 5th Trumpet |
| ___ Piccolo | ___ Con. Bassoon | ___ 2nd Trombone | ___ Viola | ___ 1st Trombone |
| ___ 1st Flute | ___ Bb Sop. Sax | ___ 3rd Trombone | ___ Cello | ___ 2nd Trombone |
| ___ 2nd Flute | ___ 1st Eb A. Sax | ___ Euph. B.C. | ___ Contrabass | ___ 3rd Trombone |
| ___ 3rd Flute | ___ 2nd Eb A.Sax | ___ Euph. T.C. | ___ Piano | ___ 4th Trombone |
| ___ 1st Oboe | ___ Bb Tenor Sax | ___ String Bass | ___ Harp | ___ 5th Trombone |
| ___ 2nd Oboe | ___ Eb Bari. Sax | ___ Tuba/Basses | | ___ Piano |
| ___ English Horn | ___ 1st Cornet | ___ Tympani | **Jazz Ensemble** | ___ Drums |
| ___ Eb Sop. Clar. | ___ 2nd Cornet | ___ 1st Percussion | ___ Conductor | ___ Guitar |
| ___ 1st Bb Clar. | ___ 3rd Cornet | ___ 2nd Perc. | ___ 1st Alto Sax | ___ Bass |
| ___ 2nd Bb Clar. | ___ 4th Cornet | ___ 3rd Perc. | ___ 2nd Alto Sax | ___ Aux. Percussion |
| ___ 3rd Bb Clar. | ___ 1st Trumpet | ___ 4th Perc. | ___ 1st Tenor Sax | ___ _____ |
| ___ 4th Bb Clar. | ___ 2nd Trumpet | ___ _____ | ___ 2nd Tenor Sax | ___ _____ |
| ___ Eb Alto Clar. | ___ 3rd Trumpet | ___ _____ | ___ Baritone Sax | ___ _____ |
| ___ Bb Bass Clar. | ___ 1st Horn | ___ _____ | ___ 1st Trumpet | LGC 2000 |
| ___ Eb Contra Cl. | ___ 2nd Horn | ___ _____ | ___ 2nd Trumpet | |

Grade _____    Performance Time _____    Library No. _____

Maintaining a card file of all titles will help the director and librarians find music in the library. Several publishers have three-card sets available that facilitate finding pieces by Title, Composer, or File (or catalog) Number. Examples may be found in Figure 5-6. Some directors prefer to use only the Title and Composer cards. File card information should also be entered into a computer database file. Be sure to back up files regularly so that important data is not lost. Many programs allow users to design a database specific to their needs. Basic information for the database would include catalog number, title, composer, arranger, and publisher. Other helpful information might include grade level, dates performed, type of work (march, Christmas, oboe solo with band, etc.), special needs (requires 12 bassoons, etc.), and a miscellaneous field to allow for extra comments. One example of a useful database file for a music library is found in Figure 5-7.

*Figure 5-7. Band Music Library Database File*

| | |
|---|---|
| **File #** | CB-844 |
| **Title** | Concertino for Solo Percussionist and Band |
| **Composer (Last, First)** | Curnow, James |
| **Arranger (Last, First)** | |
| **Grade** | 6 |
| **Publisher** | Curnow Music Press |
| **Character** | percussion solo with band |
| **Dates Performed** | 4/29/03 |
| **Misc.** | Three movements (tympani/mallets/multiple). Requires mature soloist. Accompaniment well-scored. |

When using a database file to store music library information you will find it helpful to keep field entries brief. It may be necessary to shorten or abbreviate long titles, to use only last name and first initial for composers and arrangers, and to shorten publisher names. The advantage of brief entries is that it is easier to place all of the file information in a "report" format for printing. When the name of a piece starts with an article—"The," "A," or "An"— the general practice is to list the rest of the title first, followed by a comma and the article—this allows correct alphabetizing of all titles. Be sure to keep one or more back-up copies of your library file on floppy disk, Zip disk, CD-R, etc.!

Store instrument music library music in file cabinets or on shelves. Several publishers sell filing envelopes in various sizes to protect music in file cabinets, but plain manila envelopes can be used for that purpose. Hanging file folders also hold music in file cabinets effectively and neatly. Music filing boxes can be used for either file cabinets or bookshelves. Filing boxes are the most efficient and attractive way to store music on open shelves.

## *Solo and Ensemble Music*

Filing solo and ensemble music is certainly a greater challenge than filing band and orchestra music. The complexity of music type, instrumentation, etc., calls for a cataloging system that can, by the catalog number, identify all or most of this important information. Much time can be wasted trying to find a particular type of ensemble music in a poorly designed solo and ensemble catalog, and unnecessary duplicate purchases of music drain the music budget.

I recommend a seven-digit cataloging system for solo and ensemble music. This system identifies instrument type, number of parts in the ensemble (or whether it is a solo), and the sequential number of that type of solo or ensemble. Two letters are used to identify the instrument (see Figure 5-8), and the next two digits identify the number of players needed (01 for solo, or 04 for a quartet, etc.). A dash is useful before the final three numbers that identify the sequential catalog number of this type of music (e.g., 105 would indicate that this is the one hundred fifth piece of this instrument type and instrumentation cataloged in this library). The catalog number **FL04-025** would indicate that this piece is flute quartet number 25 in the school solo and ensemble library. Likewise, **TR01-010** identifies trumpet solo number 10 and **BR08-004** identifies brass octet number four. All solo and ensemble music could then be filed in score order from solos to largest ensemble size within each instrument type (i.e. flute solo, duet, trio, quartet, etc.).

*Figure 5-8. Instrument Identification by Letters*

| | |
|---|---|
| Flute: | FL |
| Oboe: | OB |
| Bassoon: | BN |
| Clarinet: | CL |
| Saxophone: | SX |
| French Horn: | FH |
| Trumpet/Cor.: | TR |
| Trombone: | TB |
| Euphonium: | EU |
| Tuba: | TU |
| Perc.: | PE |
| Violin: | VN |
| Viola: | VA |
| Cello: | VC |
| String Bass: | SB |
| Harp: | HP |
| Guitar: | GU |
| Woodwind*: | WO |
| Brass*: | BR |
| String*: | ST |
| Mixed*: | MX |

*used for large ensembles of varying instrumentation

All solo and ensemble music can be filed in regular manila file folders. The complete solo and ensemble library should be entered into a computer database (see Figure 5-9) and/or placed in a card file. The computer database can be used to generate self-adhesive mailing labels with the catalog number, name of piece, composer, arranger, etc., and these labels can be placed on the tabs of the file folders. It is also helpful to add a small sign-out card (see Figure 5-10) on the front of all folders. When a student signs out a solo or ensemble, the music librarian or director simply lists the student's name and date on the sign out card and retains the empty file folder.

*Figure 5-9. Solo and Ensemble Library Database File.*

| | |
|---|---|
| **File #** | FL05-002 |
| **Title** | Chansons du Berceau |
| **Composer (Last, First)** | Rice-Young, A. |
| **Arranger (Last, First)** | |
| **Instrumentation** | 5 C flutes (1 piccolo), (Bass & Alto Optional) |
| **Grade** | 4 |
| **Publisher** | Alry |
| **Character** | |
| **Dates Performed** | 5/11/03 |
| **Misc.** | |

*Figure 5-10.*

**ASBURY COLLEGE - Solo & Ensemble Sign-out**

| due date | name |
|---|---|
| | |
| | |
| | |
| | |
| | |
| | |
| | |
| | |
| | |
| | |
| | |
| | |

## *Music Library Facilitation*

You will soon discover that the multiplicity of responsibilities in teaching bands and orchestras requires the help of students and parents. You will need to train the students in correct library procedures and give them frequent direction, but this is the kind of task that many middle school and high school students will enjoy. Since many school instrumental music programs include some kind of awards program, it would be appropriate for these student workers to receive some extra points toward those awards in recognition of their work. However, many students will volunteer to help the band and orchestra program simply because they want to be involved and be helpful to a program that is meaningful to them, without regard to any reward.

Student music librarians should be trained to process and catalog new music; distribute music to ensemble folders; and collect, repair, and re-file music after performances. When music is collected after performances, music librarians should place all music back in correct score order, check for missing parts, erase any large or distracting markings on the music, tape any tears in the music, and promptly re-file the music. Any lost parts that cannot be located should be reported to the director so replacements can be ordered immediately, which will ensure that the set of parts is complete and ready for use at any time. Any photocopies of music that you have made with the permission of the publisher should be discarded at this time. Never retain copies with your music—it is illegal.

All students in musical ensembles must be taught the proper care of music. The cost of new music is constantly rising, but the school music budget usually does not rise at the same rate, so remind your students that music should always be transported in their assigned music folders (not in instrument cases). Many publishers sell durable "leatherette" folders, which can be imprinted with the name of the band or orchestra. Local music dealers often supply cardboard folders with the name of the dealer at no charge. Many directors find that a sign-out card (see Fig. 5-11) placed in each folder, to be signed and left at the school whenever the folder is taken home, will help keep track of all ensemble folders.

Remind students to mark music in pencil only, and that all marks on music should be made neatly and carefully. It is helpful to have a pencil placed in every music folder. Students should ask music librarians to repair torn music so that more serious damage is not done. Good habits learned about care of music can transfer to improved attitudes about other aspects of the ensemble experience and the music program as a whole.

*Figure 5-11. Folder Sign-out Card Example*

## The Asbury College Concert Band

Folder No._____

### Folder Sign-out Card

Leave your folder on your stand following rehearsal if you are not taking it with you for practice. Please sign and date this card in consecutive order whenever you take this folder with you after rehearsal. Be sure the folder is returned for the next rehearsal! Folders and music are very expensive; please handle both with care. Thank you!

**Be sure to have a pencil at every rehearsal! Use only pencil to mark music**

| Date | Name | Date | Name |
|------|------|------|------|
|      |      |      |      |
|      |      |      |      |
|      |      |      |      |
|      |      |      |      |
|      |      |      |      |
|      |      |      |      |
|      |      |      |      |
|      |      |      |      |
|      |      |      |      |
|      |      |      |      |
|      |      |      |      |
|      |      |      |      |
|      |      |      |      |
|      |      |      |      |
|      |      |      |      |
|      |      |      |      |
|      |      |      |      |
|      |      |      |      |
|      |      |      |      |
|      |      |      |      |

Borrowing and loaning music among schools is a great way to stretch the music budget, and it may be the only way to perform a piece that is permanently out-of-print. Special care must be taken with borrowed music to ensure that no damage is done to any part and that all parts are returned to the lender. It is wise to use a Music Loan Form (see Figure 5-12) any time music is loaned to another school.

**Figure 5-12. Music Loan Form**

---

### ASBURY COLLEGE MUSIC DEPARTMENT
1 Macklem Drive
Wilmore, KY 40390

#### Music Loan Agreement

Name of person borrowing music: _____

Representing what organization: _____

Address (Street, City, State, Zip): _____

_____

Telephone (Area Code & Number): _____

• • • • •

*We are happy to loan this music for your ensemble. Please note the following:*

1. *Please do not loan the music to anyone else and please return it to us as soon as you finish with it.*
2. *Please ask your students to only use pencil to mark the music (never ink). Please erase any excessive marking before returning it to us.*
3. *We try to keep our music in good repair and will try to send it in good condition. Please tape any torn music.*
4. *Please replace any lost or badly damaged parts or scores.*
5. *Please comply with the copyright law.*

*Thank you!*

• • • • •

Name of Music:_____

Composer/Arranger: _____ File #: _____

The following number of parts are being sent to the person listed above:

• • • • •

| | | | | |
|---|---|---|---|---|
| ___ Full Score | ___ Solo Clarinet | ___ French Horn 2 | ___ Trombone 1 | ___ Violin 2 |
| ___ Cond. Score | ___ Clarinet 1 | ___ French Horn 3 | ___ Trombone 2 | ___ Violin 3 |
| ___ Db Piccolo | ___ Clarinet 2 | ___ French Horn 4 | ___ Trombone 3 | ___ Viola |
| ___ C Piccolo | ___ Clarinet 3 | ___ Eb Horn 1 | ___ Bass Trombone | ___ Cello |
| ___ Flute 1 | ___ Alto Clarinet | ___ Eb Horn 2 | ___ Euph. T.C. | ___ String Bass |
| ___ Flute 2 | ___ Bass Clarinet | ___ Eb Horn 3 | ___ Euph. B.C. | ___ Harp |
| ___ Oboe 1 | ___ Eb CB Clarinet | ___ Eb Horn 4 | ___ Tuba | ___ Piano |
| ___ Oboe 2 | ___ Bb CB Clarinet | ___ Cornet 1 | ___ Snare Drum | ___ _____ |
| ___ Eng. Horn | ___ Alto Sax. 1 | ___ Cornet 2 | ___ Cymbals | ___ _____ |
| ___ Bassoon 1 | ___ Alto Sax. 2 | ___ Cornet 3 | ___ Bass Drum | ___ _____ |
| ___ Bassoon 2 | ___ Tenor Sax. | ___ Trumpet 1 | ___ Tympani | ___ _____ |
| ___ Contra Bassoon | ___ Bari. Sax. | ___ Trumpet 2 | ___ Mallet Perc. | ___ _____ |
| ___ Eb Clar. | ___ French Horn 1 | ___ Trumpet 3 | ___ Violin 1 | ___ _____ |

Date Music Sent: _____ Sent by: _____ Date Returned: _____ OKd: _____

Two copies of the Music Loan Form should be made, with one retained at the lending school. This form becomes a contract that indicates the name and address of the borrower, requested care of the music, and a complete list of number of parts sent to the borrower. In this way both the borrower and the lender share information and expectations, and the lending process is more trouble-free.

## Summary

One of my former college presidents often reminded faculty and students that since there is only so much time available to read, why not use that time to read the very best literature. The same is certainly true about the music we choose for our ensembles. We have so little time available to rehearse and perform—we should fill our time with the very finest literature written for our ensembles. Our students and our audiences will be musically richer as a result of a conscientious and thorough effort to find appropriate, first-rate music for our ensembles.

### For Discussion or Assignment

1. Evaluate a score assigned by your professor for its appropriateness with the band or orchestra from your former high school or present college. Use the checklist found in the section "How to Select Good Music," the Ensemble Evaluation Form in this chapter, and any other criteria you deem appropriate.

2. Discuss and evaluate the "Core Repertoires" found in this chapter. Name other repertoire that you believe should be on those lists.

3. Complete a mock Purchase Order for 10 pieces of music appropriate for a high school band or orchestra playing Grades Three and Four music. Indicate if the music is "on approval" or if the P.O. confirms an earlier telephone order.

4. Design a computer file program to list orchestra or concert band music. Use any database program to which you have access. Decide on appropriate categories and layout. Compile a library file of 50 entries of appropriate full ensemble music and an additional 10 entries of method books, or technique and warm-up books. On 15 of the 50 concert pieces, listen to a recording while following the score and include those observations in your data file. (**Note to faculty**: this is a major project that will require several weeks to complete.)

5. Design a computer file program for your personal library of solo and/or chamber music for your principal instrument. A minimum of 20 entries is assumed. Use the catalog system discussed in this chapter or an exemplary system of your own design.

6. Find an Internet Web site that includes information for musicians about copyright law. Print a copy for your files. Several national music organizations have this information.

## For Reference and Further Reading

Byrne, Frank P., Jr. (1987). *A Practical Guide to the Music Library*. Cleveland, OH: Ludwig Music Publishing Co., Inc.

Colwell, Richard J. and Goolsby, Thomas (1992). *The Teaching of Instrumental Music (2nd ed.)*. Englewood Cliffs, NJ: Prentice-Hall, Inc.

Cooper, Lynn G. (1995). Finding quality music for our bands. *Bluegrass Music News*, *47*, 1 (October), pp. 22, 49, and 53.

Dvorak, Thomas L., *et al.* (1986). *Best Music for Young Band*. Brooklyn, NY: Manhattan Beach Music.

Dvorak, Thomas L., et al. (1993). *Best Music for High School Band*. Brooklyn, NY: Manhattan Beach Music.

Dvorak, Thomas L., et al. (2000). *Best Music for Beginning Band*. Brooklyn, NY: Manhattan Beach Music.

Garofalo, Robert (1983). *Blueprint for Band*. Ft. Lauderdale, FL: Meredith Music Publications.

Harris, Brian. "Young Band Repertoire Project" (CD and booklet). San Antonio, TX: Institute for Music Research at The University of Texas as San Antonio.

*How to File and Find Music*. Philadelphia, PA: J.W. Pepper & Son, Inc. (1966).

Kinyon, John (1982). *The Instrumental Music Director's Source Book*. Sherman Oaks, CA: Alfred Publishing Co., Inc.

Kreines, Joseph (1989). *Music for Concert Band*. Tampa, FL: Florida Music Service.

Miles, Richard (ed.) (1997). *Teaching Music through Performance in Band (Vol. 1)*. Chicago: GIA Publications, Inc.

Miles, Richard (ed.) (1998). *Teaching Music through Performance in Band (Vol. 2)*. Chicago: GIA Publications, Inc.

Miles, Richard (ed.) (2000). *Teaching Music through Performance in Band (Vol. 3)*. Chicago: GIA Publications, Inc.

Miles, Richard and Dvorak, Thomas (eds.) (2001). *Teaching Music through Performance in Beginning Band* . Chicago: GIA Publications, Inc.

Moss, Bruce. (1995). Curnow on composing. *The Instrumentalist*. April, pp. 11-15.

Neilson, James. What Is Quality In Music? Kenosha, WI: G. Leblanc Corp.

Neidig, Kenneth L. (1964). *The Band Director's Guide*. Englewood Cliffs, NJ: Prentice-Hall, Inc.

Norris, Phil (1997). *Sacred Instrumental Published Music List*. Wheeling, IL: Christian Instrumentalists and Directors Association.

Reimer, Bennett (1970). *A Philosophy of Music Education*. Englewood Cliffs, NJ: Prentice-Hall, Inc.

Reynolds, H. Robert (1993). Guiding principles of conducting. *BD Guide*, 7/4, pp. 2-12.

Rocco, Roger (1991). Band music and the paper-plate mentality: An interview with W. Francis McBeth. *The Instrumentalist*, 46/5 (December), pp. 12-15.

*Selective Music List for Bands (4th ed.)* (1997). Nashville, TN: National Band Association.

Sheldon, Deborah A. (1996). Selecting music for beginning and developing bands. *Journal of Music Teacher Education*, 6/1, pp. 6-16.

Singleton, Ira C., and Anderson, Simon V. (1969). *Music in the Secondary Schools, 2nd ed*. Boston: Allyn and Bacon, Inc.

Thomson, John (1995). Teaching with goals, not answers: an interview with John Whitwell. *The Instrumentalist*, 50/5 (December), pp. 11-15.

Walker, Darwin E. (1989). *Teaching Music: Managing the Successful Music Program*. New York, NY: Schirmer Books.

Wallace, David, and Corporon, Eugene (1984). *Wind Ensemble/Band Repertoire*. Greeley, CO: The University of Northern Colorado School of Music.

Wise, Phillip C. (1996). *So. . .You're the New Band Director: Now What?* Needham Heights, MA: Simon & Schuster Custom Publishing.

# Chapter Six

# RUNNING EFFECTIVE REHEARSALS

## Quality Rehearsals

Too many people—including school administrators and parents—judge an instrumental music program solely by the quality of its public performances. While public performances of high quality are certainly one of the goals of any music program, the quality and content of the teaching that occurs daily in the rehearsal room is of greater importance. Performance level—including festival or contest performance and rating—does not always accurately reflect the quality of rehearsals. If poor performances and low festival ratings continue, however, there may be cause for concern.

I believe that the true measure of quality in any instrumental music program is the quality of its rehearsals. The total time you have with students in rehearsal far exceeds the time you devote to performance. Are your students becoming more musical in the time they spend with you in rehearsal? Are they learning about music history, literature, and theory? Are they developing new technical skills? Are they having a genuine aesthetic experience—learning to understand, appreciate, and love music through your rehearsals? Are you exhibiting to them a love for music, a wide knowledge of music, and a genuine desire to impart those things to your students?

All these considerations, particularly the attitude and seriousness of purpose you display to your students every day, will determine the quality of the experience they take from their years in band or orchestra. Performance constitutes the public face of your instrumental music program. It also offers periodic rewards to you and your students for your diligent work. But the essence of your program is to be found in the experiences generated by your rehearsals.

## A Success Plan

Singleton and Anderson (1969) list "four principals of rehearsal preparation":

- Choose quality music
- Get a full score and study it carefully
- Practice [conducting]
- Study tape recording of your daily rehearsals

They also write:

> Furthermore, a director's first six months of rehearsals are crucially habit-forming. If these rehearsals go smoothly and efficiently because of his total command of the situation, with parts and score in complete presence of mind, the young conductor establishes a professional behavior that will carry him well as the years go by. Like other modes of behavior, excellence can become a habit. (pp. 94-97)

We often hear teachers remark that they wish they had just one more week of rehearsals before the next concert. You will soon discover that there is never enough time to accomplish all that you hope for in a rehearsal. All you can do is learn to manage time well. Having only a finite number of rehearsals forces you to plan rehearsals more efficiently; and encourages students to work more consistently rather than save their individual practice time until the last few days before a performance. Establish a policy of avoiding extra rehearsals before a performance. That will make both you and your students more accountable for the regular scheduled time.

To be an effective teacher you must plan thoroughly by making long-range, weekly, and daily lesson plans. The long-range plans may be for a full year, semester, or the block of time scheduled before the next concert. These plans will be primarily general in nature ("be able to technically play Piece X by week 3," etc.). A weekly lesson plan should be a more detailed sketch of what you intend to accomplish in each rehearsal ("work on technical accuracy of brass in Piece A"). The daily rehearsal plan should list those *specific* things needing attention, a plan for accomplishing the goal, and the amount of time allotted for the work ("10:15-10:25—correct the trumpet rhythm at letter C: demonstrate the correct rhythm, have them echo the rhythm vocally, and then play on instruments. If necessary, play it at half tempo and then gradually increase to full tempo").

Preparation of daily lesson plans is an indispensable guide, providing the opportunity for you to thoughtfully consider the quality of teaching and learning that has been taking place, make prescriptions for musical improvement, and establish priorities for rehearsals to follow. Plan daily and revise constantly. While your aim is to anticipate as many problems and solutions as possible, invariably unexpected problems will occur during a rehearsal. By being knowledgeable and well prepared, you can remain flexible and on-top of the situation. Donald Metz (1980) wrote that "The ability to plan with purpose and focus is often singled out as the factor which best describes the truly effective teacher" (p. 77).

Commenting on rehearsal preparation in *The Art of Successful Teaching* (1992) Tim Lautzenheiser wrote:

> We will spend hours selecting the "perfect" music for the upcoming concert, but will not extend that same detailed preparation in the planning of the rehearsal format. Not only is this self-defeating, but it becomes a vicious circle leading to personal stress, poor performances, strained rehearsals, and a constant battle for program survival. (p. 25)

## The Daily Plan—Rehearsal Content

There are almost as many approaches to rehearsal design as there are teachers. One widely accepted model, however, is to begin with a warm-up and tuning time, followed by a technique-building time, and then a time when the major problems of the day are addressed. After that there may be review of other literature, a sight-reading session, and then a complete play-through of at least a major section of a piece to conclude the rehearsal. This final element is critical—especially for young ensembles—for establishing a positive last impression and sense of accomplishment. The major portion of the rehearsal—especially with younger ensembles—typically will be spent working on the major problems that need to be corrected.

## Warm-up Strategies

Younger ensembles will need more direction from you in their individual warm-up time. Many successful elementary and middle school instrumental music teachers do not allow their students to warm-up individually before class. Warming up systematically ensures that only appropriate warm-up procedures and techniques are used and prevents the typical rehearsal room chaos that occurs before many young band or orchestra rehearsals. Establishing a policy of quiet and order from the moment students enter the room has many beneficial residual effects throughout the remainder of the rehearsal. An alternative is to teach a small repertoire of small individual warm-ups for each instrument and earmark a specific period of time (one minute, perhaps less) for individual warm-up immediately preceding full-ensemble warm-ups.

If the students are quiet, the few minutes needed for younger students to assemble instruments at the beginning of a rehearsal can be combined with other activities, such as giving announcements, taking attendance, or doing listening activities that help develop the students' broader musical understandings and knowledge. Listening activities might include playing a recording of music that relates to pieces being studied in class (same style, or period, or composer, etc.) and guiding students to make discoveries about that music. You might play recordings of outstanding soloists on the various instruments as models of tone, phrasing, musicality, etc.; or begin rhythm reading drills with flash cards or rhythm pattern slides as soon as the bell rings—encouraging students to join in the drill as soon as their instruments are assembled. There are many possibilities for use of this valuable time prior to the first note being sounded.

Effective ensemble warm-up is critical for the success of a rehearsal for two reasons. Students and their instruments literally become "warm" and ready to function well, but the second reason for a warm-up period may be even more important: Now is a time to establish a seriousness of purpose about what is to follow. Insist on the best tones, fine intonation, correct hand and body positions, good breath support, and intense concentration. Focus instrument, body, and mind on the total process of making fine music. Selection of scales, rhythm drill patterns, chorales, and etudes should relate to the literature scheduled for rehearsal. The warm-up should have a structure appropriate for the maturity of the ensemble. Younger groups will require a relatively consistent warm-up routine, while evolving approaches can challenge more mature groups. A brief initial tuning of the ensemble prior to the planned ensemble warm-up routine will underscore the importance of developing ensemble listening skills.

Because this is a time to warm-up, not wear-out, the old admonition of "low, slow, and soft" is a good guide. Use this time to work on balance, blend, and development of fine, characteristic tones throughout the ensemble. Encourage students to listen intently to their own sound, then their neighbor's sound, and then gradually expand their aural awareness to include the entire ensemble. This is a valuable technique in the development of a full and unified ensemble sound. Students who play with a good characteristic tone and are developing and using good listening skills are more likely to be in balance with the rest of the ensemble and will have a far greater chance of being in tune.

McBeth (1972, p. 5) has written that achieving good balance in the ensemble will lead to good pitch. His "balance pyramid" concept is a valuable aid in developing good balance and pitch. Simply put, lower pitches should have more dynamic "weight" than higher pitches—within each section and throughout the entire ensemble. McBeth's book, *Effective Performance of Band Music*, is an excellent resource for directors of bands and orchestras.

A major factor in the development of in-tune playing is in-tune singing. Begin by having the band or orchestra sing scales. Once students are comfortable and confident with the scales, have them sing the chord progression discussed below and the chorales you use during your warm-up time. Teaching an instrumental ensemble to sing well, and *in tune*, will lead to an ensemble that plays with better intonation, blend, and phrasing.

During the warm-up time, use long-tone scales and scale patterns in the key centers of the music to be rehearsed. Use simple chorales to work on balance, blend, and ensemble tone. Also, to improve the balance, blend, and tone of your ensemble drastically, teach students to play a simple I-IV-V-I chord progression that can be used in any key. Insist that students play with their best tones at all times—it really is true that "you can't tune a bad tone."

Teach this simple chord progression to your ensemble in just four steps:

1. Establish an understanding of scale step numbers by having the ensemble play a major scale as you state the scale step numbers ("'DO,' or the 1st step; 'RE,' or the 2nd step"; etc.).
2. Assign the four-note sequence found in Figure 6-1. Remind the ensemble to play in a comfortable range—not too high, not too low.
3. Play the chord progression as whole notes or with a fermata on each pitch.
4. Once the ensemble knows the scale step numbers for their part, they can play the progression in any key. Try it!

121

*Figure 6-1. A basic I-IV-V-I Chord Progression to be used in any key*

**Part One (soprano):** Play scale steps 8, 8, 7, 8.
(Violin 1, Flute, Clarinet 1, Alto Sax 2 [low octave], Cornet/Trumpet 1, Horn 3 [low], Trombone 2)

**Part Two (alto):** Play scale steps 5, 6, 5, 5.
(Violin 2, Oboe, Clarinet 2, Alto Sax 1, Cornet/Trumpet 2, Horn 1, Euphonium)

**Part Three (tenor):** Play scale steps 3, 4, 2, 3.
(Viola/Violin 3, Clarinet 3, Alto Clarinet, Bassoon 1, Tenor Sax, Cornet/Trumpet 3, Horn 2, Trombone 1)

**Part Four (bass):** Play scale steps 1, 4, 5, 1.
(Cello, String Bass, Bassoon 2, Bass Clarinet, Baritone Sax, Horn 4, Trombone 3, Tuba)

These chord progressions should also be played at varying dynamic levels. Almost every instrumental ensemble will play with proper balance at the "piano" level. A useful technique is to play a tonic chord at "piano" and ask the ensemble to listen to how their note relates dynamically to the other pitches being played throughout the ensemble. Then ask them to play a crescendo while maintaining the same dynamic relationship with the other parts in the ensemble. This should dramatically improve the ensemble tone and balance at louder dynamic levels.

## Ensemble Intonation

A thorough warm-up that teaches intense listening will encourage your band or orchestra to play more in tune. The formal tuning period will require less time as students come to understand that tuning is a continuing process—"a journey, not a destination." The initial tuning of the ensemble should be done with the concert master, principal oboist, or principal clarinetist sounding a pitch (A for orchestra and Bb, F, or A for band), allowing the ensemble to first quietly hum to internalize the pitch, and then play the pitch to check how it relates to the pitch standard.

One approach to tuning an ensemble is to begin with lower sounding instruments, followed by successively higher instruments until all have entered. Tuning a band to the tuba helps keep the pitch level from rising, and develops a darker, more balanced band tone. Another technique is to allow each section to tune to its most appropriate note. Some teachers allow section leaders to tune first, followed by the full ensemble. Using a tuning chord (such as the tonic chord scoring noted in Fig. 6-1 above) is a wise ensemble tuning technique, as ensemble members commonly find it easier to hear their own pitches while sounding them in a chord.

An electronic tuner, a valuable aid to tuning that allows the process to move along quickly, should not replace reliance on the ear in solving tuning problems. Perhaps the best use of an electronic tuner is to enable individual players to check pitches throughout the range of their instruments to find the natural tuning tendencies of their instruments. The students then understand the "built-in" tuning problems on their instruments and can begin to learn to adjust for those problem notes.

The amount of time required for the warm-up and tuning will vary with the age of the ensemble and the time of year. Young ensembles often need a longer warm-up and tuning period. More mature ensembles may find that they will spend less time on this activity as the year progresses. As with all good teaching, the goal is to help students become independent musicians by teaching them correct warm-up and tuning procedures. This should be an intentional process, not one of those "caught, not taught" kind of experiences. Be sure to teach your students the physical and aural processes required to tune their instrument—what to "push or pull" to alter pitch, how to listen for "beats" when two pitches are sounding, how "flat" sounds, etc. You will be surprised at how many students are unsure of this process.

## Technique Building In The Ensemble

Following the warm-up and tuning period, most young ensembles will spend some time in a technique book to work on the sequential building of skill and technique that is so necessary for the young instrumentalist. This is a vital ingredient in the thorough development of mature performers. Unfortunately, this type of organized training is often absent in many high school instrumental ensembles because most of the instrumental method book series contain only three or four levels of materials, and those have been completed by the end of middle school. Also, the performance pressure for high school ensembles becomes greater and the sequential development of skills and techniques often becomes a victim of that pressure. Creative and effective teachers will be diligent about finding appropriate technical development material, and may even have to write some material to meet the unique needs of their students.

Too many high school students learn advanced skills (high note fingerings, alternate fingerings, multiple tonguing, etc.) through experimentation or the advice of other players in the section. Try to anticipate the need for advanced skills in new performance music and use that opportunity to teach those new skills to the entire section. In fact, you may want to search for music that can be used to teach specific skills and understandings to your students.

## Problem-Solving Time

The "problem-solving" time of the rehearsal is generally the largest block of time. It is during this time that you will work to correct or improve those sections of music identified during your planning as being in need of focused work. Go directly to the sections needing attention instead of simply beginning the piece and then stopping to correct problems as they occur. Simply starting at the beginning of a piece and then stopping repeatedly to correct problems interrupts momentum, and frustrate ensemble members. Another strategy to consider is to work on specific problem areas that occur near the end of a piece, then make your way backward toward the beginning. To prevent momentum frustrations, be sure to play at least a major portion of a piece straight through to give ensemble members the opportunity to feel the satisfaction of completing a piece. Also, beware the tendency to work on problem areas at the expense of working on the continuity of the entire piece. Much *music* is lost in the search for notes.

Telling students the specific problems to be addressed in the rehearsal helps focus their attention. It is also helpful to make a study assignment of the material you intend to work on at the next rehearsal. John Whitwell (see Thomson 1995) reminds us "Students are usually willing to do the outside preparation once they understand what the director wants" (p. 11). Posting a list on Monday of pieces to be rehearsed each day of the week will greatly assist individual students in preparing for rehearsals. It is also helpful to have a form like Figure 6-2 ("Notes to Myself") in each band and orchestra folder so that students may keep a record of any sections in the music that they need to practice.

As you review the results of each rehearsal, and continue your score study, you may find it useful to make a list of specific corrections,

*Figure 6-2. Notes to Myself.*

## The Asbury College Concert Band • "Notes to Myself"

**Name:** _____

On this form keep notes to yourself about sections of our music you need to practice. Also note those sections the conductor has indicated need to be learned. Write the date by which you want to have this music learned. Put a check in the last column when the music is learned. Section leaders should use this form to identify music for sectional rehearsal.

**Be sure to have a pencil at every rehearsal!**

| Date of this note | Music title and measure # or rehearsal letter | Date due to be learned | OK! |
|---|---|---|---|
| | | | |
| | | | |
| | | | |
| | | | |
| | | | |
| | | | |
| | | | |
| | | | |
| | | | |
| | | | |
| | | | |
| | | | |
| | | | |
| | | | |
| | | | |
| | | | |
| | | | |
| | | | |

suggestions, or questions for your students about each piece. Putting those in the form of "Rehearsal Notes" (see Figure 6-3) and placing it on each stand before rehearsal for review by students can save much valuable rehearsal time.

*Fig. 6-3. Rehearsal Notes*

---

**Anyplace High School Band**
**Rehearsal Notes - March 22**

**Shepherd's Hey—Grainger:**

1. All: most of this piece is staccato ("chippy") unless marked otherwise (important).
2. All: some are still behind in mm. 2-5 (do we need to thin this out?).
3. A. Sax/Euph: mm. 6-9 is still not quite together consistently.
4. Clar.: staccato at mm. 10-13 please!
5. Tuba/Euph/B. Clar: at mm. 24-25 we are not always together (play softer & tongue lighter).
6. Horn/Oboe: at mm. 58-65 be sure to match pitch better & do not slow down.
7. Low Brass: keep the articulation light and do not slow down at mm. 70-73.
8. All: very "chippy" in mm. 74-80!!
9. All: we need a full crescendo from everyone at m. 81!

---

File a copy of all "Rehearsal Notes" with the conductor's score when re-filing music after a performance. The notes will be useful in preparation for the next time the work is programmed. Even when working with a completely different group, you will find that many rehearsal notes still hold true. If nothing else, those notes will remind you of the problems you had to solve the last time you rehearsed and performed the piece.

## Ensemble Sight-Reading

If you are going to teach your students to become truly independent musicians—a most worthy goal for any music teacher—then you must teach them to sight-read. Being able to figure out musical problems independently is a valuable and essential skill. Colwell (1970) writes "In music, as in other subjects, learning proceeds most efficiently when the student becomes competent enough to discern his own errors and deficiencies" (p. 16).

Although a systematic approach to sight-reading is valuable, one key to success in sight-reading is to simply do it often. Regular sight-reading experience in rehearsal—beginning with very easy examples and progressing to more complex music—is the best way to improve sight-reading skill. I recommend sight-reading at least two or three days with your ensembles during a typical five-day rehearsal schedule. This consistent approach to sight-reading allows it to become a familiar and successful experience. A discussion about how to teach good ensemble sight-reading skills is found later in this chapter.

## Rehearsal Closure

Every rehearsal of school ensembles should end with a large-scale, complete, musical experience. It might be reading entirely through a familiar piece, or it might be playing through a major section of a piece that is "under construction." The importance of providing this feeling of completion and success for your ensemble at the end of the rehearsal cannot be overstated.

Every day of the school year you will find that several announcements need to be made to the ensemble. Write all of them down to make sure that these important reminders are not forgotten. Writing down the announcements also lets you consider the most concise way to give each announcement. Many teachers save announcements until the end of the rehearsal so that the concentration and focus that they have worked so hard to achieve will not be interrupted. There will, however, be times when some variety in the placement of announcement will be appropriate—such as using them to diffuse a difficult or tense situation.

A few suggestions concerning rehearsing the ensemble:

- Be careful not to talk too much in the rehearsal. Use your conducting gestures to indicate your musical ideas. Avoid "small talk"—rehearsal time is precious! Your students want to play—let them!
- Have a sense of humor and admit mistakes quickly. Be quick to laugh at yourself and *very* slow to blame others. *Never* humiliate them—you will destroy their courage.
- Make practice assignments and hold students accountable.
- Have a pencil in every folder (including yours!) and teach students how and when to mark instructions in their music.
- Use full rehearsal time for large-group problems, not for individual or small group problems. Work on those in sectionals or in an individual session with students.

- Take attendance—and do other clerical duties—without wasting rehearsal time. Some people take attendance as students enter the room and then silently verify their record as the rehearsal progresses. Others have an assistant or secretary silently take attendance. Do remember, however, that your record of attendance is an official school record and must be accurate.
- Set high, but attainable, standards for your students and yourself.
- Be well prepared for every rehearsal—it is your professional responsibility.
- Know the score!

You should be especially vigilant about planning and evaluating rehearsals during your first several years of teaching. The development of your processes and self-expectations during this critical time will determine the type of mature teacher you will become. It is the time to put first things first and form the habits that will lead to a satisfying and successful career in instrumental music education.

## Rehearsal Environment

An attractive and orderly rehearsal room helps establish a good rehearsal attitude in ensemble members. It should be a special place where great music is rehearsed and studied, and should present an inviting first impression by having the entire set-up in place for each ensemble with only the correct number of chairs and stands. Students can be assigned on a rotating basis to set up their row or section correctly at the beginning of each class period. All stands should be tightened and in good working order. Appropriate chairs that encourage good posture and good playing habits should be in place. A tuner should be ready and available for students in older ensembles to check pitch before rehearsal begins. The rehearsal order and any special announcements should be written on the board before class begins. This allows ensemble members to get their music in rehearsal order and to note the announcements. It also allows percussionists to set up and organize the instruments needed for the rehearsal.

Every instrumental music rehearsal room should have adequate and orderly storage for instruments, equipment, and music folders; and students should be taught to keep the storage areas in order. Every rehearsal room should have a high quality music playback system so that students can 1) hear excellent musical reproductions they will want to model, and 2) hear realistic representations of their own recorded rehearsals and performances. Memorabilia (plaques, pictures, trophies, awards, etc.) can be a source of group pride, a reminder of past accomplishments, and an encouragement to work for future success. It is possible for excessive displays of old trophies to become rather gaudy, dusty, and distracting—good judgment is needed to prevent that situation.

Many teachers like to display fine art in their classrooms. It not only speaks of the relatedness of all of the arts, but also helps maintain a civilizing presence in the rehearsal room. Students should be taught that the rehearsal room is a place to make serious music. It is not a place to run and play games.

# Teaching Ensemble Sight-Reading

## *Importance*

According to Elizabeth A.H. Green, in her book *Orchestral Bowings and Routines*, "Since the ability to sight-read is a basic factor for any orchestra player, it is a wise teacher who makes a real attempt to teach this thing." Sight-reading is a true test of independent musicianship. If you want to prepare your students to both desire and to be capable of participation in music after they leave high school or college, then you must help them become independent musicians. Good sight-reading skills enable students to form chamber ensembles, play successfully in church ensembles, and participate confidently and successfully in community bands and orchestras. Isn't that a wonderful goal for school music programs?

## *Skill Development*

I define successful sight-reading as a recognizable performance of a piece of music that is unknown to the ensemble. For me, this means that notes, rhythms, dynamics, pitch, tone, and style are performed at an acceptable level. All teachers should develop an intentional and sequential program of sight-reading to ensure initial and continued success. Success leads to more success!

Teaching ensemble sight-reading skills should be a long-term project. It must never become a last minute "crash course" the week before band or orchestra festival. That will *not* be successful. In fact, John M. Long (see Franks, 1996) suggests that you avoid sight-reading with an ensemble in the last three days before a festival or contest because sight-reading tends to make students careless. He also suggests "Sight-reading at the end of rehearsal is more productive because the careless playing will not carry over to another aspect of rehearsal" (p. 18).

Start your sequential sight-reading program early in the year with pieces the ensemble can easily sight-read from a technical standpoint. When they find they are successful, encourage them to do more—to be more expressive, improve balance and blend, etc. Be encouraging, but provide more challenge! As the year progresses, sight-read increasingly more difficult literature and continue to encourage them to do more than just play notes. Try to make sight-reading experiences as musically rewarding for students as possible. To demonstrate to your ensemble how they might have played the piece better, you might want to work on a section of music that the ensemble has just sight-read. This is also an opportune time to teach about music: something about the composer, other works of the composer, the time period, other similar pieces, the form, the principle key centers, etc. Seize this chance to greatly enrich the musical lives of your students!

## *Suggestions*

The only way to learn to sight-read is to sight-read! Do it regularly and you will find success. Tips and techniques for improving ensemble sight-reading (especially for music festivals) follow:

1. Most students concentrate better if not allowed to talk as they study a new piece. Encourage students to silently point out things to their stand partner during this silent study. (Some directors allow quiet talking about the music if the students find it necessary or helpful.)

2. Students will be more successful in silent study if they have an established study procedure. Encourage students to look for the following:

- Key (and all changes)
- Meter (and all changes)
- Tempo (and all changes)
- Style at the beginning (and all changes)
- Dynamic levels (and all changes)
- All repeats (especially D.S.'s, D.C.'s, and any Coda)
- Solos (study carefully)
- Technically difficult sections (analyze and practice silently)

I have observed directors who check to make sure their students have studied a piece well by asking a series of questions:

- "What is the key at the beginning?" (ensemble responds)
- "Any key changes?" (ensemble responds)
- "Where are the key changes?" (ensemble responds)
- "What is the meter at the beginning?" (ensemble responds)
- "Any meter changes?" (ensemble responds)
- "Where are the meter changes?" (ensemble responds)

and so forth through the list above. This is also a good check to make sure *you* have not missed anything—it happens!

3. After a period of quiet or silent personal study, an effective technique is to have the entire ensemble sing the piece while fingering the notes on their instruments (and "shadow bowing" or "air bowing" for strings or "playing in the air" or "air playing" for percussion). Insist that **everyone** sing in the *correct style*, at the *correct dynamic levels*, *in balance*, and *with correct rhythms*—correct pitch is too much to ask for (but wouldn't that be nice?). By doing this in your study period, the ensemble has already "sight-read" the piece—the only thing they haven't done is produce the pitches on their instruments. The other great benefit is that you get feedback during the study period regarding the level of understanding held by the band or orchestra about this new piece, so you can then correct many problems before actually playing the piece. This is a definite advantage during festival sight-reading!

4. Teach students to word a question in a concise and clear manner. (ex. "After letter 'C' five measures, is the note on beat 4 a concert D-flat?") Actually, it is a good idea to encourage students to try to answer their own question first. Ask that all questions be held until you request them. Many student questions asked during sight-reading do not appreciably improve the performance.

5. Know the rules of the festival in which you are sight-reading. Some festivals do not allow directors to talk during actual sight-reading, some will allow the director only to call out rehearsal letters, and some allow directors to "sing, hum, or whistle" and do anything but play an instrument! *Do* whatever is allowed! I encourage you to read the rules several times every year so that you are familiar with all the rules and are aware of any changes in rules.

6. If the students know and use appropriate musical terminology it will save time in the preparation or study period.

7. Students must not waste full ensemble study time with questions about unknown fingerings. Encourage them to quietly check with their stand partner.

8. Point out any similarities between the sight-reading music and other music the students may have recently played. This often helps students better understand a new piece.

9. In preparing to sight-read at a festival or contest, practice the entire process prescribed by the rules. Read any rules statement that will be read to students at the festival, adhere to the times allowed for study, and have someone give the timings aloud during the study period—in short, practice the exact procedures the students will encounter at the music festival. They should know what to expect and feel as comfortable as possible in the process.

Prof. Green offers some other suggestions about sight-reading in *Orchestral Bowings and Routines*:

1. Teach the child to keep going in sight-reading. . . .
2. Teach the child to recognize the first beat of each measure . . .[and be sure you *show* it clearly!].
3. Simplify time-counting for the child. . .*what to do on each beat* [teach a good counting system, and teach them to read note groups on each beat and full measures—not individual note values]. (pp. 84-85)

## Final Thoughts

Develop a mindset of looking forward to the sight-reading portion of music festivals. You can enjoy the personal challenge of quick score study and getting your students successfully through the process. Sight-reading at festivals is an appropriate means of evaluating your own teaching effectiveness in the essential area of independent musicianship.

Colwell and Goolsby, in *The Teaching of Instrumental Music*, write that "Time spent on sightreading, ear training, listening, and drilling on musicianship rather than technique may in time produce musicians capable of the more difficult numbers, if the conductor has patience" (p. 123). Band and orchestra directors have an obligation to the students and their parents, and the larger musical community, to prepare students to be musically independent. Good sight-reading skills and musicianship are major keys to success in musical performance.

## *For Discussion or Assignment*

1. Submit a timed rehearsal plan for a high school band or orchestra playing Grade Four music. The rehearsal period is 55 minutes, and is being held three weeks before District Festival. Include announcements, your full rehearsal outline with sections to rehearse in the literature you select, and an indication of which National Standards for Music are being addressed in this rehearsal plan.

2. Read "Solution I" in *Effective Performance of Band Music* by McBeth. Discuss your reactions to the chapter and how these concepts could be integrated into the rehearsal.

3. Read "Solution VI" and "Solution VII" in *Effective Performance of Band Music* by McBeth. Discuss your reactions to some of the major points in these two chapters.

4. Develop "Rehearsal Notes" for a piece your college band or orchestra is now rehearsing. Include at least 12 items. Borrow a score—do it right!

5. On pages 127 and 128 are "A few suggestions concerning rehearsing the ensemble." Develop your own list of suggestions based on your experience and observation.

## *For Reference and Further Reading*

Colwell, Richard (1970). *The Evaluation of Music Teaching and Learning.* Englewood Cliffs, NJ: Prentice-Hall, Inc.

Colwell, Richard J. and Goolsby, Thomas (1992). *The Teaching of Instrumental Music (2nd ed.).* Englewood Cliffs, NJ: Prentice-Hall, Inc.

Franks, Earl (1996). Without wasting words or time: An interview with John M. Long. *The Instrumentalist.* February, pp. 18-22.

Garofalo, Robert (1983). *Blueprint for Band* (revised ed.). Ft. Lauderdale, FL: Meredith Music Publications.

Goldman, Richard F. (1946). *The Concert Band.* New York, NY: Rinehart & Company, Inc.

Gordon, Edwin (1988). *Learning Sequences in Music.* Chicago: GIA Publications.

Green, Elizabeth A.H. (1966). *Orchestral Bowings and Routines.* Ann Arbor: Campus Publishers.

Hoffer, Charles R. (1983). *Teaching Music in the Secondary Schools* (3rd ed.). Belmont, CA: Wadsworth Publishing Company.

Kennell, Richard (1989). Musical Thinking in the Instrumental Rehearsal. In *Dimensions of Musical Thinking*, ed. by Eunice Boardman. Reston, VA: Music Educators National Conference. (pp. 83-89).

Kinyon, John (1982). *The Instrumental Music Director's Source Book*. Sherman Oaks, CA: Alfred Publishing Co., Inc.

Lautzenheiser, Tim (1992). *The Art of Successful Teaching*: A Blend of Content and Context. Chicago: G.I.A. Publications.

Leonhard, Charles, and House, Robert W. (1972). *Foundations and Principles of Music Education*. New York: McGraw-Hill Book Company.

Lisk, Edward S. (1991). *The Creative Director: Alternative Rehearsal Techniques (3rd ed.)*. Ft. Lauderdale, FL: Meredith Music Publications.

McBeth, W. Francis (1972). *Effective Performance of Band Music*. San Antonio, TX: Southern Music Co.

Metz, Donald (1980). *Teaching General Music in Grades 6-9*. Columbus, OH: Charles E. Merrill Publishing Co.

Moss, Bruce. (1995). Curnow on composing. *The Instrumentalist*. April, pp. 11-15.

Neidig, Kenneth L. (1964). *The Band Director's Guide*. Englewood Cliffs, NJ: Prentice-Hall, Inc.

Pautz, Mary (1989). Musical Thinking in the Teacher Education Classroom. In *Dimensions of Musical Thinking*, ed. by Eunice Boardman. Reston, VA: Music Educators National Conference. (pp. 101-109).

Reynolds, H. Robert (1993). Guiding principles of conducting. *BD Guide*, 7/4, pp. 2-12.

Rocco, Roger (1991). Band music and the paper-plate mentality: An interview with W. Francis McBeth. *The Instrumentalist*, 46/5 (December), pp. 12-15.

Shuler, Scott C. (1989). Music learning sequence techniques in instrumental performance organizations. from *Readings in Music Learning Theory*. Chicago: G.I.A. Pub.

Singleton, Ira C., and Anderson, Simon V. (1969). *Music in the Secondary Schools, 2nd ed*. Boston: Allyn and Bacon, Inc.

Thomson, John (1995). Teaching with goals, not answers: an interview with John Whitwell. *The Instrumentalist*. December, pp. 11-15.

Walker, Darwin E. (1989). *Teaching Music: Managing the Successful Music Program*. New York, NY: Schirmer Books.

Williamson, John E. and Neidig, Kenneth L., ed. (1998). *Rehearsing the Band*. Cloudcroft, NM: Neidig Services.

Wise, Phillip C. (1996). *So. . .You're The New Band Director: Now What?* Needham Heights, MA: Simon & Schuster Custom Publishing.

Chapter Seven

# PERFORMANCES AND PROGRAMMING

## The Performance Schedule

A public performance is a kind of final exam for a performance group. Students demonstrate *publicly* (talk about authentic assessment!) their mastery and understanding of the music (the "text" and "curriculum") they have been studying and rehearsing. Thorough preparation on the part of teacher and students is essential for performance success. Thoughtful and intense rehearsals, with intelligent individual practice, lead to effective and successful public performances.

Performances by school instrumental music ensembles fall into several categories: concerts, festivals or contests, community events (parades, performances for local civic organizations, etc.), and school or athletic-oriented events (such as marching band, pep assemblies, graduation). The dates for some of these events, such as football games, pep assemblies, and local parades, will be scheduled by others. In the case of athletic events, you should discuss scheduling concerns with the athletic director to avoid situations such as five straight home football games at the beginning of the season!

When planning the school concert year for a middle school or high school band or orchestra, probably you will find that two or three concerts per year is an appropriate number. The major concerts for bands and orchestras are typically a winter concert (usually just before Christmas vacation), a festival concert (just before or just after a district festival or contest), and a spring concert (near the end of the school year). High school bands usually are involved in many additional school and community performances. High school orchestras commonly perform for local civic clubs or PTA meetings. Be sure to consider these other commitments and any traditional activities in your community when developing the calendar of events for your ensembles. I suggest that you develop a file or notebook of programs from previous years to help guide your planning for each new performance calendar. A program notebook also becomes a valuable part of the printed history of your ensemble.

It is important that you consider whether the number of performance responsibilities you require of students is appropriate. You should decide—from an educational point of view—if all the activities and performances that you'd like to schedule are actually related to your curriculum. Are they *necessary* to the educational program, or are you simply trying to keep the students and parents so busy that they won't have time to choose other things in which to become involved and perhaps drop band? Is the level of commitment required of students in your program so draining that it leads them to decide not to continue playing their instruments after high school? If so, perhaps you should consider reevaluating your music education philosophy, your performance schedule, and extra time requirements. Would your teaching change if the success of your teaching were evaluated on the basis of how many of your former students continued to play their instruments after high school?

A major issue in program scheduling is ensuring that enough time is planned between performances to allow adequate rehearsal time before the next performance. If you are directing a young or inexperienced ensemble, you might want to schedule fewer performances to allow for more rehearsal time and more successful performances. Mature school groups may be capable of performing more frequently. Whatever the number, each performance should be of high quality so that both students and teacher can continue building on success.

Calendar decisions must be made no later than early spring for the next school year. Most school districts will have a scheduling procedure in place. A good way to approach scheduling may be that all of the people responsible for major events get together and try to resolve schedule conflicts. If there is a pecking order for scheduling, typically athletics will be scheduled first (because of the large number of events), then music, drama, forensics, and school clubs. Know which administrator is responsible for maintaining the master calendar in your school, and know and follow all the procedures related to scheduling.

Be aware of any events already on the school calendar—national testing dates, school proms, senior trips—that may affect your ensemble members, their parents, or the community. You will be wise to not schedule the spring concert the night before the SAT—or the night before the Senior Prom! Another factor in concert scheduling is being aware of traditional community events—such as an annual Lions Club fundraiser. Finally, be aware of the mid-week church night in your community and avoid scheduling events on that day. Certain scheduled events may have become established over many years and are now "traditional" dates on a school calendar. Make changes in a traditional schedule only after much thought and consultation with students, parents, and administrators.

With all these factors in mind, *plan early* and get all music activities on the master calendar. After the schedule is approved by the administration, you should distribute it to students and parents right away—before the end of the school year—so that students and parents can plan family activities around their major school responsibilities.

## Concert Logistics and Concerns

One important performance issue is what to do if the ensemble does not have uniforms. What would give the most uniform appearance at the least cost to students and parents? You may want to consider for male students: white long-sleeved shirts, black dress pants, and a particular tie; and for female students: white blouses (closed neck, long sleeves), black skirts (which can be made by the students or parents) or slacks. Black shoes are a must, with black socks for males and hose for females. This is a relatively inexpensive solution that provides a unified and dignified look. Be sensitive to the economic hardship any of these suggestions might cause the students. Some situations may require that you simply ask students to wear clothes they would wear to church or a nice party.

Male teachers should wear a black suit with the same tie as band members; or, if the ensemble does have a uniform, a tuxedo is appropriate concert wear. Female teachers often choose a simple long black dress with long sleeves. Concert wear choices for teachers should be dignified and should not draw attention to themselves.

The pre-performance routine is critical to the success of an ensemble performance. You should plan this well, and include time to warm-up the ensemble, tune all members, spot check and set tempos for all pieces, and give final reminders about the performance. Perhaps your *greatest* responsibility during this time is to put the ensemble members at ease. To do that, maintain a calm and controlled demeanor, display an appropriate sense of humor, and exhibit confidence in yourself and in your ensemble members.

Plan the ensemble stage entrance carefully. Is an orderly single-file entrance appropriate in your performing area or is a simple "mob on" more efficient? There is no universal answer. Many school communities (parents and administrators) prefer a single-file entrance—it seems to speak of order and discipline. If you perform on a gym floor or on a stage without a curtain, the single file entrance may be the only logical choice. However, if your stage does have a curtain, the "mob on" entrance certainly does save time. Older, mature ensembles usually use an unplanned stage entrance with individual warm-up and tuning. Most school groups, however, will want a planned entrance.

The ensemble should do only a simple tuning after entering the performance area. This is not another warm-up time with chorales or scales. Use your usual tuning procedure with your principal clarinet, oboe, or concertmaster. This is just a final check and a chance for the ensemble members to get a feel for the performance area one more time. Individual tuning should *not* be done on stage, in front of the audience, except in the most unusual and dire situations. An "offending culprit" can usually be located by having a section or part of a section play after which the problem can be quietly corrected.

Be sure to remind your ensemble members that their focus during a performance must be on the conductor and music making. They should not try to locate family members and friends in the audience. (You may not be able to keep them from looking for their family and friends, but do insist that they not wave at them!) Students must be taught not to do anything during a performance that might be a distraction to others. This includes talking during the concert, noisily emptying the water from instruments during quiet sections of music, making loud page turns, tapping their feet, and making excessive body movement while playing.

Percussionists often have to move from instrument to instrument during a piece, and their physical movement can be a distraction—often at just the wrong time! Percussionists, if they play at all during a piece, should stand by their instrument(s) for the entire piece; and whenever possible they should set up a personal work station that includes all of the instruments they will need for the piece. If they must move during the piece, they should do so as inconspicuously as possible. Unnecessary or poorly timed movement can be a distraction. Teach percussionists to hold up instruments such as the triangle, tambourine, or crash cymbals, at the proper time so that the attention of the audience is drawn to see—and, as a result, better hear—the instruments being played.

You must decide and be consistent about when and how your students bring their instruments up to playing position before they begin a piece. Some conductors have ensemble members bring their instruments to a uniform "rest position" as the conductor steps on the podium—moving to playing position as the conductor raises his or her arms. Other conductors, especially with older, mature groups, may skip the "rest position" and just make sure that the ensemble members are alert to bring their instruments up to playing position when so directed. You will need to choose the method that is most appropriate for the maturity of the ensemble and meets any strongly expressed desires of parents or administrators. There is no single right answer.

Be sure to rehearse procedures for standing to accept audience applause for soloists and/or the full ensemble. Most student groups do not accomplish this task well. A mature ensemble knows to watch the conductor carefully at the end of a piece for any indication to stand. They should stand immediately, face the audience, and smile. They should not change music or talk with their neighbor. Their signal to be seated should come from you, or from the concertmaster if you have left the stage. Music should be changed only after all applause has ended. Student soloists should be taught not only the correct way to bow and accept applause, but also the correct procedures for entering and exiting the stage, and for recognizing the conductor and ensemble members.

The exit from the stage may be a reverse of the plan used to enter the stage. If you are sharing the concert with another group, some changes in the exit may have to be made to accommodate the entrance of the other group. Be sure that ensemble members refrain from talking until they are out of the performing area.

You should rehearse all logistics in the actual performance hall. It is advisable to hold several rehearsals in the performance hall during the last few days before a concert. Younger ensembles will need more rehearsal time in the performance site than more mature ensembles. Be sure to insist on correct concert procedures and concert etiquette during these important rehearsals. Also, be sure that the exact ensemble set-up used in rehearsal is used in the performance hall. Any last minute changes in set-up can disorient and confuse young players. Make sure that percussionists and string basses are set up close to the rest of the ensemble. Many experienced teachers will place chairs for a less experienced ensemble just a little closer together during a performance—it seems to have a positive effect on the confidence level of young players.

Having a reception for ensemble members and the audience after a performance is a "win-win" situation! Ensemble members have the opportunity to be immediately congratulated and affirmed by a large group of people, and the audience appreciates the opportunity to meet the ensemble members and conductors, and to mingle with other audience members. The Booster Club should be given total responsibility for this event. They can reserve the school cafeteria (or another large, nearby area); arrange for parents to donate punch and cookies or other snacks; purchase supplies; get volunteers for set-up, clean-up, and serving; and so forth. You will not have time to be involved in any of the preparation for this event, but you can show much appreciation to the boosters afterward. This will retain their support and enthusiasm.

If possible, all public performances should be recorded—video and audio. It provides a continuing record of the accomplishments of the ensemble and is a means to evaluate the progress of each ensemble. A library of tapes from past performances serves not only as a recorded ensemble history, but also serves as a motivation tool for present ensemble members, and is a source of recorded examples of unfamiliar music for current band members.

Whenever possible, hire a professional to record your concerts. If this is not possible, train a band parent to fill this important responsibility. There are many sources for learning about good recording techniques and appropriate equipment. Two basic rules are: 1) mount two microphones on a single extension stand placed close enough and high enough to make the microphones fairly equidistant from each ensemble member, and 2) buy the very best microphones you can afford. When a choice has to be made between a professional quality recorder (cassette, DAT, or recordable CD) and professional quality microphones, the first purchase should be the best microphones your budget will allow. Most recording engineers believe that a pair of high quality microphones is essential for a fine recording.

## *Reminders for Conductors*

You should enter the concert stage after all on-stage tuning is completed. Enter quickly and confidently—without running!—and go to center stage before recognizing the audience applause. An appropriate gesture is to include the ensemble in accepting this initial applause by motioning for the ensemble to stand before you take your bow. When accepting applause, do so confidently and sincerely. Think through each piece before a concert to consider whether soloists, sections, or the full ensemble should be recognized at the end of the piece. Do not rely on memory for this important task—anyone can forget things in the "heat of battle!" Attach a small card or Post-It to the last score page as a reminder of whom you should ask to stand before you turn to accept the applause. At the conclusion of a concert that has included other groups, be sure to ask the other ensemble directors—or any guest soloists or guest conductors—to come on stage for a final recognition. Do not leave the stage too quickly or you may stifle applause. However, leave while applause is still strong enough that you may "need" to re-enter the stage! This is not an easy thing to learn to gauge, but with experience a conductor can learn how to draw out applause, and as a result, bring encouragement to ensemble members. One final caution: never leave the stage so late that the applause has stopped before you are off stage—those last few steps can be *very* lonely!

## Audience Development

You will choose literature that expands the musical experiences of students and audiences and helps you teach technique and musicality. That is as it should be. Still, you must balance those values with considerations for developing a large, appreciative audience over time. Be careful not to perform so much new or esoteric music as to burden your audience unduly, and be sure your ensemble members are sold on the pieces you perform: students will transmit their enthusiasm to family and friends, making them more receptive. You might also talk briefly to the audience about each piece, particularly a new or unusual piece, to help them become oriented to what they are about to hear.

McBeth (1997) writes, "A program should not be a potpourri of compositions the conductor likes, but a dramatic progression to somewhere" (p. 45). As with a fine musical composition, a well-balanced program will have some variety, unity, and contrast. Variety may be achieved by selecting music of different styles, composers, and compositional periods, the addition of soloists and guest conductors, and so forth. Unity may be achieved by selecting a theme for the concert—such as "A Night at the Opera," "Music from Around the World," "Christmas Around the World," or "Mostly Mozart." Pops concerts and patriotic music concerts always find enthusiastic community support. Contrast will be found in selecting literature with different tonal centers, meters, moods, structure, ethnic origin, and so forth.

In programming, I find that placing a relatively short, up-tempo piece at the beginning seems to make a confident, authoritative opening statement by the ensemble. Many band festivals have included a requirement for each band to begin their performance with a "warm-up march." (A short opening selection also allows latecomers to be seated sooner.) Beginning with a shorter piece allows the ensemble to settle in and prepare for the more lengthy pieces to follow, a kind of full ensemble warm-up.

Marches are an important part of band heritage, and the very best should be a regular part of band concert programs. Most audiences, especially older audiences, respond very favorably to performances of the vast variety of march-types. I believe that almost all band concerts should include at least one march.

The major work on a program will generally be positioned next. Soloists are often programmed after a major work. If the program is of a length that requires an intermission, it is advisable to end the first half with a lighter piece, and begin the second half with another brief, up-tempo piece. The last portion of a typical school concert should be lighter in character than the first half, as the audience may begin to tire. It is also advisable to program music that is technically easier late in the concert—both for the benefit of the players and the enjoyment of the audience.

Audiences appreciate a program that includes a lot of variety—not only a variety of styles, forms, and musical periods, but a variety of ensembles: full orchestra and string orchestra; a large ensemble and chamber ensembles. Exposure to the wide variety of literature available for large and chamber ensembles is also an important part of a thorough, well-rounded education of the students in our ensembles.

Programming soloists and guest conductors with our ensembles can be a valuable experience for students. I have found that featuring truly outstanding older high school students also has many benefits. Showcasing "homegrown" talent is a positive reflection on the school music program and the fine private teachers in a community. An added bonus is the encouragement these performances give to younger students, who may then aspire to one day being selected as a student soloist. What a great incentive to take up an instrument and to practice!

An ensemble gains much from working with a guest conductor. This might be a college or university conductor from the area, a local community band or orchestra conductor (which has the added benefit of making students aware of post-high school performance opportunities), student teachers, or former high school students who are now school band or orchestra teachers. Asking other music teachers in the school system to guest conduct your ensemble wins the support of your colleagues and their students. You might also consider a "band director exchange" with a friend in another school district. This has the advantage of giving you valuable experience working as a guest conductor. A guest soloist—instrumental or vocal—can add excitement to performances, be a model for ensemble members, and expose students to a type of music and a performance level that they would not otherwise have opportunity to experience.

Be sensitive to the physical comfort and attention span of the audience. When a gymnasium is used for school performances, most in the audience will tire within one hour from sitting on wooden bleachers. Even in comfortable theatre seats, school music audiences will lose their attention span after 75-90 minutes. A school concert—even with an intermission—should never exceed 90 minutes. A 60-minute concert is, perhaps, ideal for most. The advice of Colwell and Goolsby (1992) is that "Few concerts can be too short" (p. 100).

Schools that schedule several ensembles on the same program will need to be especially careful about the total time needed to produce the concert (entrances, exits, music, and announcements) so that they do not exceed the good will of their audience. For the same reason, only in very rare instances should a school music group perform an encore. Be careful not to mistake the kindness of an audience with a desire to hear more music!

Choosing, rehearsing, and performing a wide variety of quality music will provide a broad educational experience for our students, and a fulfilling and enjoyable performance for our audiences. But even the most thoughtful selection of literature, soloists, and guest conductors for a concert will not ensure a large, supportive audience unless it is accompanied by a thorough public relations effort to inform your community of the concert. This will be discussed in Chapter 11.

## Programs and Ushers

Every school performance should include an attractive printed program. The program should indicate the complete date (month, day, year), time, and place of the performance, the names of each performing ensemble and conductor, full correct name of each composition, full name of the composer, and full name of any arranger. Opus numbers, date of composition, and composer dates may also be included. The correctly spelled name of every student performing in the concert should appear on the program along with a listing of any special awards they have received or significant involvement (such as solo and ensemble festival participation or college honor bands). This is a good way to recognize special achievement and to encourage more of those extra efforts.

Printed programs also provide an opportunity to recognize booster club officers, student officers of the ensembles, ushers, secretaries, and any others who assisted in any way with the production of the program or concert. Be sure to list your building administrators on the program, as well as the school system superintendent and school board members. A list of future concerts scheduled for your ensemble or other musical ensembles from your school and community can be a service to the audience and a means of recruiting an audience for those future performances.

There are many style options for programs. Consider using all uppercase letters for the titles of pieces. Most people list the name of the composition first. Program notes can be placed in the program under the titles or on an additional sheet, or not be used at all. Whatever your preference, adopt one style and use it consistently.

Figure 7-1 and 7-2 are examples of patriotic music concerts. Figure 7-3 is a typical pre-festival concert at a school with three concert bands. Figure 7-4 is an example including program notes in the printed program. Note that the program in Figure 7-4 includes music for full band; for percussion only; for brass and percussion; and for woodwinds. Figure 7-5, a theme concert ("A Night at the Opera"), includes several soloists.

A well-scripted set of program notes gives the audience information about the music they will hear and about the composer. Whether printed in the program or announced during the performance, the notes will provide the audience with a greater understanding of what they are hearing. You can find many sources for information about the music as you prepare a score for ensemble rehearsals. In addition to the information about the composer and music provided by publishers on most full scores, consult music history books, books on specific composers, books on recommended literature, books of program notes, program notes collected from other performances, and the wealth of information available through Internet searches. An exceptional option for contemporary pieces is personal contact with the composer.

Verbal announcements during a performance can help focus the attention of the audience and give a desirable "flow" to the concert. Many audience members appreciate hearing the conductor give the announcements. It can make a desirable connection between the conductor and audience, so you may wish to consider this if you have the

*Figure 7-1. Patriotic Concert*

# Asbury College

presents

# *America, the Beautiful*

## A Celebration of God and Country

**The Concert Band**
Dr. Lynn G. Cooper, conductor

Spring Tour • March 5-8

### — Program —

(to be selected from the following)

THE STAR SPANGLED BANNER............Francis Scott Key & John Smith
arranged by John Bareham

LIBERTY FANFARE ...................John Williams/arranged by James Curnow

WHERE NEVER LARK OR EAGLE FLEW ......................James Curnow

DEEP RIVER, from *Folk Suite* .........................................William Grant Still

ON A HYMNSONG OF LOWELL MASON................David R. Holsinger

AMERICAN CIVIL WAR FANTASY....................................Jerry H. Bilik

AMERICANS WE, march......................................................Henry Fillmore

ARMED FORCES SALUTE................................arranged by Bob Lowden

GOD BLESS AMERICA..................Irving Berlin/arranged by Erik Leidzen

AMERICA, THE BEAUTIFUL............Bates and Ward/arranged by Dragon

THE STARS AND STRIPES FOREVER, march.............John Philip Sousa

*Figure 7-2. Outdoor Concert*

# The Ypsilanti Community Band

presents an

## *Independence Day Celebration*
### a concert in the park

7:30 p.m. • July 4th • Recreation Park

### — Program —

THE STAR SPANGLED BANNER .................arranged by Henry Fillmore

AMERICANS WE, march.......................................Henry Fillmore

LIGHT CAVALRY OVERTURE.........................................Franz von Suppe

SELECTIONS FROM "ANNIE" ...................................Strouse and Charnin
arranged by Philip J. Lang

12th STREET RAG............................................................Euday L. Bowman
arranged by John Higgins

*- Intermission -*

AMERICAN OVERTURE FOR BAND....................Joseph Willcox Jenkins

SELECTIONS FROM "THE MUSIC MAN"...................Meredith Willson
arranged by Philip J. Lang

PATRIOTIC SING-A-LONG ...........................................James D. Ployhar

GOD BLESS AMERICA...........................................................Irving Berlin
arranged by John Warrington

THE STARS AND STRIPES FOREVER, march.............John Philip Sousa

*Figure 7-3. Pre-festival High School Band Concert*

# The Ypsilanti High School Bands

present a

## Winter Band Concert

Lynn G. Cooper, conductor

7:30 p.m.  •  YHS Auditorium  •  February 28

### — Program —

#### Concert Band

KING ARTHUR SUITE......................................................Henry Purcell

transcribed by Arnold Freed

    1. Jig
    2. Air
    3. Dance

THE RAKES OF MALLOW, from *Irish Suite* ......................Leroy Anderson

ORANGE BOWL, march ......................................................Henry Fillmore

#### Freshman Band

MONTEREY, march ...................................................................Karl L. King

DENBRIDGE WAY ...........................................................James Swearingen

LYRIC OVERTURE .............................................................Frank Erickson

#### Symphony Band

PRELUDE, SICILIANO AND RONDO............................Malcolm Arnold

arranged by John P. Paynter

MASQUE.................................................................................W. Francis McBeth

MANHATTAN BEACH, march .........................................John Philip Sousa

*Figure 7-4. Band and Orchestra Concert.*

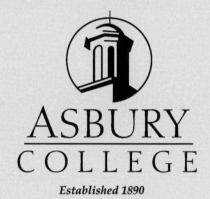

ASBURY COLLEGE
Division of Fine Arts

*presents the*

# Concert Band

Dr. Lynn G. Cooper, conductor

ASBURY
COLLEGE

*Established 1890*

7:30 p.m.  •  Hughes Auditorium  •  November 19

# — Program —

FANFARE FOR THE COMMON MAN (1944)...................Aaron Copland
*The Brass and Percussion*
Aaron Copland was one of the finest American-born composers of this century. Among his most famous works are *Appalachian Spring, Billy the Kid, Rodeo*, and *A Lincoln Portrait*. The *Fanfare* is one of his most performed pieces.

AMERICAN OVERTURE (1956)..............................Joseph Willcox Jenkins
This overture was written for the U.S. Army Field Band. It is written in a neo-modal style, being flavored strongly with both Lydian and Mixolydian modes, and in a very free adaptation of sonata form. This was Jenkins' first and most successful piece for band.

AN ORIGINAL SUITE (1928)..............................Gordon Jacobs
1. March
2. Intermezzo
3. Finale
The British composer Gordon Jacob wrote a number of pieces for the concert band including *Music for a Festival, William Byrd Suite*, and *Giles Farnaby Suite*. *An Original Suite* was was his first work for concert band and, given his great interest in folk music, many believe that the title was selected to make sure that audiences knew that this was newly composed music for band.

HYMN TO YEREVAN (1968)..............................Alan Hovhaness
The ancient city of Yerevan, at the foot of majestic, towering Mount Ararat, is the home of Armenians who found refuge there from many massacres. The music is composed in an ancient mode and hymn style of the Armenian church. A solemn contrapuntal motet expresses sorrow, strength, and spiritual resurrection. A middle section, in free rhythmless chaos of bells and roaring trombones, celebrates a dauntless defiance of tragedy. A solemn hymn returns, heroic, and triumphal.

ITALIAN IN ALGIERS, overture .....................................Gioacchino Rossini
arranged by Lucien Cailliet
Rossini (1792-1868) was one of the great composers of the Italian operatic school. His 35 operas were written within a span of two decades and after 1829 he did not write another opera. Some of his most famous operas include *The Barber of Seville, La Gazza Ladra, William Tell,* and *Italian in Algiers.*

AIR (ca. 1723)................................................................Johann Sebastian Bach
*The Woodwinds and Horns*
This arrangement of the familiar second movement of the *Suite No. 3* by Bach was scored for woodwinds and horns by Mark Hindsley, who was Director of Bands Emeritus at the University of Illinois.

MOSAICS (1975) ..........................................................................Jared Spears
*The Percussion Section*
Dr. Jared Spears is Professor of Music and Chairman of the Composition Department at Arkansas State University in Jonesboro, Arkansas. He writes extensively for the concert band and is noted for his effective writing for percussion.

COUNTRY GARDENS (1918).............................Percy Aldridge Grainger
setting by Tom Clark
Percy Grainger (1882-1961) was a remarkable innovator, using irregular rhythms before Stravinsky, pioneering in folk music collection at the same time as Bartok, writing random music in 1905, and predating Varese in experimentation with electronic music. This setting of a simple English folk song has become his more popular light piece. This arrangement for band was completed in 1931.

GEORGE WASHINGTON BICENTENNIAL, march ...John Philip Sousa
This march was commissioned for the 200th anniversary celebration, in 1932, of the birth of George Washington. The premiere performance was one of the last two conducting appearances by Sousa (1854-1932) before his death. It is considered to be one of his finest marches.

Flute
Andrea Brown *
Marybeth Cresse
Julie Cooper *
Tanya Kragh
Cindy Keckler
Jennifer Stutzman
Lora Zeller
Vanessa Carlisle

Oboe
Julie Dishon
Catherine West
Esther Hovey

Bassoon
Michael Israel

Clarinet
Amy Hiett
Charlotte Hortin
Rhonda Ferris
Melissa Kirby
Gregory Matthews

Bass Clarinet
Stephanie Oswald *

Saxophones
Rodney Patterson, alto
Adam Evans, tenor
Cathi Greenwood, baritone

French Horn
Marcy Oswald
Kent Hayward
Mandy George
Kim Schmucker +
Kevin Welch

Cornet/Trumpet
Vince Schmucker *
Vance Drakeford
Brack Dodd
John Herrington +
Glenn Stallsmith
Christopher Dempsey

Euphonium
Ross Reitz
Ginger Ulery
Doug McClure

Trombone
Nathan Farrell
Gregory Cox
James Fogal
Gareth Lewis +
Jim Barkley *+
Bart Bruehler, bass

Tuba
Johnson Cannon
Keith Zane *+
Tom Bratten

Percussion
Heather Howland +
Matt Olmstead
Matthew Myer
Steven Evans *
Jennifer Weed
Russ McGee *+
Julie Shrout

* = Senior
+ = Band Staff

151

**Figure 7-5. Theme Concert**

# Asbury College

presents

# *A Night At The Opera*

7:30 p.m.  •  Hughes Auditorium  •  October 24

## — Program —
### The Orchestra
Dr. Ronald W. Holz, conductor

SYMPHONY, from *The Fairy Queen* ............................................Henry Purcell
    Maestoso
    Allegro-Adagio-Allegro

MEDITATION, from *Thais*.......................................................Jules Massenet
               Prof. Lori Everson, violin

LIGHT CAVALRY OVERTURE.........................................Franz von Suppe

YOU'LL NEVER WALK ALONE, from *Carousel* .................Richard Rogers
             Dr. Beatrice Holz, soprano

SWORD DANCE, from *Rienzi* .................................................Richard Wagner

### - Intermission -

### The Concert Band
Dr. Lynn G. Cooper, conductor

TANCREDI, overture .........................................Gioacchino Antonio Rossini
                  transcribed by Leonard Falcone

Non piu andrai, from *Marriage of Figaro* ......................................W. A. Mozart
                  arranged by Edgar L. Barrow
          Dr. Craig Hodges, bass-baritone

ELSA'S PROCESSION, from *Lohengrin*................................Richard Wagner
                  transcribed by Lucien Cailliet

Quando men vo, from *La Boheme*................................................Giacomo Puccini
                  arranged by Edgar L. Barrow
         Prof. Virginia Bowles, soprano

WEST SIDE STORY, selections.............S. Sondheim and Leonard Bernstein
                  arranged by W.J. Duthoit

EL CAPITAN, march .........................................................John Philip Sousa voice and personality to pull it off. The primary disadvantage of giving your own announcements is that you do not have much time to mentally prepare for the next piece or to communicate with ensemble members.

One aspect of the concert that is often overlooked is the use of ushers. An agreement with other ensemble directors in your school to provide ushers for each other's concerts is a great solution to the problem. Another solution is to ask booster club members or parents to usher. This is a good way to involve parents in the activities of their children, and it provides more mature leadership.

Ushers must have a clear understanding of what is expected of them—when they should arrive, how they should greet the public, how long they are on-duty, when they should admit late arrivals, etc. Providing a printed set of instructions to the ushers (see Figure 7-6) will head off many potential problems. Recruit ushers early enough to include their names on the program as a way to publicly say "thank you" to a very important support group.

*Figure 7-6. Instructions for Concert Ushers*

**Anyplace High School Music Department**
**Instructions for Concert Ushers**

Thank you very much for helping! The following information will help make this a positive experience for all who attend the concert today.

1. Please arrive at least 30 minutes early.
2. Pick up a handful of programs in the music office and go to the auditorium. Hand out programs to anyone already in the auditorium.
3. There will be two ushers at each of the doors in auditorium.
4. Auditorium doors should be open until the lights dim at the beginning of the concert. Doors should be open during intermission, and while the curtain is closed for a set-up change.
5. As people arrive, please welcome them sincerely. All adults get a program, but give one only to children who request one.

153

Latecomers should be admitted between pieces or during applause, but not during a piece.

6. If the auditorium fills up, try to locate empty, unsaved seats and make them available to people who are still arriving. Extra chairs may be set up in back, but do not block any avenues of exit in order to remain in compliance with fire codes.

7. You should know the location of the restrooms and water fountains.

8. Please be sensitive to those who may need special assistance. Those in wheelchairs may need help with doors. They may find the most comfortable place for them is at the center aisle in back (where the floor is most flat)—but they may certainly sit wherever they choose.

9. Noisy young children are sometimes a problem. There is very little we can do unless the parent realizes that it is a distraction and takes the child out. It is generally best if you ignore the problem. If there is a major problem, simply let the parent know the location of the water fountains in the hall "in case your child might like a drink of water."

10. Please help discourage children from going in and out during a performance.

Again, thank you for volunteering to usher at our concert. Your helpful and friendly interaction with our audience plays a vital part in the success of this concert!

## Summary

The key to success in ensemble performance is careful and thoughtful planning on the part of the director, and effective and productive rehearsals. Each aspect of the performance—from scheduling through appropriate literature selection and careful preparation of the ensemble to producing the concert program—is important. The complete experience should generate educational and musical growth for the ensemble members, positive audience response, and strong long-term support of the instrumental music program.

## *For Discussion or Assignment*

1. Give the titles for three "theme" concerts (not listed in the text) and list five appropriate pieces for one of those theme concerts.

2. Select literature for a concert by your future high school band or orchestra. Turn in a complete four-page program for that concert. This does not have to be a theme concert. Feel free to use fake names for the school and ensemble members, but use the real thing for the music!

3. Write a program note for a piece that your college band or orchestra is preparing for a concert.

## *For Reference and Further Reading*

Colwell, Richard J. and Goolsby, Thomas (1992). *The Teaching of Instrumental Music (2nd ed.)*. Englewood Cliffs, NJ: Prentice-Hall, Inc.

The Community Band—A Manual of Organization and Operation (1977). Barrington, IL: The Northshore Concert Band.

Dvorak, Thomas L., et al. (1993). *Best Music for High School Band*. Brooklyn, NY: Manhattan Beach Music.

Dvorak, Thomas L., et al. (1986). *Best Music for Young Band*. Brooklyn, NY: Manhattan Beach Music.

Goldman, Richard F. (1946). *The Concert Band*. New York, NY: Rinehart & Company, Inc.

Hoffer, Charles R. (1983). *Teaching Music in the Secondary Schools (3rd ed.)*. Belmont, CA: Wadsworth Publishing Company.

Kinyon, John (1982). *The Instrumental Music Director's Source Book*. Sherman Oaks, CA: Alfred Publishing Co., Inc.

Kreines, Joseph (1989). *Music for Concert Band*. Tampa, FL: Florida Music Service.

Lautzenheiser, Tim (1992). *The Art of Successful Teaching: A Blend of Content and Context*. Chicago: GIA Pub.

Moss, Bruce. (1995). Curnow on composing. *The Instrumentalist*. April, pp. 11-15.

Neidig, Kenneth L. (1964). *The Band Director's Guide*. Englewood Cliffs, NJ: Prentice-Hall, Inc.

Norris, Phil (1997). *Sacred Instrumental Published Music List*. Wheeling, IL: Christian Instrumentalists and Directors Association.

Rehrig, William H. and Bierley, Paul E. (ed.) (1991). *The Heritage Encyclopedia of Band Music (in 3 volumes)*. Westerville, OH: Integrity Press.

Reimer, Bennett (1970). *A Philosophy of Music Education*. Englewood Cliffs, NJ: Prentice-Hall, Inc.

Reynolds, H. Robert (1993). Guiding principles of conducting. *BD Guide*, 7/4, pp. 2-12.

Rocco, Roger (1991). Band music and the paper-plate mentality: An interview with W. Francis McBeth. *The Instrumentalist*, 46/5 (December), pp. 12-15.

*Selective Music List for Bands (4th ed.)* (1997). Nashville, TN: National Band Association.

Singleton, Ira C., and Anderson, Simon V. (1969). *Music In The Secondary Schools (2nd ed.)*. Boston: Allyn and Bacon, Inc.

Smith, Norman (1989). *March Music Notes*. Lake Charles, LA: Program Note Press.

Smith, Norman and Stoutamire, Albert (1979). *Band Music Notes (revised ed.)*. San Diego, CA: Kjos West.

Thomson, John (1995). Teaching with goals, not answers: an interview with John Whitwell. *The Instrumentalist.*, *50/5* (December), pp. 11-15.

Walker, Darwin E. (1989). *Teaching Music: Managing the Successful Music Program*. New York, NY: Schirmer Books.

Wallace, David, and Corporon, Eugene (1984). *Wind Ensemble/Band Repertoire*. Greeley, CO: The University of Northern Colorado School of Music.

Wise, Phillip C. (1996). *So. . .You're the New Band Director: Now What?* Needham Heights, MA: Simon & Schuster Custom Publishing.

# Chapter Eight

# CONSIDERING SOME CORE ISSUES

## Motivation and Discipline

### The Problem

The single greatest reason that promising young teachers leave the field of education is the frustration of dealing with discipline problems. Rozmajzl and Bourne (1996) cited a study by Lawrence Vredevoe from the 1960s that found discipline to be the issue of most concern, even for prospective teachers. The same is certainly true today (see Leriche, 1992, p. 77).

Virtually all education majors in every curriculum take a course in classroom management. Many books have been written and careers made around the issue of classroom discipline or management. Every *Phi Delta Kappan* survey about education since 1969 has listed "discipline" at or near the top of what the public perceives as the biggest problems in schools. And newspaper stories about school discipline problems abound. All told, school discipline is a highly visible topic—one that mystifies some, frustrates many, and yet finds a few who wonder what all the fuss is about.

Your discipline problems will be different from those of classroom teachers, who may have only 20 to 25 students. The theories, strategies, and techniques taught in classroom management courses may not apply to a musical ensemble rehearsal with 30 to 100 students of different grade levels holding "noise makers" in their hands. You will need to understand basic theories of discipline and motivation, but know also that you will have to modify much of what you learn to fit your teaching circumstance—not to mention your personality, level of confidence, preparedness, and other variables.

One way you can stack the deck in your favor is to be well prepared and task-oriented. Berry (1993, p. 38) reminds us of a piece of advice that Thaddeus Giddings gave to Joseph Maddy nearly a century ago, advice that is yet good today: "Less talking, more singing; less teaching, more learning." Students actively engaged in something they find enjoyable and of worth seldom cause discipline problems. Mihaly Csikszentmihalyi (1993), in *Talented Teenagers: The Roots of Success and Failure*, states that:

> Whether a teenager will want to devote a great deal of time to studying chemistry or music depends also on the quality of the experience he or she derives from working in the lab or practicing an instrument. . . . The main reason they do what they do is that they enjoy it. (pp. 7-8)

Holz and Jacobi (1966) remind us that "The teacher is responsible for setting the tone of the class and creating an atmosphere in which the desired learnings may take place" (p. 51). They also wrote an exceptional definition of teaching: "If learning depends on wanting to learn, *then teaching is the art of making students want to learn*. . ." (p. 50). Can we motivate youth?

**Motivation** consists of whatever causes a student to want to take part in an activity: motivation is a matter of desire. **Discipline** consists of whatever causes a student to conform to rules and complete tasks: discipline is a matter of behavior. Motivated students are disciplined, because they monitor their own behavior through healthy self discipline. Unmotivated students need discipline imposed by a teacher.

But how effective is externally-imposed discipline? Tim Lautzenheiser (1992), noted music educator and motivational speaker, writes that "Motivation is, at all times, an individual choice" (p. 66) and "The truth is: We cannot give students motivation" (p. 108). Perhaps Lautzenheiser's statement heads us in the direction of a more complete and accurate thought about motivation and discipline. While we cannot give students motivation, we can give them a learning environment from which they will take motivation. That, in turn, generates self-discipline, which is infinitely more effective than any discipline we can give them externally.

How motivated are you as a teacher? The plain truth is that unless you are motivated to learn and grow (and to help your students learn and grow) you will not be able to create a learning environment that they find motivating. Csikszentmihalyi (1993) wrote that

> Students will learn only if they are motivated. The motivation could be extrinsic—the desire to get a well-paying job after graduation—but learning essential to a person's self must be intrinsically rewarding. Unless a person enjoys the pursuit of knowledge, learning will remain a tool to be set aside as soon as it is no longer needed. Therefore we cannot expect our children to become truly educated until we ensure that teachers know not only how to provide information but also how to spark the joy of learning. (p. 195)

Alfie Kohn, in his insightful book *Punished by Rewards* (1993), made this helpful observation:

> One of my epiphanies as a teacher came with the realization that students' disruptive acts were less a sign of malice than of a simple desire to make the time pass faster. No strategy for classroom management can hope to be effective in the long term if it ignores the fact that misbehavior often reflects students' lack of interest in much of what we are teaching. They can't get out, so they act out. Ironically, the very strategy that is intended to keep a tighter grip on the classroom is often responsible for behavior problems. The connection between the two, however, is not always obvious. (p. 217)

To spur students to be motivated you will need to keep the bar high but reachable, and remind them periodically of your expectations, but that is only one side of the equation. You also will need to be attuned to the students' expectations. In the classic motivation-inducing learning environment, teacher expectations and student expectations are at least compatible, if not perfectly aligned. As a teacher, you will find yourself engaged in balancing acts—trying to challenge students without discouraging them; trying to make success possible without boring them; trying to lead them to worthy educational objectives while being faithful to as many of their personal objectives as possible. These observations square with two classroom conditions that Csikszentmihalyi (1993) identifies as interfering with learning: anxiety and boredom. He writes that "Anxiety occurs primarily when teachers expect too much from students; boredom occurs when teachers expect too little. When curricular expectations are out of sync with students' abilities, not only does motivation decrease, but also achievement" (p. 10). Like Goldilocks in the cabin of the Three Bears, we music teachers are forever looking for something that feels "just right."

While searching for the ideal, you also have to give yourself a break now and then. Everything that goes wrong can be your fault only if everything that happens is under your control, and of course that is not the case. Realistically, some student misbehaviors are attributable to factors other than your learning environment. Students bring outside burdens and problems with them to class. While creating a motivating learning environment is your first line of defense against student misbehavior and boredom, you will need to be alert to student's personal problems as well. Your first reaction to misbehavior, then, must be to understand its source. When the source is you or your teaching, you have the power to make immediate improvements. When the source is external to you, you may have to seek help from counselors or administrators.

## *Some Solutions*

*Preparation*

According to R. Louis Rossman (1989) "The best discipline device is to be well prepared for every rehearsal and class presentation" (p. 24). Teachers who are fully prepared for class will encounter fewer surprises and accomplish more of their goals. A simple three-part approach to rehearsal and lesson planning is this:

- Plan what you want to do
- Plan what could go wrong
- Plan how to fix what could go wrong

Anticipating problems—and their solutions—helps prevent most discipline problems in the rehearsal. Donald Metz (1980) reminds us that "Perhaps the heart of the matter lies not in class size or differences in ability, but in the music teacher who doesn't know precisely what to do once attendance is taken and the class is quiet" (p. 3).

*Engaging Attention*

Hiam Ginott, in his book *Teacher and Child* (1972), reminds us in his words that we, the teachers, are the keys to establishing and maintaining a productive classroom atmosphere:

I have come to a frightening conclusion. I am the decisive element in the classroom. It is my personal approach

*"Success built in fear is not long lived."*

that creates the climate. It is my daily mood that makes the weather. As a teacher I possess tremendous power to make a child's life miserable or joyous. I can be a tool of torture or an instrument of inspiration. I can humiliate or humor, hurt or heal. In all situations it is my response that decides whether a crisis will be escalated or de-escalated, and a child humanized or de-humanized. (pp. 15-16)

Another important key to creating a motivating classroom environment is consistency. Not only must you be consistent about enforcement of all classroom rules, but your interactions with students, your educational expectations of them, and your personal attitude must all be consistent from day to day. Treat students with courtesy and avoid "temper tantrums" in rehearsals. We have all heard stories of conductors who rant and rave in rehearsal, and often find "success" with their ensembles. Even though conductor tantrums can produce results faster than courtesy in the rehearsal, success built on fear is not long lived. Fine music is not made in an environment of fear and conducting is done with a delicate baton, not a heavy club.

Holz and Jacobi (1966) remind teachers that "Young students rarely make errors on purpose. Their errors are usually honest mistakes, caused by lack of experience, the awkwardness of unfamiliar instruments and positions, the inherent mysteries of notation, or (tragically often) the failure of the instructor to make his meaning clear" (p. 56). Students will behave better if you are clear in your expectations and instructions, if you display patience, and if you encourage private practice.

Besides curricular and classroom issues, you will need to think about the effect of your personal relationships with students on their motivation, discipline, and over-all learning experience. It may be difficult for you as a young teacher to adjust to the fact that you are the adult, and that it is your responsibility to establish and maintain professional and appropriate teacher-student relationships. You need to understand that students need a teacher who is friendly, but not necessarily a friend. Be particularly careful about acting in a way that could be misunderstood by students. Inappropriate relationships with students are never excusable.

## *Some Specific Suggestions to Enhance the Learning Environment*

**161**

- Know the names of all your students and use them in rehearsal.

- Choose a balance of fine music that students will enjoy rehearsing and performing.
- Be organized and well prepared. Everything should have its place!
- Start rehearsals on time and end on time.
- Start your rehearsal only after you have everyone's attention. Foster maximum learning by following this principle: "When I talk, you listen; when you have the floor, you talk and I will listen."
- Treat students with the same courtesy you ask of them.
- Talk primarily through your baton, secondarily through verbalization.
- Keep the rehearsal moving and everyone involved as much as possible. Stop only if you are sure of the problem, have a solution, and know exactly what you are going to say.
- Display a positive attitude and a good sense of humor. Avoid sarcasm: students sometimes misunderstand and think you are serious!
- Whenever possible use non-verbal techniques (such as eye-contact and proximity) to prevent discipline lapses.
- When behavior lapses occur—and they will—focus on the behavior, not the student.
- Teach students what you want them to know rather than wasting time, energy, and good humor wishing they knew it.
- Give clear assignments for practicing so students will understand your expectations.
- Praise students publicly, but correct behavior problems privately when possible.
- Try to solve your own discipline problems. Send students to the office only as a last resort.
- Keep your classroom rules simple, post them, and enforce them. Increase student respect for the rules by involving students in their formulation and by dropping any rule that you will not or cannot (for lack of administrative backing) enforce.
- Give students the security of knowing what you expect of them. Here, for example, is a starting point for a list of rehearsal expectations:

    1. Come to rehearsal with a positive, supportive, and helpful attitude.

2. Come to rehearsal ready to play your music well and ready to learn. Practice as much as necessary to be prepared. Remember that a rehearsal is a "rehearing," a working together on what we have been practicing and hearing individually.
3. Focus your attention on the music and the conductor, and avoid talking.
4. Be intent on improving as the semester progresses.

Other contributors to motivation are discussed elsewhere in this book: performances, festivals and contests, competitions (a two-edged sword), awards, auditions, tests and grades, parent involvement, praise (from teachers, parents, family, friends, etc.), esprit de corps, social activities, chair position, individual and group successes, and recognition of accomplishments. Success as an ensemble—reinforced by positive letters from administrators and others, trophies from festivals and contests, plenty of pictures of group musical and social activities, other memorabilia, and recordings of ensemble performances—are particularly effective motivators of middle and high school students.

Course grades and a well-defined awards program can be positive motivators too, even though they are extrinsic. You may find, as many teachers have, that desirable extrinsic motivators commonly lead to the more preferred intrinsic motivation. In particular, many students who gain mature independent musical skills through their experiences in band or orchestra develop a greater love of music and a desire to continue their involvement in musical endeavors beyond their high school and college years.

# Major Events

## *Festivals and Contests*

Participation in music festivals or contests should not be a matter of blindly following tradition, but rather should relate to your personal philosophy of music education and whether it is in the best interest of your band or orchestra students. Working together to prepare for music festivals can be a valuable experience for you and your students. It is also an opportunity to receive an independent evaluation of your performance, and it can be an effective motivator. In fact, Colwell (1970) believes that adjudicator comments ". . .can be the most meaningful evaluation of performance the student receives" (p. 105). He also warns that "The judgments may not be valid, they may be based on too little evidence, but they are realistic, for performing skills in all areas are judged on a single display—one concert, one solo, one recital" (p. 105).

Although participation in music festivals can be a valuable part of a total performance program, they should *not* be the primary or most important activity. The evaluation of the performance is very important; but it is essential for director, students, parents, and administrators to remember that it is *only* an evaluation by three or four adjudicators of *one* performance by your ensemble on *one* day. While the advice received from adjudicators may be very important, continual evaluation of the total program over the course of many months (or even years) is a more valid and valuable evaluation.

The terms "festival" and "contest" are often used interchangeably, but are actually two very different events. Both usually have a required concert performance evaluated by three adjudicators, and an optional or required sight-reading experience evaluated by a fourth adjudicator. (See Chapter Six for a discussion of teaching ensemble sight-reading skills.) At a music festival, ensembles are given a "divisional rating" based on a certain performance standard. In theory, every band or orchestra could earn a Division I rating, as they are being evaluated against a *standard* of performance. At a true "contest," ensembles are awarded a numerical rating (usually on a 100-point scale) and placed in numerical order to determine their ranking. A contest has a "first place" winner. By whatever name, most concert events function as festivals and most marching events as contests.

Typically at festivals, division ratings of I (the highest) through V (the lowest) are awarded based on the average (or sometimes the predominance) of the adjudicators' ratings. Division ratings are often defined as follows:

- Division I: an excellent [or "superior"] level of performance
- Division II: a good [or "excellent"] level of performance
- Division III: a fair performance, but not outstanding
- Division IV: a poor performance that is lacking in many essential qualities
- Division V: an unsatisfactory (inadequate) performance (from the Michigan School Band and Orchestra Association)

In actual practice, only Divisions I, II, and III are used at most festivals. Only the most seriously flawed performances now receive a Division IV rating. In almost 30 years of adjudicating band and orchestra festivals I do not recall having seen a Division V rating assigned by an adjudicator.

Figure 8-1 is an example of an adjudication form used by the Michigan School Band and Orchestra Association. On this sheet the categories of **Tone**, **Intonation**, **Rhythm**, **Technique**, and **Interpretation** are awarded letter grades; and the predominance of letter grades is translated into a final divisional rating. Adjudicators are given adequate room to write comments about the performance on both sides of the sheet. Other states use Roman numerals for both the category ratings and the final rating; and some states use a weighted numerical system to arrive at a final rating or score.

## MSBOA Band and Orchestra Adjudication Form

Event No. _____ Classification _____ School _____

Name of Performing Group _____

City _____ Date_____ Festival City _____

March or String Number _____

Required Composition _____

Selected Composition _____

### FINAL RATING

DO NOT USE
PLUS OR MINUS
( _____ )
I, II, III, IV, V
Circle Roman Numeral

Judge's Signature

**ADJUDICATOR'S COMMENTS**

TONE
Beauty
Control
Balance

INTONATION
Melodic Line
Chords
Individuals
Sections

RHYTHM
Accents
Metre
Precision
Interpretation of
    Rhythmic Figures

TECHNIQUE
Fluency
Articulation
Bowing
Ensemble
Accuracy

INTERPRETATION
Phrasing
Expression
Tempo
Dynamics
Style
Tradition

SECTION DOES NOT AFFECT THE RATING
DO NOT USE THIS CATEGORY
    IN SIGHT READING

GENERAL SPIRIT
Taste
Contrast

SELECTION
Musical Value
Suitability

STAGE DEPORTMENT
Appearance
Discipline
Posture
Stage Efficiency

OVERALL
PERFORMANCE

FORM BO W11 1997 MSBOA

165

Know the philosophy of festivals or contests in your state, the festival rules, and the generally expected performance standards. Do not forget to plan for enough time during your festival experience to have all your students listen to other ensembles. This is a valuable opportunity to compare performance standards, hear fine ensemble models, hear new literature, and develop listening skills. Too many directors overlook this opportunity for musical development.

## *Festival Hosting*

Working together to host music festivals can be a rich and rewarding experience for you, your students, and their parents, and can benefit the music program in many ways. Parents who are involved and active in the program are usually more supportive, and in turn can influence their children to be more supportive. Hosting a festival eliminates transportation costs for your band or orchestra, and provides a fundraising opportunity with concessions income. It also gives a "home court" advantage to your ensembles, as they will be performing in their own facility. Students usually take pride in helping organize and run a music festival at their school. It is a motivating tool for developing student leadership.

The key to success in hosting a festival is organization. You will need a set of form letters, a well-conceived timeline of duties, good student and parent help, and a thorough job description for your workers. A set of form letters and instructions will be found in Figures 8-2 through 8-8. Many of these examples were developed by Kenneth L. Bowman, retired band director and master teacher from Lincoln High School in Ypsilanti, Michigan. Others I developed myself after many years of hosting festivals.

Figure 8-2 is an example of a letter to band and orchestra directors who plan to bring their ensembles to your festival site. Included in this mailing would be a map to your school, a layout of the building with all important rooms and performing areas clearly marked, and a master schedule of the festival program. Figure 8-3 is an example of a letter to adjudicators. This letter includes information about motel reservations, reporting times, and financial and meal arrangements—along with the enclosures sent to band and orchestra directors. Band and orchestra directors who will be working at your festival site should also get a letter (see Figure 8-4) listing their assignments, reporting times, special instructions, etc. Many district and state music organizations require that all directors of participating ensembles work one-half day at a festival site. This provides essential adult assistance in

**Figure 8-2. Festival Letter to Ensemble Directors**

# The Ypsilanti High School Bands

2095 Packard Road
Ypsilanti, Michigan 48197
743-___-____

February ___, ____

Dear Colleague:

We are very happy to be your host for the District Band and Orchestra Festival to be held on March ___ and ___, ____. Enclosed you will find a map showing directions to Ypsilanti High School, a floor plan of the school, and a performance schedule.

Here is some additional information:

1. **Arrival:** Please sign-in at Headquarters and meet your guide before you unload your buses. Unload buses at the "flagpole" entrance.
2. **Coat-rooms:** Your band has been assigned room _____ from _____ to _____ as a coatroom. You may leave instrument cases and any items that you want left in a safe place. Your guide will have the room locked when you leave to perform. Please remember: NO PLAYING in the coatrooms or in the halls.
3. **Warm-up:** Your guide will escort you to the warm-up room 35 minutes before your playing time. Music stands will be provided in the warm-up room. You will be notified when to send your set-up crew to the performance area. REMEMBER: The 25 (or 30) minute performance time begins when your set-up crew enters the performance area.
4. **Performance:** The performance room is our auditorium. Your band will enter and exit from the right as the audience faces the stage.
5. **Sight-reading:** The band room will be used for sight-reading.
6. **Ratings:** Ratings will be posted in the cafeteria.
7. **Departure:** Please sign-out at Headquarters before leaving. Please personally check your coatroom to make certain that it is in the order you found it.
8. **Food Service:** The school cafeteria will be open for your students.
9. The Ypsilanti Public Schools cannot be help responsible for any loss or damage of equipment incurred by your students while attending this festival.

If you have questions not covered in these instructions contact me at Ypsilanti High School (___-____) or at home (___-____). I hope you enjoy your visit to Ypsilanti High School and that you experience a successful day.

Cordially yours,

Lynn G. Cooper
Director of Bands

running the event site, and is a valuable "in-service" opportunity for directors as they observe other directors and their ensembles perform and sight-read.

*Figure 8-3. Festival Letter to Adjudicators*

# The Ypsilanti High School Bands
2095 Packard Road
Ypsilanti, Michigan 48197
743-___-____

February __,____

Dear Colleague:

We are pleased that you will be adjudicating at our sections of the District 12 Band and Orchestra Festival on March __ and __, ____. A map to Ypsilanti High School is enclosed along with a floor plan of the school. Motel reservations have been made at the _____ (743-___-____) for those requiring overnight lodging. The District will prepay the motel bill.

Our Friday evening briefing meeting will begin at 5:30 p.m. at our high school. The Saturday morning briefing will begin at 7:30 a.m. and we will provide coffee, juice, and donuts. Our noon luncheon will also be at the school. District 12 will reimburse you for Friday and Saturday evening meals (maximum of $10 per meal).

If you have any questions not covered in this mailing please call me at Ypsilanti High School (734-___-____) or at home (734-___-____).

I hope that you have an enjoyable visit to Ypsilanti High School.

Cordially yours,

Lynn G. Cooper
Director of Bands

168      enc.

*Figure 8-4. Festival Letter to Site Workers*

# The Ypsilanti High School Bands

2095 Packard Road
Ypsilanti, Michigan 48197
734-___-____

February ___, ____

Dear _____:

You have been assigned work in the _____ [performance room or sight-reading room] on March __ in the [a.m. or p.m.] for the District Band and Orchestra Festival.

The briefing meeting for all workers on March __ will begin at 5:30 p.m. at the high school. The briefing meeting for morning workers on March __ will begin at 7:30 a.m. Afternoon worker on March __ will be briefed at the noon luncheon at the high school. It is **absolutely essential** that you be at the briefing meeting.

Please review the "Instructions for MSBOA Workers" which was sent with your festival program.

We look forward to seeing you on March __ or __.

Cordially yours,


Lynn G. Cooper
Director of Bands

enc.

The letter in Figure 8-5 informs teachers at your school about the festival, noting which classrooms will be used as coatrooms for visiting bands. Be sure to personally ask teachers if you may use their rooms as coatrooms rather than assume availability. It is important that teachers at your school are treated with respect, that their wishes are honored to the best of your ability, and that they are kept well informed of festival plans in order to keep them on your "team." You should make sure their rooms are returned to the same (or better) condition. A follow-up letter to faculty (Figure 8-6) keeps them aware of your

169

appreciation for their help and your concern about the care of their rooms. You should send a personal thank-you note immediately following the festival to any others who assisted you (administrators, custodians, secretaries, parents, etc.).

**Figure 8-5. First Festival Letter to Classroom Teachers**

# The Ypsilanti High School Bands
2095 Packard Road
Ypsilanti, Michigan 48197
734-___-____

February ___, _____

Dear Colleague:

The Ypsilanti High School Bands are hosting two sections of the District Band Festival in our building on Friday evening, March ___, and Saturday, March ___. Twenty-one high school bands from Wayne, Washtenaw, and Monroe counties will be performing at 25-30 minute intervals from 6:00 p.m. to 8:30 p.m. on Friday evening and from 8:00 a.m. to 4:30 p.m. on Saturday. Well over 1,600 high school musicians, their parents, and friends will be in our building for the festival.

Our Freshman Band will perform at 7:25 p.m. on Friday and our Symphony will perform at 9:30 a.m. on Saturday. You are invited to come and hear them perform or to stop by any time during the festival. There is no admission charged for the festival.

All bands will perform in the Auditorium and then they will sight-read in the band room. We will also use several rooms in the Math Department and Foreign Language Department as coatrooms. We would appreciate your help in clearing the desk area in your room of any valuables, loose papers, etc., and please put away all chalk and erasers. Thank you!

Cordially yours,

Lynn Cooper

*Figure 8-6. Second Festival Letter to Classroom Teachers*

# The Ypsilanti High School Bands
2095 Packard Road
Ypsilanti, Michigan 48197
734-___-____

March __, ____

Dear Colleague:

The District Band and Orchestra Festival, which we hosted on Friday and Saturday, was very successful! Thanks to all of you for your interest and cooperation.

If your room was used as a coatroom we tried to make sure it was left in the same condition we found it. If there is a problem please let me know right away.

Thanks again!

Cordially yours,

Lynn Cooper

Recruiting good student workers for festivals will have considerable impact on the success of the event. Some work positions require more maturity than others, so carefully match the assignment to the worker. A sample worker assignment form is found as Figure 8-7. Note that the location and time for the assignment is listed.

*Figure 8-7. Student Worker Assignment Form for Festival*

**MSBOA Band Festival - March __ and __, ____**
**STUDENT WORKER ASSIGNMENTS**

<u>FRIDAY - March —</u>
• <u>Set-up Crew</u> (Friday, 2:00-4:30 p.m.)

| | | |
|---|---|---|
| 1. Kathy Jellema | 4. Raquel Logan | 7. Theresa Gregory |
| 2. Scott Ossenheimer | 5. Lisa Proskey | 8. Mike Wallis |

3. Melissa Smart     6. Deena DeButts     9. Don Burnett

- Band Guides
  1. Anderson 9th - Christine Weikel
     (4:45-7:00 p.m.)
  2. Chelsea FB - Sheryl Francis
     (5:00-7:30 p.m.)
  3. Saline Band - Scott Ossenheimer
     (5:30-8:00 p.m.)
  4. Chelsea SB - Shryl Francis
     (6:00-9:00 p.m.)
  5. Saline WE - Scott Ossenheimer
     (6:30-9:30 p.m.)

- Performance Room Usher - Auditorium, 5:30-9:30 p.m.
  1. Liz Fenelon                        2. Teresa Barnes

- Sight-Reading Room Workers - Band Room, 6:00-9:30 p.m.
  1. Pam Braman                     3. Matt Cooper
  2. Kathy Jellema                    4. Stacey Barker

- Office Assistant - Main Office, 5:30-9:30 p.m.
  1. Tammy Bos

- Warm-up Room Monitors - South Great Room Doors, 5:15-8:30 p.m.
  1. Lisa Ratliff                         2. Dennis Hayes

SATURDAY - March —-
- Band Guides: Morning
  1. Thurston HS CB - Liz Fenelon
     (7:00-9:00 a.m.)
  2. Flat Rock HS - Shawn Stovall
     (7:30-9:30 a.m.)
  3. Edsel Ford HS FB - Angie Brown
     (7:45-10:00 a.m.)
  4. Bentley HS SB - Lisa Hawkins
     (9:00-11:00 a.m.)
  5. Thurston HS HB - Liz Fenelon
     (9:30-11:30 a.m.)
  6. Edsel Ford HS CB - Angie Brown
     (10:15 a.m.-12:15 p.m.)

  Band Guides: Afternoon
  7. Northville SB - Natalie Raymond
     (11:30 a.m.-1:45 p.m.)
  8. Dearborn HS - Lisa Ratliff
     (12:00-2:15 p.m.)
  9. Huron HS CB - John Howes
     (12:30-3:00 p.m.)
  10. Stevenson HS SB - Dennis Hayes
     (1:00-3:30 p.m.)
  11. Catholic Central - Shryl Francis
     (1:30-4:00 p.m.)
  12. Wayne Mem. - Christine Weikel
     (2:00-4:30 p.m.)
  13. John Glenn HS SB - Stacey Barker
     (2:30-5:00 p.m.)
  14. Franklin HS SB - Cheryl Ensign
     (3:00-5:30 p.m.)

- Concert Room Ushers - Auditorium
  Morning (7:45-11:45 a.m.)
  1. Jane Carr
  2. Annette Leacox

  Afternoon (12:30-5:00 p.m.
  1. Colleen Pailthorp
  2. Laura Turner

172

- Sight-Reading Room Workers (Band Room)

| Morning (7:30 a.m.-12:15 p.m.) | Afternoon (12:45-5:30 p.m.) |
|---|---|
| 1. Lauren Bird | 1. Pam Braman |
| 2. Carolyn Zavrel | 2. Katen Steadman |
| 3. Shryl Francis | 3. Kathy Jellema |

- Office Assistant - Main Office

| Morning (7:30-12:30 a.m.) | Afternoon (12:30-5:30 p.m.) |
|---|---|
| 1. Kelli Bristol | 1. David Drow |

- Warm-Up Room Monitors - South Great Room Doors

| Morning (7:30-11:15 a.m.) | Afternoon (12:15-4:30 p.m.) |
|---|---|
| 1. Troy Erby | 1. Carol DeNio |
| 2. Becky McCarter | 2. Matt Cooper |

- Clean-Up Crew - Saturday, 4:00-6:00 p.m.

| | |
|---|---|
| 1. Kathy Jellema | 4. Liz Fenelon |
| 2. Scott Ossenheimer | 5. Tracey Clayton |
| 3. Dennis Hayes | 6. Liza Wilson |

Students will need a list of specific instructions for their positions, available in printed form so they can refer to them during their assignments. Figure 8-8 is a sample instruction sheet. Students will take great pride in being part of a smooth-running event like this. It helps them develop confidence in leadership skills, contributes to high esprit de corps, and fosters cooperative learning.

**Figure 8-8. Student Worker Instruction Sheet for Festival**

### Ypsilanti High School
## MSBOA FESTIVAL - STUDENT WORKER INSTRUCTION SHEET

I. General Instructions - Keep this information with you on the day of the festival.
  A. Report to the Clinic for your identification badge **on time (early)!**
  B. Dress neatly!
  C. Please phone if you can't make an assignment (___-____).
  D. Try to answer all guest questions you can. If you are uncertain of an answer or directions, refer the party to the office.

F. A custodian will be on duty. If you need custodial service, go to the office.

G. Conduct yourself—on the job and in your free time—as a mature, competent student of Ypsilanti High School. RE-MEMBER: We are the official hosts for the band festival. We must make sure the day runs   smoothly and efficiently. Our headquarters is the Clinic.

II.  Ushers

A. Get your identification badge and report to the Auditorium. Introduce yourself to the Concert Room Chairman.

B. Seat guests <u>only</u> between performances. Remind children of the importance of <u>quiet</u> if necessary. Assist the judges by sharpening pencils or, if desired, providing coffee or doughnuts (from the Main Office).

C. Close all doors just before the band tunes and stand by your door. NO ADMITTANCE during a performance. Help on stage if necessary. Be courteous to the audience, but firm.

D. One usher should remain outside during performances to help keep the doors closed and to help keep people in the halls nearby quiet. One usher should go get the next band from the Warm-up Room as the performing band is about to finish its last number. Each band has 25-30 minutes to warm-up. Don't rush the Director unless he/she runs over time. Do not call a band so soon that they have to stand in the hall and wait any length of time before being able to enter the auditorium.

III. Band Guides

A. Get your identification badge and report to the Main Lobby to wait for your band. Be available well before your scheduled time in case your band arrives early.

B. After the director signs-in, show the band to their coatroom. Remind the director (if necessary) that there is to be no playing in the coatrooms.

C. Once the coatroom is unlocked remain at that room until it is time to take your band to warm-up. Have the office lock the room at that time and have it unlocked after sight-reading.

D. Always keep your band to the right in the halls.

E. Take your band to the Warm-up Room (The Great Room) 35 minutes before its scheduled performance time.

F. <u>Five</u> minutes before your band is scheduled to perform, inform the band director that he/she should send their set-up crew to the auditorium.

G. Guide your band to the Auditorium door by Room 221 and stay with them during their performance. Ask the director for his/her judges scores and give these to the Concert Room Chairman when you enter the Auditorium.

H. After the performance take your band to Sight-Reading (the Band Room). After sight-reading take your band back to their coatroom. If the director does not need additional assistance, your duties end at this time.

IV.   Sight-Reading Assistants

A. Get your identification badge and report to the Sight-Reading Room (the Band Room) and introduce yourself to the Sight-Reading Chairman.

B. Assist entering groups in any way necessary. Be friendly and put our guests at ease—this is a stressful time!

C. Sharpen pencils for the judge when needed. Provide the judge and room chairman with coffee and doughnuts from the Office if desired. (Ask them!)

D. Distribute and gather up the sight-reading music as directed by the Sight Reading Chairman.

E. Rearrange music in proper order for the next group.

F. Don't make remarks about other groups or the music! Stay in the back of the room or in the music library when the groups are playing.

G. Arrive early so that you can speak with the Sight-Reading Chairman about any problems that have arisen during the day.

V. Office Assistants

A. Get your identification badge and report to the Office. Introduce yourself as an office assistant.

B. Assist the Section Chairman with carrying messages.

C. Cover any important assignments open due to worker absences or make arrangements for filling them.

D. Give directions to directors regarding bus parking. Bus parking is in the front lot near the Administration Building.

E. See that directors sign-in and sign-out.

F. Answer the telephone: "Ypsilanti High School—may I help you?"

VI. Set-up Crew (Friday, 2:00-4:30 p.m.)
  A. Post signs in the school (coat-room signs, cafeteria signs, etc.).
  B. Set-up chairs and stands in performance, warm-up, and sight-reading rooms. Check all coatrooms. Put away chalk and all loose materials.
  C. Set up tables and chairs for judges in the Auditorium and Band Room.
  D. In general, make final preparations for the festival to start.

VII. Clean-up Crew (Saturday, 4:00-5:30 p.m.)
  A. Return stands and chairs.
  B. Remove signs posted for the festival.
  C. Clean-up the building as needed. Check all coatrooms.

VIII. Warm-up and Sight-Reading Room Monitors
  A. After a group enters the room, close the door and stay outside to keep people from trying to enter.
  B. There is NO ADMITTANCE to sight-reading without the verbal permission of the director of the performing group.

## Suggestions For Festival Performances

The following is a list of "Do's and Don'ts for Festival Day."

1. Train your crew carefully. Setting up the stage for your performance must be orderly and well planned. Take all extra chairs and stands off stage. Make sure there are enough stands and chairs for percussionists placed near their playing area.

2. Do not play a chorale on stage just before your performance. The warm-up room is the place for chorales. Only sound a tuning pitch and tune as an ensemble. No individual tuning on stage—it takes too long and merely draws attention to any problems of intonation and tone. If you are unfamiliar with the acoustical characteristics of the stage, you might consider playing the "Warm-up Chord Progression" found in Chapter 6.

3. Require uniformity and conformity in ensemble dress. This includes black socks and black shoes. Appearance is important.

4. Be positive and supportive. Do not be negative, and do not scowl! One of your major responsibilities at festivals—or for any performance—is to keep your students at ease, calm, and confident.

5. Be aware of the proscenium on a stage and try to be completely in back of it or completely in front of it to help the ensemble hear itself better and produce a more blended sound.

6. Arrange the ensemble set-up exactly the same as at "home," with the exception that chairs could be a little closer together for younger bands (it helps them feel more secure).

7. Make sure the percussion and string bass sections are positioned in their regular placement. For some reason many of these sections set up too far from the back of the band or orchestra, causing many ensemble problems.

8. Remind percussionists to stand by their instrument for the entire length of each piece. No distractions to the performance should be allowed.

9. Make sure the music is in performance order before you begin to play!

10. Realize that the time allotted for your group to warm up at festival is never enough to complete all that should be done. On festival day plan for plenty of time at your school rehearsal room to thoroughly warm up, tune individually, set tempos for each piece, and spot-check any troublesome sections. The warm-up room at festival should be used for a final tuning check, a thoughtful run-through of a familiar chorale to focus on balance and blend and—if time permits—another brief review of the opening tempos for each festival piece.

11. Remember that your performance on stage is timed. Take only enough time between pieces for your ensemble to prepare for the next piece. Do not worry about whether the adjudicators are ready for you to continue. They will catch up!

12. Try to remember that the festival or contest is not a "life and death" situation! Keep it all in perspective.

Personal growth in maturity, self-discipline, musical ability, and confidence only begin the list of advantages to be gained by participation in music festivals (band and orchestra, solo and ensemble, jazz ensemble, and marching band). It can be a rewarding and educational experience, so give it serious consideration. Go, grow, and enjoy.

## *Ensemble Tours*

Tours can be principally a sightseeing experience with a single performance, or multiple performances with some sightseeing. Sometimes tours are sponsored by tour companies and are associated with specific "tourist" events, such as the Cherry Blossom Festival in Washington or the many football bowl games and parades.

Many directors use tours as an incentive or motivator—or as a reward for student effort during the year. Tours can be a day trip to an amusement park, a two-day (one-night) tour, or tours of up to 10 or more days. A good average seems to be four days (three nights) for most school groups. Longer tours will usually need to be scheduled during vacations. Your decision on tour length should take into consideration the purpose of the tour, the destination, and the amount of money you can (or want to) spend. If you are taking a band or orchestra on its first tour, you should limit the length to two or three days, to gain touring experience before undertaking long tours.

Be careful not to get in the "can you top last year's tour?" syndrome. It is best to travel only every three or four years if the tours are a week or longer. Four or five-day tours are best done only every two or three years. A pattern of every-year tours will be very difficult to change once it is established.

A four-day tour during the school year works well on a Friday, Saturday, Sunday, and Monday schedule. You must have the approval of your administration and the support of the faculty to make it work. Faculty and administration need to be fully informed of your tour schedule, the reasons for the tour, and your expectations for students' completion of missed coursework.

As you plan a tour, be sure to get permission from your administration *before* you begin to talk with students or parents. Do not forget to check with your school administrators to determine if a special "trip insurance" policy should be purchased. Keep the cost of the tour reasonable and plan adequate fund-raising opportunities for students to pay for tour costs. Any tour lasting more than two days is best planned through a tour agent who specializes in tours for music ensembles. Agents will understand your unique needs and know of available performance sites. Once you outline your tour, assuming that a particular tour company does not sponsor it, get at least three bids from different companies.

A letter like the one in Figure 8-9 informs parents and students of tour plans and fund-raising opportunities. The return form at the bottom of the letter indicates their commitment to the tour. About two weeks before tour departure, distribute a detailed "tour booklet" to students and parents. Issuing two booklets allows parents to have all tour information (including motel telephone number) at home. A sample tour booklet is found in Figure 8-10.

**Figure 8-9. Tour Letter and Confirmation**

# The Ypsilanti High School Bands
## Ypsilanti, Michigan 48197

November __, ____

To all Marching Band Members and Parents:

The bids for our tour to Disney World (May 16-19) have arrived! The best bid is $____. This includes all transportation, three nights lodging, all meals, a full day at EPCOT Center, a full day at the Magic Kingdom on the day of our performance, a half-day at "Wet "N Wild," a visit to the beach, and a few other planned activities.

The Band Boosters are anxious to help make this tour successful and want to help defray some of the cost. This will be discussed at the next Band Boosters Club meeting on Tuesday at 7:30 p.m. in the band room.

We want every Marching Band member to be able to go on tour and we will have three fund raising events so they can earn all or part of their tour fee. The first fundraiser is a candy sale that starts this Thursday. Each student will earn 50% profit on all candy sales and that profit will be credited to their tour fee.

I must have a commitment now for this exciting tour. Your reply is confidential. Please return the form below by this Friday. Thank you!

Cordially yours,

Mr. Lynn Cooper
Director of Bands

---

(Please detach and return by Friday!)

Name_____ Date_____

___ My son/daughter will go on tour.

___ My son/daughter will not be able to go on tour. (If possible, please state the reason.)

Comments:

Parent Signature_____ Student Signature_____      179

*Figure 8-10. Tour Bulletin*

# The Ypsilanti High School Marching Band

# Walt Disney World Tour

May __-__, ____

| | |
|---|---|
| **Director of Bands:** | Lynn G. Cooper |
| **Drum Major:** | Paul Bird |
| **Flag Corps Captain:** | Pam Jennings |
| **Chaperones:** | Mr. John Elliott |
| | Mrs. Sue Elliott |
| | Mr. Tony Comazzi |
| | Mrs. Lynne Comazzi |
| | Mrs. Ruth Ann Tinkham |
| | Mrs. Jean Wells |
| | Mrs. Joan Ratliff |
| | Mrs. Mary Wooden |

April __, ____

To all YHS Band Members:

The Ypsilanti High School Marching Band tour to Disney World will be one of the highlights of your high school years! We will perform at Disney World, and visit EPCOT Center, Wet 'n Wild, and Cocoa Beach Jetty Park. All entry fees and meals have been paid for by your tour fee except lunch on Thursday. You may want to plan just a light snack in view of all the excitement of the first day. A meal allowance will be issued to everyone on Friday, Saturday, and Sunday mornings. Plan meal spending wisely. Food in a wide price range is available. You will want to bring some spending money for souvenirs or snacks but not so much that it becomes a financial disaster if it is lost.

The itinerary, behavior guidelines, and other important information are found in this tour bulletin. We ask that all students and parents read this material, sign the form at the back of the bulletin and fill out the Health Information Form. Both forms should be returned to Mr. Cooper immediately.

You have received two copies of this bulletin so that you can keep one with you on tour and leave the other one at home for your parents.

**Reporting Time:** 6:45 a.m. on May 16 (Thursday) at YHS. We will board our buses and leave for Metro Airport as soon as attendance is taken and some additional instructions are given. You should "dress up" for our flight to Florida and the flight home.

**Return Time:** 8:51 p.m. on May 19 (Sunday) at Metro Airport on Delta Flight #368. PLEASE NOTE: Parents are to pick up your son or daughter at Metro Airport on Sunday, May 19th, at 8:51 p.m. You may want to arrange carpools and be sure to plan to arrive early to avoid any traffic congestion.

**Motel:** We are staying at the Sheraton Twin Towers in Orlando (305-351-1000).

**Luggage:** Each student is allowed, and responsible for, one medium sized suitcase, their instrument, and their marching band uniform. Each case or garment bag is to be clearly marked with your complete name and address on the outside <u>and</u> the inside of the item. The suitcase size and weight must not exceed the student's ability to carry it. Remember to save room in your suitcase for souvenirs.

<u>Instrument</u>: You are responsible for your own instrument (including flags). Make sure it is in good playing condition and that you have an adequate supply of reeds, valve oil, etc.

<u>Miscellaneous Information</u>: Be sure to read the brochures on the bulletin board in the band room so that you know what things are available and what you most want to see at EPCOT Center and Disney World. You will not be able to see everything, so plan ahead.

Don't forget to bring your camera and film. You will probably find that it will less expensive to buy your film here in Ypsilanti, instead of at "tourist stores." You may want to have your camera with you on the plane.

There is to be absolutely no playing of instruments in motel rooms, in the halls, or outside the motel. On Thursday evening, when we have a rehearsal near the motel, please wait to play your instrument until the rehearsal actually begins. We do not want to disturb any other motel guests.

You will get guidebooks for Disney World and EPCOT Center when we arrive. Use them to plan your visit and be sure not to lose them—they make a good souvenir! Always stay in groups of at least 4-6 people.

Florida weather can be very hot and humid in the Spring. Be sure to drink plenty of liquids and eat before our performance. Be sure to use sunscreen before the performance.

You will be given a $10.00 meal allowance (for two meals) on Friday and Saturday, and a $5.00 meal allowance (one meal) on Sunday.

If you need to see Mr. Cooper or a chaperone when we are at Disney World on Friday, one of us will be at the front of the Cinderella Castle at 12:00, 4:00, and 6:00 p.m. On Saturday, when we are at EPCOT Center, we will be at the bus stop on The World Showcase Plaza at 12:00, 4:00, and 6:00 p.m.

## CHECKLIST OF WHAT TO BRING:

1. This bulletin.
2. Three or four complete changes of clothes (casual but not "sloppy"). Coordinate your colors and combinations to minimize your wardrobe needs.
3. Comfortable shoes for touring.
4. Your complete marching uniform (in your garment bag—with your name and address on the bag).
   Don't forget your black socks and black (shined) shoes.
   Note: you may pack your entire uniform in your suitcase if you have room, but bring the band garment bag and hanger to transport your uniform to Disney World.
5. Instrument and music (including flags and poles). Don't forget reeds, valve oil, and extra drumsticks.
6. Personal wear: underwear, pajamas, bathrobe, slippers, etc.
7. Conservative swimsuit with cover-up—also a beach towel (and a hat?).
8. Sunscreen and sunglasses.
9. Lightweight jacket or sweater—the nights can be cool.
10. An alarm clock and a hair dryer (at least one per room—check with your roommates).
11. Two plastic bags (for dirty laundry, and wet swimwear and towels).
12. Toilet articles: toothbrush and paste, deodorant, shampoo, brush and comb, other personal items.

### Disney World Tour — Behavior Guidelines

1. As representative of our bands, school, parents, and community, we must at all times conduct ourselves in a manner that can only increase the good reputation of those we represent.

2. We will be in contact with many people on this tour and as representatives of our community we should not wish to offend anyone. Therefore, it is requested that everyone dress in a conservative manner. This includes swimwear.

3. Our schedule will be very tight at times and it is essential that everyone report to the designated areas at the <u>exact</u> times indicated on the itinerary. "To be 'on time' is to be late; to be <u>early</u> is to be 'on time'."

4. Everyone must refrain from bringing back <u>any</u> "souvenirs" from the motel (towels, ashtrays, coat hangers, etc.). We also need to be quiet and courteous guests so that we do not disturb other motel guests.

5. On each evening after our return to the motel you are to be in your rooms at the designated times and remain in your rooms. If you have a problem contact your chaperone by phone. "Lights out" <u>means</u> LIGHTS OUT! There will be regular room checks.

6. There is to be no smoking at any time. The use of alcoholic beverages or drugs is expressly forbidden.

7. All students must participate in all scheduled activities—we must know when to reach students at all times.

8. You should <u>always</u> be in groups of 4-6 (or more) when doing sightseeing on your own. Never go out alone or just in pairs.

9. No boys are allowed in girl's rooms and no girls are allowed in boy's rooms at <u>any time</u>, for <u>any reason</u>. The girl's rooms and the boy's rooms are on different floors and students should <u>only</u> be on the floor to which they are assigned. If you are meeting your boyfriend or girlfriend, meet in the motel lobby.

10. Students must follow the directions of the chaperones and the band director at all times.

11. All students will eat breakfast and will report to the dining room on time.

12. Room phones are <u>not</u> to be used for calls home or for any between-room "prank" calls.

13. Any "pranks"—of any kind—are expressly forbidden.

14. Students are responsible for any damage to public or private property.

15. If a problem arises see a chaperone first, then to Mr. Cooper if they can't solve it.

16. All school rules and YHS Band Handbook rules are in effect.

17. **The basic rule is not to do anything that could cause embarrassment to yourself, your parents, or the band.**

Violations of the above rules may result in the student being sent home at their own expense.

## CHAPERONE RESPONSIBILITIES:

1. Each chaperone has a group of students for which they are responsible. Your main responsibility is to help the student have a safe and enjoyable trip.

2. At the motel chaperones will check to see that their group is situated properly and comfortably in their rooms.

3. Check your group at curfew and report to Mr. Cooper as soon as possible that all is OK.

4. Periodically patrol the motel hallways after curfew.

5. Double check with your group regarding all instructions in this bulletin.

6. Help at rest areas, restaurants, sightseeing attractions, and at the beach as situations require.

7. Make sure your group is awake each morning for breakfast.

8. Discipline will not be a major problem. Rules and regulations are spelled out clearly but students may need to be reminded of them occasionally.

9. Distribute meal money to your group.

It is expected that our students will behave in a mature and responsible manner. All of our students are expected to assume a lot of individual responsibility on this tour.

## Chaperone Groups:

Mrs. Wells - Rooms 2, 3, and 4          Mrs. Ratliff - Rooms 15, 16, and 17
Mrs. Tinkham - Rooms 5, 6, and 7        Mr. Comazzi - Rooms 20 and 21
Mrs. Comazzi - Rooms 8, 10, and 11      Mr. Elliott - Rooms 22, 23, and 24
Mrs. Wooden - Rooms 12, 13, and 14      Mrs. Elliott - Rooms 25 and 26

## DISNEY WORLD TOUR—ROOM ASSIGNMENTS

Room #1
1. Mrs. Tinkham
2. Mrs. Wells

Room #6
1. Tish Baker
2. Melissa Smart
3. Pam Jennings
4. Erin Taylor

Room #11
1. Denise Weikel*
2. Sue Work
3. Debbie Arnold
4. Robin Arrick

Room #16
1. Sarah Wooden*
2. Shryl Francis
3. Michelle Boprie
4. Michele Kassarjian

Room #2
1. Tammy Bos*
2. Kathy Jellema
3. Natalie Raymond
4. Cathy Means

Room #7
1. Kris Miley*
2. Lisa Skrobe
3. Teresa Barnes
4. Cheryl Ensign

Room #12
1. Jennifer Smith*
2. Cyndi Roe
3. Lisa Ratliff
4. Pam White

Room #17
1. Theresa Gregory*
2. Dawn Towler
3. Lisa Proskey
4. Margo Gendin

Room #3
1. Angie May*
2. Michelle Towler
3. Vickie Musgrave
4. Tara Blackburn

Room #8
1. Kris Waite*
2. Deena DeButts
3. Christine Weikel
4. Stacey Barker

Room #13
1. Tammy Robinette*
2. Shelly Mashburn
3. Angie Bryant
4. Renee McCombie

Room #18
1. Mrs. Wooden
2. Mrs. Ratliff

Room #4
1. Angie May*
2. Colleen Tinkham
3. Marcie Skinner
4. Doreen Dudley

Room #9
1. Mr. Comazzi
2. Mrs. Comazzi

Room #14
1. Gina Comazzi*
2. Marcia Porter
3. Kelly Nichols
4. Laurie Sternbergh

Room #5
1. Pam Braman*
2. Deana Wells
3. Jennifer Calhoun
4. Michele Robbins

Room #15
1. Liz Fenelon*
2. Alberta Richardson
3. Shawn Stoval

Room #19
1. Mr. Elliott
2. Mrs. Elliott

Room #22
1. Mike Kazmierski*
2. David Ceilkaszyk
3. Chris Johnson
4. Jim Warren

Room #24
1. Sam Avery*
2. Jeff Hawkins
3. John Hildebrandt
4. Tony Markins

Room #26
1. Mark Hause*
2. Erik Pedersen
3. Mike Benns
4. Jim Elliott

Room #20
1. Dennis Hayes*
2. Bryan Girbach
3. Scott Ossenheimer
4. Mike Kennedy

Room #23
1. Chris Zavrel*
2. David Drow
3. Paul Bird
4. George Gladding

Room #25
1. Thor Johnson*
2. Matt Cooper
3. Don Burnett
4. Philip Lopez

Room #27
1. Mr. Cooper
2. Mrs. Cooper

Room #21
1. John Terris*
2. Eric Taylor
3. Scott Opland
4. David Fredrick

*Key person: This person will pick-up room keys when we check-in at the motel and turn them in on Saturday.

## WALT DISNEY WORLD TOUR ITINERARY

| | | |
|---|---|---|
| May 16 | 6:45 a.m. | Report to the Band Room with luggage, instrument, and uniform. |
| THURSDAY | 7:00 a.m. | Board buses and leave for Metro Airport. |
| | 8:40 a.m. | Leave Metro Airport via Delta Flight #645. |
| | 10:55 a.m. | Arrive in Tampa and change planes. Follow tour guide instructions. |
| | 11:35 a.m. | Leave Tampa via Delta Flight #523. |
| | 12:03 p.m. | Arrive in Orlando. |
| | 12:45 p.m. | Transfer to motel. |
| | 1:15 p.m. | Arrive at the Sheraton Twin Towers. Key people only off the busses on signal to get room keys. Take bags to rooms and have a light snack if desired. Change to swimsuits, grab your beach towel and head back to the buses. |

|  | 2:30 p.m. | Leave for the beach. |
|  | 3:30 p.m. | Arrive at Cocoa Beach at Jetty Park. Enjoy the beach and sun! |
|  | 5:30 p.m. | Bus to the motel via Davis Brothers Cafeteria for dinner. |
|  | 7:30 p.m. | Arrive at the motel. |
|  | 8:30 p.m. | Rehearsal in the motel parking lot and then enjoy the pool until curfew. |
|  | 11:00 p.m. | Everyone in your rooms. |
|  | 11:30 p.m. | Lights <u>out</u> and room checks by chaperones. |
| May 17 FRIDAY | 7:45 a.m. | Breakfast at the motel. (Plan your own wake-up time and be <u>on time</u> for breakfast. Every one MUST eat breakfast everyday. Meal money for the day will be distributed at breakfast.) |
|  | 8:30 a.m. | Leave for Walt Disney World. Have your instrument and your uniform in the band garment bag (with hat, black socks, and black shoes). |
|  | 9:00 a.m. | Arrive at Walt Disney World. Instructions from the park staff. Lunch on your own—be sure to eat and drink liquids before we perform. |
|  | 1:45 p.m. | Report to the Staging Area and change into uniforms in the Changing Rooms. Apply <u>sunscreen</u>. Warm-up time. |
|  | 3:00 p.m. | Perform in the "Mickey Mouse Character Parade." After the parade change out of uniforms and return instruments and garment bags to buses. Enjoy Walt Disney World until closing. Dinner on your own. |
|  | 8:30 p.m. | Meet in the Town Square. We will take the Monorail to our buses and exit the park. Attendance taken by Chaperone Groups. |
|  | 9:00 p.m. | Return to the motel. Pool time! |
|  | 11:00 p.m. | Everyone in your rooms. |
|  | 11:30 p.m. | Light out and room checks by chaperones. |
| May 18 SATURDAY | 8:00 a.m. | Breakfast. (Meal money distributed.) |
|  | 9:00 a.m. | Leave for EPCOT Center. |
|  | 9:30 a.m. | Passport admission to EPCOT Center. (Sunscreen, hat?) You will not be able to see everything so plan ahead to visit the exhibits you most want to see. Lunch and dinner on |

|  |  | your own. |
|---|---|---|
| | 8:30 p.m. | Meet at the Entrance Plaza to exit EPCOT Center. Attendance taken by Chaperone Groups. |
| | 9:00 p.m. | Return to the motel. Poolside <u>pizza and cokes</u>! |
| | 11:00 p.m. | Everyone in your rooms. |
| | 11:30 p.m. | Lights out and room checks by chaperones. |
| <u>May 19</u><br>SUNDAY | 8:00 a.m. | Breakfast. (Meal money distributed.) |
| | 9:00 a.m. | Check out and place luggage in late checkout room. |
| | 9:45 a.m. | Leave for Wet'n Wild for a day of enjoying yourself in the pools and on the slides and rides! (Lunch on your own.) |
| | 3:30 p.m. | Return to the motel, get bags and change for the trip home. |
| | 4:30 p.m. | Leave for the airport. |
| | 6:30 p.m. | Leave Orlando via Delta Flight #368 (non-stop) with dinner in flight. |
| | 8:51 p.m. | Arrive at Detroit Metro Airport! Take all luggage, instruments and uniform bags home with you and bring the instruments back to school on Monday. |
| <u>May 20</u> | 7:35 a.m. | EVERYONE WILL BE IN YOUR FIRST HOUR CLASS. Please do not abuse our privilege of missing school on Thursday and Friday to go on tour. To protect our ability to take future tours it is essential that <u>no one</u> miss school on Monday (or the day before tour!). |

## BUS ASSIGNMENTS:

Bus #1: Rooms 2, 3, 4, 5, 6, 7, 8, 20, 22, 23, 24, and Mr. and Mrs. Cooper, Mr. Phillips, Mr. and Mrs. Comazzi.

Bus #2: Rooms 10, 11, 12, 13, 14, 15, 16, 17, 21, 25, 26, and Mr. and Mrs. Elliott, Mrs. Tinkham, Mrs. Wells, Mrs. Ratliff and Mrs. Wooden.

Do not change buses at any time. Do not leave the buses at a destination until instructed to do so, and only after you know the time you are to return to the buses.

The front two seats on each side at the front of the buses are reserved for the chaperones.

# THE YPSILANTI HIGH SCHOOL BANDS

## Walt Disney World Tour

Please sign and return this form and the Health Information Form to Mr. Cooper immediately.

1.  I give my permission for my child to attend to attend the Walt Disney World Tour with the Ypsilanti High School Marching Band on May 16-19. I have read this tour booklet and am aware of the policies and rules for this tour.

_____     _____

(date)                  (signature of parent/guardian)

Phone during the day: _____

Phone at night: _____

2.  I have read the tour booklet and I agree to follow the stated rules and policies during the Walt Disney World Tour.

_____     _____

(date)                  (signature of parent/guardian)

# THE YPSILANTI HIGH SCHOOL BANDS
## Health Information Form

Student's Name: _____ Age: _____
Parent's Name: _____
Address: _____ city_____ zip_____
Home Phone: _____ Parent's Work Phone: _____

### Emergency Contact Person:
Name: _____ Phone: _____

Family Physician: _____ Phone: _____
Health Insurance Co.: _____
Policy Number: _____

1. Please list any significant health problems that chaperones should know of:
_____
_____

2. Does this student have allergies to any drugs or foods?
_____
Please list:
_____
_____

3. Please list any medications this student is taking now and will take along on this trip:
_____
_____

*******************************************************************

### Permission for Emergency Treatment
(to be used only if the parent cannot be reached by phone)

Permission is hereby granted for this student to receive necessary treatment by a qualified physician, in his/her office or in a hospital emergency room, in the event of an accident or serious illness.

_____        _____
(date)                (signature of parent/guardian)

191

Thorough planning spells the difference between disaster and delight. In an article about music festival participation and tours, Richard Mark Heidel (1999) listed several suggestions.

- Create an itinerary that works and make sure parents have a copy with the phone numbers of where you can be reached.
- Create a "director's binder" with all the information about the trip, including rooming lists, schedules, emergency telephone numbers, etc.
- Take a school administrator with you so that he or she can gain a better understanding of your program.
- Take plenty of sponsors or chaperones. A ratio of one per 10 students is good.
- Try to recruit some parents who are doctors or nurses to go as chaperones.
- Put all student medical information forms and trip permission forms in a binder and have it with you at all times.
- Take an emergency medical kit.
- Delegate—do not try to do everything yourself.
- Take a cellular telephone with you in case of emergencies.
- Have some emergency cash with you on the trip.
- If you are staying in a motel, plan every moment and allow very little free time at the motel. Have procedures in place to ensure that students remain in their rooms after curfew.
- Have a mandatory pre-tour meeting of students [parents] and chaperones. Explain all expectations and consequences. (p. 20)

## Competition For Music Groups

Competition has always been a part of music (auditions to get into an ensemble, auditions for chair positions, auditions to play a solo at a concert, concerto competitions, conducting competitions, etc.). In fact, although there were a few school bands as early as the mid-1800s, the real public call for bands in the schools was fueled by wide-spread public interest in and support of the National Band Contests that began in 1923. These competitions—and later competitions for orchestra, choir, and solos and ensembles—focused public interest on establishing music programs in local schools. Thanks in large part to these early competitions, we have active music programs today in virtually every public school in the United States (Holz and Jacobi, 1966, pp. 4-8).

Even though school music programs today owe a debt of gratitude to earlier competitive influences and to those that continue to occur in the schools, many band and orchestra directors have begun to question the long-term impact of competition on an artistic endeavor. Paul R. Lehman (1995), a major voice in music education, believes that

> Historically, these competitions have served a useful purpose by generating interest and promoting high standards. Beyond a certain point, however, their influence may become less positive when it produces cutthroat competition or when it undermines the balance of the program by placing excessive emphasis on certain specialized aspects. (p. 18)

Alfie Kohn (1992), a strong critic of competition in the schools, writes

> Strip away all the assumptions about what competition is supposed to do, all the claims in its behalf that we accept and repeat reflexively. What you have left is the essence of the concept: mutually exclusive goal attainment (MEGA). One person succeeds only if another does not. From this uncluttered perspective, it seems clear right away that something is drastically wrong with such an arrangement. (p. 9)

*Music is not a zero-sum game*

Tim Lautzenheiser (1994) reminds us that "It is easier to be better than someone else than to be the best we can be" (p. 2). He asks "Is it possible to turn the *competitive* spirit inward and, rather than using it to outdistance an opponent, could it be used as a measuring stick of *→ Drumline* self-improvement? If so, then the benefits of competition could be enjoyed without the scars of defeat" (p. 2). Nancy G. Thomas (1992) believes that "...the motive 'to do one's best' or 'just enjoy,' as opposed to being 'better than' the next person, may be not only desirable but essential to maintaining students' continuing motivation in music" (p. 430). Competition *can* be an effective motivator of middle and high school students. Regular playing tests (with grades and new chair positions assigned) encourage students to practice assigned music, and leads to technical and musical progress on their instruments. Music festivals cause ensemble directors and students to work a little harder and achieve a little more than for usual concerts. When handled with care, competition can be an effective motivational tool. But each of us must be sure of our own philosophy about competition, and pursue that philosophy with confidence and expertise.

I believe that the acknowledged high level of burnout for high school band directors relates to the fact that many have created a monster—over-scheduling. Adding six marching band competitions each fall means choosing marching band music and preparing the arrangements in March or April, beginning the drill in May or June, starting band camp in July, having sectionals three or four days per week after school in September and October, scheduling two or three evening rehearsals per week in September and October, and taking a full day (8:00 a.m. to 12:00 p.m.) on six to eight Saturdays in the fall to either participate in a contest or to watch one. All that time spent is in addition to the Friday football games, the parades, the concerts, the festivals, band banquets, fundraising events, etc.

Why do we build these monsters? After we build them it is almost impossible to back off from some of the "hyperactivity" because students, parents, administrators, and the community begin to expect it of us. You need to establish and believe in your own philosophy of music education. From that position of strength you can evaluate whether you should or should not participate in various activities. Difficult decisions can be made somewhat easier if you compare each opportunity with its potential contribution to learning about and performing fine music.

Every bit as important as the concern for teacher burnout is the problem of *student* burnout. Many students drop out of programs that over-emphasize competition (with its attendant over-commitment) at the expense of *music* education. College band directors find that many students who come from such programs do not continue to play their instruments in college or later in life—they are tired of all of the activity and lack the *intrinsic* motivation needed to continue to play. But students who know about music, listen to fine music, love music, and possess the skills, techniques, and understandings to be mature, independent musicians will continue to participate in music even after they graduate from their school music program, because music has become important to them.

Remember balance. It is important in the ensemble, and it is important in life.

194

## *For Discussion or Assignment*

1. Develop a set of basic classroom rules or expectations to use in a beginning instrumental music class; another set for middle school band or orchestra; and a third set for high school band or orchestra.

2. Develop a list of things you, as a teacher, could do to motivate students.

3. What motivates you and your friends in music? How would you try to develop self-motivation in your future students?

4. Develop a list of things that bore students in band or orchestra. How would you try to prevent this boredom?

5. Make a list of the pros and cons for attending a music festival with your future high school orchestra or band. Using your professional beliefs and understandings (your Philosophy of Music Education) explain why you would choose to attend (or not attend) music festivals.

6. List some techniques and strategies (not discussed in this chapter) that you have observed being used by band or orchestra directors at music festivals in performance or sight-reading. Evaluate their potential effectiveness and usefulness in your own teaching.

## *For Reference and Further Reading*

Asmus, E.P. (1985). Sixth graders' achievement motivation: Their views of success and failure in music. *Bulletin of the Council for Research in Music Education*, 85, 1-13.

Asmus, E.P. (1986). Student beliefs about the causes of success and failure in music: A study of achievement motivation. *Journal of Research in Music Education*, 34, 262-278.

Asmus, E.P. (1989). The effect of music teachers on students' motivation to achieve in music. *Canadian Journal of Research in Music Education*, 30, 14-21.

Berliner, David (1985). What do we know about well-managed classrooms? Putting research to work. *Instructor*, 94/6.

Berry, John (1993). The legacy of Maddy and Giddings. *Music Educators Journal*, (March), pp. 36-40.

Canter, Lee (1976). *Assertive Discipline*. Los Angeles: Lee Canter Associates.

Charles, C.M. (1996). *Building Classroom Discipline, 5th ed*. White Plains, NY: Longman Pub.

Colwell, Richard (1970). *The Evaluation of Music Teaching and Learning*. Englewood Cliffs, NJ: Prentice-Hall, Inc.

Csikszentmihalyi, Mihaly, et al. (1993). *Talented Teenagers: The Roots of Success and Failure*. New York: Cambridge University Press.

Franks, Earl (1996). Without wasting words or time: An interview with John M. Long. *The Instrumentalist*, February, 18-22.

Ginott, Hiam G. (1972). *Teacher and Child*. New York: The Macmillan Company.

Glasser, William(1990, 1992). *The Quality School (2nd ed.)*. New York: HarperCollins Publishers.

Glasser, William (1992). The quality school curriculum. *Phi Delta Kappan*, May, 690-694.

Glasser, William (1993). *The Quality School Teacher*. New York: Harper & Row.

Heidel, Richard M. (1999). Music festivals: a worthwhile experience. *NBA Journal*, 39/3, 18-20.

Hoffer, Charles R. (1969). *Teaching Music in the Secondary Schools*. Belmont, CA: Wadsworth Publishing Co.

Holz, Emil A. and Jacobi, Roger (1966). *Teaching Band Instruments to Beginners*. Englewood Cliffs, NJ: Prentice-Hall, Inc.

Kohn, Alfie (1992). *No Contest: The Case Against Competition (revised ed.)*. Boston: Houghton Mifflin Co.

Kohn, Alfie (1993). *Punished by Rewards: The Trouble with Gold Stars, Incentive Plans, A's, Praise, and Other Bribes*. Boston: Houghton Mifflin Co.

Langer, S. (1941). *Philosophy in a New Key*. Cambridge: Harvard University Press.

Lautzenheiser, Tim (1992). *The Art of Successful Teaching: A Blend of Content and Context*. Chicago: G.I.A. Pub.

Lautzenheiser, Tim (1994). Competition or cooperation: what's best for our students? *Fanfare*, 7/3 (December), 2.

Lehman, Paul R. (1995). Control of K-12 arts education: who sets the curriculum? *Arts Education Policy Review*, 97/2 (Nov./Dec.),16-20.

Leriche, Leo (1992). The sociology of classroom discipline. *The High School Journal*, December/January.

Madsen, Charles H. Jr., and Madsen, Clifford K. (1983). *Teaching/Discipline: A Positive Approach for Educational Development (3rd ed.)*. Raleigh, NC: Contemporary Publishing Co.

Metz, Donald (1980). *Teaching General Music in Grades 6-9*. Columbus, OH: Charles E. Merrill Publishing Co.

Moore, James (1992). A philosophy of attitude management. *Today's Music Educator*, Fall, 14-15.

Moss, Bruce. (1995). Curnow on composing. *The Instrumentalist*, April, 11-15.

Neidig, Kenneth L. (1964). *The Band Director's Guide*. Englewood Cliffs, NJ: Prentice-Hall.

Neiman, Marcus L. (1992). It's not what you do, but how you do it that counts—classroom management or mismanagement. *Today's Music Educator*, Fall, 12-13.

Rossman, R. Louis (1989). *TIPS: Discipline in the Music Classroom*. Reston, VA: Music Educators National Conference.

Rozmajzl, Michon and Bourne, Patricia (1996). On classroom management for the music educator. *Journal of Music Teacher Education*, 5/2, (Spring), 21-29.

Singleton, Ira C., and Anderson, Simon V. (1969). *Music in the Secondary Schools, 2nd ed.* Boston: Allyn and Bacon, Inc.

Thomas, Nancy G. (1992). Motivation. In *Handbook for Research on Music Teaching and Learning*. New York, NY: Schirmer Books, 425-436.

Thomson, John (1995). Teaching with goals, not answers: an interview with John Whitwell. *The Instrumentalist*. December, 11-15.

Walker, Darwin E. (1989). *Teaching Music: Managing the Successful Music Program*. New York: Schirmer Books.

# Chapter Nine

*"Efficiency is enhanced when everything has a place"*

## ORGANIZING AND ADMINISTERING THE PROGRAM

## Program Organization

A well-organized, well-administered program has a much greater chance of becoming a successful program. Organization will save you a great amount of time. While it may take considerable effort to *get* organized and *stay* organized, efficiency is enhanced when "everything has a place" and you do not have to waste time searching through unorganized files looking for a report or a score. You will do better to spend that time on educational and musical matters with students. Robert House (1965) wrote that "Administration facilitates the teaching process" (p. 3). A high level of personal and classroom organization allows you to focus on being a more effective teacher. Many teachers leave the profession because they cannot deal with the organizational aspect of the job, not because they are poor teachers.

*"Administration facilitates the teaching Process"*

*Interesting →*

Program organization includes such timesaving strategies as development of a set of forms to help administer the program; the use of student helpers; the use of parent support and helpers; and the use of appropriate technology to maintain inventories, financial records, correspondence, and student grades. Organization also includes establishing program goals, policies, and procedures under which your band or orchestra operates. When students, parents, and administrators are aware of these goals, policies, and procedures, they will better understand your expectations. At the outset you may wonder if all such planning is too much busy-work, but experience will prove that

*Awareness for others → they better understand your expectations*

organization is the fine-tuned (no pun intended), timesaving machinery that keeps the program (and you) humming along smoothly—yielding more time for music education.

## *Band and Orchestra Handbooks*

Many band and orchestra directors have found that publishing a handbook is an effective way to present students and parents with the basic requirements and procedures of band or orchestra. Such a handbook is a valuable tool that requires you to thoughtfully identify the big issues in your ensemble and articulate them in a concise but thorough manner.

Do not establish any policies or procedures until you are sure that they comply with the all-school policies and procedures that the school administration supports. You might even consider inviting your school principal to write a brief statement to be included at the beginning of the handbook, which indicates approval and support. Talk with your principal about your ideas before you talk to students or parents. Include students in the development of new policies and procedures. They will have a unique view of these issues and can offer valuable insight and advice. Actually, you may find that students want more stringent policies and procedures than you have proposed, and you might need to moderate their suggestions! If a handbook is in use from previous years, make changes to existing policies and procedures gradually—and only after thorough discussions with your administration, students, and parents.

What are the basic elements of an ensemble handbook?
- A statement of philosophy and goals or objectives
- Classroom policies and procedures
- Attendance policy
- Grading policy
- Student officer or staff structure and duties
- Any awards system (with any merit and/or demerit system)
- A calendar of events for the year

Band and orchestra handbooks can vary in length. While it is good to have everything in one place, your ensemble members may never read a handbook of 30 pages! It is possible to be thorough and concise! Figure 9-1 is an example of a minimalist approach to a band handbook.

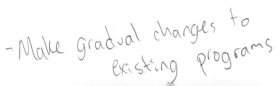

*Figure 9-1. Sample Band Handbook*

# The Ypsilanti High School Bands
## Ypsilanti Public Schools
## Ypsilanti, Michigan

# Band Handbook

### *A Commitment To Excellence*

This handbook is planned to acquaint every member of the Ypsilanti High School Bands with its traditions, activities, rules, and administration.

In order that our band may function smoothly, it is necessary to have these regulations, with a fair and firm method of having them respected. These rules and regulations are not a threat, but a means of protecting each member and should bring us closer to the finest band possible.

**PURPOSE:**

It is an honor and privilege to be a member of the Ypsilanti High School Bands. As a member of our organization each individual must assume responsibility to maintain our reputation for reliability, efficiency, and the highest standards of musical performance. You should take pride in our accomplishments and seek to improve yourself, and thus contribute to the success of the bands.

**OBJECTIVES:**

1. To help students learn about the content of musical works through discussion, analysis, and performance with a goal of developing aesthetic responses to music

2. To increase aesthetic sensitivity to music by using music of varying forms and styles

3. To develop high standards of musical performance and to maintain a well-organized band program

4. To encourage the student to continue his or her musical experiences in post-school years

5. To provide opportunities for development for those who may make music a profession

201

6. Students should find satisfaction and enjoyment in their participation in band

7. To encourage parents participation and support in musical activities and to encourage fine music in the home

### The Ypsilanti High School Band Council

The Ypsilanti High School Band Council will consist of the President, Vice-President, Secretary, and Treasurer from the Freshman Band, Concert Band, and Symphony Band. These officers are elected in each band. The Council will also include the Drum Major, Business Manager, Social Chair, Head Librarian, and Equipment Manager who are appointed by the Director of Bands.

President: To help supervise the activities of the bands. To be a musical and moral inspiration to the entire organization. To handle such items of business as directed by the Director of Bands. The President of the Symphony Band will preside at Band Council meetings.

Vice-President: To assist the President in the execution of the various duties of that office. To act in the capacity of the President in his or her absence. The Vice-President of each band will collect all publicity about the bands and other material for use in the band scrapbooks.

Secretary: To be in charge of checking attendance. The Secretary of the Symphony Band will keep accurate records of all Band Council meetings or other meetings called into session by the Director of Bands.

Treasurer: To keep the books on all the proceeds and expenditures of special band activities. To see that incoming money is deposited and all bills incurred are promptly paid.

Drum Major: The field officer in charge of the Marching Band. The Drum Major must be well versed in all marching fundamental skills and must be thoroughly familiar with the execution of all maneuvers and with the verbal or parade commands for each. The Drum Major will assist the band director in rehearsing the band and will assist members of the band having special difficulty.

Business Manager: To help organize and promote all band sponsored activities such as concerts, fund raising activities, etc. These responsibilities include securing ushers for all concerts, distributing concert posters, and notifying students, faculty, staff, and administration of coming events.

Social Chair: To plan and organize the social activities of the bands. To organize and direct the activities of the Social Committee.

<u>Head Librarian</u>: To oversee all handling of music. To keep all music cataloged and filed, and to supervise the activities of the Library Staff members. To keep an accurate record of all music handed out and to report any lost music to the band director. To keep the entire Music Library in top condition.

<u>Equipment Manager</u>: To see that all property used by the bands is carefully handled. To oversee the handling of all equipment on trips. To keep the storage areas in proper order. To supervise the Equipment Staff members and to have the rehearsal areas in order and prepared before each rehearsal.

<u>Band Awards — Merit and Demerit System</u>

<u>Awards</u>:

| | | |
|---|---|---|
| 9th Grade | Freshman Pin | 25 merits |
| 10-12th Grades | Band Letter | 75 merits |
| 11-12th Grades | Junior Pin | 125 merits |
| 12th Grade | Senior Key | 200 merits |

<u>John Philip Sousa Award</u> and the <u>National Arion Foundation Award</u>:

1. These awards are given to outstanding Senior members of the Ypsilanti High School Bands on the basis of (a) Musicianship, (b) Leadership, and (c) Service to the bands. The primary emphasis of the Arion Award is Leadership and Service, and the primary emphasis of the Sousa Award is Musicianship and Service.

2. The recipients must have been members of the Concert Band or Symphony Band for three years.

3. The recipients must be a Senior in good standing.

4. A Senior must have 200 or more merits to be nominated. The recipients are determined by a vote of the Concert Band and Symphony Band, and must have the approval of the Director of Bands and the High School Principal.

<u>Merits</u>:

Orchestra, per performance (if not in the class)...............................2
Commencement Band.......................................................................4
Solo at Solo and Ensemble Festival (District or State)....................20
Ensemble at Solo and Ensemble Festival (District or State)...........12
Accompanist at Solo and Ensemble Festival (each event)...............12
Attending Concerts (college or professional—turn in the
program—each concert) ................................................................1
Tag Day (per hour)...........................................................................2
Greens Sale (per $5 worth of orders).................................................2
Private Lessons (per semester)........................................................16
First Chair (90% of the year)...........................................................10

Rank Leader during marching season (Freshman Band is 3)......10
Squad Leader during marching season (Freshman Band is 2).......6
Concert Soloist.................................................25
July 4th Parade and Heritage Festival Parade (each one).............8
Usher for concerts (each time).....................................2
Jazz Band (if it is not a class)..................................30
Pep Band (per game)................................................2
Assistant Drum Major.............................................25
Flag Corps......................................................25
Flag Corps Captain..............................................50
Flag Corps Lieutenants..........................................35

People serving on the Social Committee and other committees will receive merits in relation to the amount of work done. Unusual situations requiring extra work will earn merits at the discretion of the band director. Merits are accumulated from one year to the next.

Merits for Band Council:
President (elected)......................15 (20 for Symphony Band President)
Vice-President (elected).............10 (15 for Symphony Band President)
Secretary (elected).....................10 (15 for Symphony Band President)
Treasurer (elected)....................10 (15 for Symphony Band President)
Drum Major (elected)..............................50
Social Chair (elected)...............................30
Business Manager (appointed)...................25
Head Librarian (appointed )....................50
Equipment Manager (appointed)..............50

Merits for Band Staff:
Librarians (appointed)...............................30 (on recommendation of
                                                    the Head Librarian)
Equipment Staff (appointed).....................30 (on recommendation of
                                                    the Equipment Manager)
Uniform Staff (appointed)..........................15 (on recommendation of
                                                    the Band Booster Club
                                                    Uniform Committee)

Merits are issued by the Director of Bands.

Demerit System:
    The issuance of any demerits must be approved by the Director of Bands. Demerits will be posted and should be worked off the following week. They may be worked off at one hour per demerit. Any demerit not worked off in a marking period will lower a students grade one-third mark (three demerits not worked off will low a grade one full mark, etc.). If a student has six or more demerits at the end of a marking period which have not been worked off he/she will receive a failing grade for that marking period. A student who receives demerits during the last week of a marking period will have one

week to eliminate them.

Demerits:
1 - Tardiness at an extra rehearsal without an excuse.
3 - Absence from an extra rehearsal without an excuse.
2 - Absence from a sectional or ensemble rehearsal without an excuse.
2 or 3 - Tardiness at a pubic performance.
6 - Absence from a performance for reasons other than illness or death in the family.
1 - Chewing gum or eating candy during a rehearsal (2 at a performance).
1 or 2 - Improper conduct at a rehearsal or sectional (2 or 3 at a performance).
1 - Failure to bring your instrument to rehearsal (includes reeds, sticks, etc.).
1 - Failure to put your music folder or instrument in its proper storage place.
1 or 2 - Failure to carry out the instructions of a rank or squad leader.
1 - Improper care of your band uniform.
1 - Incomplete uniform while in the public view (including to and from school).
1 - Smoking at any band function (in or out of uniform).

The use of any form of intoxicants or drugs at any band function (in or out of uniform) is a very serious offense which will result in 12 demerits. It will also be reported immediately to the appropriate principal for action.

- - - - - - - - - - - - - - - - - - - - - - - - - - - - - - - - - - - - - - - - - - - - - - - - - - - - - - - - - - - - - - - - -

(detach and return the form below by Friday)

"We have read the band handbook and agree to abide by the policies and requirements listed."

_____          _____
(student signature)                              (parent signature)


_____          _____
(date)                                              (date)

Your handbook could also include:
- A brief history of the ensemble
- General information about each performing ensemble
- Audition and challenge procedures
- Uniform instructions

*Could do an "all-in-one-place" handbook!*

- Performance absence policy
- Any special policies (use of school-owned instruments, band or orchestra camp requirements, drum major and color guard auditions, etc.)
- A list of recommended private teachers
- Fundraising information
- Information about any special fees
- Information about the booster club
- A list of recommended "upgrade" instruments
- A list of recommended college band clinics or honor bands.

Obviously, many of these items can be distributed to students at various times during the school year. In fact, distributing this information when needed may be a more effective way to ensure that students and parents are attentive to those matters.

Some "all-in-one-place" handbooks even include such things as statements about the value of music education, supportive quotes from various well-known people, a discussion about the importance of good attitude, introductions of the band directors and staff, bus policies, medical consent form, and a "we have read and understand this handbook" page to be signed by parents and students. The return form—indicating that parents and students have read and understand the statements, policies and procedures in the handbook—is a good idea. If you travel with your band, medical consent forms should be on file and kept in a binder so they can easily be taken on all trips.

## Forms and Files

The consistent use of a system of forms can greatly simplify your work. Begin now to collect copies of forms used in your college ensembles and those you find as you visit area public and private schools. Keep a notebook of your collection of forms and add to it during your student teaching experience and your first several years of teaching. It is much easier to alter an existing form than to come up with an entirely new form.

*Figure 9-2. Uniform Loan Contract*

**The Ypsilanti High School Bands — Uniform Loan Contract**

Name _____ Date _____

Address _____ Phone _____

| CONCERT UNIFORM | | MARCHING UNIFORM | |
|---|---|---|---|
| | (Part Number) | | (Part Number) |
| Coat ($85) | _____ | Shirt ($36) | _____ |
| Trousers ($40) | _____ | Trousers ($48) | _____ |
| Vest ($30) | _____ | Sash and Drop ($26) | _____ |
| Bow Tie ($4) | _____ | Hat/Aussie ($16) | _____ |
| ************************************** | | ************************************** | |
| Skirt ($35) | _____ | Garment Bag ($3) | _____ |
| Blouse ($30) | _____ | Coat Hanger ($3) | _____ |
| Bolero ($30) | _____ | *($--.--) = replacement cost | |

Date Issued _____ By _____    Date Issued _____ By _____

Date Returned _____ By _____    Date Returned _____ By _____

Student Agreement

I acknowledge receipt of the above marked items and agree to assume the responsibility for any loss or damage beyond ordinary wear. I will not exchange any uniform parts with other band members.

I further agree to properly care for the uniform and clean and/or press it professionally when necessary or required. I understand that no material may be cut off the uniform during alterations.

I agree to return the complete uniforms upon the request of the band director. I agree to have the uniform professionally cleaned and pressed (no coin cleaners) and mended just before the uniform is returned. (Uniforms are to be returned in the cleaners bag.)

_____        _____
   (parent's signature)                         (student's signature)

207

*Figure 9-3. Instrument Loan Contract*

# The Asbury College Concert Band

### Instrument Loan Contract

Name: _____ Date: _____
Instrument: _____ Make: _____
Serial #: _____ List all accessories:_____
_____
_____
Condition (list all problems): _____
_____
_____
_____

"I, the undersigned, acknowledge receipt of the instrument described above and do hereby agree to be responsible for the return of said instrument to Asbury College at the end of the school year or as requested. I will return said instrument in its present condition with all accessories that are issued. It is understood that should the instrument become damaged through careless handling, faulty use, or any other causes, excluding normal wear, I agree to reimburse Asbury College the amount necessary to restore the instrument to its former condition. I will keep the instrument in good playing condition at all times. Should said instrument become lost or destroyed during the period of the present loan, I agree to pay Asbury College a sum sufficient to pay for the purchase of an instrument of equal value."

Signature: _____ Date: _____
College Address: _____ Phone Ext.: ____
Instrument issued by: _____ Date: _____
Returned to: _____ Date: _____

*[handwritten note: Using a phone picture as insurance]*

This book contains numerous examples of forms that can be time savers for the busy instrumental music teacher. Another example of a timesaving form is the attendance form. Teachers must keep accurate attendance records, but many teachers waste valuable rehearsal time by calling all names aloud at the beginning of each class period. Another way to take attendance quickly is to make copies of the seat-

208

*Don't have students take attendance, they will inevitably mess it up.*

ing chart that can be used to take attendance quickly by circling the absent (or tardy) student's name on the dated seating chart. This information can later be transferred to a grade book. Other useful forms include uniform loan contracts (Figure 9-2), instrument loan contracts (Figure 9-3), percussion music assignment charts (Figure 9-4), percussion set-up assignments (Figure 9-5), membership cards (Figures 9-6 and 9-7), and rehearsal schedules (Figure 9-8). Other forms to be discussed in Chapter 10 include audition forms, instrument inspection forms, practice records, and self-evaluation forms.

*Figures 9-4. Percussion Assignment Chart.*

**Percussion Music Assignments**

**After a Gentle Rain**
Jenn:  Piano
Abigail:  Tympani
Matt:  Vibes & xylophone
Andrew:  Bells
Kyle:  Percussion

**The Boys of the Old Brigade**
Jenn:  Crash cymbals
Abigail:  Bass drum
Andrew:  Field drum
Kyle:  Snare drum

**Where Never Lark of Eagle Flew**
Jenn:  Percussion 2
Abigail:  Mallet 1
Matt:  Percussion 1
Andrew:  Tympani
Kyle:  Mallet 2

Figure 9-5. Percussion Set-up Chart

# The Bigtown High School Bands

## Percussion Equipment Assignments

These set-up and put-away assignments are to be done every day. You are all responsible for the proper care of all instruments. Please report any damage or needed repairs immediately. Percussion instruments and equipment are very expensive—please take very good care of all our fine instruments.

| | Freshman Band | Symphony Band | Concert Band |
|---|---|---|---|
| Mallets & unlock/lock cabinets | Joe Pinsoneault | David Fredrick | Steve Arnold |
| Folders (also keep them in order) | Sabrina Wheeler | Michele Robbins | John McDermott |
| Snare drums & stands | Aaron Taratsas Brad Randall | Scott Opland Brad Jones | Eugene Browne John Hildebrandt |
| Tympani (and covers) | Scott House David Diomedi | John Ferris Tim Barnard | Tony Markins Steve Guthrie |
| Keyboard (all needed —also cover bells) | Shawn Zeddell | Scott Fairfield | Jeff Hawkins |
| ALL needed accessories | David Diomedi | Tim Barnard | Steve Guthrie |
| Substitute for anyone absent | Joe Pinsoneault Sabrina Wheeler | David Fredrick Michele Robbins | Steve Arnold John McDermott |

*Figure 9-6. Member Information Card, Example 1*

**The Ypsilanti High School Bands**
**Ypsilanti, Michigan  48197**

**Band Registration Card**

Name _____  Date _____

Address _____  Phone _____

Full Name of Parent/Guardian _____

Instrument(s) Played _____

Make of Instrument _____  Serial # _____

Class:  ___9th  ___10th  ___11th  ___12th  Birthdate _____

E-mail address _____

---

***Class Schedule — First Semester***

Class                                    Room                                    Teacher

1. _____

2. _____

3. _____

4. _____

5. _____

6. _____

(Second Semester — only list schedule changes)

_____

_____

**Figure 9-7. Member Information Card, Example 2**

# The Asbury College Concert Band
## Member Information Form

Name: _____ Date_____

Instrument(s) Played: _____

College Graduation Year: _____ Birthdate: _____

Local Address (or Dorm/#): _____ Local Phone: _____
_____(City/State/Zip)

Parents Names: _____

Home Address: _____ Home Phone: (____)_____
_____(City/State/Zip)

Local E-mail: _____Home E-mail: _____

*Please list any suggestions of music for the Concert Band to play:*
_____
_____

---

(page 2)
## Additional Information

1. High School Band Director: _____
   Name of High School: _____
   Address: _____
   City/State/Zip:_____
   *Possible Tour Contact?* YES_____ NO_____

2. Please list any possible Tour Contacts (churches, schools, etc.)
   Contact Person: _____
   Name of Church/School/Etc.: _____
   Address: _____
   City/State/Zip: _____
   Telephone (if known): __(_____)_____

*Figure 9-8. Rehearsal Schedule Form*

## The Bigtown High School Band

Tentative Rehearsal Schedule for the week of: _____

| Monday | Tuesday | Wednesday | Thursday | Friday |
|--------|---------|-----------|----------|--------|
|        |         |           |          |        |

*File things right away, not just when there's time*

Once you have developed an effective set of forms, your next challenge is to keep track of all that paperwork! File it right away. Everyone occasionally finds himself or herself in the situation that a former student of mine called "pile management." We get overwhelmed by all the paperwork that crosses our desk each day, and begin to feel good that things have even made it to the right "pile" on our desk, but it actually saves time to file things right away so that they can easily be retrieved when needed.

Some items, such as instrument or uniform loan contracts, should be filed in binders (instrument contracts in "score order" and uniform contracts in alphabetical order by students' last names), while others belong in file folders. Many types of information will be in a computer database, and a hard file may not be necessary. You may find that folders of information used regularly should be kept in your desk file drawer or in desktop file holders. Less frequently used files should go in your regular file cabinets—generally, in alphabetical order by file name. Some types of files—such as files concerning annual tours or yearly band camp—could be filed in separate file drawers. Because of confidentiality laws, you must keep individual student files (those discussed below) in a separate and locked file cabinet.

*ASBDA Curriculum Guide* — A helpful source of ideas for forms is the *ASBDA Curriculum Guide*. This lengthy book offers many suggestions for instrumental program organization from successful instrumental programs around the country. It also includes more than 250 pages of sample forms for a wide variety of uses.

An important aspect of being an organized person is to answer mail and messages as quickly as possible. Try to respond to mail within one day. Return telephone messages and answer e-mail on the same day they are received. Administrators, parents, students, and the public will appreciate your attention to their inquiries, and you will help yourself by tossing the ball back in their court, or getting a given concern entirely off your shoulders.

Being an organized person is not easy for everyone, but it is important. A high level of program organization will allow you to concentrate on teaching, and will help reduce and control the anxiety that comes from all the paperwork required of teachers. It will definitely help reduce problems leading to teacher burnout. Do not let the thought of all these details overwhelm you at the outset. Little by little, you can establish order, but sooner is better. If you begin while you are still a student yourself, you will find your first teaching position to be a considerably more satisfying experience.

## Music Student Files

An Instrumental Music Student Permanent File (IMSPF) is a valuable resource for teachers. These files should be started in elementary school when students enter the instrumental program and be transferred to their next teacher as they move through the school system. These files should contain such things as the results of standardized testing done at the beginning program level, musical achievement test results, a list of awards and recognition earned, significant correspondence with parents, and any other information that could help another music teacher better understand the educational needs of the student. Figure 9-9 is an example of a Student Information Form for the IMSPF. This form should be updated each year and kept in a locked cabinet.

## Student Awards Program

An awards program that recognizes achievement at the various grade levels and requires progressively more effort from students can stimulate success. Ensemble members enjoy displaying on jackets or sweaters the musical awards they have earned. These awards could be band or orchestra letters, medals won at solo and ensemble festivals, service ribbons or stripes, or jacket patches. You will find that a well-designed awards system can be a powerful student motivator.

Many schools will already have an awards system in place. Work to improve that awards system so that it recognizes the achievements or actions you believe to be important. Some directors honor "outstanding" or "most improved" members in their bands or orchestras. You may also find that a cumulative "highest award" is an excellent way to honor outstanding seniors, and can serve as a worthy goal for underclassmen. Several nationally recognized awards are available through *The Instrumentalist* magazine, including The John Philip Sousa Band Award, the Louis Armstrong Jazz Award, and the National School Orchestra Award. Other national professional organizations offer awards such as the National Arion Foundation Award. Several citations are available from the National Band Association, the United States Marine Band, and others.

Some directors give awards based strictly on participation—each year spent in band or orchestra earns an award. Others use a system of points or merits earned for important or extra activities. An example of a merit-based awards system is in the band handbook found in Fig-

215

*Figure 9-9. Student Information Form for Permanent File*

---

## Student Information Form
### for the Instrumental Music Student Permanent File

Ypsilanti Public Schools
Ypsilanti, Michigan

Your Name: _____ Today's date: _____
         (last name)         (first name)

Parent or Guardian Name: _____
         (last name)         (first name)

Address: _____
         (street)         (city)         (state)  (zip)

Telephone #: _____ Birthdate: _____

Instrument (with make and serial #): _____

List any other instruments you play: _____

_____

Music Aptitude Test Results and Comments: _____

_____

Music Achievement Test Results and Comments: _____

_____

Awards and Honors: _____

_____

_____

List School Ensemble Memberships (and year): _____

_____

_____

_____

**Student Information Form - page 2**

Private Lesson Teachers (and years) : _____

_____

Solo and Ensemble Festival Participation (grade & year): _____

_____

_____

_____

Honor Bands/Orchestras or Summer Camps (grade & year): _____

_____

_____

_____

Miscellaneous Comments: _____

_____

_____

_____

_____

_____

_____

_____

_____

_____

ure 9-1. This system is progressive—freshmen earn a Freshman Pin with 25 merits; sophomores, juniors, or seniors earn a Band or Orchestra Letter with 75 merits; a Junior Pin (to be worn on the Band or Orchestra Letter) is earned with 125 merits by juniors and seniors; and seniors earn a Senior Key with 200 merits. In this example the merits earned are cumulative during a student's years in band. Therefore, sophomores who earned 25 merits during their freshman year have to earn only another 50 merits to earn the Band or Orchestra Letter, and so forth to the Senior Key. There are many approaches to the type of awards given. Some people use the Band or Orchestra Letter as the base award and add chevrons each year. Others use ribbon pins or certificates to recognize various kinds of achievement.

An extensive awards program can be quite expensive, but it is an effective student motivator. Be sure that the awards system you use with your band or orchestra has been carefully planned, has the support of your administration and the booster club, and is recognized by all to be fair and meaningful.

*[handwritten: Fair & Meaningful]*

## Facilities and Equipment

*[handwritten: Floor Plans for A New Program]*

The quality of music facilities has a major impact on the educational program that is taking place in those facilities. Facilities that are attractive and inviting, acoustically appropriate, adequate in size, and well supported with adjunct spaces and appropriate equipment will encourage and facilitate music learning (Geerdes, 1976 and 1981). When designing new facilities, work with structural and acoustical engineers who understand the unique needs of music programs.

*[handwritten: Designing A Building]*

You should thoughtfully anticipate the future size and structure of your music program. Darwin Walker (1998) observes that "Buildings outlast students, teachers, and even theories of education" (p. 112). Anticipating needs—such as number of students, types and number of ensembles, or new technologies—is one of your responsibilities as a music teacher. Typically, teachers are asked to develop position papers about their views of the future of their department when beginning to plan a new facility, followed by Educational Specifications that list specific spaces or rooms needed (along with their intended use, needed square footage, electrical needs, technology needs, special equipment needed, etc). These position papers and Educational Specifications are usually developed in a group process, which includes school personnel, school board members, and community members. Educational Specifications should address such factors as desired proximity to other

*[handwritten: Responsibility to anticipate needs]*

*Rooms + Offices Need Windows*

facilities (such as the auditorium and outdoor practice areas), needed storage areas, desired technological capabilities, ceiling height, the need for visual control of practice rooms, and number and size of practice rooms. A very important issue for all rooms and offices in a music facility is that all doors have a window. This offers security and protection for teachers and students.

When completed, this report becomes the guiding document for architects and engineers who design the new facility. Planning a new music facility is a complex task that will require you to study all available resources; visit outstanding facilities; seek the input of other music teachers, students, and parents; and work closely with the architects and engineers selected to design your new facility. The floor plans of several outstanding music facilities are found in Figures 9-10 through 9-12.

Many teachers will not have the privilege of designing new music facilities, but all teachers can work to make their existing facilities a better place in which to teach and learn. You should evaluate your facilities relative to the five facility issues mentioned in the first paragraph of this section, then seek needed improvements.

- Attractive and inviting—Is the room color warm and pleasant? Is room temperature and humidity comfortable, and is the system quiet? Is the lighting adequate and quiet?
- Acoustically appropriate—Is the decibel reading at acceptable levels when the loudest ensemble is playing full volume? Can ensemble members hear each other easily? Are the walls non-parallel? Is there good sound isolation to prevent disturbing people in other areas? *Learn more about acoustics*
- Adequate in size—Does the size of the room and the height of the ceiling provide the space volume necessary for the largest ensemble rehearsing in that room? Have you anticipated size needs to allow for program growth?
- Adequate support spaces—Are there appropriate and nearby storage areas for all instruments (including storage for all percussion instruments)? Do storage areas and instrument lockers provide safe storage for all instruments? Is the space for traffic-flow in and out of storage rooms appropriate? Is there adequate and secure storage space for music (and work areas), uniforms, and unassigned school-owned instruments?
- Appropriate room equipment—Is there an adequate number of chairs (which encourage proper posture) and stands? Are

219

*Figure 9-10. Music Suite at Ypsilanti (MI) High School*

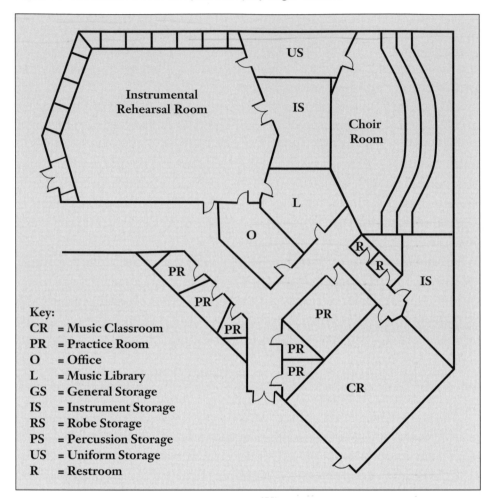

there appropriate chairs or stools for tuba, cello, and string bass players? Is there a high-quality sound system? Is the room wired for appropriate technology? Are there racks for chair and stand storage? Is there storage for music folders?

Many items on the above list can be improved or corrected in an existing facility. Changing the room color is a relatively inexpensive undertaking, and a lighting upgrade can be as simple as changing the fluorescent light ballast to a silent type—however, if your room lighting is inadequate, you may have to replace the existing fixtures or install additional light fixtures. Unfortunately, solutions for air conditioning and humidity problems are seldom easy or inexpensive; but rooms with adequate air and humidity control provide a much better atmosphere for effective rehearsals and offer protection for sensitive wood instruments.

*Figure 9-11. Music Suite at Greenville (MI) Senior High School*

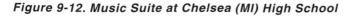

*Figure 9-12. Music Suite at Chelsea (MI) High School*

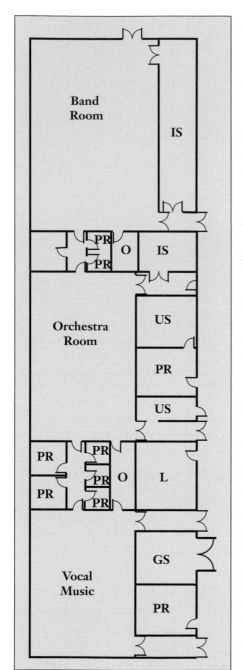

The issue of excessively high decibel levels in instrumental rehearsal rooms is important for teachers and students. While teachers are more at risk, spending a greater number of hours each day in the rehearsal room, students may also face hearing damage caused by prolonged and cumulative exposure to high decibel levels. A number of companies manufacture wall and ceiling panels that can improve the acoustical properties of rehearsal and practice rooms. These companies generally offer consultation services to schools seeking solutions for their acoustical problems. You will find that a well-designed application of such sound panels will not only help control the volume of sound produced, but will enable ensemble members to hear the other instruments better. The application of carpeting can have a dramatic effect on noisy music rooms. Anything you can do to improve sound isolation—changing to sound deadening doors, using sound absorbing panels on walls adjoining other classrooms, sealing electrical boxes and other conduit pipes—will be appreciated by those who teach in nearby rooms.

Obviously, you will not be able to do much about the size of an existing rehearsal room. Sometimes removing a drop ceiling will improve the acoustical properties of a large rehearsal room, and simply painting the entire ceiling area (including all mechanical lines and equipment) will make it aesthetically "neutral."

Some inadequate storage facilities can be improved by replacing open-shelf storage with new "cage-type" storage lockers. Placing some of those cage-type lockers in the rehearsal room or a large hallway can dramatically add to your instrument storage capacity. If your rehearsal room is adequately large, you might consider adding storage closets for storing large percussion instruments.

Solving problems by adding appropriate room equipment requires a supportive administration. It is important that only chairs that encourage good posture be used in music rooms, and that an adequate number of music stands be available so that no more than two students share a single stand. Special chairs for tuba and cello players and appropriate stools for string basses and tympani should be purchased. Rolling storage racks will protect your chairs and stands, get them off the floor so that custodians can more easily clean the floor, and make it easier to move those items to your performance area.

Every music rehearsal room and classroom should have a high quality sound system. Modeling is an important teaching technique in music: you should be able to play recorded examples for your students that are of the highest sound quality. Music rooms without a high quality sound system are like geography classrooms without maps or globes. It should not be! A "boom box" is not an acceptable solution.

*Opportunity-to-Learn Standards for Music Instruction: Grades PreK-12* was published by the Music Educators National Conference (Paul R. Lehman, Project Director) in 1994. This publication—part of a series related to the National Standards for Music—presents recommendations for school districts concerning (1) curriculum and scheduling, (2) staffing, (3) materials and equipment, and (4) facilities (p. vi). The premise of these "opportunity-to-learn" standards is that if students are to be held accountable for what they are to learn, and teachers for what they teach, then appropriate and adequate support must be provided by the school. Standards are suggested at four levels: pre-kindergarten and kindergarten, elementary school, middle or junior high school, and high school. These opportunity-to-learn standards can be a persuasive argument when used as a tool to convince a school to provide adequate resources, equipment, and facilities. The publication states that "Both practice and history support the belief that there is a high correlation between effective student learning in music and the existence of the favorable conditions specified in the opportunity-to-learn standards (p. vii)."

Many things can be done to improve inadequate music classrooms. Be knowledgeable about possible solutions and be politely persistent in your requests to your school administrators. Emphasize that you recommend the improvements solely to benefit the students in the music program and to provide them with enhanced educational opportunities.

# School-Owned Instruments, Equipment, and Uniforms

## *Instruments and Equipment*

Bands and orchestras collect a sizable inventory of music, instruments, uniforms, and equipment. Even a small instrumental program could have an inventory worth 100,000 dollars. Managing those inventories is a major responsibility of the instrumental music teacher. Accurate record-keeping— and good parent and student help—will make this important job easier (procedures for managing the music library were discussed in Chapter 5). You will need accurate and complete records for insurance purposes and to allow more precise planning for the instrument, equipment, music, and uniform needs of your program. Be sure to make several backup copies of these database files and store them in locations both in and out of your building. Your school business office should have a hard copy of at least your instrument and equipment inventory as well as your music library master list. These documents would become invaluable in the event of a catastrophic loss.

*Figure 9-13. Instrument Inventory Database*

| | |
|---|---|
| **Instrument Type** | Bassoon |
| **Brand Name** | Fox Renard |
| **Model Number** | 230 |
| **Serial Number** | 30605 |
| **Accessories** | seat strap, neck strap, crutch, 2 bocals, 2 swabs |
| **Date Purchased** | June 2000 |
| **Purchase Price** | $4,795.00 |
| **Current Value** | |
| **Present Condition** | like new |
| **Repair Record** | June 2001: replace bocal pad & adjust — Sept. 2002: replace top tenon cork |

Database computer programs like the one shown in figure 9-13 will help you maintain an accurate inventory listing of school-owned instruments. By including an accurate instrument repair history with a thorough record of any major dents or other problems, you will help yourself plan a preventive maintenance repair schedule and establish responsibility for damage done to these expensive school-owned instruments. Other information, such as the name of the student assigned each instrument, could be included in the database. An Instrument Loan Contract (figure 9-3) should be completed for each student who is assigned a school-owned instrument. A regular schedule of instrument inspections, as discussed in Chapter 10, will dramatically improve the level of instrument care for both privately owned and school-owned instruments.

School-owned instruments not currently issued should be kept out of sight in locked, dust-free closets. All privately owned and school-owned instruments that are issued to students should have an assigned storage space for safekeeping. Storage may be simple open-shelf cabinets (which provide no security for the instruments) or individual lockers or storage units. As discussed earlier, individual lockers are preferred. Many companies make specially designed lockers for music rooms, lockers that can be secured with a padlock. Some basic lockers are of the oversize metal locker style; others are made from a variety of wood and composite materials with solid or "cage-style" wire-mesh doors. These lockers provide safe and effective storage for instruments and help maintain order in the rehearsal room. If you do have individual instrument lockers at your school, I suggest buying a complete set of "gym-locks"—numbered combination locks that also have a master key—so that you can have access to the lockers when necessary. These locks can be issued to students for a small deposit fee.

Percussion instruments are some of the most difficult to store and keep from "walking away." Larger percussion instruments (various drums and keyboard instruments) should, if at all possible, have a lockable storage area. They should not be left out in the rehearsal room where they are a great temptation for other students to play. Most of these larger instruments will have serial numbers, and should also be discreetly marked with your school name and any school inventory number.

Smaller percussion instruments present many problems for the teacher related to inventory control and care. Almost all small instruments (such as wood blocks, wind chimes, guiro, and maracas) and equipment (stands, mallets, etc.) can be marked with a distinctive tape or paint, or can be etched carefully with your school name or initials.

Some instruments (such as triangles and cymbals) may not be easily marked—except with paint or marker—without damaging the playing characteristics of the instrument. All small percussion instruments need an assigned storage place—which also makes taking a regular inventory much easier. Small instruments used regularly in rehearsals should be kept in a lockable percussion cabinet with wheels, and stored in the rehearsal room. Another option is to use a large trap case that can easily be wheeled from rehearsal room to performance room or onto a truck for travel. Whatever storage system is used, you will need to teach students to store all instruments properly—wood instruments only with other wood instruments, and metal instruments with other metal instruments. By teaching students the proper care, maintenance, and storage of instruments, you will spend less money on repair and replacement and waste less rehearsal time looking for missing instruments or equipment. Figure 9-14 is a list of preventive maintenance procedures for percussion instruments. Training your students to complete these procedures on a regular schedule will prolong the life of your percussion instruments and give your percussionists a greater sense of "ownership" of school-owned instruments and equipment.

**Figure 9-14. Preventive Maintenance for Percussion Instruments**

## Percussion Maintenance
### by Lynn Cooper

Every band or orchestra director has experienced the frustration of finding percussion instruments, mallets, and equipment that have been damaged by careless or inappropriate use. The cost of repair or replacement places a great strain on budgets already stretched to the breaking point.

Much of the damage or careless use can be the result of handling by students who do not own the instruments and therefore do not feel any great obligation to exercise care in their use. How can we remedy the situation? I believe that when students are made aware of the high cost of instruments and mallets, and are taught proper preventive maintenance techniques, a more "professional" attitude toward those instruments and mallets will result, and much less damage will occur.

Let's teach our percussionists how to care for all of that expensive equipment and make them responsible for its care. The first step is a program of instruction. That could be as simple as giving a hand-out with maintenance suggestions to each percussionist. It will be much more effective, however, if a series of instructional sessions is scheduled to reinforce the maintenance hand-out. That will give students some actual "hands-on" experience in maintenance techniques. We may want to ask them for their suggestions so that they will feel more a part of the whole process.

I have found the following information an essential first step in a preventive maintenance program. It is brief, yet complete, so that middle school and high school students will take the time to actually read and study it. After the instructional sessions I have found it works best to assign each person in the section some specific duties so that these maintenance procedures are regularly followed on all school-owned instruments. It is amazing to see a sense of pride develop in young percussionists! It is equally gratifying to see how much money can be saved on the repair budget!

### Percussion Maintenance and Mallet Information

I. Care of sticks and mallets
  A. Sticks: no rough edges, not warped, clean beads.
  B. Mallets
    1. General
      a. Don't touch the mallet heads: perspiration, dirt, etc. can damage them.
      b. Don't lay them on the floor or stands and get them dirty. Use a trap table or drape a towel or carpet piece over the horizontal desk of a music stand.
      c. Keep them in a mallet bag.
    2. Timpani (also some marching quads or quints mallets)
      a. Never use on a suspended cymbal (use yarn mallets)
      b. Don't rub felt heads: it causes them to pill and then they must be trimmed.
      c. Keep mallet heads covered when not in use.
      d. Mark the seams on the head covers and do not play on them.
    3. Keyboard
      a. Rubber: keep the heads clean
      b. Plastic and brass: don't abuse them, do not pound

with them.

    c. Yarn and cord: don't touch the fabric or get it dirty, keep the heads  covered when not in use, and store them in a mallet bag, replace the yarn when it is badly worn.

4. Bass drum and gong

    a. Keep the heads clean by not touching them or laying them on the floor or a stand.

5. Chime

    a. Do not abuse or run down the edges of a rawhide mallet head.

6. Wire brushes

    a. These must be handled with extreme care—they are easily destroyed.

    b. Store in a "closed" position or in a storage tube.

II.    Keyboard Instrument Care – A general rule: Never use a mallet which is harder than the surface being played.

  A. Chimes

    1. Use rawhide or Lucite mallets only.

    2. Play ONLY on the caps of the chime tubes. Never play on the tube itself.

    3. Check all fittings every month for tightness and wear. Especially check the dampening mechanism.

    4. Replace roping when worn.

  B. Orchestra Bells

    1. Use poly, lucite, acetol, phenolic,plastic, rubber, or brass (when specified)    mallets. Never use brass mallets on aluminum bells.

    2. Use brass mallets carefully to avoid damage to the bars.

    3. Be sure to keep the instruments covered when not in use.

  C. Xylophone

    1.Use wood, rubber or poly mallets only – never brass. Note that some synthetic and some hard wood mallets may damage some rosewood bars.

    2. Never strike the bars with drum sticks or any object other than those listed above.

    3. Check all fittings every month for tightness.

    4. Clean and polish the bars every month with a commercial furniture polish.

5. Be sure to keep the instrument covered when not in use.

D. Marimba

    1. Use yarn or cord wound mallets of soft rubber mallets ONLY.

    2. Marimba bars are easily abused. Use caution, care, and only the mallets listed above.

    3. Check all fittings every month for tightness.

    4. Clean and polish the bars every month with a commercial furniture polish.

    5. Be sure to keep the instrument covered when not in use.

E. Vibraphone

    1. Use only yarn wound or rubber mallets, NEVER brass or plastic: the bars will dent!

    2. Check all fittings every month for tightness.

    3. Oil the motor bearings, pivot pins, etc., every month with a light machine oil.

    4. Check the tension on the drive belt every month and replace it if necessary.

    5. Keep the instrument covered when not in use.

III. Membrane Instruments

A. Snare Drum

    1. Keep heads clean and free of writing.

    2. Tension the heads evenly (tensioning in rotation as you do when putting on a car tire.)

    3. Tension snares evenly (leave snares *on* when the instrument is stored.)

        a. Clean the snares off occasionally with a soft brush.

    4. When changing heads, clean all lugs with WD-40 and lubricate with "Lug Lube" or "3-in-1" oil.

    5. Heads should be replaced when necessary (usually at least every two years.)

        a. When replacing a head clean off the shell rim (bearing edge) completely (use emery cloth lightly) and lubricate lightly with Vaseline.

        b. Be sure to "seat" the head properly.

        c. Tighten all inner fittings while the head is off.

    6. When a snare strand becomes stretched or bent remove that single strand completely and promptly.

    7. Do not abuse the drum. Handle and play it with care.

    8. Clean the outside of the shell and hardware as needed by wiping with a cloth dampened with WD-40. Do not use

an abrasive metal polish on any surface.

9. Do not set the drum on any hard, rough, or sharp surface or object – this is especially a problem with marching drums.

10. Always store the snare drum carefully—in a case, if possible.

B. Bass Drum

1. Keep even tension on the heads (see under Snare Drum)
2. Keep the heads clean and free of marks. A slightly damp cloth works well.
3. Tighten fittings and lubricate lugs once a year (see instructions under Snare Drum).
4. Play only with a covered mallet (never a snare drum stick.) Wooden bass drum mallets are rarely needed in concert band music.
5. Keep covered when not in use.

C. Bongos, Timbales, Tom-toms, tenor drums, marching quads and quints, etc.

1. Keep heads clean and evenly and properly tensioned (see under Snare Drum.)
2. Lubricate lugs once a year and tighten all fittings (see Snare Drum).
3. Clean and lubricate the shell rim when replacing a head or as needed (see under Snare Drum.)

D. Timpani

1. Keep the heads evenly and properly tensioned.
2. Keep the heads clean and free of writing.
3. NEVER adjust the tensioning at the base of the timpani without instruction and permission.
4. Tighten all fittings once a year.
5. Lubricate the lugs every year.
6. Clean the rim of the shell and lubricate when replacing the head or as needed (use special Teflon tape on the bearing edge).
7. Be careful not to dent or scratch the bowl. Dents may be carefully removed with a large rubber hammer such as he type used in an automobile body shop.
8. Lubricate the pedal once a year.
9. Keep the timpani covered when not in use. Store the covers carefully when they are off the drums. Do not allow the fiber board (which touches the timpani head) to get dirty.

10. If the drums have plastic (mylar) heads, store with the pedal up (all the way tight). If they have calfskin heads, store with the pedal down (head loose).

IV. Other
  A. Cymbals
    1. Polish as needed with a non-abrasive polish—never buff on an electric buffing wheel.
    2. Use the proper stand (in good condition) for suspended cymbals.
    3. Crash cymbals should be held by a proper rack/holder during rehearsals—they should not be placed on the floor or on a chair.
    4. Store all cymbals in a cabinet or closet—do not leave them set up in the band room.
  B. Temple Blocks
    1. Use soft rubber mallets ONLY—never use snare drum sticks.
    2. Use care in playing and handling temple blocks.
    3. Store in their case (if available) or in a cabinet or closet.
    4. If painted: repaint them lightly when needed.
  C. All stands
    1. Keep the rubber and plastic guards in place for the protection of the instrument.
    2. Use care with lugs and screws so that they are not stripped. Use a light lubricant as needed.
    3. When placing a drum on a stand be careful not to puncture the snare head with the stand and be sure the stand is adjusted snugly to the drum.
    4. Make sure a good pad and a plastic or rubber rod cover are used on the suspended cymbal stand.
  D. Woodblock
    1. Use only a rubber mallet.
  E. Storage of all equipment
    1. Never store instruments and equipment carelessly or on top of each other.
    2. Keep wood instruments stored together and metal together—NEVER mixed together.
    3. Organize your percussion storage cabinets or closets and label storage areas so that instruments may be quickly located and correctly stored. LOCK your cabinets or closets immediately after every re-

> hearsal.
> 4. Never leave percussion instruments or equipment set up between rehearsals. Keep them away from "untrained hands."

## *Uniforms*

Band and orchestra uniforms are a major investment for a school district. If they receive excellent care, uniforms should last 10 to 15 years or even more. Maintaining and issuing uniforms is an appropriate task for parent volunteers. A parent uniform committee (sometimes referred to as "Box Moms," or "Bag Ladies"!) should be given the responsibility to fit and assign uniforms to students, provide needed repairs, arrange dry cleaning when needed, and maintain an orderly uniform storage area. This is a major responsibility, which—when given to a hard-working and conscientious parent group—can relieve you of an incredibly time-consuming task.

You will need to make several decisions about uniform use and care:

- Are uniforms to be turned in and reissued each year or assigned to a student for his or her full high school career?
- Are uniforms to be stored at school (and issued just before each performance) or kept by the student at home?
- Are uniforms to be dry cleaned only by direction of the parent uniform committee or by the students as needed?
- May students have their assigned uniforms altered or should alterations be done only by the parent uniform committee?

It is certainly easier on the parent uniform committee to issue a uniform for a student's entire school career—but students grow. Be sure to refit students at the beginning of each school year to ensure that they all have a well-fitted uniform. Uniforms stored at school and dry cleaned by the parent uniform committee will last longer because they will receive more consistent and appropriate care. That approach will require a large uniform committee and a major time commitment to distribute and return all uniforms before and after each performance. Fortunately, many parents are eager to volunteer for this work—and bless them for it! Storing all uniforms at the school will require private changing rooms for students near your rehearsal room and additional on-site time before and after performances.

If uniform alterations are allowed, students should receive some kind of instructions. Even a basic "No material is to be cut from the uniform during alterations" may help prevent losses. The best policy may be to allow only a member of the parent uniform committee to alter uniforms—or to prohibit any alteration other than changing pant length. Major alterations may interfere with sizing students to that uniform in the future.

When students are issued a band or orchestra uniform they should sign a Uniform Contract such as in Figure 9-2. You may wish to fill out this contract in duplicate so that students may keep a copy of this agreement. It is a good idea to include the replacement cost for each uniform part so that students understand the extent of their financial obligation in the event of a lost or badly damaged item. The parent signature is necessary, because a minor may not be considered legally responsible for this or other contracts. You will probably find it helpful to keep all of the uniform information (the size of each uniform item, to whom it is issued each year, and perhaps a record of any major alteration or repair) in a computer database.

# Student Helpers

## *Student Staff*

The responsibilities of leading an instrumental music program are complex and time-consuming. You will soon learn that there are simply not enough hours in the day to answer personal correspondence, make curriculum and literature decisions, order music, answer messages, fill the music folders, set up the chairs and stands for rehearsals, issue school-owned instruments, take instruments to be repaired to the shop, publicize concerts, issue uniforms, and so forth. The first four items on this list are duties that can be done only by you. You should consider assigning routine tasks to student assistants. Tim Lautzenheiser (1992) offers this list of things an instrumental music teacher does not need to do:

1. Stuffing and emptying music folders.
2. Entering data into your band computer.
3. Being the financial guru of the fund-raising project.

4. Serving as superintendent of ensemble properties—more commonly known as "straightening up the band room."
5. Getting caught in the undertow of correspondence. DO NOT TRY TO BE YOUR OWN SECRETARY.
6. Now that you're "on a roll" let's not "take roll!" (p. 128)

Many students will cheerfully volunteer to help you by serving on a student music library staff (process new music, file music, pass out music), an equipment staff (keep an accurate inventory of school-owned instruments and equipment, issue instruments, sell reeds and equipment to students, set up chairs and stands for rehearsals), or a uniform staff (with parent supervision maintain, repair, and issue uniforms). Some teachers like to combine each of the preceding groups into a single Band Staff or Orchestra Staff. Having a single student staff group is particularly a good idea in a smaller school system, but in large schools you may prefer to divide the duties so that more students can be involved in this work. Students can also help with concert publicity, production of a newsletter, maintenance of your ensemble history with scrapbooks, and in many other ways.

When you appoint your working staff, select students who have a good attitude, are willing to work hard, and want to do their job well. Maintain high standards for student workers and ask them to be thorough and precise in their work. They will rise to the level of your expectations. In other words, teach them their roles and help them to establish those same high goals for themselves. Train them adequately for their job and make sure they understand what they are doing and why they are doing it. If you, like I, think it is important to have your ensemble set up exactly the same each day, then teach your student workers what they need to do to meet your expectations. Select the most mature (usually the oldest, but not always), hard-working, and supportive students to lead each staff group. The student leader can keep workers focused on their tasks, find new ways to make your job easier (always a good thing!), and help train new workers. Stephen Covey (1992) wrote that "The basic role of the leader is to foster mutual respect and build a complementary team where each strength is made productive and each weakness made irrelevant (p. 246)." So, choose, and train effective leaders.

After you select good workers and leaders, and train them in their roles, empower them to be successful by letting them work without constantly checking up on them. At least, do not be obvious about it!

Give them some independence and encourage initiative. You will be pleased and perhaps surprised at the results.

Be sure to recognize and thank student workers. A listing of workers on concert programs is a good way to do this, and you may want to verbally express appreciation at the last concert of the school year. If you use a merit system to earn awards, give merits for working on the band or orchestra staff. When you notice student workers complete a job for you, be sure to thank them for the quality of their work. That will encourage them to continue producing high quality results.

Get as many students as possible involved in working for the band or orchestra—as a staff person, an officer, or on a fundraising project. A shared workload is a lighter workload. More important, Covey (1990) noted that "Without involvement, there is no commitment" (p. 143). Students who are active are more likely to enjoy their involvement, remain active members throughout their school years, be positive ambassadors for the program in the school and community, desire to become better musicians, and encourage others in the ensemble to be positive members. This is a "win-win" situation!

## Student Leaders

The student leadership of your ensembles will include elected officers, students in appointed staff positions, section leaders, seniors, and other members of the ensemble who have gained the respect of their peers. The instrumental music program will benefit if these student leaders are supportive of each other, the instrument music program, and the instrumental music teacher. You can set that tone by treating students with respect, setting clear and attainable goals, encouraging and supporting positive student behavior, and assigning student leaders specific responsibilities and letting them carry them out without interference.

The process of developing future student leaders is an important responsibility. When younger students with leadership potential are identified, try to involve them by inviting them to serve on the student staff or help in some other way. Student workers who demonstrate a hard-work ethic and commitment should be rewarded with greater responsibility. Meet with your student leaders regularly to discuss your program goals and expectations, talk about upcoming activities, discuss their needs or questions, and encourage their continued positive leadership.

# Parent Helpers

Parents—in an organized group or as individuals—can be a great help to their children's music program. Even without a booster club, parents can help by organizing fundraising events, taking photos or videos of marching band shows and concerts, assisting with public relations efforts, chaperoning social events and trips, or helping with the care and distribution of uniforms. Parents who work for the music program will be more supportive of the music program and the teacher. Their support will also encourage a good attitude and higher level of involvement by their son or daughter. Another win-win situation!

## *Booster Clubs*

An organized band and/or orchestra booster club is extremely important to an active program. You cannot be an effective and organized teacher when you are also busy planning and administering fundraising events, issuing uniforms, maintaining an instrument inventory, etc. An organized booster club can assume many of the burdensome extra responsibilities of the instrumental music teacher—and usually do them more effectively and efficiently.

If a booster club is not already organized at your school, be sure to talk with your school administrators to gain their support for such a group. With administrative support, invite a small group of supportive parents to attend an informal meeting to determine if adequate parental support of a booster club exists and to establish a plan for beginning the club. It is usually a good idea to have your administrator attend the first organizational meeting to welcome parents and express support for a booster club. Some temporary organizational structure will need to be established until a constitution and by-laws are developed and approved. Usually, only a president, secretary, treasurer, and two or three board members will be needed. This group can also serve as the constitution and by-laws committee. A sample booster club constitution and by-laws is found in Figure 9-15. Some teachers find that a combined band and orchestra booster club is most effective in their school, while others prefer a separate booster club for each program. It is a decision that should be made based on the needs of your program, school, and community.

*Figure 9-15. Booster Club Constitution and By-Laws.*

# Ypsilanti High School Band Boosters Club

## Constitution

### Article I
### Name

The name of this club shall be the Ypsilanti High School Band Boosters Club.

### Article II
### Objectives

The objectives of the Ypsilanti High School Band Boosters Club shall be:

1. To promote family and community interest in the Ypsilanti High School Bands.

2. To encourage the school administration in the adequate financing of the High School Bands.

3. To further the interest of the students in the High School Bands.

4. Provide such funds, when possible, to enrich the program of the High School Bands.

### Article MIII
### Membership

Members shall be parents or guardians of past or present Ypsilanti High School Band members and any other interested community members.

The High School Band Directors are ex-officio members.

237

## Article IV
**Officers**

The officers shall consist of a President, a Vice-President, a Secretary, and a Treasurer.

The officers shall be elected in accordance with Article II of the By-Laws. The term of Office shall be one year.

Terms of Office shall be held for no more than two consecutive years by the same person.

# By-Laws

## Article I
**Meetings**

Regular meetings shall be held on the second Tuesday of the months of September, November, February, and May, at 8:00 p.m. The Executive Board may change the meeting night and time of meeting for the current year.

Special meetings may be called by the President after giving due notice to the membership. Said notice shall be by publication in the local newspaper or by postcard or letter.

A quorum shall consist of ten (10) members and must include the President and the Vice-President. No meeting shall be held without a quorum present.

## Article II
Election of Officers

The officers shall be elected at the regular meeting in May from a slate presented by the Nominating Committee or from nominations made from the floor.

The person receiving the highest number of votes cast shall be declared elected.

The new officers shall assume office at the regular meeting in September. The outgoing President shall preside at the beginning of the first meeting in September to finalize the year's activities and then turn the meeting over to the new officers.

The Nominating Committee shall consist of five (5) members. Two (2) members shall be appointed by the Executive Board and three (3) members shall be appointed by the President. The chairman of this committee shall be appointed by the Executive Board.

### Article III
### Duties of Officers

The President shall be the executive head of the Ypsilanti High School Band Boosters Club with full authority to enforce the Constitution and By-Laws. He/she shall preside at all meetings and shall be a member Ex-officio of all committees except the Nominating Committee. He/she shall be authorized to countersign disbursement checks.

The Vice-President shall act as Publicity Chairman, preside in the absence of the President, and shall perform such other duties as pertains to this office. In the event of the death or resignation of the President, the Vice-President shall become President. He/she shall be authorized to countersign disbursement checks issued by the Treasurer.

The Treasurer shall receive all monies accruing to the Club and shall deposit same in a depository approved by the Executive Board to the account of the Ypsilanti High School Band Boosters Club. The Treasurer shall issue all disbursement checks in accordance with Article IV of the By-Laws. The Treasurer shall keep an accurate record of all receipts and disbursements and present a financial report at the regular meeting each month. A written copy of this report is to be filed with the Secretary. The Treasurer shall be bonded in the amount of Two Thousand Dollars ($2,000). Cost of said bond is to be paid by the Club. The Treasurer shall submit the financial records to the Audit Committee at completion of current year's business.

## Article IV
### Funds

A receipt in duplicate shall be issued for all monies paid to the Treasurer. A copy of each receipt is to be retained in a bound pre-numbered receipt book. All monies should be deposited promptly and the Treasurer should retain a duplicate copy of each deposit slip.

All disbursements over $25 must be approved by majority vote of the quorum present at any regular meeting. Checks shall be signed by the Treasurer and countersigned by the President, Vice-President, or Secretary.

Special accounts may be established when authorized by the membership.

## Article V
### The Executive Board

The Executive Board shall consist of the officers of the Club, the chairman of the standing committees, the High School Band Directors, and one (1) member elected by the membership.

The Executive Board shall meet prior to the regular meeting of the Club and each month to transact such business as may come before it, and to make recommendations to the membership.

The outgoing President who retains membership in the Club shall become a member Ex-officio of the Executive Board.

A majority of members shall constitute a quorum at a Board meeting.

## Article VI
### Standing Committees

There shall be the following standing committees: Ways and Means, Social, Publicity, Audit, and such others as the Executive Board find necessary.

The Ways and Means Committee shall consist of the Green Sale Chairman, Tag Day Chairman, and the Candy Sale Chairman. They shall be responsible for fund raising activities of the Club. They shall submit fund raising activities of the Club. They shall submit fund raising plans to the Executive Board for approval before presentation to the membership.

The Social Committee shall consist of two (2) chairpersons appointed by the President. They shall be responsible for all social affairs of the Club.

The Publicity Committee shall consist of two (2) members appointed by the President, of which the Vice-President shall be chairman. They shall be responsible for all publicity of the Club. All press releases, etc. shall be cleared by this committee. The Audit Committee shall consist of three (3) members appointed by the Executive Board. They shall be responsible for auditing the financial records of the Club at the conclusion of current year's business.

### Article VII
### Amendments

This constitution and By-Laws may be amended at the regular meeting of the Club by a majority vote, provided that members have been duly notified of the amendment at the previous meeting or not later than two (2) weeks prior to regular meeting by mail.

The most visible role of the booster club is to raise money to support the band or orchestra program. As a general rule, the money raised by the booster club should not be used to purchase those things that ought to be in the school board budget. Booster club funds should not be used to buy instruments, music, or uniforms, or for any part of regular professional staff salaries. It is sometimes appropriate for booster clubs to buy special instruments (such as flugelhorns for marching band and jazz ensemble or a keyboard for the jazz ensemble), or special color guard uniforms. It might also be appropriate for the booster club to fund special instruction such as color guard and percussion instructors for the marching band. Many booster clubs are very involved in funding special trips for their bands or orchestras. The regular travel that is curriculum-related (festivals, attending college or professional concerts, etc.) should be paid from the regular school budget. Band and orchestra uniforms should be purchased by the school board. The football team does not have to raise money to buy helmets and uniforms. Because band and orchestra are curricular subjects, the needed course supplies—including uniforms—should be provided by the school district. The usable life of most uniforms is 10-12 years, making this a reasonable investment by the school board.

While the position affirmed in the preceding paragraph is philosophically correct, the reality in too many school districts is that their bands and orchestras would not be able to participate in many of their regular activities without the financial support of a booster club. It is unfortunate that the funds raised by booster clubs often must be used to purchase needed uniforms, instruments, or equipment, instead of funding enrichment activities or programs. If you find yourself in such a situation, you probably will need to launch a long-term, low-key effort to "educate" a school board and administration about the correct use of booster club financial support.

Other activities that could be funded by the booster club include
- Scholarships (for summer music camps or college)
- Special clinics by local professional musicians
- Private lesson scholarships (especially for students who transfer to oboe, bassoon, French horn, viola, and string bass)
- Summer camp scholarships for drum majors and color guard members
- Commissions of new music

These suggestions will benefit the individual band or orchestra member and the entire program. Commissioning new music has the potential to bring important and significant music into the repertoire.

The community in which you begin to teach may have a band and/or orchestra booster club already organized. In that case, you and the booster club need only come to an understanding of your respective roles. Be openly appreciative of the many hours of work and commitment given by parents to support their children's music program. You may want to ask for advice from the booster club concerning plans for the band or orchestra, and you will want to explain thoroughly how any fundraising money is to be spent. The booster club budget should be developed by the teacher and the booster club officers. Officers sometimes ride a fine line between offering advice and telling the music teacher what to do—which is an inappropriate and dangerous situation. Booster groups must understand that you are the professional educator hired by the school system and given the authority to make the educational decisions. The right balance has booster clubs supportive of the teacher, the students, the program, and the school.

There may be times (such as threatened program reduction or change) when it is appropriate for the booster club to lobby with the administration and school board. This should be rare! A unified lobbying effort mounted by a parent group may be positively received by a school board or administration—especially if that group is not a "regular" in presenting requests or concerns to the board. An overly active lobbying group can lose its effectiveness. In addition, if they are often successful in getting their way with the school board, they may decide that they should (or could) also control you!

What happens when the relationship between you and the booster club deteriorates? You have four choices:
- Go along (let the boosters exert control)
- Move along (get a new job and do not make the same mistakes!)
- Restore an appropriate relationship (this is easier said than done)
- Disband the booster club (this is a drastic option that must have the support of your administration)

The first choice would create an unhealthy situation for any band or orchestra program. The second choice is selected by many teachers who find themselves in such a predicament. If the relationship between teacher and booster club is severely strained, this may be the best alternative to an open struggle for control of the program. Sometimes the best-learned lessons are the hardest.

Restoring an appropriate relationship with an out-of-control booster club is quite challenging. It will require great character and patience, and the support or intervention of the school administration. But if you can accomplish it, you will grow in personal strength and maturity at the same time you regain healthy control of your program.

243

If you decide to stay at your present position and cannot resolve the conflict, you may find that you need to disband the booster club. This is a very difficult thing to do: it publicly announces a major relational problem and may alienate a significant number of band or orchestra parents and students. Only in rare instances should this be the solution. Thoroughly discuss the situation with your administrators, present your view of the available options to resolve the situation, and ask for their suggestions. If your administrators agree that the only solution is to disband the booster club, you should inform the entire booster organization by mail and ask your administrators to co-sign the letter. You should wait at least two or three years before inviting a small group of supportive parents to organize a new club. In the meantime, ask specific groups of parents to help organize fundraising activities, work on a uniform committee, or help with other organizational tasks.

It is important that a positive, cooperative, and respectful relationship be established between you and the booster club. Everyone should be seeking the same major goal—a positive, meaningful musical experience for students in the instrumental music program.

## *For Discussion or Assignment*

1. Describe two teachers you have observed at opposite ends of the organization skills spectrum. Discuss how their organizational skills have affected their teaching effectiveness.

2. Do a web search and find three or four high school band or orchestra Web sites that include their band or orchestra handbooks. Download those handbooks and evaluate their content and usefulness.

3. Design your own Instrumental Music Student Permanent File (IMSPF) form.

4. Write a short paper offering your viewpoint on the following: Should band or orchestra awards be based on a merit-type system, should every child get an award for each year in an ensemble, or should no special awards be given to ensemble members?

5. Discuss what you believe to be the most important items in an outstanding music facility.

# For Reference and Further Reading

Covey, Stephen R. (1990). *The Seven Habits of Highly Effective People*: Restoring the Character Ethic. New York: Fireside

Covey, Stephen R. (1992). *Principle-Centered Leadership*. New York: Fireside.

Gary, Charles, ed. (1966). *Music Buildings, Rooms and Equipment*. Reston, VA: Music Educators National Conference.

Geerdes, Harold P. (1975). *Planning and Equipping Educational Music Facilities*. Reston, VA: Music Educators National Conference.

Geerdes, Harold P. (1976, January). *Music facilities: how to make the best of them*. Paper presented at the Midwestern Conference on School Vocal and Instrumental Music, Ann Arbor, MI.

Geerdes, Harold P. (1981, January). *Your music rooms: asset or liability?* Paper presented at the Midwestern Conference on School Vocal and Instrumental Music, Ann Arbor, MI.

House, Robert (1965). *Instrumental Music for Today's Schools*. Englewood Cliffs, NJ: Prentice-Hall.

Lautzenheiser, Tim (1992). *The Art of Successful Teaching: A Blend of Content and Context*. Chicago: GIA Pub.

McCabe, Donald W. et al. (1973). *The ASBDA Curriculum Guide*. Pittsburgh, PA: Volkwein Bros.

*Opportunity-To-Learn Standards for Music Instruction: Grades PreK-12 (1994)*. Reston, VA: Music Educators National Conference.

Singleton, Ira C., and Anderson, Simon V. (1969). *Music in the Secondary Schools, 2nd ed*. Boston: Allyn and Bacon, Inc.

Walker, Darwin E. (1998). *Teaching Music: Managing the Successful Music Program*. New York: Schirmer Books.

Chapter Ten

# ORGANIZING AND ADMINISTERING YOUR TEACHING

## Rehearsal Organization

### *Seating Plans*

The seating plan you use in your ensemble will change from year to year. It may change because the number of students in each section has changed, or because of changes in the performance ability of the sections, or to reflect your desire for a slightly different sound from your ensemble. Obviously, the size and shape of your performance area will influence your seating plan decisions. The way you seat the ensemble directly affects the balance and quality of the full ensemble tone.

The jazz ensemble set-up discussed in Chapter 4 (figure 4-2) is probably the most common set-up for school jazz ensembles. Some directors will alter the rhythm section placement (such as moving guitar and bass closer together and drum set more toward the front) or the order of saxophones (moving tenor sax 2 to between alto sax 2 and baritone sax to put the traditional saxophone soloists—tenor sax 1 and alto sax 1—closer to the rhythm section).

The orchestra seating plan has developed into a traditional plan over the years. Figure 10-1 is typical of most full orchestra seating plans. Violin I and violin II sections are grouped together on the conductor's left so that their sound (projecting from the violin f-holes) is more easily heard. Figure 10-2 could be used to project the viola section sound for better balance with the rest of the string section. The placement of the winds and percussion is standard, though some alteration may be needed if sections are larger or smaller than normal. Note that first chair or principal players in each wind section are placed toward the center of the set-up (they are identified by a "dot"). This groups principal players together for improved wind section pitch, style, and balance. The placement of the principal player for each section in each of the following examples is identified by a dot.

**Figure 10-1. Full Orchestra seating plan**

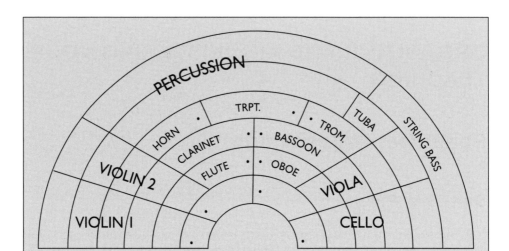

**Figure 10-2. Full Orchestra with split violins**

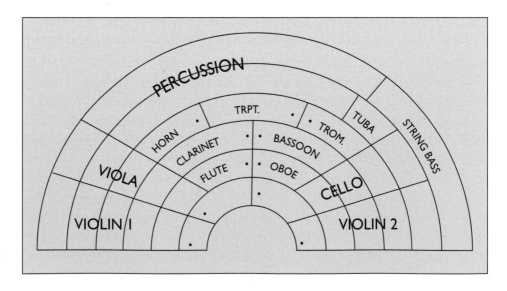

A basic set-up for a string orchestra is found in Figure 10-3.

**Figure 10-3. String Orchestra seating plan**

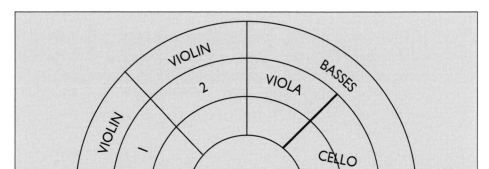

The set-up used by bands is certainly *not* standardized. Variables—age of the players, numbers in each section, the lack of some instruments, etc.—make a "traditional" band set-up impossible. It may be best just to give some guidelines and suggestions—with a few possible plans—to consider when designing an appropriate band seating plan.

- Keep together sections that play similar parts (alto saxophones near French horns; bass clarinets near baritone saxophones and bassoons; euphoniums near trombones; tenor saxophones near euphoniums; etc.).
- Place trombones, and trumpets and cornets, according to the strength of those sections and the kind of band sound that you prefer. Because these instruments are directional, you will hear a more "unfiltered" sound if they are placed in the middle of the band and facing the audience, but their sound seems to be more blended—even less harsh—when placed at the sides of the band. Obviously, a trumpet and cornet section that contains mostly cornets will also have a markedly different sound than one with mostly trumpets.
- Place the tuba section near the tympani. This will improve the fundamental pitch accuracy of the band. Also, place the bass drum near the tympani to improve rhythmic accuracy and cohesion.
- Place flutes in the front row for better projection, with the first chair player on your left.
- Place the first-chair person on the outside in sections seated at the sides of the set-up.

249

- Place keyboard percussion instruments near the outside of the set-up for better projection. Those instruments with less projection (chimes, vibes, and marimba) should be closest to the audience.
- Read *Effective Performance of Band Music* by W. Francis McBeth for important insights about achieving a balanced band sound. You will improve section balance if you place more players on the low parts and fewer on the high parts. In an 18-member clarinet section, that might mean having four players on the first part, six on the second part, and eight on the third part.

**Figure 10-4. Young Band with Incomplete Instrumentation**

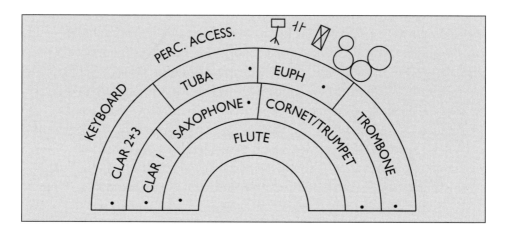

**Figure 10-5. Large Band seating plan No. 1**

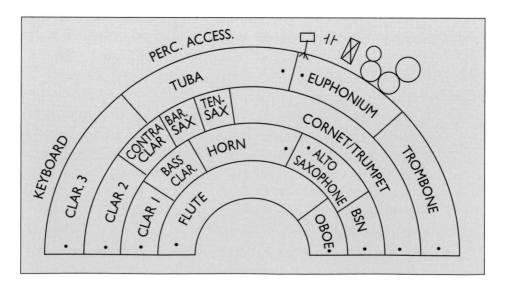

*Figure 10-6. Large Band seating plan No. 2*

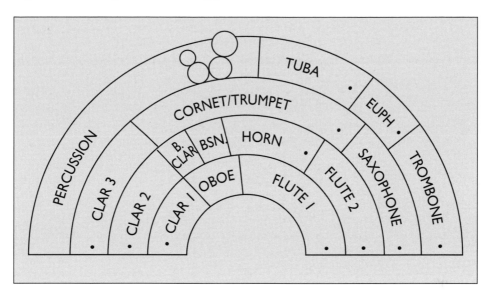

Figure 10-4 is an example of one possible set-up for a young band with incomplete instrumentation. One possible set-up for an older band with complete instrumentation is found in Figure 10-5. Again, note that first chair players are identified by a "dot" where appropriate. There could be many variables in this set-up because of unusually large or small sections, or missing sections (such as contra-alto or contra-bass clarinets and bassoons). Note the placement of tubas and bass drum near the tympani; snare drum and cymbals near the bass drum; and mallet percussion near the audience. Also, alto saxophones and horns are seated together; and tubas, bass clarinets, contra-clarinets, and baritone saxophones are in close proximity. In this set-up the bassoon is placed at the outside of a row, not near the other low wood-winds, because it is difficult to project the bassoon sound over a full band sound. In Figure 10-6 the cornets and trumpets are in the middle of the set-up, flutes are split in two rows on the conductor's right, bassoons and bass clarinets are placed together (since they often play similar parts), and saxophones are placed on the outside of their row.

Many successful band directors prefer a wind ensemble concept for their bands. Generally, this means the use of only one player per part except in clarinets and possibly flutes. Some directors add an extra tuba, trombone, trumpet, horn, or euphonium to improve ensemble balance. The wind ensemble concept is based on the model of an orchestral wind section. Therefore, an expanded version of the orchestral winds seating plan is often used for the basic wind ensemble seating plan.

**Figure 10-7. Wind Ensemble seating plan No. 1**

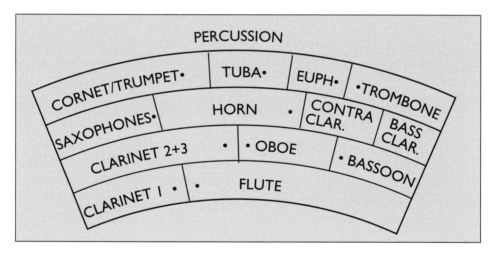

**Figure 10-8. Wind Ensemble seating plan No. 2**

Figure 10-7 is an example of the "wedge" set-up that resembles the orchestral winds model. Note the placement of first-chair players to the inside of the set-up so that they can better hear each other. Figure 10-8 is a more open, wider set-up with slightly different placement of some sections. The rows in this set-up are slightly arched and have more players per row. There are many variations to these two basic wind ensemble set-ups.

## Auditions and Challenges

The assessment of student performance is an important diagnostic and planning tool. Only after assessing the performance of each ensemble member can you accurately complete the Ensemble Evaluation Form mentioned in Chapter 5 (Fig. 5-1). Understanding the strengths and weaknesses of the individuals in your ensemble helps you design instruction (including planning how to address any discovered performance deficiencies) and choose appropriate literature.

*Figure 10-9. Placement Audition Form*

**THE YPSILANTI HIGH SCHOOL BANDS - Placement Audition Form**

Name _____

Instrument _____ Class _____

Score _____

Grade _____

Band _____

| I. **Solo** (50 points) | | II. **Scales** (25 points) | |
|---|---|---|---|
| Tone | (10) __ | _____ (5) _____ | |
| Intonation | (10) _____ | _____ (5) _____ | |
| Rhythm | (10) _____ | _____ (5) _____ | |
| Technique | (10) _____ | _____ (5) _____ | |
| Interpretation | (10) _____ | _____ (5) _____ | |
| Sub-Total _____ | | Sub-Total _____ | |

III. **Sight-Reading** (25 points) _____     **Comments:**

Most instrumental music teachers use performance assessments to assign grades and playing positions (part and chair) for their students. This is an important kind of "accountability" check to make sure that students are practicing regularly and are making musical progress on all assigned literature. You will do well to use a standardized audition or performance assessment form. Figure 10-9 is an example of a Band Placement Form that you might use for a large-scale assessment near the end of the school year (or earlier) to assign band and chair placement for the next school year. You might use a form like Figure 10-10 for regular performance assessments, and then give copies of the forms to students so they can use your written comments to improve their performance. A useful form for large-group chair placement auditions is found in Figure 10-11. This form has two blank columns to allow the addition of scales or sight-reading to the performance criteria. A form like this—since it contains the evaluation and grades of each student in a section—should not be reviewed by students.

*Figure 10-10. Performance Assessment Form*

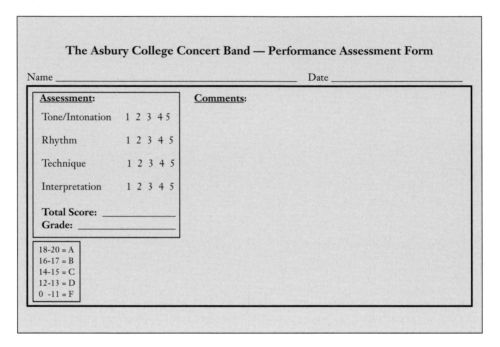

Many teachers allow students to challenge for the chair position of others in their section, either by on-the-spot challenges of anyone in the section on assigned days or by carefully prescribed procedures that allow students to challenge only one chair position at a time. A challenge allows students to improve their chair position—a very positive thing for students who simply had a bad day at the last assessment; and it almost guarantees a heightened level of practice for both students involved.

One challenge system that a number of public school teachers use is to allow students to challenge the next chair position after a performance assessment is completed, but not within one or two weeks before a concert. This prevents unsettling changes just before performances. To initiate a challenge, both the challenger and the challengee go to the teacher at the same time. Usually it is a good idea to schedule the challenge for one week later to give both students adequate preparation time. Both students should choose music (which you approve) to be used for the challenge. You may want to have a policy that during a challenge you may add any of the literature or technique

**Figure 10-11. Chair Placement Test Form**

| The Ypsilanti High School Bands — Chair Placement Test | | | | | | | | | | |
|---|---|---|---|---|---|---|---|---|---|---|
| Name | Tone | Intonation | Rhythm | Technic & Artic. | Style/Musician. | | Total Points | Comments | New Chair | Grade |
| | | | | | | | | | | |
| | | | | | | | | | | |
| | | | | | | | | | | |
| | | | | | | | | | | |
| | | | | | | | | | | |
| | | | | | | | | | | |
| | | | | | | | | | | |
| | | | | | | | | | | |
| | | | | | | | | | | |
| | | | | | | | | | | |
| | | | | | | | | | | |
| | | | | | | | | | | |
| | | | | | | | | | | |
| | | | | | | | | | | |
| | | | | | | | | | | |
| | | | | | | | | | | |
| | | | | | | | | | | |
| | | | | | | | | | | |
| | | | | | | | | | | |
| | | | | | | | | | | |

Band_____ Section_____ Music_____ Date_____

studies currently being used in rehearsals—or even a sight-reading excerpt—if the challenge is very close or tied.

The time to hear a challenge would usually be at the very end of a rehearsal, before school, after school, or during lunch hour. Have both students go with you to a practice room. Ask the challenger to play first, then have the students alternate playing all of the assigned material as you use one of the various evaluation forms to determine the challenge winner. Add up the points and make your decision right away—it never gets any easier when you put it off, and the point sys-

255

tem should clearly determine a winner. Tell the students your decision before they leave the room. Students may set another challenge right away, but it is best to call for a little break after a student unsuccessfully challenges the same person two or three times. A challenge system should not become harassment! You may find a Challenge Form (Figure 10-12) to be helpful in keeping track of the entire challenge process.

You may want to consider using a "blind" challenge system. In this system one of your student leaders or another teacher monitors the challenge and assigns a number or letter to both performers, and announces the start of each performance. You would then evaluate the performance of "Student A" and "Student B" and decide the challenge winner. At that point the monitor would disclose the names of the two students. This system is helpful in maintaining the highest level of confidence, by students and parents, in the impartiality of the challenge process.

*Figure 10-12. Challenge Form*

## CHALLENGE FORM

_____has challenged
(challenger's signature)

_____
(challengee's signature)

The challenge will be heard on _____at _____
(date)                  (time)

The music for the challenge will be:_____

Approved by director:_____Date_____
(signature)

**Challenge Rules:**
1. The challenger will give the challengee a one week notice.
2. Both the challenger and challengee will select music for the challenge.

3. Anyone who refuses a challenge will automatically forfeit his or her chair.
4. You may only challenge one chair position at a time.
5. Scales, other music in the folder, and sight-reading may be added by the director.
6. No challenges will be heard in the two weeks before a performance.

I do not recommend holding challenges in front of the rest of the section or the full band. We have all heard (or been part of) such challenges, and we know that they produce a very high level of anxiety that usually compromises the musicality of the performance. Fine music is not made in a climate of fear. Many students, especially lower achieving students, will find this system to be embarrassing or even harassing. Certainly there are times to hear students play individually in the full ensemble rehearsal, but these times should be infrequent and justified by strong pedagogical pay-offs. Grading or chair position changes should rarely, if ever, be a part of these live assessments. Having students play individually in the full rehearsal may become necessary when expected progress is not being made; when there are significant technical, stylistic, or pitch differences in the section; or when it is obvious that some people are not able to play a part of the music accurately and must be asked not to play it again until it is learned.

The use of a fair and organized challenge system can be a strong motivator for students and a means for students to demonstrate improvement. Be sure you have explained the reasons for challenges. Although a challenge system can encourage students to practice and improve on their instruments, be careful not to let competition become too intense. A challenge system mishandled can create unneeded and unhealthy tensions between friends and throughout the band.

## Assessment and Grades

Taking accurate class attendance and assigning grades are important tasks for any teacher. You will need a system for marking attendance (some schools require that all teachers use the same system); and you must establish clear, measurable, and realistic criteria for assigning grades. Any ambiguity in your plan to assign grades invites conflict and dissension in your classes.

257

First, a basic premise: It is a grade, not a guess. Too many music teachers assign grades solely on the basis of daily attendance, class behavior, and performance attendance. While all of these items are essential for an orderly classroom and acceptable performances, they do not provide a means for measuring individual student achievement in music or for raising the level of student achievement. It is little wonder that few administrators and teachers of other subjects think of music as a rigorous, academic subject. In fact, many college admissions offices disregard high school music grades when they make admissions decisions.

Meaningful testing and assessment is essential in all subjects. Colwell (1970) has written that "The real value of testing is not the ability to predict but rather the ability to improve learning by giving direction to the learning efforts of students and teachers" (p. 72).

Some educational terminology can be confusing because it seems to change slightly with new educational movements, and sometimes has slightly different meanings as applied to different grade levels or subjects. The following is a list of some terms related to evaluation of student performance for the purpose of diagnostic prescription and the assigning of student grades.

- **Measurement** is the use of an assessment instrument to objectively quantify performance of skills or demonstration of knowledge.
- In an educational setting, **evaluation** or **assessment** refers to the interpretation of data that shows student performance of educational objectives.
- **Formative evaluation** is a preliminary, diagnostic, or in-process evaluation.
- **Summative evaluation** is a final, culminating, or comprehensive evaluation.
- **Authentic** or **performance assessment** uses assessment tasks that ask the student to *do* something to demonstrate attainment of a skill or understanding. This is sometimes referred to as "praxial assessment."
- A **portfolio** is a collection of individual student work representative of that student's work over a period of time. In music performance classes, a portfolio might include written tests, completed forms from performance assessments, audio or video tapes of individual student performance, or adjudicators' rating sheets from solo and ensemble festivals.

Performance assessments, such as playing tests, are important student motivators. They also are a means of evaluating teacher effectiveness, are important diagnostic and prescriptive tools, and provide one part of the grading criteria in your ensemble. I recommend giving at least two or three performance assessments each grading period (6-week, or 9-week periods). Early in a school year you may want to focus these assessments on material from technique books or scale memorization, but later you will want to evaluate the work of students on the music programmed for concerts. Students benefit from performance assessment by getting feedback from the teacher about their current performance levels and by receiving suggestions for improvement. The teacher benefits by learning if rehearsal strategies and assignments have been effective.

Figure 10-10 is an evaluation form that works well for regular performance assessments. There is adequate space to write comments and suggestions for improvement to the student, and a simple scoring rubric to determine grades. The Total Points number could also be used to assign new chair seating. Figure 10-11 (Chair Placement Test Form) would be appropriate to use at the beginning of a semester for initial chair placement or early in a semester when playing tests are primarily on technical studies that would not require feedback to students. Use a ten-point scale for each category on this form, then total the scores and assign grades based on a percentage rubric (91-100 percent = A, 81-90 percent = B, etc.). Total Scores may be used to determine new chair placements.

One of the most efficient performance assessment procedures is to have a tape recorder in each practice room to record students during the rehearsal. Assuming that there are at least four or five rooms available for testing, a full band or orchestra of 70-80 members can be recorded in one regular class period. Assign sections to specific rooms so that a fairly equal number of students will use each room. It is usually best to place a sheet of paper on the music stand in each room, reminding students of their assignment. After your ensemble warm-up time, have the first two students assigned to each practice room go to the room. The first student should go into the room and the second should wait at the door. You should start each recorder. After the first student in each room completes the performance, that student goes back to the rehearsal room and the third student in the section leaves to wait by the practice room door. This continues through each section in each room until all students have completed their performance. Students need to be reminded not to play in the hallway as they wait for their turn to test, and they should be instructed not to turn off the tape recorder at any time. Probably you will need to establish a policy that the total score for any student turning off a tape record will be lowered by five points. This will prevent a student from entering the practice room, turning off the recorder, and practicing for 10 minutes—or, checking the taped performance and re-record if unhappy with the result! Both of these situations would prevent you from completing a full ensemble assessment during one class period, and would be unfair to other students who followed instructions.

Recording performance assessments saves an enormous amount of rehearsal time. One suggestion: as you listen to tapes, resist the temptation to rewind and listen to some of them a second time. Try to focus your attention on listening to the tapes and trust your initial judgment. Otherwise, you may double or triple the time it should take you to complete your assessments. If you were hearing a live testing performance, you would not have a rewind option.

Another way to use cassette tapes is to have each student supply a recorded cassette that is due on a certain date. The advantages of this procedure are that you use no rehearsal time (and avoid the distraction of students coming and going to practice rooms), students can re-record until they get a performance they like (guided practice time), and students can keep all their performance assessments on one cassette for future evaluation or reference. Instruct students to have their tapes cued up to the current assignment when they turn in tapes. I have also had students e-mail performances in a computer sound file format! The obvious concern about students turning in their own recording is to ensure that it is, in fact, a recording of their own performance!

While performance assessments are the principal criteria for determining marking period grades, several other items might be considered. If you think that something is important for students to know, you might consider testing that knowledge or skill and making it a part of student grades. Many teachers understand the value and importance of teaching students about the music they are preparing for performance, and that information could easily be measured and assessed through a written test. At least one written test each marking period about the music being studied in band or orchestra could be a valuable incentive for students to learn and retain valued information.

Other items you might consider in determining student grades include a daily performance grade, regular instrument inspection grade, student self-evaluation, demerits, etc. A daily performance grade is your evaluation of the student's musical proficiency in rehearsals. This is a relatively subjective grade and not as reliable as some other grading criteria. I recommend that you do instrument inspections at least once each marking period. Instruments that are well maintained spend less time in the repair shop. Parents appreciate not having to spend money for instrument repairs, and you will benefit by having fewer students unable to play in class because their instruments are in for repairs. Figure 10-13 is an example of an easy-to-use inspection form. A useful procedure for inspections is to announce the inspections at least one week before they are to begin and then ask several sections to leave their instruments (in cases) after rehearsal each day until all sections are completed. Make sure all cases have a nametag! A suggested grading scale is 9 or 10 "yes" = A, 8 "yes" = B, 7 = C, etc. It takes just a few minutes to complete an inspection using this form, and you will probably be ready to have students pick up their instrument at the end of the day.

*Figure 10-13. Instrument Inspection Form*

**INSTRUMENT INSPECTION FORM**      Name _____

Date_____      Grade_____

General:                                                                Yes   No

| General | Yes | No |
|---|---|---|
| 1. The outside of the case is clean and the latches work. | | |
| 2. The inside of the case is clean and free of extraneous matter. | | |
| 3. The outside of the instrument is clean and free of fingerprints. | | |
| 4. The mouthpiece is clean and in good condition. Brass mpc. ends are in round. | | |

Brass:

| Brass | Yes | No |
|---|---|---|
| 1. The instrument is free of major, critical dents. | | |
| 2. The inside of the instrument is clean. | | |
| 3. All slides are clean and lubricated. | | |
| 4. All valves are clean and oiled. | | |
| 5. Water key corks and springs are in good condition. | | |
| 6. Felts & corks (and strings) on valves are in good condition. | | |

Woodwinds:

| Woodwinds | Yes | No |
|---|---|---|
| 1. The instrument is swabbed and dry. | | |
| 2. There is no dirt or dust under the keys or rods. | | |
| 3. The keys have been recently oiled. The bore on wood instruments is oiled. | | |
| 4. Cork joints have been recently greased. Flute joints are clean and in round. The flute cork assembly is in the proper position. | | |
| 5. All pads, corks, and felts are in good condition. | | |
| 6. The instrument appears to be in proper adjustment. | | |

Student self-evaluation is an important piece of information. Even if it is not actually a part of the student's grade, it will give you important insights about each student in your ensemble. A Personal Rehearsal Evaluation (PRE) form (see Figure 10-14) should be completed by all students each week and recorded in the grade book. Students should also be encouraged to write at least one comment on the back of the form. Student comments can be an insightful source of feedback about your rehearsals. Since there are 20 possible points on this PRE, the average of all the PRE scores could be 20 percent of the marking period grade. You should feel free to alter the scale on the PRE or change the numbers or type of questions on the form.

*Figure 10-14. Personal Rehearsal Evaluation form*

**Personal Rehearsal Evaluation Form for Band and Orchestra**

Name _____ Date _____

| | Seldom | | Sometimes | | Always |
|---|---|---|---|---|---|
| | 1 | 2 | 3 | 4 | 5 |
| 1. I was on time and warmed-up | 1 | 2 | 3 | 4 | 5 |
| 2. I stayed "on task" with no extra talking | 1 | 2 | 3 | 4 | 5 |
| 3. I was prepared for rehearsals/I practiced as needed | 1 | 2 | 3 | 4 | 5 |
| 4. I am a positive member with a good attitude | 1 | 2 | 3 | 4 | 5 |

Total Points: _____

Note: On the reverse side please write your evaluation of the rehearsal and any helpful suggestions. Thank you!

Because of school district attendance policies, your class attendance usually will not be reflected in marking period grades. Performing ensembles, however, have additional attendance responsibilities (after school or evening rehearsals, sectionals, concerts, festivals, etc.) for which students must be held accountable. One accountability method is a demerit system like the one in the band handbook found in Chapter 9 (Figure 9-1). In that system, students are given the opportunity to "work off" any demerits by spending one hour working in the band or orchestra room for each demerit.

Students should be expected to practice regularly on their instruments in order to make musical and technical progress. Adding that practice expectation to the criteria used to determine marking period grades should encourage a regular practice routine. Many music dealers supply practice cards for band and orchestra directors, but you may want to produce your own cards to fit your particular need. Figure 10-15 is an example of a card that could be copied on cardstock or paper and distributed to students at the beginning of a marking period. One side of the card (8.5-by-5.5 inches) is the actual practice record that requires a parent's initials to verify practice time. It has a small column for the teacher to check after practice time has been recorded. The other side explains the "why" and "how" of practicing, states the grad-

*Figure 10-15a. Practice Card (side 1)*

**Bigtown High School Band and Orchestra**

**Practice Record**

The Practice Record is used as an incentive to practice regularly and to reward that regular practice routine. Obviously, we will make much more progress as a group if all of the individuals in the group are working hard and preparing their lessons regularly. There is <u>always</u> music to work on, including the warm-up and technique books used in each ensemble. Your practice period should start with a careful warm-up and then work on new music or the things that need the most attention. The easier, "fun" pieces should be practiced last. Find the time of day best for you to practice and stick with it. You should use a music stand in a well-lighted room and away from distractions.

All practice records are to be turned in during class on each Monday and are to be initialed by a parent or guardian. The time practiced each week is recorded. At the end of each grading period the practice times will be totaled and averaged to arrive at the Average Practice Time per week. A grade is given for that Average Practice Time. The Average Practice Time grade, your daily performance grade, and the grades for your regular playing tests, will determine your marking period grade.

Average Practice Time Grading Scale:
3 hours average = A
2 hours average = B
1 hour average = C
.5 hour average = D
0 hour average = F

*Figure 10-15b. Practice Card (side 2)*

**Individual Practice Record**

Name _____   Class Hour _____

| Week of: | Mon. | Tues. | Wed. | Thurs. | Fri. | Sat. | Sun | Total | Parent Signature | |
|---|---|---|---|---|---|---|---|---|---|---|
| | | | | | | | | | | |
| | | | | | | | | | | |
| | | | | | | | | | | |
| | | | | | | | | | | |
| | | | | | | | | | | |
| | | | | | | | | | | |
| | | | | | | | | | | |
| | | | | | | | | | | |
| | | | | | | | | | | |

(Enter the number of <u>minutes</u> practiced on each day and total the <u>minutes</u> for the week.)

263

ing scale, and lists the procedure for turning in cards. This is important information for your students. It is best to collect cards on the same day each week and return them the next day.

Using the system discussed above, a possible grading structure for your middle or high school band or orchestra might be:

| | |
|---|---|
| Performance Assessments (2 @ 20 points) | 40 points |
| Personal Rehearsal Evaluation (average) | 20 points |
| Instrument Inspection | 10 points |
| Daily Performance Grade | 20 points |
| Weekly practice Grade | 10 points |

Total Points Possible　　100 points

| | |
|---|---|
| 91-100 | = A |
| 81-90 | = B |
| 71-80 | = C |
| 61-70 | = D |
| 0-60 | = E [or F] |

Note: Any demerits not worked off will lower your grade.

Some schools adopt a school-wide grading scale in order to standardize numerical expressions for grading. Even in districts without a school-wide policy, you may find it best to follow the scale used by a majority of teachers in the school. Grading scales that are markedly different from those used by most teachers in a school will not be warmly received.

Administrators and teachers of other subjects sometimes remark that students do not learn new material during each of their semesters in band or orchestra. Music teachers know that students learn different literature, acquire new performance techniques, and assume greater musical leadership as they continue in instrumental music. Not only is that sometimes a "hard-sell" to non-musicians, it is sometimes difficult to quantify the progress by students in individual musical performance and understandings. Some teachers require students to memorize and perform progressively more difficult major and minor scales in each grade level. This "scale curriculum" becomes an additional item to use in determining student grades. Another suggestion is to establish a solo literature curriculum for each instrument with increasingly more challenging literature each semester. Requiring all 9th grade trumpet players to play "Piece A" in the first semester, "Piece B" in their spring semester, "Piece C" in the first semester of their sophomore year, etc. provides a means of guiding the musical and technical develop of individuals in your ensemble. All students should be required to play their piece for a grade at the end of the semester in a recital or as a "jury" after school. This adds accountability and provides additional criteria for marking period grades. A required solo curriculum is especially helpful in school districts lacking local private teachers for band or orchestra instruments.

Most schools will not have enough accompanists to work with every student on solos. "Music Minus One" is an answer to that dilemma. "Music Minus One" has an extensive catalog of recordings of standard solo literature for each instrument. The recordings contain a performance of the solo and accompaniment by outstanding professional performers, and a track with only the accompaniment. This series has a wealth of outstanding solo literature at different grade levels. You might consider purchasing a set of these recordings for your music program. A catalog and other material is available from:

Music Minus One
50 Executive Boulevard
Elmsford, NY 10523-1325
(telephone: 914-592-1188)

Other publishers, such as Curnow Music Press, are beginning to make recordings like this available in their solo catalogs. In addition, the *Smart Music Studio* (formerly *Vivace Practice Studio*) is a collection of solo literature for various instruments. The great advantage to this series is that when played on the CD-ROM player in your computer (with a microphone), the accompaniment will alter tempo to follow the soloist performance.

You could also use the chamber ensemble program discussed in Chapter 4 as part of the course requirements you establish to determine marking period grades in your large ensembles. Most rehearsals of these chamber ensembles should be before or after school, and a final performance—in a recital or a jury—should be scheduled at the end of each semester.

Some teachers find that requiring or giving extra-credit to students who complete a computer-based program for music theory, aural skills, etc., is an efficient and effective means of teaching important information. There are many excellent computer programs available in music. This is also an excellent way to address the National Standards dealing with music arranging and composition. Some teachers give credit to students who attend college or professional concerts, do book reports, watch approved concerts on television, read magazine articles about music, watch approved videos about music, listen to band or orchestra recordings, etc.

Another idea for a grading procedure in your ensemble is to establish a basic set of the above items that you feel are essential, which would earn for the students who complete the basic set a grade of "C" for the marking period. Also list items that students can select to earn a higher grade, and indicate the number of selected items required for each higher grade. You may want to have students complete a "grade contract" at the beginning of the marking period as a means to help them set goals and guide them to successful experiences.

Whatever criteria you finally establish for your ensembles and courses, they must be realistic, meaningful, and measurable. Your criteria must be age-appropriate and should reflect your own philosophy of instrumental music education. The criteria must be clearly stated in writing, have the approval of your school administration, and be distributed to students and their parents. No one should be uncertain about the academic expectations and requirements of students in your classes.

Accurate record-keeping (of attendance and grades) is an essential duty for all teachers. Many teachers now keep all attendance and grade records on a computer grading program as an efficient way to store that information. Most programs will automatically do the mathematics to arrive at marking period grades after you have assigned point values to the various items in your grading criteria. Always be sure that you keep at least one backup disk of this valuable and confidential information. Many teachers keep one backup copy at school and one in their briefcase just in case of some major disaster.

There are many options for organizing a hand-written grade book. Some teachers of ensembles enter names by section and in chair order so that attendance taking is easier. Others enter students' names in alphabetical order by last name, the way class lists arrive from the administration. An alphabetical listing facilitates accurate record keeping. The next step is to enter the dates for each day of the marking period from left to right at the top of each column of boxes. As mentioned previously, you may take attendance as students are assembling for class by simply circling the names of missing students on a copy of the ensemble seating chart. Additional notations can be made on the chart to indicate tardy students, those called to the office during the hour, etc. That information can be transferred to the grade book after class. It is important that accurate and clear records be maintained because the teacher's grade book is the official attendance record and grade list for each class.

There are many ways to record attendance. Some teachers devise very elaborate codes for attendance taking and others use just a few basic symbols. Many school districts have an established attendance code that all teachers are required to use. One simple attendance code is the use of a lower-case letter "a" to indicate an absence—a lower-case letter is used to prevent confusion with letter grades—and the letter "t" to indicate a tardy. If an absence or tardiness is officially "excused," the letter is circled. Another type of attendance code is found in Figure 10-16. Whatever system you choose to use for attendance record-keeping, be sure to be consistent, make your entries as neatly as possible, and attach a copy of your attendance code to the inside cover of your grade book.

*Figure 10-16. Attendance Code*

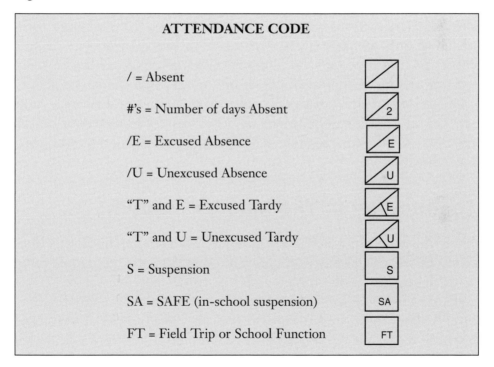

**ATTENDANCE CODE**

/ = Absent

#'s = Number of days Absent

/E = Excused Absence

/U = Unexcused Absence

"T" and E = Excused Tardy

"T" and U = Unexcused Tardy

S = Suspension

SA = SAFE (in-school suspension)

FT = Field Trip or School Function

# Private Lessons

The "secret" reason for the success of many school music programs is a strong private lesson program. Students who study privately are able to make individual technical and musical progress at a much faster rate than is usually made in an ensemble setting. In addition, students who study privately are exposed to the solo literature for their instrument, learn advanced techniques (alternate fingerings, multiple tonguing, reed-making and adjusting, etc.), and (through their teacher) have someone to emulate in their playing. Students who study privately usu-

267

ally become more involved and supportive of the school music program and are more self-confident student musicians.

An active private lesson program is a "win-win" situation for everyone—the music program benefits because students play better; students benefit because they are more likely to excel and become mature musicians; and parents benefit because of the increased involvement and opportunities that become available to their children. Many school music teachers reward students who study privately by giving "extra credit" toward their marking period grades, or by awarding merits toward band and orchestra awards.

In rural school districts, or for students who cannot afford private lessons, you may become the private lesson teacher on many of the instruments in your ensemble. In addition, check with all the band and orchestra teachers in neighboring school districts to see if they accept private students on their major instrument or if they have any fine private teachers in their community. Another idea is to arrange for a group of outstanding college students from a nearby college or university to come to your school on a certain night to give lessons. Keep a list of private teachers that you recommend and make it available to students and parents at the beginning of each semester. Private lessons are so important that you might want to consider having your boosters club provide some lesson scholarships to those students who cannot afford lessons.

## Technology In The Music Program

Many music teachers across the country are using technology effectively in the classroom to increase student knowledge and develop skills and understandings. New and exciting developments in computer software and hardware—and the promise of useful new technologies—offer teachers new tools to meet the variety of educational needs and learning styles of their students. Brian Moore (1989) reminds us that "The rapidly evolving nature of technology demands a constant awareness and revision of current practice to realize technology's potential as a learning and teaching resource" (p. 116).

Computer software useful for music educators includes programs in notation, sequencing, ear training and theory, accompaniment creation, interactive CD-ROMs for music history and listening, etc. New audio and video recording technologies may also be useful in the music classroom. You will be responsible for deciding what technology is appropriate and helpful for your students. Learn what is available, and remember the cautionary note raised by Jacques Ellul (1990) in his book *The Technological Bluff*—the "bluff" being that all technology is inevitable. Ellul suggests that we carefully decide whether a new technological development will improve our society and take us where we want to go, and then decide if we want to embrace that new technology.

The Internet has many helpful resources for music teachers. Hundreds of Web sites contain a wealth of information that can enrich your band or orchestra program. A list of music-related Web sites is found in Appendix C, but many more can be found through a search for your particular topic. As with all the information about new music publications you receive each year, you will need to sift through all that is available to find what is helpful and appropriate for your use.

We often get caught up in the dizzying procession of new technological wonders and forget that some "old" technology still is useful in our band and orchestra rehearsal rooms. Every band and orchestra room should have a high quality sound reproduction system so that students may hear examples of exemplary performances and their own performances. Small digital tuners are a valuable aid for rapidly tuning an ensemble, and can help students visualize and chart the intonation tendencies of their instrument. Metronomes are essential for individual practice and full ensemble rehearsal to teach rhythmic and tempo accuracy and consistency. Of course no technology, new or old, matters unless it is used by a capable, enthusiastic teacher.

## Teaching Away from Your Expertise

In some school districts the band teacher will also be responsible for orchestra instruction, or the orchestra teacher for band instruction. You will certainly feel most prepared to teach in your major, but many band teachers find success as orchestra teachers and many orchestra teachers find success as band teachers. Since all instrumental music education majors take instrument methods courses, they should possess the skills and knowledge to find success with a band *or* orchestra. You will probably have to work to improve weaknesses on your secondary instruments so that your students will receive excellent instruction.

If part of your job is to teach instruments with which you are marginally familiar, the first thing to do is look for help. Review instrument methods class textbooks, call friends in the same situation, read, attend clinics and workshops, practice on those other instruments, and maybe even take some private lessons on your secondary instruments. Do not try to "fake it" take the time to learn the teaching strategies and playing techniques that will make you a better teacher and your students better musicians.

In *Teaching Stringed Instruments in Classes* (1966) Elizabeth A.H. Green wrote, "Strings are not harder to teach than winds. Whereas the problem of the beginning wind player is that of building range, note by note, the problem of the string novice is the bi-manual functioning of his hands, each doing a specialized type of work. . . ." (p. 1) In addition, all of the technical concerns are visible on string instruments—unlike trying to figure out what the articulation problem is for some beginning trumpet player. This is a great help for the string teacher. Professor Green also provided a clear, sequential set of goals for the first few years of instruction (pp. 32-34) that both non-string players and string players will find of great value. It is also a model for band teachers to emulate in beginning band instruction.

Band directors teaching middle and high school strings will need to develop greater understanding of various bowing techniques and other technical skills. In the classic text *Orchestral Bowings and Routines* (1966), Professor Green—in addition to explaining the variety of possible string bowings—included an excellent listing of "The Effective Tricks of the Trade, Orchestrally." This is a list of typically encountered problems found in orchestral music along with accepted solutions. She also included suggestions for improving ensemble playing by the orchestra. You will also find a number of helpful texts published by the Music Educators National Conference (MENC) and the American String Teachers Association (ASTA).

Instrumentalists assigned to teach choir will want to know appropriate warm-up exercises, tone production techniques, choral enunciation, etc. An excellent resource is *The Choral Conductors Handbook* by Walter Ehret (1959). This text is a concise and helpful reference for anyone working in choral music. MENC also publishes a number of helpful books about teaching choral music.

If you are assigned to teach outside of your expertise, try to enjoy the experience and work hard to be an effective teacher. Also, remember that you are a *music* teacher, not just a band teacher or an orchestra teacher—you happen to be using the band or the orchestra to teach *music*. If you are a fine musician you can teach any of the music ensembles and be musically successful. If you, like many other music teachers, are asked to teach something like middle school choir to "fill out" your schedule, you may find that you can be successful in that assignment as well. You may even enjoy it!

## *For Discussion or Assignment*

1. Using MicroGrade or a similar computer grade book program, set up an imaginary class of 12 students, list course grading criteria, assign grades for those items, determine marking period grades, and print the results.

2. Find the Music Educators National Conference Web site and the Music Publishers Association Web site and locate information about copyright. Print both and place them in your course notebook.

3. At the MENC Web site, locate information about finding a job. Print that information and place it in your course notebook.

4. Monitor a Web-based chat group for band or orchestra directors for two weeks and write a summary of the issues discussed. If the site has an archive search option, find a topic of interest and print the results.

## *For Reference and Further Reading*

Boston, Bruce O. (1996). *Teacher Education for the Arts Disciplines*. Reston, VA: Music Educators National Conference.

Brimmer, Tim (2000). Choral technologies: an oxymoron? *The Resource Guide*. 6/2, 40.

Colwell, Richard (1970). *The Evaluation of Music Teaching and Learning*. Englewood Cliffs, NJ: Prentice-Hall, Inc.

Demoline, Kelly (1997). Getting started with music technology. *Canadian Music Educator*. Fall.

Demoline, Kelly (1998). What can music technology do for me? *Canadian Music Educator*. Spring.

Demoline, Kelly (1999). Choosing a composition program. *Canadian Music Educator*. Spring.

Elliott, Robert (1994). Improving ensemble recordings. *The Instrumentalist*. May, 56-64.

Ellul, Jacques (1990). *The Technological Bluff*. Grand Rapids, MI: Wm. B. Eerdmans Publishing Co.

Ehret, Walter (1959). *The Choral Conductor's Handbook*. Winona, MN: Hal Leonard.

Garofalo, Robert (1983). *Rehearsal Handbook for Band and Orchestra Students*. Ft. Lauderdale, FL: Meredith Music Publications.

Gordon, Edwin (1988). *Learning Sequences in Music*. Chicago: G.I.A. Publications.

Green, Elizabeth A.H. (1966). *Orchestral Bowings and Routines*. Ann Arbor: Campus Publishers.

Green, Elizabeth A. H. (1966). *Teaching Stringed Instruments in Classes*. Englewood Cliffs, NJ: Prentice-Hall, Inc.

Higgins, William (1992). Technology. In *Handbook of Research on Music Teaching and Learning*, ed. by Richard Colwell. New York: Schirmer Books.

House, Robert (1965). *Instrumental Music for Today's Schools*. Englewood Cliffs, NJ: Prentice-Hall.

Leonhard, Charles (1958). Evaluation in music education. In *Basic Concepts in Music Education*. Nelson B. Henry, ed. Chicago: The University of Chicago Press.

McBeth, W. Francis (1972). *Effective Performance of Band Music*. San Antonio, TX: Southern Music Co.

Moore, Brian (1989). Musical Thinking and Technology. In *Dimensions of Musical Thinking*, ed. by Eunice Boardman. Reston, VA: Music Educators National Conference.

*Performance Standards for Music: Grades PreK-12 (1996)*. Reston, VA: Music Educators National Conference.

Peters, David G. (2000). What chief school administrators should know about music technology. *The Resource Guide*. 6/2, 22-23.

Chapter Eleven

# HANDLING BUSINESS ISSUES

## A Public Relations Program

In all facets of life, two keys to success are organization and communication. Stephen Covey (1990) wrote that "Communication is the most important skill in life" (p. 237). Public relations—at its basic level—is communication; keeping people informed about your instrumental music program and interested in its success. Public relations (communication) is not a highly developed skill among school band or orchestra directors. It is, however, extremely important for the success of your program, and therefore requires a high priority in your professional work.

Public Relations can be defined as a continuing, long-term effort to inform your community (students, parents, teachers, administrators, school board members, alumni, all area residents, etc.) about the continuing activities and accomplishments of your instrumental music program. A good public relations program is much more than publicity—particularly when you consider that publicity can be positive or negative!

Obviously, a public relations program is most effective when the quality of the work being done by your ensembles is top notch. A good product will earn the respect and support of a community. Work to develop a positive image of your ensemble. You want people to think of your ensemble as one of the "quality" groups in the curriculum (Neidig, p. 61).

The booklet, *How to Promote Your Band*, published by the Selmer Company, states that "The basis of all band public relations programs is the contact between the band and the community and it is the director's responsibility to guide this contact into productive channels" (p. 20). In smaller communities this may mean that you will create the entire public relations program, but in larger communities with very active music programs, you will want to involve parents and students in a public relations committee. You will still need to guide the public relations effort to keep it compatible with your education philosophy and with school district policies concerning public relations and press releases. Some school districts have an official school information officer, and have policies in place that all school employees must follow. Learn to work with the system in place in your school district. Be sure to recruit one or more photographers (students or parents) to help visually record the events and accomplishments of your band or orchestra program.

One of the first things you might do after taking a new teaching position is meet the local newspaper editor and the education or arts writer. Ask about their deadlines for press releases and photos, and the size photo prints they prefer. Work to establish a good professional relationship with these people—and that includes following deadlines and not asking for special favors. You will probably find that if you supply the local media with timely and well written stories with real news value, they will become more supportive of you and your program. The result will be good story placement in the paper and occasional feature stories about your students. You may find that some local newspapers prefer to write their own stories from "fact sheets" that you supply to answer the questions "who, what, where, when, and how." Many newspapers now prefer to have this information submitted by e-mail or fax. Be sure to keep aware of newspaper staff changes so that your information is always addressed to the correct person. Also, do not forget to personally invite the newspaper editor and the education or arts reporter to attend your concerts.

If you use parents and students to assist in this effort, you might want to have a meeting to plan the long-term and short-term public relations needs of the band or orchestra. Start the planning with performances (concerts, recitals, festivals and contests, etc.) and events (tours, fundraising, etc.). Use a large planning calendar and write in those major events. Then, based on your knowledge of media deadlines, work backward to schedule press releases and photo sessions for each event. Make sure everyone knows who is responsible for each element of the process, and establish a checklist of items to be accomplished for each event. Figure 11-1 is an example of a concert promotion checklist. In each case, you should receive the press release to review before it is sent to the appropriate media. This oversight is essential to ensure the integrity of the information circulated about your program. You must be in control of the public relations program to control the flow of information and the amount and quality of effort, and to avoid duplication of effort.

After you have scheduled the public relations program for all of the major performances and events, you should have your committee brainstorm for possible stories about the ensemble or students. The committee may have some innovative ideas for news or special interest stories that can be scheduled in the less active weeks in the band or orchestra calendar.

**Figure 11-1. Concert Promotion Checklist**

## Concert Promotion Checklist

Name of Concert/Event _____

Date of Concert/Event: _____  Concert/Event Chair: _____

May of Last School Year:

____ Event on School Calendar

____ Facilities secured

____ Students and parents notified

Beginning of Each Semester:

____ Letter to "Friends," civic clubs and organizations, and seniors groups about semester events/concerts

2 Months Before Event:

____ Tentative program determined

1 Month Before Event:

____ Posters designed and sent to printer

____ Tickets (if needed) printed

____ Press releases prepared and approved

____ Ushers secured

____ Letters to civic clubs/seniors/etc.

____ Contact local banks/etc. about signs

3 Weeks Before Event:

____ PSAs to local radio, TV, and cable

____ Program copy to printer

____ Schedule photos for press release

2 Weeks Before Event:

____ Concert mailing to "Friends" list

____ Concert announcement to "Arts Calendar" in newspaper

____ Press release to school newspaper

1 Week Before Event:

____ Posters up in schools and community

____ Press release to all local newspapers

____ Daily PA announcements in school

____ Invitations to faculty, staff, and admin.

Day After Event:

____ Take down all posters

• • • • • • • • • •

275

## *Long-term Public Relations*

An effective long-term public relations program will include an active effort to demonstrate your credibility and your educational and musical authority in the community. This authority or credibility is not *given* to you simply by virtue of your employment in the local school district. You must earn it by your actions. Treat people well—students, parents, other teachers, secretaries, custodians, administrators, etc.—and show a genuine interest in them and their needs. If possible, join and be active in a local civic club. Be an active member of your local church, synagogue, temple, or mosque. Volunteer to chaperone school dances and other activities. Be supportive of the rest of the faculty and be involved in their social and professional activities. Your active and good-natured involvement in the total community will *earn* you credibility and authority. It will establish your position as a leader in your school and the community, a position from which you will be able to do your job with good will and greater ease.

Publish a regular booster club newsletter. One of the many computer programs available will make this job much easier and give the newsletter a professional appearance. You may find that some parents have writing experience and would be happy to help with this important project. See Figure 11-2 for an example of a basic short newsletter. A newsletter can be sent to parents, alumni, faculty, administrators, board of education members, and interested community members. Develop a "Friend of the Band" or "Friend of the Orchestra" list to use for newsletter mailings and concert announcements. This list can be developed over the years by inviting concertgoers to sign-up at the end of the concert to receive announcements of future concerts. Many schools now publish their newsletters on-line. This is a money saving idea, and it allows you to include links to further information on your Web site.

You might find that giving the board of education an annual "Progress Report to the Taxpayers" is an effective way to highlight the accomplishments of the program during the previous year. Programs by your large ensembles or chamber groups to PTA, district faculty meetings, civic clubs, and other community organizations elicit widespread public support for your program. In the school you can encourage the respect and support of the faculty and student body by such things as making bulletin boards that highlight your students' achievements, maintaining a trophy case to display recent awards and memorabilia, and even supplying a well rehearsed and enthusiastic pep band for athletic events.

*Figure 11-2. Sample Booster Club Newsletter*

# BAND BOOSTER NEWSLETTER

**Ypsilanti High School Band Booster Club**
**2095 Packard Road**
**Ypsilanti, Michigan 48197**                                    April 24

### IMPORTANT TOUR MEETING FOR PARENTS SCHEDULED

There will be a <u>very</u> important meeting for all students going on tour and at least <u>one</u> <u>parent</u> on Monday, May 6, at 8:00 p.m. in the band room. Please make sure you can attend this <u>very</u> important meeting. We will discuss our complete tour itinerary, go over all rules, meet our tour guide, and answer any questions you may have about the tour. If you have a conflict with this meeting, please call Mr. Cooper.

A few words about appropriate clothing for tour. We are representatives of our bands, school, and community. Student should dress in a tasteful and conservative manner at all times—including you choice of swim wear. If you have a question as to whether some particular clothing is appropriate, it probably isn't! We also request that you dress up a little for our flight to Florida and back home. Suits aren't necessary, but sweats are <u>not</u> appropriate!

There will be a special rehearsal for the Tour Band on Thursday, May 9, from 7:00-9:00 p.m.

### SPRING BAND CONCERT

The Spring Band Concert will be on Thursday, May 2. The concert will begin at 8:00 p.m. in the high school auditorium. We hope all of you can be with us for the concert and please invite your family and friends!

The concert will include performances by the Concert Band, Freshman Band, and Symphony Band. Also playing will be the newly formed Freshman Wind Ensemble of 40 players. Featured on the concert will be Senior trumpet player Robin Arrick.

A wide variety of music will be played, so be sure to attend! There is no admission charge.

### ROBIN ARRICK HONORED

Robin Arrick has been selected to perform in the State Honors Band! The top 100 band students from across the State were selected from those who scored 85 or above on their Proficiency Three Examination at the State Solo and Ensemble Festival. The State Honors Band will perform at Western Michigan University on May 11 as part of the Michigan Youth Arts Festival.

Congratulations Robin!

### BAND TAG DAYS

Our Annual Band Tag Days help support a variety of band projects, such as summer music camp scholarships and our special clinics program. The Tag Days are scheduled for Friday afternoon, May 10, and all day Saturday, May 11. Students will be asked to sign-up in pairs for a two-hour block of time. They also receive merits for their work. Please encourage your child to help out on this important project. Thanks!

### BAND BOOSTER MEETING

May 10th

8:00 p.m.          Band Room

### JAZZ BAND TO LANSING

The Jazz Band has been invited to play a concert on the steps of the Capitol Building in Lansing on May 22. This is part of Michigan Week activities. The band will play a 45-minute noontime concert for state government workers.

There are some extra seats on the bus if any parents would like to go with the Jazz Band. Call Mr. Cooper if you want to go. We will leave at 9:30 a.m.

### MEMORIAL DAY PARADE

The Memorial Day Parade will begin at 9:00 a.m. on Monday, May 27. The Marching Band and the Freshman Band will both march in the parade. Please plan any family travel plans to allow your child to be back in time for the parade. Thanks!

### BAND BANQUET

The Band Banquet will be held in the high school cafeteria on May 28 at 6:30 p.m. All band awards are given at that time and there is a short program. This banquet is for your full immediate family. You should bring your own table service and two dishes to pass (each dish should serve 10). The Freshmen and Juniors should bring a meat dish and either a vegetable or potato dish. Sophomores and Seniors should bring a dessert and either a vegetable or potato dish.

### BAND CONCERT

May 2                              8:00 p.m.

Invite a friend!

Concert Band                    Freshman Band
Symphony Band                Freshman Wind Ens.

---

An effective program of press releases and special interest or feature stories about your band or orchestra students will keep the name of your group in front of the public and increase its interest and support. A few suggestions of possible special interest or feature stories:

- A band or orchestra member who is a National Merit Scholar or Finalist
- The unusually high GPA of band and orchestra students

277

- A parent who has volunteered time to the band or orchestra for a great number of years or who has taken on a major responsibility
- A family with several generations who have been in the program
- The start of band camp or the new marching season
- Band or orchestra alumni with an important achievement
- A special anniversary (25, 50, 75 years, etc.) of the band or orchestra program
- A large family with children in the program at various grade levels

This type of story is limited only by your imagination and the precaution that you do not over-sell your program. Be sure to include your school newspaper in this public relations program. A good public relations effort in the school newspaper should help increase your program's visibility and support among the general student body.

## *Event Promotion*

Performance-related activities (concerts, tours, festival appearances, etc.) require a specific promotional effort to attract maximum attendance of parents and family members, school personnel, other students, and members of the general public. This effort can be accomplished in many ways: area news media (local and school newspapers, and radio and television), targeted mailings, your school or ensemble Web site, posters, paid advertising, etc.

Effective press releases answer the questions "who, what, when, where, and why." Be sure you address each question in your press releases. Also, put the most important information first; some people will not take time to read your entire article, and some editors may take the easy way to edit your release by simply deleting the last few paragraphs.

A sample press release about a concert is found in Figure 11-3. Note that a release date (or the statement "For Immediate Use") is included, wide margins and double spacing should be used to allow editor comments, a headline is suggested, the name and phone number of the contact person is listed, and the text end is identified with "end" or "###." Most press releases should be only one page. Many people suggest that short sentences and paragraphs be used, that you write at about a 7th or 8th grade level, and that you avoid specialized jargon and technical terms in the article. Figures 11-4 and 11-5 are examples of press releases for theme concerts. A short quote can add interest to any press release.

*Figure 11-3. Sample Press Release No. 1*

---

**PRESS RELEASE**—For Immediate Use
April 19, 1999

ASBURY AND CEDARVILLE BANDS TO SHARE CONCERT

The Asbury College Concert Band and the Cedarville College Symphonic Band will present a joint concert on Tuesday, April 27. The concert will begin at 7:30 p.m. in Hughes Auditorium on the Asbury College campus. There is no admission charge for the concert.

This concert is part of a concert exchange that had the Asbury College band perform at Cedarville College on March 6. Asbury band director Dr. Lynn Cooper reported that "Our joint concert at Cedarville College was quite well attended and we certainly hope that our students and the local community will come in large numbers to hear this concert."

The 90-member Cedarville band will perform the march "Rolling Thunder" by Henry Fillmore, several movements of the "William Byrd Suite" by Gordon Jacob, "How Firm Thy Friendship" by James Swearingen, and "Dublin Sketches" by James Curnow. Prof. Michael DiCuirci conducts the Cedarville band.

The second half of the program will feature the Asbury College band. They will play the "Overture to Candide" by Leonard Bernstein, "Lincolnshire Posy" by Percy Grainger, "Giving" by Stephen Melillo, and "Mannin Veen" by Haydn Wood.

This is the final concert of the school year at Asbury College. Cooper notes that "Each band has programmed a wide variety of fine band music and the concert should be a very enjoyable concert experience for everyone."

### ###

For further information contact:
Dr. Lynn Cooper
Asbury College
Wilmore, KY 40390
606-858-3511, ext. 2249
E-mail: lynn.cooper@asbury.edu

279

**Figure 11-4. Sample Press Release No. 2**

**PRESS RELEASE**—For Immediate Use
February 19, 1999

## ASBURY AND CAMPBELLSVILLE JAZZ ENSEMBLES PLAN CONCERT

The Asbury College Jazz Ensemble and the Campbellsville University Jazz Ensemble will play a joint concert on Thursday, February 25. The concert will begin at 7:30 p.m. in Akers Auditorium and there is no admission charge.

The concert will feature a wide range of jazz music from the 1940s to some recent jazz compositions. The Campbellsville Jazz Ensemble will perform "Swingtime" by Benny Goodman, "Cute" by Neal Hefti, "Blue Rondo a la Turk" by Dave Brubeck, and other big band pieces.

The Asbury College Jazz Ensemble will open the second half of the concert with "Rain Delay" by Dean Sorenson. The Asbury band will salute Duke Ellington, on the occasion of the centennial of his birth, by playing two of his most popular pieces, "Take the 'A' Train" and "Satin Doll." They will also play "Get Out and Stay Out" by Ian McDougall and a jazz waltz arrangement by Bill Himes of "Amazing Grace."

This concert is part of a number of exchanges planned for the future. The Asbury Jazz Ensemble will play at Campbellsville University during the 1999-2000 school year. In addition, this semester the Asbury Concert Band will play at Cedarville College on March 5 and the Cedarville band will play here on April 27.


### ###


For further information contact:
Dr. Lynn Cooper
Asbury College
Wilmore, KY 40390
606-858-3511, ext. 2249

*Figure 11-5. Sample Press Release No. 3*

**PRESS RELEASE**—For Immediate Use

The Asbury College Orchestra and Concert Band will present a combined concert on Thursday, October 24. The concert will begin at 7:30 p.m. in Hughes Auditorium and there is no admission charge.

The concert is titled "A Night at the Opera" and will feature well-known opera overtures and selections from a wide variety of operas, operetta, and Broadway musicals. Also featured will be three members of the voice faculty at the college. Dr. Beatrice Holz will sing "You'll Never Walk Alone" from the Broadway musical Carousel with the Orchestra. Performing with the Concert Band will be Professor Virginia Bowles, who will sing "Musetta's Waltz" from La Boheme, and Dr. Craig Hodges, who will sing "Non Piu Andrai" from The Marriage of Figaro.

The Orchestra, conducted by Dr. Ronald Holz, will also perform the "Meditation" from Thais featuring faculty violinist Professor Lori Everson, the "Sword Dance" by Wagner, and the "Light Cavalry Overture" by von Suppe.

Dr. Lynn Cooper will lead the Concert Band in performances of the "Overture to Tancredi" by Rossini, "Selections from West Side Story," and "El Capitan March" by John Philip Sousa.

### ###

For further information contact:
Asbury College Music Department
Wilmore, KY 40390
859-858-3511, ext. 2250

Pictures add interest to a story. Most newspapers prefer black and white 8-by-10 inch or 5-by7 inch photos that are crisp and clear, and have high contrast. Many newspapers prefer to receive photos electronically, so be sure to check on local preferences. Color photos usually are limited to special feature stories (although most newspapers will take your color photo and print it in black and white). Photos of two to six students engaged in some activity are much preferred over static, posed shots or large group photos. Newspapers sometimes will send a photographer for a story, but this will require greater lead-time to schedule the photo. An important consideration with photos of students is that many school districts require parents' permission for their child's photograph to be published. You may want to have parents sign a photograph permission form at the beginning of each school year.

Concert or event promotions should also include Public Service Announcements (PSAs) to all local radio and television stations. These should be written as 30-second announcements (See Figure 11-6). Stations are required to give a certain number of PSAs regularly, and most are pleased to use well written and easy to understand announcements. Also, do not forget to send a PSA or notice to the local cable television company to include on its community bulletin board channel. Some community access cable channels may even be interested in a live or delayed broadcast of some of your concerts—it never hurts to ask! Concert announcements should certainly be listed on your school and band or orchestra Web site.

*Figure 11-6. Sample Public Service Announcement*

## PSA for Local Band Concert

[For Use Between May 1 and May 10]

The Annual Spring Concert at Smalltown High School is scheduled for Thursday, May 10, at 7:30 p.m. The concert will include performances by the high school and middle school bands, orchestras, and choirs. Featured soloist with the high school orchestra will be Dr. Frank LaRue, professor of violin, at Bigtown College.

There is no admission charge for this concert. For further information contact the high school music department office at 222-1122.

end -

Many music educators send mailings or e-mails announcing concerts and events to their "Friends" list (see Figure 11-7). In addition to individual community members, these "Friends" letters should go to civic clubs (Kiwanis, Lions, Ladies Literary, etc.), veteran's organizations (VFW, American Legion, etc.) and senior citizen's organizations and homes. People in these organizations will enthusiastically support and attend local music events. You might consider sending a concert invitation letter to area churches and houses of worship (Figure 11-8) and ask that they include a brief announcement in their bulletin or newsletter. Another idea (see Figure 11-9) is to have ensemble members address and sign postcards to their family and friends with a simple "I hope you can come to my concert next Thursday evening at the high school!" Also, be sure to send an invitation to all faculty and staff in your school. Visually pleasing and easy-to-read posters placed in the school and around the community can also draw attention to your concert.

Another effective idea for concert promotion is to print "tickets" to your free concerts! These tickets are really nothing more than reminders to people of "who, what, when, where, and why." Give each ensemble member 10 tickets to give away and see if attendance increases at your next concert. This brings up the question of whether you should charge for school concerts. The two primary responses to this question are (1) "people don't come to 'free' events because of the impression that they are not of 'worth' (besides, it's a little money for the budget)" or (2) "since our school is supported by the tax-payers, they have already 'paid' for concerts and should not be charged again." You will need to reach your own decision about charging for concerts, based on the circumstances in your community. One effective alternative is to have a benefit concert for some local charity, or ask concertgoers to bring, as the price of admission, a canned good that can be donated to a worthy local cause.

Professionally printed posters placed in all the school buildings in your district and in local businesses are an effective way to attract an audience for concerts. Be sure your poster design is not too "busy" with excessive text or graphic design, and that the basic concert information is easily readable from a distance. Posters larger than 8.5-by-11 inches will be more noticeable and allow you to use larger printed text. A student committee can be recruited to place your concert posters in the schools and throughout the community. After the concert, send that same committee back to take down the posters. That gesture will make businesses more willing to support your program in the future, and it will also help create a positive image for your program.

*Figure 11-7. Sample Concert Letter*

October 21

Dear Colleague:

I would like to invite you and your students to attend our major ensemble concerts at Asbury College this semester. The first concert will be our Fall Concert on Thursday, October 28. This concert will include performances by our Concert Band, Men's Glee Club, Handbell Choir, and Concert Choir. It will begin at 7:30 p.m. in Hughes Auditorium and there is no admission charge.

The Concert Band will open the concert with "Hands Across The Sea, march" by Sousa, "Sinfonietta" by James Curnow, "Variations on a Korean Folk Song" by Chance, and "American Riversongs" by LaPlante. Our Men's Glee Club will sing "Two Dvorak Biblical Songs," "Stout-hearted Men," and "Ride the Chariot." Next, the Handbell Choir will play "Canticle" by Sherman and "The Easy Winners" by Scott Joplin. The program will conclude with the Concert Choir performing "Rejoice and Sing Out His Praises" by Hayes, "Ubi Caritas" by Duruflé, "Cantique de Jean Racine" by Fauré, and "Come Thou Fount of Every Blessing" arranged by Wilberg.

The other major ensemble concerts scheduled this semester are:
- November 11 - **Fall Preview Collage** (Jazz Ensemble, Women's Vocal Ensemble, and Chorale), 8:00 p.m., Akers Auditorium
- December 2 - **Jazz Ensemble Concert**, 7:30 p.m., Akers Auditorium
- December 12 - **Festival of Christmas Music** (Women's Choir, Concert Choir, Concert Band, Men's Glee Club, Percussion Ensemble, Brass Sextet, plus soloists), 3:00 p.m., Hughes Auditorium

Would you please post the enclosed poster and encourage your students to attend these concerts? I hope to see you there!

Cordially yours,

Lynn G. Cooper, Ed.D.
Director of Bands

284

*Figure 11-8. Sample Letter to Churches*

April 12

Dear Pastor:

I would like to invite you and the members of your church to attend the final two large ensemble concerts of the semester at Asbury College. Our Concert Choir, Men's Glee Club, Handbell Choir, and Orchestra will perform their Spring Concert on Thursday, April 15. The concert will begin at 7:30 p.m. in Hughes Auditorium.

On Tuesday, April 27, our Concert Band will host a joint performance with the Cedarville College Symphonic Band. That concert will also begin at 7:30 p.m. in Hughes Auditorium. There is no admission charge for either concert.

Our Concert Band performed at Cedarville College during our recent spring concert tour and we look forward to their performance on our campus. The Cedarville band will play the *William Byrd Suite* by Gordon Jacob, *How Firm Thy Friendship* by James Swearingen, *Rolling Thunder March* by Henry Fillmore, and *Dublin Sketches* by James Curnow. The Asbury College Concert Band will perform the *Overture to Candide* by Leonard Bernstein, *Lincolnshire Posy* by Percy Grainger, *Giving* by Stephen Melillo, and *Mannin Veen* by Haydn Wood.

I hope you can join us for these two final concerts of this school year. Thank you for your support of our music program at Asbury College!

Cordially yours,


Lynn G. Cooper, Ed.D.
Director of Bands

P.S. Would you please announce these concerts to your students and post the enclosed poster on your bulletin board? Thank you!
Also, would you consider adding the following brief announcement to your church newsletter or your church bulletin for April 18 or 25?

*The Asbury College Concert Band will host the Cedarville College Symphonic Band from Cedarville, Ohio in a joint concert on Tuesday, April 27. The concert will begin at 7:30 p.m. in Hughes Auditorium on the Asbury College campus in Wilmore. There is no admission charge.*

285

enc.

*Figure 11-9. Sample Postcard From Band Members*

April 20

Dear

   I would like to invite you to attend my concert next Tuesday evening (April 27) at 7:30 p.m. in Hughes Auditorium. Our Concert Band will be playing a joint concert with the Cedarville College band.

   The concert will include a wide variety of music including overtures, sacred music, and a march. Featured on the concert will be "Lincolnshire Posy" by Grainger, the "Overture to Candide" by Bernstein, "Rolling Thunder March" by Fillmore, and "Dublin Sketches" by Curnow.

   I hope you can join us for this free concert on Tuesday evening at 7:30 p.m.! And bring your friends!

   Another publicity idea for school use is "table cards" placed on cafeteria tables during the week of a concert. Table cards (see Figure 11-10) are simply 8.5-by-11-inch designs with your concert information repeated in each of three columns (in "landscape" view) and printed on brightly-colored cardstock. The cardstock is folded in thirds and the sides taped together to form a three-sided table card that will attract student and faculty attention as they eat lunch.

   Concert programs (discussed in Chapter 7) can also be considered as an important part of a total public relations program. A fine concert program not only informs the audience of the order of the music to be performed and the names of all ensemble members, but also lists the school administration, the booster club officers, the names of all concert ushers, and the names of anyone else who has helped in preparing the concert. Be sure to acknowledge your building secretaries and custodians—they do a lot each day to make it possible for you to do a better job as a teacher. An attractive concert program with all this important information included—and all text spelled correctly—makes an important contribution to the public image of your band or orchestra.

*Figure 11-10. Table card sample*

The Asbury College

**COLLAGE 2000**

This Friday at 7:30 p.m. in Hughes!

featuring the

**Concert Band
Concert Choir
Women's Choir**
and outstanding soloists

*Don't miss it!*

(No Admission Charge!)

The Asbury College

***All-Star Band Clinic Concert***

**Saturday, Nov. 18**

at 3:00 p.m.

in Hughes Aud.

High School All-Star Band
and
College Chamber Ensembles

(No Admission Charge!)

The Asbury College

**Jazz Ensemble**

***Friday!***

November 17th

in the Grille
at 9:30 p.m.

(No Admission Charge!)

Do not forget to send a written "thank you" to everyone who helped make your public relations program, concert, or other event a success. They will appreciate your extra effort to recognize their contribution to the band or orchestra program.

A well-planned and professionally presented public relations program will present the good news about your band or orchestra to your community. The result of an effective public relations program is that your community—in and out of your school building—is more likely to support your band or orchestra, believe in your program and your students, and consider it a valued part of the community.

# Business Skills and the Ensemble Director

## Budget Practices and Procedures

Budgeting practices and requirements vary greatly from school to school and state to state. Become familiar with the policies and procedures in your school district and follow them carefully. While some procedures may seem cumbersome, or even odd, they have been developed to ensure that taxpayer money is spent wisely and accounted for precisely.

Two suggestions for any program, in any school: Plan ahead and document. Maintain accurate inventory lists of instruments, equipment, uniforms, and music. Use those lists (and repair records for instruments and equipment) to plan for the future needs of your program. It is best to have a long-range plan developed for large purchases such as instruments and uniforms. The repair record for each instrument, along with your inspection of its current condition, will help you decide if it is best to continue to maintain the instrument or plan for its replacement. The same is true for uniforms. In both cases (instruments and uniforms), you will have to anticipate large purchases and, at least for instruments, suggest a multi-year plan for replacement. I once worked in a school district in which the middle school instruments were 20 to 30 years old and in very poor condition. We made a presentation to the school board emphasizing our responsibility to supply students with instruments in good playing condition, and gave the board members a copy of the instrument inventory (with date of purchase and current condition) and a suggested three-year plan to replace the entire inventory. We expected the board to approve only a portion of the plan and require a five-year duration, but they were so appreciative of the clarity and thoroughness of the report that they approved the entire request as presented!

Know the budget categories and account numbers used in your school district, and use the correct terms and numbers in all your requests. Although different categories may be used in different schools, many school budgets will include:

- Instructional Supplies: this would include music, and could include paper, pencils, valve oil, drum sticks, reeds, etc. (Some schools have a separate category called Expendable Supplies for paper, pencils, etc.)
- Textbooks: sometimes this can be used for the ensemble director to purchase method, technique, and warm-up books
- Repair: for instrument repair, piano tuning (sometimes even for the replacement of broken drum heads or mallets)
- Transportation: to festivals, off-campus performances, etc. (usually not extra tours that are funded by the boosters club or student fundraising)
- Capital Outlay: new instruments, large equipment, uniforms, etc.

Be sure to list items in the correct categories, and be reasonable in your requests. Why ask for $3,000 for new music this year (even with a woefully deficient music library) if you could not possibly play all that music in a single year? Submit your request to the building administrators well before the due date. Some school districts will not ask for budget items from the band or orchestra director—they seem to feel all that is needed is to simply increase the budget figures by a set percentage. In such schools it might be necessary to meet with the principal to discuss your budget needs and ask if you may put those needs into a formal budget proposal.

Budget proposals for school district funds should have a cover letter discussing the broad needs of the program and a list of current needs in each budget category. The cover letter should include any helpful explanations about the item requested—especially if it is an unusual or expensive item. Some directors even include pictures of the instruments requested and an indication of the average "life-span" of requested instruments and equipment. Additional needs to be met via the booster club would not be a part of this proposal, but rather would be presented to the booster club separately. In the sample budget found in Figure 11-11 you will note that requests listed in each budget category include the basic information about how much music is to be purchased or the number and distance of trips, etc.

*Figure 11-11. Sample Music Department Budget*

**Budget Request for the Middletown High School Band**

I. Instructional Supplies
    A. Concert Band (3 concerts/4 new pieces each @ $80)  $960.
    B. Jazz Band (4 concerts/4 new pieces each @ $50 )    $800.
    C. Solo and Ensemble Literature (30 @ $15 )    $450.
    D. Marching Band (4 shows/3 new pieces each @ $50 )  $600.
                                        $2,810.

II. Repair Budget
    [could list specific known repair needs or a general figure
    based on past needs]    $2,000.
                                          $2,000.

III. Transportation
    A. District Band Festival (160 miles round trip @ $2 /
        mile - 2 buses and 1 truck)    $960.
    B. Marching Band Trip (200 miles round trip @ $2/
        mile - 2 buses and 1 truck)    $1,200.
                                          $2,160.

IV. Capital Outlay
    A. Two (2) Holton French Horns (H179), @ $3,500  $7,000.
    B. One (1) pair Sabian 18" Hand-Hammered
        Crash Cymbals    $400.
    C. Two (2)BessonEuphoniums (BN968GSS), @ $4,500. $9,000.
                                          $16,400.

                                Sub-Total    $23,370.

V. Contingency Fund (10 Percent)    $2,337.

    TOTAL BUDGET REQUEST    $25,707.

Most school boards understand that to initiate and sustain a music program requires a sizable investment. Sometimes, however, it may be helpful to ask that the business office provide a comparison of total costs and per-pupil costs in the music program, the athletic program, and the over-all school program. This type of study often helps administrators and board members understand the relatively low per-pupil cost for a fine music program. One caution—do not ask for this study unless you are sure it will show that favorable information!

The separate budget request to the booster club would typically include the proposed expenditures and estimated receipts from booster club fundraising activities. Typical expenditures from the booster club would be for such things as summer camp scholarships, private lesson scholarships, new color guard flags or uniforms, etc. Estimated receipts would be from such sources as concessions at athletic events or music festivals, member dues, student fundraising, and gifts from local businesses or civic organizations. As stated in Chapter 9, booster clubs should not—unless circumstance is severe—buy those things directly related to the curriculum. The local school board should pay the salary for all certified faculty and for all basic instruments, music, uniforms, fees, curriculum-related travel, etc. There may be brief periods of time, such as during a financial crisis in a school district, when the boosters must help fund those program needs normally budgeted by the school district. Those periods should be extremely rare, temporary, and of short duration.

After your budget proposal is accepted by your administration, you will need to solicit bids from local music retailers. Most school districts require that all items over a specific dollar amount ($400 or $500) be let for competitive bids. Items below that figure should be purchased from the local dealer who provides you with timely and excellent service. In addition, when bids are very close you might consider recommending the bid of the dealer who services your school regularly. That dealer's investment in store personnel who travel to your school and meet your daily program needs should be rewarded by your purchases when possible. Figure 11-12 is an example of a Request for Quotation, and Figure 11-13 is a typical Compilation of Bids, with teacher recommendations. School administrators will make purchase decisions based on this information, and will issue then a Purchase Order to the accepted bidder for the items needed. Figure 5-5 is an example of a purchase order issued by a school business office. For items not on bid, you would send a memo or a Requisition for a Purchase Order (see Figure 5-4) to the business office with all of the

*Figure 11-12. Request for A Quotation*

**REQUEST FOR QUOTATION**

(This is not an order)             from             (This is not an order)

Smalltown High School
Music Department
4321 Main Street
Smalltown, MI  49999

To:     Matt's Music Mart
        5555 Main Street
        Smalltown, MI  49999

Dear Sirs:

   Please quote itemized prices and delivery time for materials listed below F.O.B. Destination. This inquiry is in duplicate. One copy must be returned to us properly completed, with the duplicate to be retained for your files. The right is reserved by the Board of Education to reject any or all quotations. Unless otherwise stated, we assume you will accept an order on any items listed. If you are unable to furnish goods as specified and wish to offer a substitute, brands must be clearly stated and of similar quality. Please return quotation by February 15, 2003.

| Quantity | Item | Unit Price | Total Price |
|---|---|---|---|
| 2 | Fox Renard Bassoon, Model 220, w/case | | |
| 1 | Jupiter Alto Flute, Model 519S, w/case | | |
| 1 | Fox Renard Oboe, Model 330, w/case | | |
| 2 | Yamaha French Horn, Model YHR-667, w/case | | |
| 1 | Yamaha Euphonium, Model YEP-321S, w/case | | |

Delivery to be made within _____ days after receipt of order.

Date of quotation _____

Name of Bidder_____

Per _____

necessary information—name and address of the store, the complete information about the item you are purchasing, the item prices, the total price, and the account to be charged for these items.

   Keep your own ledger for each account. Enter the total cost of each item and any other costs such as shipping and handling. In this way you will be sure to remain within your budget allocation for the year. Just as it is important not to go over your budget allocation, it is also important not to fall appreciably short of the budget. Unfortunately, some administrators assume that if you did not need all of your budgeted money one year, they should cut your budget for the next year. Many people recommend that school budgets be expended no later than early in the second semester to avoid any school-wide budget cutoffs.

*Figure 11-13. Compilation of Bids*

Smalltown High School
Music Department
4321 Main Street
Smalltown, MI 49999

**Compilation of Bids — April 20, 2003**

| Quantity | Item | Matt's Music | Music Shoppe | Local Music |
|---|---|---|---|---|
| 2 | Fox Renard Bassoon, Model 220, w/case | | | |
| 1 | Jupiter Alto Flute, Model 519S, w/case | | | |
| 1 | Fox Renard Oboe, Model 330, w/case | | | |
| 2 | Yamaha French Horn, Model YHR-667, w/case | | | |
| 1 | Yamaha Euphonium, Model YEP-321S, w/case | | | |

*Recommended Bid

Total Bid:

## Fundraising

Fundraising has become a regular part of most programs in the schools. It has become an increasingly important part of instrumental music programs as band and orchestra programs try to supplement sometimes shrinking school district budgets. Unfortunately, it seems that some school group or club is selling something to the community about every week of the school year. There is certainly a concern about "market saturation," and a possible public perception that schools are more about raising funds for various groups than giving children a high-quality education.

In answer to concerns about excessive fundraising, some school boards have adopted policies to regulate sales in schools and throughout the community. For example, some schools allow candy sales only in school and not in the community, while others prohibit candy sales

293

in the school building during school hours. Some schools prohibit door-to-door sales, and some prohibit sales outside school district boundaries. Be aware of all related school district policies about fundraising, and follow them completely.

Students involved in a fundraising project should have a clear understanding of the purpose and intended use of profits. A worthy project is more likely to be supported by the community. I also suggest limiting the total number of projects and completing them early in the year, before fundraising activities saturate the community and while your students are still "fresh." The other advantage, obviously, is that the funds are then available for use early in the year.

Generally, funds are raised for one of three purposes:
- For general band or orchestra funding
- For specific instrument, uniform, or equipment needs
- For a special band or orchestra trip or summer camp

In the case of a trip or summer camp, students are usually raising funds to cover their own expenses. For obvious reasons, the booster club treasurer must maintain accurate records of these individual accounts. In the case of general fundraising for the program, a prize program may be necessary to encourage participation. Some fundraising companies provide such programs with either merchandise or cash as the prizes, or the local school group may decide to set aside some of its profits to fund a prize program. Other schools have a special "fun trip" (such as a day at an amusement park) for everyone who has attained a minimum number of sales. Those schools with merit system programs leading to band or orchestra awards might consider giving merits for a certain number of sales.

Whenever possible, the booster club should be in total charge of fundraising projects. This will relieve you of an enormous responsibility and allow you to focus more on teaching. It is best if students pick up all fundraising products (such as candy) at designated booster club member homes in the community and turn in all money at those homes. This is better for your educational program and is safer than having students carry large sums of money to school. Actually, you should avoid handling any money, if at all possible, and should not be able to co-sign booster club checks. That will eliminate the chance of someone questioning your honesty. Your role should be only to distribute the information about a fundraising project and motivate

students to participate in the venture. If your school does not have an active booster club, try to recruit a committee of interested and hard-working parents to take charge of fundraising.

When deciding on a product to use for fundraising, ask yourself if the percentage of profit is acceptable (50 percent or better is good), if the product is of value and needed in the community, and if the project is repeatable. You might decide to sell a product that yields a slightly lower profit margin if the projected quantity of sales seems high.

When choosing a fundraising company consider these points:
- The integrity of the local sales representative and the company
- Company services (such as a computer tabulation of orders, company owned truck delivery, a prize program, etc.)
- The product return policy (no returns, only unopened cartons, etc.)
- Delivery time (for order-taking projects)
- Delivery time for reorders

Many reputable and efficient fundraising companies across the country help school groups meet their program needs. Talk to other music teachers in neighboring schools and get their recommendations. When interviewing prospective fundraisers, you may want to include some students and parents. Their perceptions may be helpful.

In addition to various kinds of candy, you may want to consider some of the following fundraising projects:

- Dinners—pancake, spaghetti, fish, etc.
- Run-A-Thon (or Bike-, Golf-, Walk-, Swim-, Play-, etc.)
- Community calendars (this works well in smaller communities—sell ads to local businesses, and birthday and anniversary listings to residents)
- Tag Days (sell tags to hang on jackets or automobile mirrors stating "I support the Anywhere High School Orchestra" for a donation)
- Fruit (highly repeatable if the fruit is good!)
- Pizza mixes, cheese and sausage, etc.
- Concerts by professional musical groups
- Concessions at athletic events, marching band contests, concert festivals, etc.
- Christmas greens sale (wreaths, holly, etc.—if the greens are fresh this really is supported by the community)

Fundraising has become a necessity in most schools. Be sure to choose a fine company and a needed product, motivate your students to participate, secure an excellent booster club committee to manage the sale, and have a very good use for the funds to be raised. And be sure your students can articulate that need to their potential customers.

## The School Music Dealer

The school music representative who visits your school each week can help you get your job done efficiently and effectively. Particularly in more rural schools, "school reps" will save you a tremendous amount of time by taking instruments in for repair, bringing supplies to sell to your students (reeds, drum sticks, mouthpieces, etc.), and even ordering music for you and your students. They may also be the only contact you have on a regular basis with another music professional, so they can keep you informed of recent developments in the field—including positions that are going to be available in the area.

When you start your recruiting program for the beginning band or orchestra program, invite the school music representatives to attend so parents can rent instruments at the school instead of having to travel to the nearest music store. In addition to the convenience for parents, this system helps ensure that students will be renting only instrument brands that you have approved. Your local music store may also be able to supply you with recruiting aids and cardboard music folders for your ensembles.

In many areas of the country, only one music store services a school. But when possible, having a good working relationship with several dealers encourages price competitiveness and offers a wider range of instruments and merchandise. Using several music stores also helps you maintain a correct professional relationship. No one objects to small gifts (like a box of candy) at Christmas, but beware of dealers who offer special pricing for personal purchases, or even a "rebate" on instrument rental fees. This is an illegal and unethical practice, and you should report any improper suggestions like this to your administrator and cease doing business with that company.

Music dealers can be a double-edged sword in your recruiting of beginning band or orchestra students. They provide quality instruments (usually with a rent-to-own program) and service those instruments. Some dealers will even go to the homes of prospective students and recruit them into your program. Although this may initially seem like a good idea, remember two things: The music store wants to rent or sell a lot of instruments (and may not be as concerned about whether an instrument is physically appropriate for a student or if there is an appropriate instrumentation in the class); and *you* are the professional hired by your local school district to administer and teach your program. Do not leave such an important task as fitting students to instruments and achieving instrumentation balance in the hands of someone who primarily wants to rent or sell instruments.

Froseth (1974) cites four dimensions of music dealer service to consider: quality products, acquisition plans, instrument repair service, and general service. You will expect your local music dealer to supply quality instruments and accessories for your beginners, upgrade instruments for older students, and supply high quality instruments for your school needs. The acquisition plan for your beginners could be either a "continuous" or "three month" rental-purchase plan. The continuous plan (with all payments going toward the final purchase of the instrument) does not force parents and students to decide whether to continue in instrumental music after just three months of instruction.

A skilled and efficient repair facility is a vital attribute for any full-service school music dealer. A good dealer will deliver high-quality repairs at a reasonable cost, and within a reasonable time (generally no longer than one week). Instruments in the repair shop for a week or more cause children to lose valuable instructional and practice time. Some dealers supply a loaner instrument when repairs will take longer than a week. Most music dealers will "subcontract" the more major repairs (complete overhauls, refinishing, etc.) to manufacturer shops or to a major full-service repair facility.

Following are four general service issues to consider in choosing a local music dealer:
- A competent and knowledgeable staff
- Adequate inventories of music, high-quality instruments, and accessories
- Regular store representatives to call on schools (weekly preferred)
- Quick service on all needs such as product information and competitive bids on school purchases.

## *For Discussion or Assignment*

1. Design and produce a Band or Orchestra Boosters Club newsletter for your future ensemble. Produce appropriate stories and other

material for this one-page newsletter. Scan at least one image into your newsletter.

2. Develop a budget proposal for your future high school band or orchestra. Use the budget categories discussed in this chapter and research current pricing. Include a cover letter justifying your proposal.

3. Develop a list of recommended brands of instruments, mouthpieces, and accessories for a beginning band or string class.

4. Write a press release for a recent or future concert by your college band or orchestra. Follow the format presented in this chapter.

## *For Reference and Further Reading*

Covey, Stephen R. (1990). *The Seven Habits of Highly Effective People: Restoring the Character Ethic*. New York: Fireside

Froseth, James O. (1974). *The NABIM Recruiting Manual*. Chicago: GIA Publications, Inc.

*How to Promote Your Band* (1980). Elkhart, IN: The Selmer Company.

Neidig, Kenneth L. (1964). *The Band Director's Guide*. Englewood Cliffs, NJ: Prentice-Hall, Inc.

# Part III:

# The Big Picture

# Chapter 12

# KNOWING THE PROFESSION TODAY

## Education Reform

"For years we have heard that there are only two things certain in life: death and taxes. We know now there are three: death, taxes, and school reform" (Adams, 1994, p.2). Semi-annual curriculum revision has become a fixture in many schools. We deal with such things as block scheduling, flexible scheduling, year-round schools, Quality Schools, Charter Schools, Objectives-Based Education, character education, school-based councils, portfolios, authentic assessment, and many other programs and issues under that much-used category of "educational reform." It is easy to become wary and weary of frequent reform efforts. However, as Paul Lehman (1992) reminds us, we must become involved in the reform process because "If we don't, education will be reformed by bureaucrats and businessmen, and it probably won't be to our liking" (p. 4).

The admirable desire of the American people to improve its schools and the student learning process has caused enormous changes in the way schools operate. More and more is being required of teachers and administrators relative to documentation of planning (long-term and short-term), assessment strategies, standardized test preparation, and public accountability. Teachers are being asked to do more, often with less time, less disciplinary support, and less parental and public support. The current uncertainties and demands in education have kindled such high levels of stress among teachers and administrators that many may leave the profession prematurely. How unfortunate!

What is needed to encourage talented teachers to stay in the classroom, where they can be part of the solution to our educational problems?

For America's schools and teachers to succeed, I believe they need
1. broad-based community and parent support,
2. motivated and interested learners,
3. a rigorous curriculum,
4. adequate resources,
5. supportive administrators,
6. and appropriate and accurate assessment strategies.

These are the characteristics of many of the best schools in this country. Schools seeking improvement will work toward these goals. A wise music educator will support improvement in the total educational program in their school, because educationally strong schools are more likely to also have outstanding music programs.

You can help guide the school change process by becoming involved in committee work, and by staying informed of local, state and national issues in education. Become knowledgeable about the broad issues in education, and about those specific to music education. Try to be an educational leader who sees the "big picture" in education, and not just a special interest advocate. Remember: You must be involved in the process to be part of the solution. You can make a difference in your school district.

Of major concern is the need for a strong curriculum in our schools.

> This point, however, seems to be lost on critics who think the most important way to improve our educational system is to increase the length of the school year (or the school day) or to pile on more homework. What they fail to grasp, what a ten-year-old might tell them, is that their efforts would be better spent trying to improve the content of the curriculum that fills those hours and notebooks (Kohn, 1993, p. 216).

The National Association of Secondary School Principals (NASSP), in the book *Breaking Ranks: Changing an American Institution* (1996), stated that ". . .high schools must offer students a curriculum of substance, courses that require students to do serious work" (p. 8). In the same book, the NASSP stated their belief that "The success of high school reform depends on rigorous standards" (p. 87).

The National Standards for Music Education were discussed earlier in this book. These standards, developed by the Music Educators National Conference (MENC), can serve as a model for music curriculum development. In fact, many school districts and state departments of education already have used the National Standards for Music Education as models in developing local or state standards and curricula.

Stanley Pogrow (1996), in a discussion of school reform, wrote that "The ultimate reality is that the only way to improve education significantly is by the use of more powerful forms of curricula in the hands of very good teachers who are trained to teach better. All three of these conditions must exist" (pp. 661-662).

There are actually four curricula in the schools. As Paul Lehman (1995) put it:

> The first is the official curriculum. That is the one that exists in the statutes and the curriculum guides. The second is the curriculum that teachers teach. That is not necessarily the same as the official curriculum. The third is the curriculum that students learn. That is sometimes sharply at odds with the curriculum that teachers intend to teach. The fourth is the curriculum that's tested. That can be different from the other three, and it is important because test results often serve as a basis for policymaking. (p. 16)

The challenge for anyone writing curricula is to eliminate as many differences as possible between these four.

Even the finest, most innovative, and thorough curriculum will not be successful unless it is taught by well-trained and committed teachers. Too often teachers are viewed, by the "experts" and the public, as the weak link in the process of education. While it is undeniably true that there are unqualified and unmotivated teachers in classrooms across the country, most educators want to improve American public and private education. It is not helpful, or correct, to paint teachers in general with the broad-brush of obstructionism. Lehman (1995), writing about education reform, stated that

> The solution is for districts to hire only well-qualified teachers, give them the authority and responsibility that should accompany professional status, and then let them do their jobs. . . . Too many reform proposals suggest that teachers are a part of the problem. Teachers aren't part of the problem,

303

they're part of the solution. They must be. If they aren't,
then there is no solution because there is no one else who
can implement it. (p. 19)

Finding, training, and facilitating outstanding teachers is the
responsibility of music teacher education programs, and public and
private school administrators. According to Lehman (1986) "The
solution lies in securing extraordinary performance from ordinary
people" (p. 7).

In a 10-year study of American education, Laurence Steinberg, *et
al* (1996) found: "An extremely high proportion of American high
school students do not take school, or their studies, seriously" (p. 18).
If we educators take our calling seriously, let's find the key to change
students' attitudes and actively engage them in the learning process.

Learners will be motivated and interested if they are taught by
inspiring teachers and if the program has the support of parents, school
authorities, and the community. I believe that if parents are sold on the
value and quality of a program, their children are likely to follow suit.
If the program is supported enthusiastically by the school board and
administration—through their monetary support, good scheduling
practices, etc.—students and their parents will be affirmed in their
support of the program. Likewise, community support—the school
community and the general community—reinforces the value of the
program. Finally, when schools have assessment strategies in place that
accurately measure student learning, they will have more of an
understanding of whether they are successful in the teaching-learning
process.

## Program Goals

Any discussion about goals and objectives in education needs to begin
with a brief definition of some terms, since they often cause confusion
even among veteran teachers. Through the years the terms *goals*,
*objectives, performance objective, instructional objective, social objective,
content standard, achievement standard, learning goals, culminating objectives, enabling objectives, outcomes, purposes*, and many others have
appeared in educational literature. Many of the terms are used interchangeably and without specificity. The use of these terms changes
with various educational philosophies and with the passage of time. It
can, indeed, be confusing to new and veteran teachers alike!

**304**     In *Music Matters*, David Elliott writes that "In the jargon of curriculum theory, the term objective usually indicates an exceedingly spe-

cific level of intention (or target) compared to a moderately definite *goal*, or a broad *aim*" (p. 245). Many educators use all three of these terms interchangeably, and that can lead to confusion. Because these are the three central terms for this discussion, we should look at their most common current definitions.

Broad *aims* are "big picture" items linked to the development of your personal philosophy of music education. *Goals* might be more specific accomplishments or understandings that we want students to attain in a specified time period. *Objectives* are the relatively specific, and usually short-term, means that enable us to achieve our goals. You will find that time spent setting aims, goals, and objectives will be time well spent. Thoughtfully considering your beliefs about what you would like students to know, understand, and be able to do will help you prepare a list of program aims and ultimately develop a meaningful personal philosophy of music education.

After setting broad aims consider the major goals you want to establish for your music education program. These major goals become real "lighthouse statements" that lead you to thoughtful educational decision-making. Some goals will be for a single semester and some for a year; others will take several years to reach. Tim Lautzenheiser (1992) wrote that ". . . it is evident that successful teachers maintain a serious disciplined pattern when it comes to short- and long-term goal setting" (p. 25). He also made several suggestions about setting goals:

> Goals must be specific.
> Goals must be realistic.
> Goals must match our values.
> Visualize the goals in detail.
> Goals must be measurable.
> Read and review the goals daily. (p. 26)

To reach the major goals you have established for your program you need to meet a series of specific objectives. Objectives can be short-term (daily, weekly, monthly) or more long-term (a grading period, a semester, or an academic year). Thoughtfully written objectives serve as your roadmap to achieving major program goals. It is important that objectives and goals be realistic and measurable. While "winning the state marching band championship" may be a measurable goal (you either win it or not), it may not be realistic or educationally valid. It is important that you develop a means to assess or measure your goals and objectives. Predetermined assessment items provide a yardstick against which to measure your success in meeting your goals and objectives. (See Figure 12-1 for assessment item examples.)

Developing your own personal aims, goals, and objectives helps you focus and define your most desired and important educational ends. If you have not established educational goals and objectives, your music program may flounder as you bounce from one educational fad to another. Leonhard and House (1972) wrote that

> . . .honestly held objectives are the most practical tools of the music teacher. They are the foundation of a strong and consistent music program and serve as reference points for every professional decision and action. (p. 178)

An example of an aim, with goals and objectives relating to that aim is found in Figure 12-1.

*Figure 12-1. Example of a High School Band Aim, Goals, and Objectives*

**Aim:**
The Anywhere High School Band will perform literature of recognized quality and depth at a performance level demonstrating student and director understanding of the literature.

**Goals:**
1. The Anywhere High School Band will program outstanding literature with at least three pieces at the grade 3 level during the 2003-2004 school year; three pieces at the grade 4 level during the 2004-2005 year; and two pieces at the grade 5 level during the 2005-2006 school year. The pieces selected must be represented on at least three graded music lists from major band organizations or professional sources.
2. The director will develop a systematic and comprehensive approach to the rehearsal and performance of fine literature. Topics to be addressed will include biographical information about the composer, analysis of the piece (including form, harmonic structure, style, interpretation, and rhythmic construction), listening activities, and the significance of the work from an historical and musical perspective.

Assessment of Each Goal:

1. The selected literature will be listed on at least three of the following lists: the State Music List, the *Teaching Music Through Performance* series by Richard Miles, *Music For Concert Band* by Joseph Kreines, and *Best Music for High School Band* by Thomas Dvorak.

2. A lesson outline will be used that includes the items listed under Goal 2 in planning specific lessons.

**Objectives:**

1. The students will be required to maintain a portfolio of class notes, handouts, and related information about the pieces being studied.

2. Student playing will be evaluated by the director using regular taped playing tests.

3. Concert performances will be evaluated by band members in a systematic way and those evaluations will be included in their portfolio.

4. All public performances will be recorded and archived as a permanent record of the achievements of the Anywhere High School Band.

Assessment of Each Objective:

1. The student portfolio will be graded at the end of each grading period and the contents verified.

2. Students will include in their portfolio a copy of the director's written evaluation of their playing tests on the pieces being studied.

3. A teacher-designed checklist will be used in class discussion and individual reflection. This will be included in the portfolio.

4. The recorded archives of the Anywhere High School Band will be stored in the band room and available for student reference and study.

# National Standards for Arts Education

We live in a time when students, teachers, administrators, parents, communities, and states are increasingly being held accountable for their educational program. That accountability may take the form of state- or community-adopted goals or standards, school-based-councils, comprehensive testing of students, funding based on test scores, etc. Howard Gardner (1991) believes that "Indeed, the question is no longer whether there will be national standards and curricula but, rather, what those standards and curricula will be and who will determine them" (p. 256). While some question the inevitability—or even the wisdom—of required standards, it does seem prudent for music educators to be involved in the development of goals or standards that might be recommended or required for use in their local school. If nothing else, our involvement in a thoughtful and deliberate process of establishing goals or standards should lead to a stronger and more comprehensive music curriculum in our schools.

Respected arts educators disagree about the need for establishing national standards in the arts. For example, Elliot Eisner (1995) warns that "The aim of education is not to train an army that marches to the same drummer, at the same pace, toward the same destination" (p. 763). And, Richard Colwell (1995) believes that ". . .it is necessary to ascertain before implementation whether the national standards have sufficient clarity and foundation in theory, philosophy, and empirical research to succeed. Mandating an arts program for all students in the public school system is a risky venture under optimum [sic] conditions" (p.3). But, at the other end of the spectrum is Will Schmid (1996), who writes that "The Standards—one of the most important developments in the history of American music education—should serve as a beacon for years to come" (p. 4).

The National Standards for Arts Education were developed by the Consortium of National Arts Education Associations and published in 1994. The Consortium includes the American Alliance for Theatre and Education, the Music Educators National Conference, the National Art Education Association, and the National Dance Association. The development of National Standards for Arts Education was precipitated by the passage of *Goals 2000: Educate America Act* and the desire to establish meaningful, bold, and comprehensive standards in the arts. The Standards for these four arts disciplines were published in *National Standards for Arts Education*, and MENC has published a series of its own books about the National Standards for Music Education. The following books, all published by MENC, will help you better understand and apply the National Standards:

- *Opportunity-to-Learn Standards for Music Instruction*

- *The School Music Program: A New Vision*
- *With One Voice: A Report from the 1994 Summit on Music Education*
- *Performance Standards for Music*

In general terms, **standards** define what students should understand and know about a subject and what they should be able to do. **Content standards** broadly define the knowledge, skill, or understanding identified as important for students to learn and know, and **achievement standards** specify levels of achievement desired for students within each grade-level group.

The nine content standards for music are as follows:
1. Singing, alone and with others, a varied repertoire of music
2. Performing on instruments, alone and with others, a varied repertoire of music
3. Improvising melodies, variations, and accompaniments
4. Composing and arranging music within specified guidelines
5. Reading and notating music
6. Listening to, analyzing, and describing music
7. Evaluating music and music performances
8. Understanding relationships between music, the other arts, and disciplines outside the arts
9. Understanding music in relation to history and culture

The content standards listed above are used for each grade-level group, with age-specific achievement standards established for each group (grades K-4, 5-8, and 9-12). A listing of the content and achievement standards for grades 5 through 8 is found in Figure 1-3.

The National Standards for Music Education raise some questions:
- Can all the standards be taught to all children?
- Should all the standards be taught?
- Are there other items that should be on the list?
- Are some standards more difficult than others to teach?
- Would a refocus of music education on teaching the standards lead to a de-emphasis of performance skill development in ensembles?
- Would implementation of the standards be met by teacher resistance?

These questions and others cause concern among current teachers, teacher educators, future teachers, and other supporters of strong music performance programs.

The question of whether devotion to the present National Standards will impair performance group development is a realistic concern, because many of the standards are viewed as oriented toward a more "general music" or "listening" approach. Still, many of these standards fit very nicely into a Comprehensive Musicianship approach that includes teaching *about* music (theory, history, etc.) in the full performing ensemble rehearsal. The series *Teaching Music Through Performance* will help you make sure that performing ensemble rehearsals are more than just learning to play music well—that within rehearsals, students learn why and how the literature they are preparing for performance was composed. This series of books offers valuable information, techniques, and materials—from some of the most respected music educators in the country—to make your rehearsals a complete and meaningful musical experience.

An important factor in adopting the National Standards is that they may require teachers to teach unfamiliar subjects and exercise unfamiliar skills. Some teachers will feel inadequate and unprepared to teach such things as music composition and improvisation. As Scott Shuler (1995) wrote "teachers do not teach what they cannot do themselves. . . ." (p. 3). People are naturally reluctant to expose their own shortcomings to their students. Older teachers who have never had to teach subjects or skills called for by the Standards may be particularly vulnerable. Younger teachers may need to add to their already heavy workloads to develop—through college course work, attendance at workshops, or individual skill development—some of the new skills required by the National Standards.

Some of these standards are easier to teach than others, and difficulties vary from one student to another. We will need to develop strategies and techniques to meet children where they are and advance them sequentially through concepts and skills appropriate to each grade level. School districts will need to supply funding for materials, instruments, and equipment. Success in meeting the National Standards will not occur without the financial commitment of local, state, and national governments. *Opportunity-to-Learn Standards for Music Instruction* is an essential reference in this matter.

If you decide to follow the National Standards in your music program, you will need to be flexible in the initial stages. Of course you will be able to introduce what you have already been teaching to all grade levels simultaneously. Standards 1 (singing) and 2 (performing on instruments) may require only the introduction of a more varied repertoire, while Standard 5 (reading and notating music) should already be integral to all music classes. Standards 6 (listening, analyzing, describing) and 7 (evaluating) will require the use of age- and course-appropriate terminology and concepts, some of which may be new to your curriculum. Standards 8 and 9 (understanding relationships) probably will require some new approaches to teaching. Likewise, Standards 3 (improvising) and 4 (composing and arranging) are not now a part of most curricula in the public schools. Therefore, you might introduce Standards 1, 2, 5, 6, and 7 in all grades at the same time, while you probably will incorporate Standards 3 and 4 most effectively by starting in earlier grades with basic concepts and then moving up through the grades each year with the given achievement standards. You might incorporate Standards 8 and 9 in all grades at the same time, but—assuming no prior knowledge base—you should work at about the same depth at each grade level during the first year. Each successive year you can introduce more complex concepts to each grade level and course.

The National Standards document will need to change as educational conditions change. It is a starting place. At the very least, it is a document that will cause the music education community to honestly and thoroughly analyze what we do, why we do it, how we do it, and whether we should be doing something else in an entirely different way. We might find, in the phrase of Stephen Covey (1990), that we are "in the wrong jungle"—that our aims, goals and objectives are not the *right* ones for our students and us. Implementation of these or any standards may be a controversial issue, but as Susan Byo (1999) reminds us, "The national standards movement has brought heightened awareness to issues of curriculum, as well as a window of opportunity for improving the music education of our students" (p. 121).

The Consortium of National Arts Education Associations has sought to allay the fears of many about National Standards in its publication *Teacher Education for the Arts Disciplines* (1996).

> The Standards represent a consensus view of educators from professional associations in arts education about what constitutes a good education in dance, music, theatre, and the visual arts. They are not rules but guidelines, not regulations but benchmarks, not compulsory but voluntary. They are shaped by the well-validated educational principal that students respond to the level of expectation set before them (p. 5).

Shuler (1995) wrote that "teachers must continue to learn. It is impossible for teachers to learn everything necessary for lifelong success during their undergraduate years, both because of time limitations and because the profession will evolve during the many years that the teacher will spend in music education" (p. 4). *We* must be life-long learners if we want our *students* to be life-long learners. We have an obligation to the profession, our students, and ourselves, to remain current in the field. What we do, why we do it, and how we do it, continues to change. If the content of our courses is to remain meaningful and help prepare our students to be capable, enthusiastic music makers and music consumers, then we must continue to learn, to grow, and to expand our knowledge and skill base as teachers.

## Music Education Research

In my observation, practicing music educators do not, as a whole, exhibit much faith in the work of music education researchers. Band and orchestra teachers seem to be people who want to get things done in the quickest, most efficient, way. They are "doers," who tend to think of music education researchers as "lookers" or "thinkers." Likewise, many researchers in higher education seem to consider public and private school teachers as a group in great need of help—and researchers think they have the answers to the questions. They also think they know the questions that need to be answered. Unfortunately, some of the questions being asked and answered by higher education researchers are not considered important or helpful by music educators.

The NASSP, in *Breaking Ranks: Changing an American Institution* (1996), has stated that "Research in education should generally have links to learning and practice. Scholarship should play a role in informing and reforming the work of practitioners who strive to improve schools and school systems" (p. 87). There can, and should be, a *cooperative* effort to improve music instruction in the schools. Unfortunately, music research too often is focused on narrow issues difficult to generalize to the profession as a whole. As Richard Colwell (1995) has written

> Research in music education consists primarily of unpublished doctoral dissertations, most of which have been focused either on investigating the effect of a relatively trivial behavioral stimulus or on a descriptive or ethnographic study. These descriptive studies, while interesting, are not

helpful in convincing the supporters of music education that specific instruction, other than practices of private instruction, makes an actual difference (p. 7).

In short, there is too often a disconnection between practitioners and researchers. If a dialogue could be maintained between the two groups, researchers might look at very different topics and practitioners might have a greater interest in the results of that research. In addition, research will find a larger and more receptive audience when research results are published in a more accessible format, one that can be read and understood readily by music education practitioners. If we are to make the greatest positive impact on reforming and improving music education in this country, then we need the unified work of practitioners and researchers. When "informed practice"—the wisdom gained from years of success in the classroom—and scientific research on the large issues in music education work in tandem, we should see improvement in what we do in the schools.

You and your profession will benefit when you regularly read such publications as the *Journal of Research in Music Education* (from MENC), the *Journal of Band Research* (from the American Bandmasters Association), *Update* (from MENC), *Arts Education Policy Review* (formerly *Design for Arts in Education*), and *Phi Delta Kappan*. While the improvement of education is, indeed, a large puzzle, small pieces will be found in the research reported in these publications. Many of these publications are now on-line, making them much more accessible for music educators. Part of your professional responsibility is to keep current. Keep up to date on the results of the most recent research that pertains to your teaching. Your students will be the beneficiaries.

## For Assignment or Discussion

1. Reflect on the strengths and weaknesses of your high school educational program. Why do you believe these strengths and weaknesses developed, and what are the program changes you would recommend for your high school?

2. What educational reform efforts are being made in your high school? Discuss your opinion as to their effectiveness.

3. Should National Standards in music education be voluntary or required? Support your position.

4. In your opinion, are the current National Standards for Music Education appropriate for all students? Should there be different standards? If so, please list them.

5. Do you believe that adoption of the National Standards will decrease emphasis on performing ensembles? Is that positive or negative?

6. Read and reflect on a research article in the *Journal of Research in Music Education*, the *Journal of Band Research*, *Arts Education Policy Review*, or *Phi Delta Kappan*. Share this one-page, typed reflection with your colleagues in class.

## *For Reference and Further Reading*

Adams, Bobby (1994). How should band directors deal with school reform? *Strategic Planning for Instrumental Education* (1993-94 *Task Force Committee Report*). The American Bandmasters Association.

Bennett, William J. (1992). *The De-Valuing of America: The Fight for Our Culture and Our Children*. New York: Summit Books.

Breaking Ranks: *Changing an American Institution* (1996). Reston, VA: National Association of Secondary School Principals.

Byo, Susan J. (1999). Classroom teachers' and music specialists' perceived ability to implement the national standards for music education. *Journal of Research in Music Education*, 47/2, 111-123.

Colwell, Richard (1970). *The Evaluation of Music Teaching and Learning*. Englewood Cliffs, NJ: Prentice-Hall, Inc.

Colwell, Richard (1990). The posture of music education research. *Design for Arts in Education*. (May/June), 42-52.

Colwell, Richard (1992). *Handbook of Research on Music Teaching and Learning*. Reston, VA: Music Educators National Conference.

Colwell, Richard (1994). Thinking and walking backwards into the future. *Arts Education Policy Review*. 95/5 (May/June).

Colwell, Richard (1995). Will voluntary national standards fix the potholes of arts education? *Arts Education Policy Review*, 96/5 (May/June).

Consortium of National Arts Education Associations (1994). *National Standards for Arts Education*. Reston, VA: Music Educators National Conference.

Consortium of National Arts Education Associations (1996). *Teacher Education for the Arts Disciplines*. Reston, VA: Music Educators National Conference.

Coostanza, Peter and Russell, Timothy (1992). Methodologies in music education, in *Handbook of Research on Music Teaching and Learning*. Reston, VA: Music Educators National Conference.

Covey, Stephen R. (1990). *The Seven Habits of Highly Effective People: Restoring the Character Ethic.* New York: Fireside

Eisner, Elliot W. (1995). Standards for American schools: help or hindrance? *Phi Delta Kappan.* June 1995 (758-764).

Elliott, David J. (1995). *Music Matters: A New Philosophy of Music Education.* New York: Oxford University Press.

Forsythe, Jere L. (1987). The blind musicians and the elephant, in *Applications of Research in Music Behavior* (edited by Clifford K. Madsen and Carol A. Prickett). Tuscaloosa, AL: The University of Alabama Press. pp. 329-338.

Flohr, John W. (1999). Recent brain research on young children. *Teaching Music.* 5/6 (June) (41-43, 54)

Fullan, Michael G. and Miles, Matthew B. (1992). Getting reform right: what works and what doesn't. *Phi Delta Kappan.* June (745-752).

Gardner, Howard (1991). *The Unschooled Mind: How Children Think and How Schools Teach.* New York: Basic Books.

Gfeller, Kate (1992). Research regarding students with disabilities, in *Handbook of Research on Music Teaching and Learning.* Reston, VA: Music Educators National Conference.

Glasser, William(1990, 1992). *The Quality School (2nd ed.).* New York: HarperCollins Publishers.

Glasser, William (1992). The quality school curriculum. *Phi Delta Kappan.* May (690-694).

Gordon, Edwin (1971). *The Psychology of Music Teaching.* Englewood Cliffs, NJ: Prentice-Hall, Inc.

Humphreys, Jere, et al (1992). Research on music ensembles, in *Handbook of Research on Music Teaching and Learning.* Reston, VA: Music Educators National Conference.

Kohn, Alfie (1993). *Punished by Rewards: The Trouble with Gold Stars, Incentive Plans, A's, Praise, and Other Bribes.* New York: Houghton Mifflin Co.

Lautzenheiser, Tim (1992). *The Art of Successful Teaching: A Blend of Content and Context.* Chicago: GIA Pub.

Lehman, Paul R. (1986). Teaching music in the 1900's. *Dialogue in Instrumental Music Education.* 10/1 (Spring) (3-18).

Lehman, Paul R. (1992). Winning and losing in the struggle to reform education. *Design for Arts in Education.* May/June (2-12).

Lehman, Paul R. (1995). Control of K-12 arts education: who sets the curriculum? *Arts Education Policy Review.* 97/2 (Nov./Dec.) (16-20).

Leonhard, Charles and House, Robert W. (1972). *Foundations and Principles of Music Education (2nd Ed.).* New York: McGraw-Hill Book Co.

Leonhard, Charles (1958). Evaluation in music education. In *Basic Concepts in Music Education.* Nelson B. Henry, ed. Chicago: The University of Chicago Press. (pp. 310-338).

Lisk, Edward S. (1994). How should band directors deal with school reform? *Strategic Planning for Instrumental Education (1993-94 Task Force Committee Report)*. The American Bandmasters Association.

Manno, Bruno V. (1995). The new school wars: battles over outcome-based education. *Phi Delta Kappan*. (May, 720-726).

Moody, William J. (ed.) (1990). *Artistic Intelligences: Implications for Education*. New York: Teachers College Press.

Music Educators National Conference (1994a). *Opportunity-to-Learn Standards for Music Instruction*. Reston, VA: Music Educators National Conference.

Music Educators National Conference (1994b). *The School Music Program: A New Vision*. Reston, VA: Music Educators National Conference.

Music Educators National Conference (1995). *With One Voice: A Report from the 1994 Summit on Music Education*. Reston, VA: Music Educators National Conference.

Music Educators National Conference (1996). *Performance Standards for Music*. Reston, VA: Music Educators National Conference.

Pogrow, Stanley (1996). Reforming the wannabe reforms. *Phi Delta Kappan*. June (656-663).

Pranaitis, Shanna and Ashley, Richard (2000). The elusive search for proof that music improves the mind. *The Instrumentalist*. 30-32, 77 (Dec.).

Rutkowski, Joseph (1996). Conducting research in the music classroom. *Music Educators Journal*. (March), 43-45 and 62.

Schmid, Will (1996). Parting shots. *Teaching Music, 3/6*, 4-5.

Schmidt, Charles P. and Zdzinski, Stephen F. (1993). Cited quantitative research articles in music education research journals, 1975-1990: a content analysis of selected studies. *Journal of Research in Music Education. 41/1*, 5-18.

Shuler, Scott C. (1995). The impact of national standards on the preparation, in-service professional development, and assessment of music teachers. *Arts Education Policy Review. 96/3* (Jan.-Feb.).

Steinberg, Laurence (1996). *Beyond the Classroom—Why School Reform Has Failed and What Parents Need to Do*. New York: Touchstone.

Weerts, Richard (1992). Research on the teaching of instrumental music, in *Handbook of Research on Music Teaching and Learning*. Reston, VA: Music Educators National Conference.

Chapter Thirteen

# EXPLORING PERSONAL ISSUES FOR THE MUSIC EDUCATOR

## The Job Search

Completing a college instrumental music education program should prepare you for a successful job search. The content of all those methods courses should provide the knowledge, skills, and understandings to prepare you to find—and be successful in—that first job. Let's take a look at the three aspects of the job search: "where are the jobs?," "how do I do the paperwork?," and "how can I do an impressive interview?"

### Where Are The Jobs?

Every area of the country needs teachers every year. In fact, some parts of the country will experience a significant teacher shortage. An important part of a successful job search is to decide where you would like to teach. Many people like to go "home" to teach, but you will have a much better chance of finding, and landing, the kind of job you really want if you are open to moving around the country. That is not to suggest that it is a bad idea to want to teach in the area you call "home"—there are many very important and valid reasons to go back to your home state to teach. You simply have to realize that deciding to do that may limit the kinds of jobs available to you.

How do you find out about jobs in music education? The obvious answer is the Career Center at your college or university. That is a good place to check, but you should realize that they do not get all the job listings from all areas of the country. Many jobs are filled before they get to any Career Center. There are other, probably more important, sources of job listings. For instrumentalists, there is a "job listings" section in every issue of The *Instrumentalist* magazine. Most state departments of education maintain a Web-based listing of known job openings in their state. Many state or regional professional organizations also offer a job listing service. A number of state associations of private or church-related schools maintain Web sites that include a listing of open jobs. Some state, regional, or national music organizations have job fairs at their conventions. There are also several music employment agencies that charge a fee for their service.

If you plan to look for a teaching position in your home state, you might consider contacting the state department of education and purchasing a set of mailing labels for all school districts in that state. You could then send letters of inquiry to all those districts in which you have an interest. Another source for this information is *Patterson's American Education*. All school districts in the United States are listed, along with the correct mailing address and the names and phone numbers of the school administrators. This resource is probably available in your college education department or the college library. A new edition is published each year. You can find the same information on individual school Web sites. While these two ideas will identify school districts in a particular geographic area, probably you will want to use a more specific approach to increase your chances of finding the best job for you.

Most jobs are obtained through networking. For information about job openings in your home area, talk with friends already in the business and to your high school band, orchestra, or choir director. Probably the least used—but sometimes best—source of information is salespeople from local music stores. They often know if someone is leaving a position long before that person submits a resignation. Some music stores even maintain a master list of available music positions that is more accurate and up-to-date than the list at the state department of education!

## The Paperwork

You will need a well-written and professional looking résumé. It should be one page long (longer only for teachers with several years experience), and I recommend that you print it on a light colored (tan, ivory, or even a very light blue or green) or textured paper to help make it stand out in a group of stark-white résumés. Just be careful not to go overboard with the color! Choose an attractive business-like font and print your résumé on a high quality laser printer.

A number of fine books and software programs are available to help you prepare an attractive and informative résumé. Your college Career Center will probably own several. Here is the basic information for a résumé:

- Your full name, address and telephone number (If you list your college address as your current mailing address, be sure to also include your home address or other permanent mailing address. Also include your e-mail address.)
- Your employment goal or objective
- Your educational record (List your college and location, with year of graduation. List degree earned and include your GPA only if it is above 3.0.)
- Experience—with place, position, and dates of association (The heading of "experience" allows you to include volunteer positions—especially those that involve working with children. Use action words in a sentence fragment describing your duties for each position.)
- Collegiate and professional recognitions, awards, and memberships (including scholarships earned, offices held in organizations, etc.)

Some optional categories include

- Relevant courses listed under the education section
- Community involvement and honors
- Special skills (advanced computer or technology skills, speaking fluency in a foreign language, etc.)
- Publications
- A list of three or four references with address and telephone number (These should be the people you have asked to write references for your reference file at your college. This can be on a separate sheet of the same paper used for your résumé. Indicate their role in your life: methods teacher, student teacher supervisor, student teaching cooperating teacher, etc.)

List items beginning with the most recent, and include dates where applicable. Figure 13-1 is an example of a résumé for an instrumental music education major. Use action verbs (achieved, completed, developed, designed, etc.), concrete nouns, and positive modifiers (competence, consistent, versatile, etc.) in brief incomplete sentences to describe your duties and accomplishments for each "experience" position. Use action verbs, concrete nouns, and positive modifiers to describe your employment goal or objective. Your employment goal should be concise, realistic, and not too "boastful." Two examples of employment goals or objectives are:

- Instrumental music educator for a public or private school system
- Instrumental music educator using my creative, organizational, and leadership skills.

After you have prepared your résumé and identified some available positions, you will need to contact potential employers. The letter should be typed and personalized—it should not be a "form letter." This letter of inquiry should be brief and should express your interest in applying for their open position, should tell where you heard about the position, should give a very brief self-introduction, and should ask for an application (see Figure 13-2). It is essential that the letter be cleanly typed and have absolutely no spelling or grammatical errors. Remember, this letter is your "first impression"—make it a good one! Actually, the real first impression will be the envelope that contains your material—make it neat, business-like and *typed*.

After you fill out the application (again, it should be typed or neatly printed), return it with a brief cover letter, your résumé, your Philosophy of Music Education, copies of recent recital or concert programs (if you played a major role), and performance recordings (if requested). Your cover letter (see Figure 13-3) should state that you are available for an interview, that you look forward to visiting their community, and that your reference file and transcript are available (some school districts will ask that you include those with your application). I recommend that your cover letter include a request that the school district return an enclosed stamped postcard notifying you that they have received your material. This helps establish some very important two-way communication. It is usually best not to call a school district to check on the status of your application—you don't want to be viewed as a pest!

**Figure 13-1.  Sample Résumé**

# Michael J. Brown
michaelbrown@emailcity.com

*College Address*                                   *Permanent Address*
Smalltown College                                1234 Madeline Drive
College Post Office Box 231                   Anytown, OH  33333
Smalltown, MI  44444                            (540) 455-1234
(859) 887-5555

**Objective**
   High school band and orchestra teacher.

**Education**
   Bachelor of Music Education (May, 2003)          (GPA: 3.65)
   Smalltown College, Smalltown, MI
   Major:  Instrumental Music

**Experience**
   Student teacher:  Smalltown High School, Smalltown, MI (Spring 2003)
     • *Taught the elementary band and strings.*
     • *Assisted with the high school band and orchestra.*

   Conductor:  Anytown Community Band, Anytown, OH (Summer 2002)
     • *Directed sixty member volunteer band in a six-concert series.*

   Camp Counselor:  Camp Vivace, Littletown, KY (Summer 2001)
     • *Administered archery and tennis instruction for the entire camp.*
     • *Directed all cabin activities for twelve campers.*

   Volunteer:  Smalltown Elementary School, Smalltown, MI
   (September-May 2001-2002)
     • *Provided small groups of students with remedial help in reading*
       *and math during the 2001-2002 school year.*

   Trumpet Teacher:  Smalltown School District, Smalltown,
   MI (September-May 2000-2002)
     • *Instructed 10-12 students in an after-school private lesson pro-*
       *gram.*

**Honors and Awards**
   Outstanding Music Education Major:  Smalltown College (Spring 2003)

   President, Collegiate Music Educators National Conference.
   Smalltown College (2002-2003 school year)

   President, Smalltown College Orchestra (2002-2003 school year)

*Figure 13-2. Sample Letter of Inquiry*

## Michael J. Brown
1234 Madeline Drive
Anytown, OH 33333
(540) 455-1234
michaelbrown@emailcity.com

May 3, 2003

Dr. George Towers, Principal
Great City High School
Great City, IN 33456

Dear Dr. Towers:

The Career Center at Smalltown College has informed me of an open position for a band director at your high school. I would like to apply for that position.

I am a recent graduate of Smalltown College with a degree in instrumental music education and a strong background in band (marching, concert, pep, and jazz) and orchestra. My successful student teaching experience—in the Smalltown (Michigan) School District—was in a school district very similar to your district.

I look forward to receiving the application and talking further with you about the position.

Cordially yours,

Michael J. Brown

*Figure 13-3. Sample Application Cover Letter*

**Michael J. Brown**
1234 Madeline Drive
Anytown, OH 33333
(540) 455-1234
michaelbrown@emailcity.com

May 15, 2003

Dr. George Towers, Principal
Great City High School
Great City, IN 33456

Dear Dr. Towers:

Enclosed is my application for the position of band director at Great City High School. I have also enclosed a copy of my resume, my Philosophy of Music Education, and copies of some recent programs. Also enclosed is a recording of an excerpt from my senior trumpet recital and of two pieces performed by the Smalltown (Michigan) High School Band which I conducted on their recent Spring Concert.

I am available for an interview and would enjoy talking with you about this position. I believe that I meet all of the qualifications stated for the position and I believe that my background and education have prepared me to be very successful in such a position. I look forward to visiting your community and interviewing for this exciting position.

My placement file and academic transcript are being sent to you by the Smalltown College Career Center.

Dr. Towers, would you please send the enclosed stamped and self-addressed postcard which will notify me that you have received my application materials? Thank you.

I look forward to hearing from you soon.

Cordially yours,

Michael J. Brown

Be sure to keep copies of all information and correspondence about each position for which you apply. This can be kept in a manila file folder for each position or in a binder with dividers. Be organized and keep track of the paperwork.

Typically, though you send many applications, you will be invited to only a small number of interviews. Do not be discouraged. Many open positions will have 50 or more applicants, and all that paperwork can severely overload school offices. The result is that many school districts will not acknowledge receipt of your application or even let you know who got the job. Do not take it personally—while some people may be rude and insensitive, most are simply overworked.

## The Interview

Let us assume that you have been scheduled for an interview. You will, obviously, know that personnel at the interviewing district are serious about your candidacy for the position. Most school districts will interview only three or four candidates for a position, so you should feel very good about being invited to interview.

These suggestions will help you prepare for you interview

1. The interview is the "deciding factor."
2. Be prepared for it, be poised, and be confident.
3. Dress conservatively and neatly—personal appearance is very important for music educators.
4. Arrive 10 minutes early for your interview, but no more than 20 minutes early.
5. Never be late!
6. Introduce yourself to everyone on the interview panel and try to remember—and use—their names during the interview.
7. Use first names only if invited to do so by those on the interview panel.
8. Let the lead interviewer indicate where you should sit.
9. It is important that you communicate and interact during the interview.
10. Look directly at a person asking a question and try to establish eye contact with each person on the interview panel.

11. Do not just give basic one- and two-word answers to questions, yet be careful not to "ramble."
12. Avoid slang and casual terminology—use professional and mature language.
13. Be sure to sit up tall in your chair, be aware of arm and hand position, and avoid distracting mannerisms.
14. Be optimistic and positive in your answers.

Prepare thoroughly for the interview. Know as much as possible about the school district and community. You may want to arrive early for your interview and spend some time talking to people around town—at gas stations and other local businesses. You should read the local newspaper. It also helps, of course, if you know someone familiar with the community who can give you insight into the school district and community. Showing familiarity with their turf tells them that you are as interested in them as they are in you.

Anticipate questions that might be asked in the interview and think through possible answers. Be ready for questions about how you would handle discipline, how you would work with parents and boosters groups, and what you believe to be your "strong" and "weak" points (which is an awful question but is frequently asked). The willingness to answer this question reveals a self-awareness and a desire to improve. As a band director candidate you will often be asked about your marching band style and philosophy (including the question of competition), and whether you can work with coaches. You should also be prepared to recommend teaching materials (both textbooks and performance literature for ensembles) and explain why you would use them. Figure 13-4 is a list of typical interview questions for a position in instrumental music education. While not an exhaustive list, it covers most of the topics discussed in a typical job interview. Obviously, some questions are quite technical in nature and would be asked only by music professionals on the interview panel.

**Figure 13-4. Typical Job Interview Questions**

1. Would you please tell us a little about yourself and why you want to teach instrumental music?
2. What techniques do you consider effective for classroom management in the large groups you would typically encounter in instrumental music?

3. What are your strengths and weaknesses? Please evaluate and discuss each.

4. How would you describe your teaching style?

5. What are your career and personal goals, and how will they be attained through employment in this school district?

6. What do you know about our community and our schools, and why would you like to teach here?

7. In a few sentences, please state your philosophy of music education.

8. What are some of the beginning band (or string) methods books you would recommend that we consider using with our 5th grade beginning band (or strings)? [Title and author, publisher is helpful.]

9. Could you please recommend two or three pieces of fine band (or orchestra) music for our 8th grade middle school band (or orchestra)? They are now playing Grade Three music. [Title and composer, publisher is helpful.]

10. Our high school band (or orchestra) is playing Grade Five music. Could you recommend several fine pieces of literature for this group? [Title and composer, publisher is helpful.]

11. Our high school marching band now competes in about seven contests each fall. What is your personal philosophy about marching band competition?

12. Our high school music program (in a high school of 1,200 students) consists of one band and one choir. We would like to expand our program and involve more of our student body, while at the same time offering some enrichment courses for our students already involved in the program. What would you suggest we add to the program?

13. Do you have some examples of your work that you would like to show us?

14. I am hearing a lot about National Standards in music. Would you please tell us what you know about these standards and how they might effect your teaching?

15. This position in instrumental music may also include teaching one middle school choir. Do you feel that you would be qualified to add that responsibility?

16. Our high school band & orchestra boosters club is a very hard-working group that has raised a lot of funds to support the program. Unfortunately, in the last few years there has been some tension between them and the previous director. How would you go about improving that situation?

17. In the last few years we have had more and more students involved in both the band and orchestra program, and the athletics program. This has sometimes caused conflicts between the band and orchestra directors and the coaches because some events were scheduled at the same time. How would you work to resolve that situation?

18. Have you thought about how you will plan for personal professional development after you begin your teaching career?

19. We have had a few years of tight budgets in our school district, and the band and orchestra boosters have helped out by funding some things that were previously funded by the Board of Education. We are now trying to sort out what kinds of things are appropriate for each group (the Board and the boosters) to fund. What are your thoughts on this subject?

20. I notice that we have very few oboes, bassoons, and French horns in the band. What steps would you take to fix that problem? Or, is it a problem? [or orchestra: very few violas and string basses.]

21. How would you determine grades for the band or orchestra for each marking period?

22. Our previous instrumental music teacher often used the term "comprehensive musicianship." I never really understood what he was talking about but he seemed to think it was important. Can you tell me what he meant by "comprehensive musicianship"?

23. In the last few years several knowledgeable parents, and a number of music festival adjudicators, have mentioned that our band [or orchestra] does not play very well in tune. How would you work to solve that problem?

24. The percussionists in our band always seem to be getting into trouble. What strategies or techniques would you suggest to solve this problem?

25. When our band plays it seems to have a very harsh sound, and about all you can hear are the drums, flutes, and first trumpets. How could you solve this problem?

26. I am a former history teacher and I think that knowing about our past is a great way to guide our present work and, hopefully, prevent us from repeating some of the mistakes of the past. Who are some of the most important names in the history of music education in this country and what are some of the most significant events in that history?

27. Our previous band and orchestra director did not take the students to solo and ensemble festivals. Should our students attend these festivals?

28. How do you get band and orchestra members to practice their instruments on a regular basis?

29. How do you motivate students?

30. What important things did you learn from your student teaching experience?

31. How do you plan to involve special needs children in instrumental music?

32. What kinds of technology do you use in your classroom and in your office?

33. What does the word "diversity" mean to you, and what impact does it have on your teaching?

34. Would you please briefly describe what you believe to be an effective recruiting program for a beginning band or orchestra class?

35. Do you have some questions for us?

36. When this committee is reviewing all candidates in preparation for our final hiring recommendation, what one thing about you would you like us to remember?

Your interview could be a series of one-on-one interviews with such people as the school principal, the music supervisor, the curriculum director, the personnel director, the assistant superintendents, the superintendent, or even the full Board of Education in some smaller districts. If you are interviewed by a committee it will usually have four to eight members, including administrators, other teachers, and, possibly parents and students.

You should take several things to an interview, just in case you need them. Take your portfolio with examples of your very finest work in both education and music education classes. Include examples of assignments and projects related directly to your preparation as a future teacher. Your college department of education may help you develop your portfolio and may recommend that you incorporate standards or issues mandated by the state department of education or by "learned societies" in the profession. You may want to include examples of your work that relate to the National Standards of Music Education from the Music Educators National Conference to show that you are attuned to the work of leading music educators in this country.

You may also want to take your personal "program book" to the interview, with copies of all your major recital and concert programs. Take copies of any journal articles you have written; performance tapes (if not previously sent); names, addresses, and telephone numbers of your references; several copies of your Philosophy of Music Education; a copy of your transcript; a copy of all the correspondence with that school district; and a written list of questions you want to ask during your interview. You may be asked to play an audition for the interview panel, so have your instrument with you and a couple of audition pieces (in divergent styles) prepared.

In the interview you should be sure to answer all questions forthrightly. Do not try to figure out the answer that the committee wants to hear. If your educational philosophy or teaching methods are vastly different from the rest of that school district, then you probably would not be happy or successful at that school. Your working relationship is a bit like a marriage in that both parties must enter the relationship honestly and with eyes wide open if you are to enjoy long-term accord.

If you do not know the answer to a question, simply say that—do not try to bluff your way through. It usually does not work! Sometimes, a simple "I have not thought about that issue before, but I would be glad to consider it and send my response tomorrow" will satisfy a questioner's concern. Be as relaxed and personable as possible in the interview. Sometimes, a few moments of "small talk" at the beginning of the interview can help break the ice and help you relax.

I think it important for you to ask questions at the interview. Have a written list and be sure to take notes as the committee responds to your questions. This demonstrates good organization and preparation on your part, not to mention sincere interest. Some questions you may want to ask are

- What are the specific job duties?
- Is there a written job description?
- Is there a written curriculum?
- How many performances per year for each ensemble?
- What is the current condition of the program?
- What do they expect from the program?
- What was the relationship with the former teacher to the students (and parents, faculty, administration, and community)?
- Is the school faculty supportive of the music program?
- What is the budget for the music program (music, new instruments, etc.)?
- What is the financial condition of the school district?
- What is your philosophy of music education in regard to striking a balance between learning and skill development, competition, and community entertainment?

Ask to tour the building (especially the music facility) and ask to see accurate instrument and music inventory lists. The question of salary and benefits (and extra pay for extra duty) may not be mentioned in the interview process. If it does not come up, do not ask for it at the interview. While none of us pursued music education to get rich, we do need to earn a fair wage to meet our financial obligations. Most school districts in a given geographic area will pay similar salaries, but the "extra pay" schedules often have a wide range of pay for similar duties. Particularly in states with collective bargaining laws, pay scales are readily available by mail or on the Internet.

After the interview you should send a follow-up letter expressing your appreciation for the opportunity to interview and stating that you look forward to hearing the decision of the committee soon (see Figure 13-5).

If you are offered a job, you should accept or decline in writing quickly. One important point: You should choose and accept only a job for which you are prepared. You will enjoy it more and will have more of a chance of being successful. Never accept a position that has a high chance of failure because you are not prepared to fill the complete job description.

As you start the job process, I encourage you to be organized. Approach it with the same, or more, effort than you would expend in trying to get an "A" in a very difficult college course. Study and prepare for interviews. Using a checklist such as the one in Figure 13-6 may help you organize your job search. Finding and securing the

*Figure 13-5. Sample Follow-up Letter*

---

**Michael J. Brown**
1234 Madeline Drive
Anytown, OH 33333
(540) 455-1234
michaelbrown@emailcity.com

June 10, 2003

Dr. George Towers, Principal
Great City High School
Great City, IN 33456

Dear Dr. Towers:

Thank you for the opportunity to interview for the band director position at Great City High School. I enjoyed meeting you and all the members of the committee and learning more about your school and community.

If any other information is needed please contact me at the telephone number listed above. I look forward to hearing soon of the decision of the committee.

Cordially yours,

Michael J. Brown

---

"right" job is one of the most important events in your career as a music educator. Make it a priority to do it right!

Be careful about accepting a position just because you think it might be a good "stepping stone" to a better job. You do yourself and your future students a disservice with this kind of attitude about a position. When you begin any job, it should be with the thought that it could be the only position you will hold in your 30- or 40-year career. Resolve to give your very best to that new job and your new students—do all you can, learn all you can, teach all you can, and be all you can.

*Figure 13-6. Checklist for a Job Search*

## Job Search Checklist

**Spring Semester (junior year)**

___ Attend all job fairs, résumé, and interview workshops, etc. offered by the college Career Center.

___ Revise your Philosophy of Music Education.

___ Begin your process of deciding in which geographical areas you would like to teach.

___ Establish professional contacts in the geographical area in which you want to teach.

**Summer (before senior year)**

___ Find a teaching-related summer job.

___ Continue to network with friends, relatives, professors, and former teachers who may help in your job search.

**September (senior year)**

___ Complete all registration material with the college Career Center.

___ Continue to network.

**November (senior year)**

___ Talk to those you would like to list as references and ask them to write a letter of reference. Letters of reference could wait until near the end of student teaching.

___ Revise and refine your résumé.

___ Revise and refine your letter of inquiry and application cover letter.

___ Develop a contact list of school districts in which you may wish to teach.

___ Begin to regularly check any on-line job posting services in your desired geographical area.

**January (senior year)**

___ Continue to attend all career workshops scheduled at the Career Center.

___ Continue to network with friends, relatives, professors, and former teachers who may help in your job search.

___ Use your contact list to begin to request applications.

**February (senior year)**

___ Check with the Career Center that all references and other material have been received.

___ Check the job listings in your Career Center each week.

**March (senior year)**

___ Do research for each position for which you plan to apply.

___ Continue to network with friends, relatives, professors, and former teachers who may help in your job search.

___ Subscribe to the job vacancy bulletin published by the college Career Center.

___ Be sure to send thank you notes after all interviews and to those who have helped in your job search.

___ Accept or decline (in writing) all job offers quickly.

You and your students will greatly benefit from such an approach to teaching.

A helpful brochure about careers and the job search from MENC is available at their Web site (MENC.org).

# Ethics

As a music educator you have a unique opportunity of having a significant impact on your student's lives. In small school districts, you may teach students from their elementary school years through graduation from high school. In addition, you will spend a significant amount of time with the students under a great variety of circumstances (band camp, tours, concerts, festivals and contests, etc.). They will see you, and you will see them, under the best and worst conditions—and you will see how each other responds to those conditions. And rest assured—your students *are* watching and evaluating!

The way you lead your life will speak loudly about the "real" you. Some suggestions:

- Dress—Make sure your dress is professional, appropriate for the occasion, modest, and mature.
- Speech—Be careful about good grammar and avoid slang (you often may not know the exact, latest definition anyway!), double-meaning terms, etc. Basically, keep what you say as professional and straight-forward as possible.
- Attitude—Be sure you have and display a healthy attitude concerning yourself, your students, your job, your administration, etc. It usually shows in what you say and do. Work to keep it positive! You may not have as much control over your job situation as you would like—but, you do have control over your own attitude.
- Temper—Certainly, this relates to attitude, but it is a major issue with those in the "performance" arena because of all the pressures that ensemble performance can create. Loss of temper is rarely justifiable.
- Treatment of students—Are you in control of yourself in rehearsals? Do you treat students in a humane manner—in a way you would want to be treated? Do you compromise personal relationships just for the sake of "winning"— whether that relates to seeking a superlative concert performance, a "superior" rating at festival or contest, or some other external award? Is "success" worth *any* cost?

- The influence of your spouse—If you are married, your spouse will often be with you and your ensemble as you go on trips, or to contests or festivals. He or she will have a much more significant influence on your students than you will ever anticipate. Be sure to state and show your appreciation to your spouse for the support of you and your students. It is also the kind of positive life-style modeling students appreciate seeing from their teachers.

You will face general moral issues almost every day as a school teacher. Some are more obvious than others, but all are important.

- Music selection—Play "good" music. That may include some well-arranged pop music, but make sure you know the lyrics and their intent. Also, you can play and sing "religious" music in the public schools within certain guidelines (see the MENC brochure "Religious Music in the Schools"). Be sensitive to school and community feelings, and be sure to talk it over with your building administrator. You may have to remind administrators and parents that the Constitution guarantees freedom of religion, not freedom *from* religion. Whatever religious content you put before students will constitute only an artifact of human society, not a religious statement.
- Music Copying—Do not illegally copy music. Know the copyright law and follow it. The composer and the publisher deserve to be paid for their work. A very helpful article is available online from the MENC Web site.
- Performing at "professional events" or political events—Do not do it if it takes work away from professional musicians or is an endorsement of something with which you should not be involved. In my opinion it is not ethical to play for a political rally (even for a candidate you support).
- Schedule conflicts—Avoid scheduling rehearsals or concerts on the traditional midweek "church night" in your community. Would you excuse students from your rehearsals or performances for family or church responsibilities? Advance planning can avoid conflicts. Can you reach a compromise? Can you or they change dates?

**334**     One issue that needs to be discussed more openly and thoroughly in music education courses is the developing and maintaining of appropriate relationships with students. While your extended contact with students as their music teacher—sometimes across several years—carries the advantages cited earlier, that contact also increases opportunities for inappropriate relationships to develop. Be aware that you exert considerable influence on your students and attract great loyalty from them. All the while, you need to be vigilant about your responsibility to maintain a professional, adult role—to set and maintain boundaries appropriate to a teacher/student relationship. Teachers lose reputations and even jobs because of student accusations, some false, so live above reproach. Here are some pieces of advice that might help you protect both yourself and your students.

- When you give private lessons, use a room with a window in the door.
- Never be alone with a student for an extended period of time.
- Be careful not to ask questions of students that could be misinterpreted as to their intent.
- Avoid giving students a ride without written permission from their parents.
- Touch students only for sound educational reasons, and only with their permission.
- Never touch a student in anger.

It is sad, but this is the reality of teaching today. Avoid even the possible "appearance of evil." If an incident occurs that could be questioned, be sure to discuss it with your supervisor and local teachers association representative immediately.

Also, be sure your relationships with colleagues, administrators, parents, and representatives of the music industry are strictly professional and appropriate. The same advice about relationships with students extends to these as well.

Another concern is to guard against "using" students through inappropriate scheduling. Students have lives away from band or orchestra! They have family responsibilities, religious responsibilities, part-time jobs—and other teachers who expect them to study once in a while! Try always to find a balance between keeping your band and orchestra students busy and involved with your ensembles, and demanding too much of their time. Having an active program will increase student loyalty, but avoid scheduling too many extra rehearsals and sectionals, attending an excessive number of contests, or taking elaborate tours that demand many hours of trip fundraising and rehearsals. Try to see the "big picture." You will want your students to develop a loyalty to your ensemble and have an unforgettable experience, but be sure they remember it as a part of life rather than as an obstacle to life during their school years.

Set a good example for your students by putting "first things first" in your own personal and professional life. Be sure that what you say is important in your life (family, faith, job, etc.) gets priority attention. Stephen Covey (1990) reminds us that "The key is not to prioritize what's on your schedule, but to schedule your priorities" (p. 161). Be sure that "distractions"—even laudable undertakings such as service club memberships, volunteer work, etc.—do not inhibit you from keeping your focus on those things you say are important. John Whitwell, in a interview with John Thomson (1995), said that "There should be balance between our musical work, family activities, hobbies, and physical well-being in order to have a freshness and focus in the classroom. . . .Part of staying fresh and vibrant is the ability to release what happened today so you can start the next day with a renewed spirit" (p. 15).

While we all want to make sure that we give 100 percent to our students and the music program, we do not want to realize some day that we have sacrificed some things that we say are very important to us. Ed Solomon, in his article "Strangers at My Table," wrote of the serious potential to get so wrapped up in our jobs that we neglect those closest to us—our families. The key, and the difficulty, is to keep all things in balance—and to keep "first things first."

The life you live in front of your students, their parents, your colleagues, administrators, and staff tells them who you are and what you believe. Some of your students will need a positive role model or substitute father- or mother-figure because of the lack of one in their own family—and you may not even realize that you are supplying that need. It may seem that some students just like to "hang out" around the band room, but there may be a significant reason for all that time spent in your classroom.

## Relational Skills

Tim Lautzenheiser (1992) has written that ". . .the ability to get along with others is the single most important commodity of our profession" (p. 48). A certain level of conflict between teachers, coaches, and other staff members is inevitable in the schools, because all of these people are interested in developing and sustaining support for their particular subject or activity. It is appropriate for all of these people to work hard to make their activity successful and important to the school setting.

Many young teachers are unprepared for the tensions that can develop between teachers. We have all heard horror stories of difficulties between band directors and coaches, but these same kinds of conflicts arise between band and orchestra directors, or band directors and drama teachers, or orchestra directors and choir directors. Performance pressures commonly lead to disagreement and discord. You can avoid many problems with careful and early scheduling of all major events. Be sure to avoid conflicts with all the athletic events, plays, etc. that you can. Some problems are unavoidable, but be sure that all students are kept out of the middle of conflicts. Try to work out all conflicts with the other adult (coach or other teacher). If you are unsuccessful, take the issue to your school principal for resolution. Often you will discover that one event is obviously more important than the other is. A concert is certainly more important than an athletic team practice, and a league basketball game is more important than an evening orchestra rehearsal. If things are not easily resolved between the adults, you may choose to allow the student to make the choice. If so, both of the adult leaders must agree that the student involved may make the choice without fear of any consequence from either adult.

You will also find it important to develop a good working relationship with your administrators, secretaries, custodians, and all other faculty. Work hard at this—you will need their support of your instrumental music program. Become involved in the entire school program: volunteer to chaperone a school dance or a ski trip, volunteer to serve on teacher committees, and attend faculty social activities. Find time to go to the teacher's lounge. If other teachers get to know you, they are more likely to be positive about you and your program. Never expect automatic approval and acceptance just because you are the new band or orchestra director. You have to *earn* that acceptance by your actions.

## Professional Development

A thorough undergraduate music education program will prepare you to begin to teach successfully, but it cannot prepare you to be 100 percent ready for every aspect of every teaching position. There are too many variables, and the profession keeps changing. Your assignment may change slightly, or new program standards may be adopted by your school district. It will then be up to you to "fill in the gaps" of knowledge, skill, and understanding needed for your current position.

Planning for your own professional development is an important responsibility for all teachers. Professional development may include a graduate degree, but it also includes attending state, regional, and national music education conferences. Also, many colleges and universities offer workshops and clinics that foster new skills (such as teaching improvisation in the full rehearsal, fiddling group techniques, instrument repair, etc.) or help you refine current skills (conducting, beginning band methods and materials, etc.). You will receive notices of these opportunities through the mail and by way of your professional journals. You owe it to yourself and your students to keep up-to-date in your field. Allow yourself to become professionally empowered. Avoid falling into the trap of complacency—do not be content with a familiar and "comfortable" technique or materials, because something new may revolutionize your teaching if you give it a chance. Remember that there is not just one correct way of doing most things. Find the best way for you and your students.

Belong to and become an active member of your professional organizations. The meetings and social times of these professional organizations will provide important collegial interaction that lead to conversations about unknown materials and methods. Some memberships include subscriptions to major professional journals. Be sure to read them all! A partial list of available professional journals follows.

- *The Instrumentalist*
- *Music Educators Journal* (MENC)
- *Teaching Music* (MENC)
- *Bandworld*
- *Journal of Research in Music Education* (MENC)
- *Journal of Band Research* (ABA)

Bruce Boston (1996) reminds us that "Improvement of arts education for all K-12 students in terms of the Standards cannot be achieved without consistent and vigorous attention to professional development" (p. 9). According to Mary Pautz (1989)

A thoughtful music educator will not "jump on every bandwagon" that comes along but will evaluate and analyze critically the merits of each proposal. A thoughtful music educator will search for meaningful ways to incorporate the many new ideas learned at conventions into an organized curriculum rather than viewing these ideas as simply ready-made lesson plans for the next week, with no thought of sequence or follow through. . . . In other words, the thoughtful music educator will be a life-long expert learner and thus a master teacher. (p. 102)

It has been said that the great jazz musician Count Basie left out more notes when he played than most people ever thought of. Master teachers are like that. They know and understand much more than they actually use in the classroom, but that knowledge guides and informs their teaching. We can never know too much about our profession!

## A Complete Education

Teaching instrumental music is an incredibly multi-faceted profession. It sometimes seems that you should have majored in music education, public relations, psychology, business administration, public speaking, technology, and more! You will find that obtaining some skills and understandings in many of those areas will be beneficial to your teaching career. Unfortunately, you will not have time during your undergraduate program to take many of the courses that could be beneficial. After you begin your teaching career, you will need to "fill the gaps" by personal study, seeking advice from colleagues (in all disciplines) and students (especially in technology!), attending special workshops and clinics, and reading journals and books or taking courses at a local community college.

These are some possible "gaps" in your professional preparation:

- Instrument repair (it is necessary to at least learn "band room repairs")—you can acquire these skills at clinics or by asking technicians at your local instrument repair shop if you may watch them work on Saturdays
- Public Relations—there are a number of fine books on the topic
- Interpersonal skills/counseling—again, read a lot
- Business skills—a basic business course at a local college can be very helpful
- Technology—many colleges require a "tech ed" course for all education majors (the challenge is to keep current)

You might consider some of the following subjects that are not part of a "typical" college music education curriculum to round out your professional preparation.

- First Aid (including CPR)—this could be invaluable in a time of crisis.
- A Dale Carnegie Course
- Financial Planning—general concepts and personal financial planning.
- Motivational Workshops—Tim Lautzenheiser, Stephen Covey, and many more are worth the time.

## Habits of Effective Teachers

I have heard it said that "During college we make our habits, and after college our habits make us." The good habits you develop during college can help you become a better teacher after college. Take every opportunity to work with children. Consider a summer job at a youth camp, teach church school, volunteer to work with your church youth choir, volunteer to work with your old high school band during summer camp, etc. Not only do you help other people by doing this, but you learn valuable professional and interpersonal skills.

Develop personal and musical discipline. Keep promises, meet deadlines, commit to always doing your best, set meaningful priorities, schedule your priorities, be prepared for lessons and rehearsals, and treat people with respect. These habits will serve you well as a teacher, as an employee, as a spouse, and as a friend. Work to develop your own personal musicianship. David Elliott (1992) reminds us that "To be an expert music educator one must possess an expert level of musicianship" (9). Your musicianship will be developed and refined in the practice room, in the rehearsal room, in the lesson studio, and in the concert and recital halls. Take advantage of the growth these experiences present by being thoroughly prepared for rehearsals, lessons, recitals, and concerts. Make that a personal priority as a college student. After all, isn't that what you want from your students when you begin teaching? You can set the example for that behavior as a college student and then carry through with those habits when you begin your teaching career.

## *For Assignment or Discussion*

1. Prepare your résumé in an acceptable format. Try to make it only one page long.

2. Prepare a list of four questions you would want to ask at a job interview.

3. Your teacher will conduct a mock job interview with each student in your class using the questions in Figure 13-4. Use actual open positions posted with your college Career Center in the interview. Do appropriate research about the open position prior to your mock interview.

4. What are some ethical issues in addition to those mentioned in this chapter faced by teachers today? How can you be prepared to respond appropriately?

5. List five or six additional skills and understandings not listed in this book that an instrumental teacher may benefit from knowing. Suggest ways of acquiring these skills and understandings.

6. Read "Fiddler on the Fence" in the book *Case Studies in Music Education* (1998) by Frank Abrahams and Paul Head. As a class, discuss how you would handle this situation.

## *For Reference and Further Reading*

Abrahams, Frank and Head, Paul (1998). *Case Studies in Music Education*. Chicago: GIA Publications, Inc.

*Breaking Ranks: Changing an American Institution* (1996). Reston, VA: National Association of Secondary School Principals.

Covey, Stephen R. (1990). *The Seven Habits of Highly Effective People: Restoring the Character Ethic*. New York: Fireside

Covey, Stephen R. (1992). *Principle-Centered Leadership*. New York: Fireside.

Choksy, Lois, et al. (1986). *Teaching Music in the Twentieth Century*. Englewood Cliffs, NJ: Prentice-Hall.

Elliott, David J. (1992). Rethinking music teacher education. *Journal of Music Teacher Education*. (Fall, pp. 6-15).

Lautzenheiser, Tim (1992). *The Art of Successful Teaching: A Blend of Content and Context*. Chicago: GIA Publications.

Moody, Douglas (ed.) (2002). Patterson's American Education. Schaumburg, IL: Educational Directories, Inc.

Murphy, John (1993). What's In? What's Out? American education in the nineties. *Phi Delta Kappan*, 74/8, 641-646.

O'Neil, I. Riley, and Adamson, David R. (1993). When less is more. *American School Board Journal*, *180*/4, 39-41.

Saska, Ronald (1999). Emergency instrument repairs. *The Instrumentalist*. February, pp. 58ff.

Singleton, Ira C., and Anderson, Simon V. (1969). *Music in the Secondary Schools, 2nd ed.* Boston: Allyn and Bacon, Inc.

Solomon, Ed (1989). Strangers at my table. *The Instrumentalist*. May, pp. 92-94.

Thomson, John (1995). Teaching with goals, not answers: an interview with John Whitwell. *The Instrumentalist*. December, pp. 11-15.

Chapter Fourteen

## CONTEMPLATING THEN, NOW, AND WHY IN MUSIC EDUCATION

## Historic and Current Influences

### *Introduction*

Knowing our past helps us understand why we do what we now do, and it helps us avoid repeating mistakes. Thoughtfully considering the following questions will help guide your decision-making:

- Where have we been?
- Why were we there?
- What did we learn?
- Where are we now?
- Where do we go from here?

As we look at some of the major events in music education on this continent, it becomes apparent that instrumental music is particularly indebted to:

- The Singing School movement of Colonial America
- Improvements in instrument design and manufacture
- Improvements in methods and materials for instruction
- The growth of the curriculum and the extra-curriculum
- The development of college curricula to train music educators

• The support of the public and of ensemble members

We have a musical heritage that has developed into a school music education program considered the envy of most of the world. Our music education pioneers were willing to work hard, try new methods and materials, and be flexible. We are the beneficiaries of their eagerness to learn and grow, to change and evolve. As James A. Keene (1982) notes, "The history of music education in the United States has been, generally speaking, one of reform" (p. vii).

*(In this part of the chapter concerning our music education history I will occasionally add a few sentences in parenthesis noting other national and world events or important people during that time period. These brief remarks are meant to help gain a more broad perspective of all those events.)*

## *Music in the New World*

Michael L. Mark and Charles L. Gary (1999) report that "The earliest known structured music education system in America was that of the Incas, in what is now Peru, around 1350" (p. 41). Music was a central part of the four-year course of study given in these schools for the children of the nobles and royal family.

*(At this time in Europe Giullaume de Machaut was writing secular motets during the Ars Nova period.)*

After Cortez had conquered Mexico in the early 1500s, he requested that schools be established to educate the sons of the Aztec tribal chieftains. Pedro deGante established a school in Vera Cruz in 1523 that was run by Franciscan monks. Its main purpose was to win converts to the Catholic Church. The school was patterned after the cathedral schools of Europe. Students were taught reading, writing, singing, instrument construction, how to play musical instruments, and how to copy music. In 1542 the Spanish developed schools for the Indian population in what is now New Mexico.

*(This happened during the middle of the Renaissance in Europe. The great artists of the time were Botticelli, de Vinci, Michelangelo, Raphael, and Titian. The development of the compass made possible long voyages that opened the New World.)*

The French established schools (again, patterned after European cathedral schools) in the second half of the 16th and first half of the 17th Century in Canada and the northern midwest area of what was to become the United States. These schools, with Jesuit priests as teachers, were also established to educate the Indian population and to win converts to the church. (Mark and Gary, 1999, pp. 43-44)

## The Influence of the Church in Colonial America

The Pilgrims, Puritans, and Calvinists, who settled in America in 1620-1630, were thrust into a completely new environment in this country. While the establishment of a permanent settlement was paramount, the basic problem was survival. The stark reality was that "Some 14,000 people had migrated to the colony since 1607, but the population in 1624 stood at a precarious 1,132" (Tindall, 1988, p. 55). For these people music had to be very functional (Fennell, 1954, p. 41). Although there was social music, only the sacred function of singing in the churches was well-documented.

Instrumental music was rare in the colonies for several reasons. The Pilgrims, who might have supported instrumental music in their communities, did not have room on their ships to bring large instruments to America. The Puritan movement, being a reform of what members considered the excesses of the Church (which included instrumental music in the services), rejected the use of instruments in their churches. Another problem faced by the early colonists was the scarcity of printed music. The *Ainsworth Psalter*, which contained 39 notated melodies, was brought to the colonies by the Pilgrims. The *Bay Psalm Book*, the first book printed in the colonies, was published in the colonies in 1640, but contained no melodies (for lack of typographical capabilities) until the ninth edition, published in 1698. That edition contained 13 melodies for the 150 psalms.

In the area now known as Pennsylvania, German settlements with Moravians, Pennsylvania Dutch, Lutherans, and Pietists were established. These people developed schools for their own children and were careful to include music in the basic curriculum (Britton, 1958). The Moravians, who had a strong tradition of vocal and instrumental music, were particularly known for the contributions they made to the sacred and secular musical life of their communities and for an emphasis on music education (Mark and Gary, 1999, p. 45-47).

*(Europeans were in the early Baroque period as the American colonies were being settled. Important European composers included Claudio Monteverdi [1567-1643], Heinrich Schutz [1585-1672], John Dowland [1562-1626], William Byrd [1543-1623], and Girolamo Frescobaldi [1583-1643]. It was a time of change and adventure in Europe, significant figures being Galileo, Copernicus, Descartes, Milton, and Spinoza. In the colonies, Harvard University was begun in 1636.)*

## Singing Schools

The Puritans did not initially consider the lack of tunes in the *Bay Psalm Book* to be a problem, because the people were familiar with the tunes in the *Ainsworth Psalter* and each tune was used for many psalms. The method known as "lining-out" or "deaconing" had one person read a line of the psalm and then sing that line—echoed by the congregation—as they moved through the complete psalm. As time went by fewer people could read music and singing became more improvisatory. Some of the younger Puritan ministers wanted a return to note reading or singing by "rule and art." In an effort to teach note reading, the Reverend John Tufts published *An Introduction to the Singing of Psalm Tunes* in 1721. It was the first American music textbook (Hitchcock, 1969, p. 6). During the same year Reverend Thomas Walter published his book, *Grounds and Rules of Musick Explained*.

A desire to reform the indigenous style of psalm singing prompted the development of "singing schools." These singing schools—begun as early as 1712—exerted an influence on music teaching and learning for almost 150 years. They were organized and taught by traveling "singing masters," who also sold the materials used. The "tunebooks" were compilations of tunes (psalms, hymns, and patriotic tunes) written by the singing master and tunes "borrowed" from other composers—with or without permission. Typically, the singing schools met two or three times per week for one or two months, then ended with a "singing lecture" or a "singing assembly." The singing lecture included a sermon by the local minister. Funded with fees paid by the students, the singing schools primary purpose was to teach and demonstrate singing by note. The social aspect of these singing schools was a factor in their success. They continued until the 1850s when, due to the inclusion of music in the schools, they were no longer needed. Many of the "singing masters" became teachers in the schools (Britton, 1961, p. 217).

*(In Europe in 1721, J.S. Bach was 36 years old and was composing chamber music, some keyboard music, and the six Brandenburg Concerti at Cöthen. Benjamin Franklin was 15 years old.)*

Before the Revolutionary War, most bands in America were attached to military units. The bands usually had only six to eight musicians—with a typical instrumentation of one or two horns or trumpets, one or two bassoons, a pair of clarinets, and/or a pair of oboes. These ensembles were called the "Band of Musick" (Bryant, 1975, p. 7)—an example of which continues to perform at Colonial Williamsburg, Virginia. After the war, many of these military bands became town bands. They were usually small—in the 1820s their typical instrumentation was only about eight woodwinds, five or six brass, and a drummer (Holz and Jacobi, 1966).

## The Work of Lowell Mason and Others

As the "frontier" began moving westward and people in the eastern areas of the country had more leisure time, they began to show a greater interest in music. Along with this greater musical interest came higher standards of musical taste and a desire to improve teaching methods in music.

Lowell Mason (1792-1872) traveled from Savannah, Georgia, to Boston in 1827 to teach singing schools for children (Keene, 1982, p. 105). He began his quest to have music introduced into the Boston schools in 1830. After an eight-year struggle, which included Mason supplying both his services and the materials free for one year at the Hawes School, music was placed in the Boston schools in 1838 and paid for by the city. This marks the beginning of music in the schools of the United States.

Because qualified teachers were essential to Mason's plan, he helped established the Boston Academy of Music in 1833. Its mission was to train music teachers. The Academy sponsored "music conventions," which were typically three or four day training sessions on various aspects of teaching vocal music in the schools. These music conventions were directly related to the singing schools of Colonial America. Because many singing schools had developed into "singing societies," their leaders saw a need for better training. That evolved into music conventions. The Boston Academy of Music music conventions were important models for later music teacher education programs (Mark and Gary, 1992, Chapter 7).

Mason espoused a belief in the educational principles of the Swiss educator Johann Heinrich Pestalozzi. According to Mason, the applicable Pestalozzian principles included teaching sound before symbol, teaching each element of music separately, mastering each element before moving on, involving the child actively, introducing theory after practice, and having the note reading process correspond to that used in instrumental music. This Pestalozzian approach, Mason's own pragmatic philosophy, and the child-study (or child-centered) movement—which stressed teaching the whole child through learning-by-doing activity—moved us toward the Progressive Education that was to appear in the next century.

Two important publications were introduced during this period. Mason's *Manual of the Boston Academy,* listing his principles of teaching, was the first cohesive statement on modern pedagogical principles. Luther Whiting Mason's *National Music Course* was the first complete graded textbook series. The *National Music Course*, written between 1870 and 1875, became the model for music-book series throughout the next 50 years (Keene, 1982).

*(About 1838 in Europe, Paris was the center of Romanticism; and composers of the time were Robert Schumann, Frederick Chopin, Hector Berlioz, and Franz Liszt. Europe was experiencing a time of great nationalism. In America, Martin Van Buren was President, and it was the year of the Cherokee "Trail of Tears.")*

An important development for bands was the work of instrument maker Adolphe Saxe in the 1840s. Saxe made important improvements in the valve system of existing conical brass instruments, and developed a unified family of brass instruments known as saxhorns that ranged from soprano flugelhorns to tuba. These instruments were very popular because they had a common fingering system (which allowed easy transfer between the various instruments), were relatively easy to learn to play, and were louder than woodwind instruments and strings. Their popularity led to the formation of brass bands—a tradition that dominated the instrumental music scene in America until the innovations of the great showman and musician Patrick S. Gilmore (1829-1892) in the late 1800s (Holz & Jacobi, 1966).

During the Civil War, brass bands were an important part of military life. The band served ceremonial purposes, played evening concerts for the men, and provided music for parades. Many of their instruments were over-the-shoulder models with the bells pointing

Interesting

*Patrick S. Gilmore*

backward. That model was ideal for parades, as the band was usually at the beginning (Bryant, 1975).

In 1872, Gilmore—who had staged large music events earlier in New Orleans and Boston—produced the World Peace Jubilee in Boston. It was an enormous event requiring a chorus of 20,000 and a combined band and orchestra of 2,000 musicians. Such extravagant music spectacles gained notoriety for Gilmore, but more important, they encouraged public support for music activities (Goldman, 1961, p. 130). Gilmore was also responsible for bringing some fine European bands to perform in America. These bands were well-received, and the effect was to inspire still more support for bands. Because these European bands included full woodwind sections, American band leaders began to re-think their commitment to the brass band tradition. In fact, when Gilmore became director of the 22nd Regiment Band of New York in 1873, he reorganized it in the style of the European band. That band became the model for the concert band as we know it in America (Holz and Jacobi, 1966; Keene, 1982).

*Concert Band model w/ woodwinds*

*(Influential composers of this time were Peter Ilyich Tschaikowsky [1840-1893], Johannes Brahms [1833-1897], Richard Wagner [1813-1883], Giuseppe Verdi [1813-1901], Anton Bruckner [1824-1896] and Franz Liszt [1811-1886].)*

The work of composer and conductor John Philip Sousa (1854-1932)—first as conductor of the United States Marine Band (1880-1892), and then with his own professional band (1892-1932)—was also highly influential for the band movement in America. Sousa traveled extensively with his band. Because of his high performance standards, his entertaining programming, and his employment of some of the finest woodwind, brass, and percussion musicians of the day, he received excellent musical reviews from both professionals and the average citizen. His band was enormously popular, and that popularity encouraged the development of school bands, community bands, and other professional bands.

*John Philip Sousa*

Even though the professional band had enjoyed widespread public support, and had played a vital role in securing acceptance of bands and orchestras into the public schools, their presence diminished greatly during the first part of the 20th Century. Holz and Jacobi (1966) report that "In the last decade of the 19th Century there were well over 10,000 professional and amateur bands in the United States. Yet, by the end of World War I they had all but disappeared" (p. 2). Holz and Jacobi attributed that sudden decline to three things:

*Sudden Decline*

349

*Reasons for Decline*

① • Changing popular music styles which called for different musical skills from professional musicians
② • The decline in the popularity of amusement parks that had provided employment for bands
③ • The severe economic conditions of World War I

Still, the effect of World War I on instrumental music in the schools, especially bands, was very important. The use of bands for patriotic purposes helped gain widespread public support for bands in the armed services and in the schools. Bands, highly mobile and capable of producing loud and stirring performances, enjoyed great popularity. The armed services had trained many military bandsmen during the war, and many of those trained musicians chose to become involved with teaching school bands after the war (Whitehill, 1969).

During this time, a number of school bands were begun around the country. Some of the earliest school bands were at the Farm and Trades School in Boston (1859), Christian Brothers High School in Memphis, Tennessee (1884), and in schools in Greenville, South Carolina (1893), Connersville, Indiana (1907), and Oberlin, Ohio (1913). College bands were established at the University of Minnesota (1891), the University of Wisconsin (1894), the University of Michigan (1896), Purdue University (1896), St. Olaf College (1902), and Baylor University (1906) (Keene, 1982; Bartner, 1963).

The first instrumental ensembles in schools were most often orchestras. Usually these were small groups of diverse instrumentation—basically whatever instruments were available. Early high school orchestras were formed in Middletown, Ohio (1863); Chelsea, Massachusetts (1886); Winfield, Kansas (about 1890); and Richmond, Indiana (1898). Joseph Maddy (1956/2000) reported that "there were probably at least 50 school orchestras in existence by 1900, and probably three times that many by 1910" (p. 87). Mark and Gary (1999) note the important role played by touring bands and orchestras in the development of public support for school and community groups, and especially the significant work of Theodore Thomas (1825-1905) and his touring orchestra. The importance of orchestras in American musical life is certified by the founding of the New York Philharmonic in 1842, the Symphony Society of New York in 1878, and the Boston Symphony in 1881 (Keene, 1982).

American teachers were interested in finding an efficient and inexpensive way to teach children to play instruments. A successful experiment in class violin instruction in 1898—the Maidstone Movement, begun at All Saints School in Maidstone, England—seemed to fit their needs. Holz and Jacobi (1962) report that a curate at a local church began to offer class violin to children in his parish. Music dealers supported his program and programs similar to it by offering promotional materials, low-cost instruments, and additional instructors. It was very successful, and soon spread throughout England (p. 10).

Albert J. Mitchell was one of those responsible for bringing this new violin class method of instruction to America. Mitchell was teaching vocal music in the Boston schools when he took a leave of absence in 1910 to travel to Maidstone to study the new method. Upon his return to Boston in 1911 he started his own violin classes—free of charge—after school. The classes were so successful that he was relieved of his other high school teaching duties and was asked to be a full-time teacher of instrumental music in the schools.

*(During this time Tschaikowsky composed* The Nutcracker *in 1892, and Stravinsky* The Rite of Spring *in 1913. Gustav Holst wrote the* First Suite in E-flat for Military Band *in 1908 and his* Second Suite in F for Military Band *in 1911. Other influential composers of the time were Gustav Mahler [1860-1911] and Claude Debussy [1862-1918].)*

## The Growth of Music in Schools

John Dewey, one of the founders of the Laboratory School at the University of Chicago, is credited with beginning the Progressive Education movement in 1917. That movement was to have a profound effect on education, one effect being the inclusion of orchestras and bands in the schools. The development of junior high schools (with more time for exploratory courses) and the effects of World War I (bands were needed for morale purposes) also helped establish instrumental music in the schools—even though it was as an after-school, extra-curricular activity taught by whomever was available and had an interest in the band or orchestra. Because of the extra-curricular status, these instrumental groups were not part of a vertical structure of instrumental ensembles with progressive curriculum through the grades.

Two very important events in the school band movement occurred in 1923. The first National Band Tournament was held in Chicago, and *The Universal Teacher*, by Joseph Maddy (1891-1966) and Thaddeus Giddings (1868-1954), was published.

The National Band Tournament (the first national band contest) was held in Chicago on June 4, 5, and 6, 1923 as an entertainment for a convention of music instrument manufacturers, publishers, and music dealers. According to Holz and Jacobi (1962) "The event attracted thirty school bands from thirteen states, the bands ranging

351

in size from the twenty-five boys from Paw Paw, Michigan, to the seventy or more from each high school in Gary, Indiana" (p. 6). In spite of poor and last-minute planning, it was an important and successful musical event with national media exposure.

The band directors involved in the first national contest were not pleased with the organization of the event or with the commercial connection. They asked C.M. Tremaine of the National Bureau for the Advancement of Music to reorganize and improve future events. Tremaine invited the Committee on Instrumental Affairs of Music Supervisors National Conference (MSNC—the forerunner of the Music Educators National Conference) to supervise future band contests. This process took three years, but the national band contest returned in 1926 and led to a series of grand musical events that dominated secondary school music until 1941 (Holz, 1962). The band contests gained widespread public approval, creating an acceptance of bands and other music groups. The success of the early band contests inspired orchestra contests, choir contests, solo and ensemble contests, and the formation of the National High School Orchestra of 1926. Conducted by Joseph Maddy, this outstanding group led to the development of the National Music Camp at Interlochen, Michigan in 1928. Holz and Jacobi (1966) report that "The ferment created by contests helped to secure band instruction as almost universal in American schools" (p. 7).

Will Earhart was a leader and innovator in the early school instrumental music movement. He had established a high school orchestra in the Richmond, Indiana, schools in 1898 and secured credit status for participation in orchestra in 1905—20 years before that became a common practice. "In 1911 he taught the first course in instrumental methods offered by any school in the country, and he conducted courses in musical aesthetics on the college level at a time when such classes were rarely a part of the college curriculum" (Buttelman, 1962, p. 130). According to Fennell (1954), Earhart's work in Richmond ". . .is generally considered to be the first significant instrumental activity in the public school of America" (p. 44). The second National High School Orchestra, also conducted by Joseph Maddy, performed at the convention of the National Education Association Department of Superintendence in 1927; and at that convention Will Earhart presented a paper on the value of music. Both the performance by the orchestra and Earhart's paper led to the adoption of a resolution supporting the establishment of music programs in all schools (Buttelman, 1962, p. 90).

The publication of *The Universal Teacher* in 1923 —the first heterogeneous class method—was significant for instrumentalists. It was a melodic approach to instruction that also included several pages of three-part harmonizations. According to Holz and Jacobi (1966) "Students were asked to sing first, then play, finding for themselves the fingerings that made the tunes sound right" (p. 12). The material in the books was simple—simple to teach and to learn. *Instrumental Class Teaching*, a teachers guide to *The Universal Teacher*, published in 1928, included teaching suggestions and methods. This class method book became a model for beginning instrumental class methods books to follow.

*(In the United States at this time was the introduction of Prohibition [1920], the publication of Hemingway's first novel in 1926 [The Sun Also Rises], and the beginning of the Great Depression in 1929.)*

## *Struggles for the Arts*

The Progressive Education movement was never a very well organized reform, and deteriorated to the point that most scholars disassociated themselves from it by 1940. The MSNC, however, continued to grow in numbers and influence. Societal difficulties caused by World War II put a strain on music programs in the schools. School, community, and military ensembles, however, provided an important service to the country through performances designed to support the war effort and encourage the citizenry. Just as occurred following the close of World War I, an important by-product of the active military music program during World War II was that many members of the military music program left the service with a desire to teach music in the schools. This large infusion of instrumental music teachers helped fuel a renewed interest in, and support for, music in the schools.

College band programs provided a much-needed model for public school bands in America beginning in the 1920s. The high musical standards—of people like William D. Revelli at the University of  Michigan, A.A. Harding and Mark Hindsley at the University of Illinois, Raymond F. Dvorak at the University of Wisconsin, Clarence Sawhill at the University of California at Los Angles, and Glenn Cliffe Bainum at Northwestern University—were inspirations to public  school bands. The pioneering work of these directors—and others— in instrumentation, concept of band sound, development of a unique and respected repertoire, and concert programming, set the direction for school and college bands. Also noteworthy for his contribution to

353

*Edwin Goldman*

→ the development of concert bands in America was Edwin Franco Goldman. Goldman formed his band of professional musicians in New York in 1911. He was a tireless supporter of the band movement through his own compositions, the commissioning of a lot of new music by eminent composers, innovative programming, and high performance standards.

## New Directions

*1958 → Curricular Re-evaluation*

With the launching of Russian Sputnik I on October 4, 1957, Americans realized how far behind we were in the sciences and mathematics. Curricular reforms were proposed for a return to a traditional "3 R's" approach. The launching of our own Explorer I satellite in January 1958 eventually prompted another curricular re-evaluation and an easing of the traditional approach—although the "back-to-basics" debate continues to this day.

The 1960s were a time of experimentation and reform in the schools, with much support for a definite child-centered approach to education. New college curricula prepared future music educators better. It was also a time of expansion—of the curriculum, of faculty, and of facilities. This had positive benefits for school music programs, with the inclusion of more music classes in the curriculum (Mark and Gary, 1999). It was also a decade of noteworthy events for music education. The Ford Foundation sponsored two projects that had continued positive impact on American music education. The Young Composers Project (actually begun in 1959) was the result of a desire to familiarize music educators and their students with 20th-Century music by placing young composers in schools as composers-in-residence. The project was very successful, leading the Ford Foundation to award MENC a $1.38 million grant to fund a continuation of the Young Composers Project and a series of seminars and workshops on contemporary music for music educators. A significant idea to come from one of those seminars (1965 at Northwestern University) was the movement called "comprehensive musicianship." The concept encouraged a more broad musical experience in music classes to include teaching *about* music (the "what, where, when, why, and how" questions) in the context of the rehearsal and performance of fine music.

*Identify + Solving Problems*

→ The Yale Seminar on Music Education was held in 1963 to identify the problems in music education and make suggestions for solving those problems. The conclusion was that little music of real quality was being used in the schools and, in addition, there was an over-emphasis on skill development in performing groups. Mark and Gary (1999)

354

↳ A lot of the same issues we face today

noted that "Although many changes occurred after the Yale Seminar, it is unlikely that the seminar had major influence on music education practices. One reason for this is that few music educators participated in the seminar" (p. 344). One positive result of the Yale Seminar was the Juilliard Repertory Project of 1964. Headed by the composer Vittorio Giannini, this project produced a collection of 230 vocal and instrumental works identified as outstanding literature representing the various music periods and styles.

MENC, in cooperation with the Berkshire Music Center, the School of Fine and Applied Arts at Boston University, and with a grant from the Theodore Presser Foundation, organized the Tanglewood Symposium in 1967. This 10-day symposium was convened to answer some of the charges of the Yale Seminar. It was attended by a wide range of participants, including educators, philosophers, scientists, theologians, and others. The participants agreed to what is called "The Tanglewood Declaration."

> We believe that education must have as major goals the art of living, the building of personal identity, and nurturing creativity. Since the study of music can contribute much to these ends, *we now call for music to be placed in the core of the school curriculum.*
>
> The arts afford a continuity with the aesthetic tradition in man's history. Music and the other fine arts, largely non-verbal in nature, reach close to the social, psychological, and the physiological roots of man in his search for identity and self-realization.
>
> Educators must accept the responsibility for developing opportunities which meet man's individual needs and the needs of a society plagued by the consequences of changing values, alienation, hostility between generations, racial and international tensions, and the challenges of a new leisure. (Choate, 1968, p. 139)

This philosophical declaration, the identification of major issues then facing music education, and recommendations to address some of those issues, provided guidance to music educators.

A 1964 tour of the United States by Shinichi Suzuki and 10 of his very young violin students has had an enormous impact on all instrument teaching in this country. This visit was the result of great excite-

Shinichi Suzuki

ment at the 1958 showing at Oberlin College of a concert by Suzuki's students in Japan. The tour caused American strings teachers in particular to re-evaluate their ideas about the appropriate beginning age, materials, and methods. Suzuki believed in what he called "Mother-tongue Education." He involved parents directly in the teaching of their children from a very early age. He believed that students should listen to outstanding recorded examples of the music they were to play and that the experience of learning to play the instrument should be an aural experience. While he did believe that students must eventually be taught to read music—and that parents should be taught to read music earlier so that they could help teach their children—he wanted them to focus first on developing their aural skills. Suzuki, in the brochure "How to Teach Suzuki Piano" that is found on the Suzuki Association Web site, said "The ability to read music is one important aspect of musical ability. However, the printed score must never be confused with music itself; it is nothing but a symbol of it. I believe that true music reading means discovering the composer's musical idea and expressing it aloud in a beautiful manner." One of Suzuki's important beliefs was that a beautiful tone comes from a beautiful heart. That concept also speaks to the attitude of the teacher, the atmosphere in the classroom, and the expectations the teacher should have of students.

There are now an estimated 300,000 young students involved in Suzuki educational programs just in America. The influence of the teaching philosophy of Shinichi Suzuki has had an obvious influence on many teachers of young band and orchestra students. His book, *Nurtured By Love: The Classic Approach to Talent Education,* should be read by all instrumental music educators.

## Back To Basics (Mid 1970's)

Unfortunately, by the mid-1970s low standardized test scores encouraged a return to an emphasis on the "basic" courses. Also by the mid-1970s, lower school enrollment and difficult economic times led to decreased spending for schools and the need for fewer facilities and teachers. This strain on general education had a predictable negative impact on most school music programs.

A general concern among the public about the state of education was reinforced by the 1983 publication *A Nation at Risk: The Imperative for Educational Reform* from the National Commission on Excellence in Education. This influential report set off national alarms about the quality of our educational system and the economic future of the

*Instrumental Music History = Music Found A Place In Schools Through The Hard Work of Individual Teachers in Many Schools*

country. *A Nation at Risk*, along with a number of other reports about the American educational system, has prompted numerous reform efforts throughout the 1980s and 1990s, and into the new century. We have cycled from a belief that large schools are of most benefit to children to a support for small schools; from a small core of required courses to a large core; from many experimental courses (including many in music) to basic course offerings; and from "open schools" to traditional schools. It is safe to predict that such changes will continue and that many ideas currently out of favor will return. Much of educational reform is a matter of recycling old ideas and approaches, some of which are so sound that they never should have gone out of favor, but which—alas—will no doubt go out of favor again.

*Educational Reform in a Nutshell ↓ Damn.*

## *Instrumental Music Education Today*

Charles Fowler (1991) wrote that "The successive waves of back-to-basics educational reform during the past thirty years have seriously eroded the stature of music in the schools" (p. 9). He also commented on a concern that national standardized tests evaluate only reading comprehension and mathematics—not music skills and understanding. According to Fowler "As wave after wave of reform and demands for 'back-to-basics' have washed over our school systems, accountability and testing have increased commensurately. . . . These tests define education: what is tested is what is taught and valued" (p. 10). Fortunately, since the time of Fowlers writing we have seen a number of states beginning to include music on state-wide educational testing.

*"What is tested is what is taught + valued"*

Our continuing evaluation of the problems in American schools, many of which are actually societal problems beyond the control of schools, has led to a cycle of reform and reflection. While many educational practices and philosophies have been on a cycle of influence, it seems that those cycles have become much shorter. Add to that the dichotomy of national standards and local control of education and we find there is not, and never has been, an easy road to meaningful educational reform. To help protect the interests of instrumental music education, you may want to keep yourself active in the educational reform efforts. Be knowledgeable, be open to new ideas, and be involved.

Our instrumental music education history teaches us that music found a place in the schools through the work of individual teachers in many different schools. Hard-working, dedicated individual teachers in many classrooms across the country today will find the solutions to the current and future problems in instrumental music education.

357

*Problems in Schools → Often Societal Problems*

Many "ingredients" have gone into the "stew" we call music education in America. They have helped shape and mold many disparate ideas into a rich music education heritage that is unique in the world. Leave it to Americans to want to teach music to all children and to include it in the basic curriculum of our schools!

## A Personal Philosophy of Music Education

One of the definitions of "philosophy" is: ". . .a system of principles of guidance in practical affairs. . . ." (Stein, 1988). Too often people think of a philosophy as something esoteric, an interesting exercise of college professors and philosophers, but not something that will influence the daily work of a teacher in the classroom. Some would echo the statement by David J. Elliott (1995): "As one suspicious colleague put it: 'Philosophy is like a pigeon: it's something to admire, as long as it isn't directly over your head'" (p. 9).

Humor aside, let's consider the definition that a philosophy gives us guidance in practical affairs. We all make many decisions every day—and those decisions are based on what we know and believe. In other words, our daily decisions are based on our "philosophy." Many of us have not taken time to actually write out a statement that summarizes our beliefs about a certain topic, but we do already have a belief system in place because of our educational training, our personal experience, and our conscious or unconscious deliberations about that topic.

If we already make decisions based on our belief system, why do we need to develop our thoughts into a formal philosophical statement? A thoughtfully written personal music education philosophy will be the product of a period of reflection about your most basic beliefs concerning music and music education. Taking time to ask the questions of what, why, how, when, where, etc., as it relates to music education will enable you to create a lighthouse document—one that lights your way through your future work in music education. It becomes an invaluable tool to use as you make the daily educational decisions that affect your students and their music education. Developing and refining a personal philosophy of music education will allow you—in the words of Stephen Covey—to "Begin with the end in mind."

Several years ago, while watching a stage version of the book *Treasure Island*, I was struck by a line from Long John Silver as he told his men that it was not yet the right time to take over the ship. He said: "We can steer a course, but who's to set one?" (p. 69). In other words, anyone can steer a ship (or teach music!), but who's to chart the course?

*[handwritten margin note:]* create a "lighthouse document"

*[handwritten bottom note:]* "We can steer a course, but who's to set one?"

358

If you want to be a complete music educator, one who helps "set the course" for yourself and your students, then you must develop a fine personal philosophy of music education.

A philosophy of music education is an evolving document. The document you write as an undergraduate student—without the benefit of significant teaching experience—undoubtedly will be different than the one you will write after your student teaching experience. And that document will differ from the one you will write after five years of teaching, and after 10 years of teaching. Your personal philosophy of music education reflects your education, your training, and your own experiences—and all of that changes and grows.

The topic "Philosophy of Music Education" is substantial enough to constitute a complete graduate-level course. It is a topic deserving of in-depth study and reflection. However, because it is so essential for all new teachers to have spent time developing their own personal statement, we will now consider this topic from the viewpoints of four major philosophical positions related to education: Idealism, Realism, Existentialism, and Pragmatism.

## Philosophical Positions

*Idealism, Realism, Existentialism, Pragmatism*

Idealism—identified with Plato, René Descartes, and Immanuel Kant—encourages people to search for the truth, to hold high standards, and to realize the importance of personal experience. Idealists believe that course content should focus on the accepted primary knowledge in a subject-area. They also see the teacher as an important model for students.

Aristotle, Johann Heinrich Pestalozzi, and Johann Friedrich Herbart are associated with the Realist position. Realists advocate a more "rules and procedures" approach, with an emphasis on accountability by students and teachers.

The Existentialist focuses more on the individual student, and encourages experimentation and exploration. Friedrich Nietzsche and Jean-Paul Sartre were Existential philosophers. The influence of Existentialism in education is seen in open schools and aesthetic education. In Existentialism, students and teachers commonly work together as collaborators.

Pragmatism—associated with John Dewey—views the classroom as a community of learners, and encourages hands-on, problem-solving learning in a democratic classroom. Pragmatists stress process over product and believe that learning is a lifelong process.

These educational philosophies have served as the basis of a number of educational theories. Many of the beliefs of Perennialists—who focus on the humanities, acquiring knowledge, and developing intellectual skills—refer to Realist thought. Essentialism—a conservative approach to education focusing on the liberal arts and rigorous academic standards, and exemplified by the "Back-to-Basics" movement of the 1970s—comes from both Idealism and Realism. The influence of Essentialism can be seen in the call for National Standards and required competency testing.

Pragmatism led to the development of the theories of Progressivism and the related theories of Experimentalism and Social Reconstructionism. Progressivism is noted for collaborative learning, learning by doing, self-directed learning, and use of the scientific method. Experimentalists also stress the testing of ideas, child-centered curricula, and interrelated curricula. Social Reconstructionists stress democratic procedures in the classroom and the role of education in making societal changes.

## Contributions to Music Education Philosophical Thought

Many valuable contributions have been made to music education philosophy and research into the way students learn music. Such research and thought has given us important information about what we might do in music and why we should be doing it.

Much of the field of music education philosophy is dominated by two groups: those who espouse an aesthetic experience through listening activities and those who favor a performance-oriented philosophy. The work of Bennett Reimer (1970) and of Charles Leonhard and Robert W. House (1972) has clearly and articulately presented the case for aesthetic education, with listening activities being central to developing aesthetic response. David J. Elliott (1995) has proposed an approach to aesthetic experience in which active involvement in the music-making (through performance, composition, arranging, improvising, and conducting) is the key methodology (p. 121).

Reimer (1970), in *A Philosophy of Music Education*, wrote that "Aesthetic education is the systematic attempt to help people explore and understand human feeling by becoming more sensitive to (better perceive and react to) conditions which present forms of feeling" (p. 143). He wrote that "When art is experienced aesthetically and understood aesthetically, it delights in a way that few experiences in human life pro-

360

vide" (p. 85). As to the importance of listening activities, Reimer believes that "Listening is the essential mode of musical experience. Some people will achieve a musical listening experience as they perform or compose, but *all* people will share the art of music directly through its peculiar sense modality—listening" (p. 120). "Yet it is impossible to ignore the fact that a great many people have experienced their most satisfying, most fulfilling, most significant musical experiences as *performers*, and that at least some children who perform have had similar experiences. The power of such experience is so great and its satisfaction so deep that those who have shared it are likely to be changed fundamentally in their relation to music" (p. 131).

Elliott (1995) states "In summary, past music education philosophy is remarkably weak in a fundamental regard: it neglects to consider the nature and importance of music making" (p. 32). "The best preparation for listening to musical performances in the future is full participation in music making in the present" (p. 104). Elliott promotes universal music education by affirming that ". . .music making is a unique and major way of gaining self-growth, self-knowledge, and optimal experience, both now and in the future. . . .For these reasons, music making is something worth learning to do well by *all* students" (1995, p. 122). He believes that there are four basic values of music and music education: self-growth, enjoyment, self-knowledge, and self-esteem (1995, chapters 5 and 12). According to Elliott "This praxial philosophy of music education holds that all music education programs ought to be conceived, organized, and carried out as reflective musical practicums" (1995, p. 267). And, "In sum, musical experiences are not impractical, purposeless, disinterested, or intrinsic or the one-dimensional outcomes of perceiving aesthetic qualities. And music experiences are not 'experience for the sake of experience.' People may well and rightly continue to describe musical experiences as beautiful and moving. But a truly musical experience is not aesthetic in its nature or value, as conventional music education philosophy maintains" (Elliott, 1995, p. 125).

David Elliott's writing makes a strong case for genuine musical experience for all children through the personal performance of music. The rehearsal and performance of ensembles needs to include the "what," "when," "where," and "why" kind of questions so that our students begin to know for themselves, and understand, the music they are preparing. It seems to be a logical extension of "comprehensive musicianship." I believe that this philosophy recognizes and embraces the important work of bands and orchestras in our schools, work that has attracted widespread support—from the public and from ensemble members—for music in the schools. The public performances of these groups in the schools and in the communities have been of great benefit to the entire music education program. Elliott recognizes and endorses informed performance as a route to aesthetic experience. Your work in music education—and your students'—will benefit from a study of *Music Matters.*

Edwin Gordon has made valuable contributions to music education through his research and writing about how children learn music. Darrel L. Walters and Cynthia Crump (1989) write that Gordon's "Music Learning Theory is unique in several ways. First, it is based upon a student view rather than upon a teacher view, i.e., it is based upon the premise that the nature of learning must dictate approaches to teaching. Second, it is supported by substantial educational research. Third, it has incorporated into it the collective wisdom of previous music educators and educational theorists. And fourth, Music Learning Theory is conceived by Edwin Gordon to be subject to constant growth and revision" (p. v). The design and delivery of sequential instruction is a central component to Music Learning Theory. Gordon (1988) writes that "Music learning theory is the structuring of the logical order of sequential objectives which include the music skills and content that students must learn in order to achieve the comprehensive objective of music appreciation" (p. 29). He also believes that while all students are capable of learning music, their success will be affected by their music aptitude, and that the individual learning differences in students must be taken into account by teachers (Gordon, 1988, p. 17).

The interesting work of Howard Gardner in his Multiple Intelligences Theory ("MI Theory") gives all educators valuable insight into the way people learn. Gardner (1990) defines intelligence as ". . .an ability to solve problems or to fashion a product, to make something that is valued in at least one culture" (p. 16). He explains further that ". . .an *intelligence* is a biological and psychological potential; that potential is capable of being realized to a greater or lesser extent as a consequence of the experiential, cultural, and motivational factors that affect a person" (Gardner, 1995, p. 202). An important concept in the MI Theory is that everyone possesses an array of intelligences, but that each person is more proficient in some intelligences than in others (Gardner, 1993, p.27). He identified seven intelligences (1990, pp. 18-20)—although he has written of his consideration of two additional intelligences:

- Linguistic (the use of language to communicate and inform)

- Logical-mathematical (recognizing and solving problems)
- Musical (thinking, acting, and reacting musically)
- Spatial (accurately perceiving the visual world, being able to transform or modify your perceptions, and being able to recreate aspects of your visual experience) (Gardner, 1983, p. 173)
- Bodily kinesthetic (the ability to use the body to solve problems or make things)
- Interpersonal (understanding other people)
- Intrapersonal (the understanding of oneself)

MI Theory has heavily influenced teaching in the general classroom, especially at the elementary school level, and in music classrooms. It is a valuable theory that helps us understand how students learn based on their dominant intelligences; and it is helpful for music educators as they explain the significance of music as a central element of general education. David Elliott (1990) wrote that "Howard Gardner's (1983) theory of multiple intelligences, if it becomes widely accepted, will likely result in a return in this country to a more child-centered approach to public education than has been the case in the past decade. Gardner's theory, however, has an added advantage—it calls for fundamental philosophical reform in public education *based on scientific evidence*, a consideration rare in most educational reform" (p. 142).

As you study the various philosophies you will discover that you agree primarily with one, but you still may value some aspects of others. Some people may urge you to adopt only one philosophical approach, but a more eclectic philosophy may be most appropriate. After all, it is *your* philosophy, and it may not fit into a nice, neat predetermined box. In fact, the nature of instrumental music education may *require* a more eclectic philosophy. Certainly instrumental music teachers should stress leading students to a fuller understanding of, and aesthetic response to, the music they perform; but we can not deny or discard the high level of public and student support that has been earned by the social and civic elements of these school ensembles. Students do learn important life skills through participation in band and orchestra, skills that make them better citizens. We are part of a decidedly eclectic enterprise!

## Sample Philosophies

As you begin to write your personal music education philosophy, you may find help in reading some sample philosophies from a variety of sources. The first two examples (Figures 14-1 and 14-2) are philosophies written by undergraduate students prior to their student teaching experience.

*Figure 14-1. Sample Philosophy #1*

### Philosophy of Music Education

Music education is an essential part of any child's education. Very few people live a life in which music does not play a part. Music is a gift meant for worship, communication, and celebration. Education in such a vital subject enables students to more fully understand, appreciate, use, participate in, and enjoy music, to the benefit of themselves and those around them.

A student who is well educated musically has had an opportunity to develop and apply skills that are important to all of life. Music is a subject that is a synthesis of all other academic subjects and engages all other types of intelligence—from logical-mathematical and kinesthetic, to linguistic. It is, by definition, a hands-on, experiential learning process. Students who are musically educated have acquired a love of learning that will continue after their formal education is complete.

Students should experience and learn about music with the help of a teacher who models social and life skills as well as musical ones, in an atmosphere of emotional safety, encouragement, love of learning, and enough order to make this possible. Students should be encouraged to cooperate with and be supportive of each other, and to recognize and appreciate the various areas of music in which they and others excel.

(used by permission of Carla Richardson)

*Figure 14-2. Sample Philosophy #2*

## Philosophy of Education

I believe that every child has the right to a music education. Every child needs an outlet for creativity and expression. A music education provides this and allows students to become well-balanced individuals. Music helps bring joy, hope, and emotional healing into a child's life, enhancing the quality of their life overall. Music provides an opportunity for students to grow, build their self-esteem, and reach their full potential.

Music is basic to our culture and is a vital part of any school's curriculum. It is the responsibility of the school to provide a music education for any student that shows interest. Within the school system, it is the responsibility of the music teacher to impart a love and passion for music. The teacher is to be a role model, exhibiting integrity and positive character in all that is said and done. The effective teacher will be straightforward and clear as to what is expected, yet be encouraging and sensitive to the students' needs. I believe in challenging students and pushing them to reach their full potential. At the same time though, they need to be given an enthusiasm for learning and develop a positive attitude towards music.

I believe the music teacher has a responsibility to create musically literate and musically sensitive students. The teacher should prepare students to become independent musicians. Students should become aware that music is a skill and hobby they can carry with them the rest of their lives.

Learning occurs through a variety of modes, but I believe the most effective learning will take place when students are able to experience music for themselves. Involvement in any ensemble is a necessity for students to truly understand music. I believe it is important for students to have a basic understanding of the major time periods of music, as well as key composers. Students should be exposed to a broad range of styles of music, including music of other cultures. I believe students should be able to explain the basic elements of music (melody, harmony, rhythm, form, timbre, etc.). I believe technique and skill are important if students are to function

365

as independent musicians. However, I firmly believe that the quality of the music experience that is given them will far exceed extrinsic things such as grades or trophies. The music experience that students carry with them should impart a joy and satisfaction for their entire lives.

(used by permission of Lisa Stoltzfus)

Figure 14-3, an example of a philosophy from a veteran music teacher, reflects an eclectic educational view.

**Figure 14-3. Philosophy of a Veteran Music Teacher**

### Philosophy of Music Education

I believe that the transmission of cultural heritage, knowledge, skills, attitudes and ideals to create a responsible citizenry are appropriate goals for schools in our contemporary society. By helping students develop problem solving and logic skills we will enable students to meet and solve the problems of today, and those they will meet in the future. The study of music in a fine school music program can greatly benefit the achievement of these worthy educational goals.

I believe that the music program in the schools should be diverse, offering performance and non-performance classes, to meet the diverse needs of the student population. I believe that the core musical experiences for all students should be in performance-based classes. It is through performance experiences that students will gain significant, lasting understanding and insight about music, about the world around them, and about themselves. They will develop the skill of personal discipline and reap the reward of goals accomplished. Music making encourages personal growth, enjoyment, and improves self-esteem. Students who develop fine musicianship in school ensembles will become knowledgeable and insightful listeners—and, hopefully, life-long performers—as adults. The key to musical enjoyment—as school students and as adults—is musicianship. Musicianship may be attained in a music education program that moves students through increasingly complex musical discovery and decision-making—from the beginning music program to levels of higher musical proficiency in our secondary schools.

A well-educated student is educated musically. In the study of multiple intelligences, music is identified as a subject of significance for all children at every grade level. Every child in every school district in this country deserves a quality music education curriculum that is rigorous and of high quality; and is taught by skilled teachers who have high expectations of students.

Be sure to review the philosophies in Chapter 1 by Holz and Jacobi, and from the Michigan School Band and Orchestra Association. They are well-written philosophical statements.

## Writing Your Music Education Philosophy

*This helps!*

As you begin to develop your personal philosophy of music education, make a list of what you believe about music and why you believe it. Make a list of what you believe about the value of music in the schools and explain why you believe it. List what you think students should know, understand and be able to do, and what they should experience in a fine school music program, and list why each is important.

As you develop your lists you will begin to see connections, and you may discover—through reading and contemplation—that some considerations are not as important as you originally thought. Be sure to consider the information in earlier chapters of this book, your class discussions, and related readings and materials from other education courses. You may also find that this process leads you to unexpected issues. Transfer your lists into concise and clear sentences. The central questions are: why should music be in the curriculum, and what knowledge, skills, and understanding should students learn in a school music program? Most teachers, especially new teachers and pre-service teachers, will find that their philosophy of music education fits on less than one single-spaced page. Eventually, after numerous revisions, you will develop the kind of scholarly, thoughtful, "lighthouse" document that will give you guidance and direction as a new teacher, and will explain your core beliefs about music education to school administrators, parents, and students.

## Some Quotes for Reflection

It will be helpful to read the thoughts of some of the great music educators—and others—of the past and present as you begin to formulate your personal philosophy of music education. The quotations below will enrich your thoughtful deliberation—and may even challenge, or support, your current thoughts and beliefs about music and music education.

> "Music exalts the human spirit. It enhances the quality of life. It brings joy, satisfaction, and fulfillment to every human being. It is one of the most powerful, compelling, and glorious manifestations of human culture. It is the essence of civilization itself" (*Performance Standards*, 1996, p. 9).

> "It has always seemed strange to me that we as music educators seem to be the only branch of education to deprecate performing in favor of observing and philosophizing. Who ever heard of a course in history appreciation? chemistry appreciation? or football appreciation?" (Britton, 1991, p. 184).

> "Austin A. Harding, Joseph E. Maddy, Marguerite V. Hood, William D. Revelli, and thousands of others have demonstrated over many years that the way to win children to music is to give them as much of the best of it as the day allows" (Britton, 1991, p. 187).

> "There is a serious need to match instruction in music with the interests of today's students, particularly in terms of drawing on the musical environment and culture outside schools, where music is such a large part of student life" (Boston, 1995, p. 20).

> "There is also a challenge, when writing curricula, to sustain a balance between knowing about music and doing music" (Boston, 1995, p. 21).

". . .I believe that the quality of the music we give our students will play a significant role in the public's perception of the quality and value of music education itself. That is, if we present music which is not serious to our students, we are simultaneously educating the public to understand that what we are doing is not serious" (Whitwell, 1993, p. 157).

"If we can teach Music as a language through which the individual student learns about himself, his feelings and his emotions, society will come to appreciate our discipline. Society will come to understand that it is music teachers, not philosophy teachers, who can help the student discover his real self. That it is music teachers, not English teachers, who can help the student communicate his feelings. It is music teachers, not science teachers, who help the student connect his *own* experiences and feeling with his environment. That it is music teachers, not history teachers, who can help the student associate earlier periods of time *with himself*" (Whitwell, 1993, p. 175).

"Whether a teenager will want to devote a great deal of time to studying chemistry or music depends also on the quality of the experience he or she derives from working in the lab or practicing an instrument" (Csikszentmihalyi, 1993, pp. 7-8).

"A major goal of music education is to develop students who are musically independent and can progress to the next level by themselves after they leave school" (Thomson, 1995, p. 11). [a quote of John Whitwell]

"A teacher must work from some basic beliefs about the importance and purpose of music in order to provide direction, consistency, and insight" (Metz, 1980, p. vii).

"Because discipline problems often arise in class as a reaction to the teacher's obvious lack of a sense of purpose, the teacher-to-be needs a workable philosophy" (Metz, 1980, p. 3).

"Therefore, it is reasonable to assume that musical aptitude is a product of both innate potential and musical exposure" (Gordon, 1971, p. 4).

"One of the greatest assets a man can have in his adult life is the ability, when need arises, to shake the dust of reality momentarily from his feet, and to step, by way of his own imagination, through Alice's charmed mirror into the exquisite Wonderland of Music" (Green, 1966a, p. 91).

"The National Goal of the National Coalition for Music Education: Every child in every school will receive a well-rounded education that includes a comprehensive, sequential, high-quality program of music taught by a qualified music teacher" (Boston, 1995).

"Just as words can describe events we have not witnessed, places and things we have not seen, so music can present emotions and moods we have not felt, passions we did not know before" (Langer, 1957, p. 222).

"The aesthetic experience occurs when information coming from the artwork interacts with information already stored in the viewer's mind. The result of this conjunction might be a sudden expansion, recombination, or ordering of previously accumulated information, which in turn produces a variety of emotions such as delight, joy, or awe" (Csikszentmihalyi, 1990, p. 18).

"Enjoyment of an activity for its own sake is, in my opinion, the most important educational process that happens in school" (Csikszentmihalyi, 1995, p. 18).

"Musicianship is not a talent; it is a form of knowledge that can be taught and learned. It is a form of knowing and thinking. Just as most people can learn to 'do mathematics' (and science and so on), most people can learn the procedural musical knowledge required to make music musically" (Elliott and Rao, 1990, p. 32).

"As a universal language music builds a deeply human understanding between one person and another, be it man to man or teacher to student, but to *speak* the language of music—well, one has to do that for himself" (Green, 1966b, p. 84).

"In one definition, a skilled teacher is a person who can open a number of different windows on the same concept" (Gardner, 1991, p. 246).

"Thinking, discussing, and establishing priorities for the culture is as much the responsibility of the music teacher as of the history teacher. If students can see the importance and priority of music in relationship to other subjects *while* in school, music will retain its priority after graduation" (Colwell, 1994, p. 32).

"I have come to a frightening conclusion. I am the decisive element in the classroom. It is my personal approach that creates the climate. It is my daily mood that makes the weather. As a teacher I possess tremendous power to make a child's life miserable or joyous. I can be a tool of torture or an instrument of inspiration. I can humiliate or humor, hurt or heal. In all situations it is my response that decides whether a crisis will be escalated or de-escalated, and a child humanized or de-humanized" (Ginott, 1972, pp. 15-16).

"Sarcasm is not good for children. It destroys their self-confidence and self-esteem. Like strychnine, it can be fatal. Bitter irony and biting sarcasm only reinforce the traits they attack" (Ginott, 1972, p. 66).

"Learning depends on the emotional climate engendered by empathy and civility. In their daily contacts with children, teachers must preserve these vanishing virtues" (Ginott, 1972, p. 77).

"Children often live up to what parents expect them to be, and what teachers tell them they are. It is damaging to tell a child where he will end up. Destinations may become destinies" (Ginott, 1972, p. 102).

"Teachers often ask psychologists how to motivate children to learn. The answer is 'Make it safe for them to risk failure.' The major obstacle to learning is fear: fear of failure, fear of criticism, fear of appearing stupid. An effective teacher makes it possible for each child to err with impunity. To remove fear is to invite attempt. To welcome mistakes is to encourage learning" (Ginott, 1972, p. 242).

"Teachers have a unique opportunity to counteract unhealthy influences in a pupil's early childhood. They have the power to affect a child's life for better or for worse. A child becomes what he experiences. While parents possess the original key to their offspring's experience, teachers have a spare key. They too can open or close the minds and hearts of children" (Ginott, 1972, p. 301).

"Performance can no longer sell itself on the basis of its contribution to social skills or physical health or moral behavior or citizenship training or the need for rewards such as uniforms, medals, 'A' ratings, and the like. If such unsupportable and irrelevant claims are all that performance has to offer then performance is in deep trouble" (Reimer, 1970, p. 129).

"Music education, for many people, consists of material learned and skills gained. It is being suggested here that music education should consist of musical aesthetic experiences. Of course reading, writing, practicing, talking, testing, are legitimate and necessary components of music education. But when they become separated from musical experience itself they have become separated from that which provides their primary reason for existence" (Reimer, 1970, p. 86).

"Music education has a dual obligation to society. The first is to develop the talents of those who are gifted musically, for their own personal benefit, for the benefit of the society which will be served by them, for the benefit of the art of music which depends on a continuing supply of composers, performers, conductors, scholars, teachers. The second obligation is to develop the aesthetic sensitivity to music of all people regardless of their individual levels of music talent, for their own personal benefit, for the benefit of society which needs an active cultural life, for the benefit of the art of music which depends on a continuing supply of sympathetic, sensitive consumers. These two obligations are mutually supportive: the neglect of either one inevitably weakens both" (Reimer, 1970, p. 112).

"A performance program which is essentially musical, which justifies itself accordingly, which expends its major efforts on its essential purpose, can afford to give a reasonable amount of peripheral service without endangering its status" (Reimer, 1970, p. 129).

"The parallel in educational terms is that even the best philosophy cannot be expected to predict or describe every contingency in every teaching-learning situation. No philosophy can be perfectly applicable to all practical situations" (Elliott, 1995, p. 10).

"In sum, educating competent, proficient, and expert listeners for the future depends on the progressive education of competent, proficient, and artistic music makers in the present" (Elliott, 1995, p. 99).

"In summary, music making is a unique and major way of gaining self-growth, self-knowledge, and optimal experience, both now and in the future. . . . For these reasons, music making is something worth learning to do well by *all* students" (Elliott, 1995, p. 122).

"Accordingly, a school that denies children a sustained and systematic music education curriculum is not simply incomplete; it imperils the quality of students' present and future lives by denying them the cognitive keys to a unique and major source of fundamental human life values. If a society wishes to invest in a basic education for every child, then public schools must center on the domains of thinking and knowing that are accessible, achievable, and applicable to all. MUSIC is one of these basic cognitive domains" (Elliott, 1995, p. 130).

"Not everyone who is taught how to read and write can become a Shakespeare or a Robert Frost. But schools still attempt to teach all students to read and write well. Not everyone who is taught math can become an Albert Einstein. But schools still attempt to teach everyone to do math well. Not everyone who is taught music can become (or is expected to become) a Mozart or a Jessye Norman. Nevertheless, all schools should attempt to teach all students to make and listen for music well. For the values inherent in knowing how to make and listen for music intelligently are central to making a life; self-growth, self-knowledge, self esteem, creative achievement, humanistic and cultural empathy, and enjoyment are central life goals and life values in all human cultures" (Elliott, 1995, p. 236).

"When we educate our artistic intelligences, we awaken our perceptions and levels of awareness. We put more of our mind to work. We develop our capacity to view the world from different perspectives and to absorb from it more broadly. We immediately open windows to understanding" (Fowler, 1990, p.165).

"In the process of overselling science, mathematics, and technology as the panaceas of commerce, schools have denied students something precious—access to their expressive/communicative being, the essence of their personal spirit" (Fowler, 1990, p.166).

"Development of successful teaching techniques, a meaningful philosophy, and appropriate attitudes often takes years of diligent effort" (Forsythe, 1987, p. 333).

Developing a thoughtful personal philosophy of music education will be one of the most beneficial and far-reaching actions you will take as a teacher. It will help guide you through the unexpected challenges you will meet as an instrumental music teacher. Make the time to develop a first-rate and scholarly document.

## *For Assignment or Discussion*

1. Read "A Sound Decision" in the book *Case Studies in Music Education* (1998) by Frank Abrahams and Paul Head. As a class, discuss how you would handle this situation.

2. Write your own thoughtfully considered Philosophy of Music Education. Use the content of this course and your other music education courses, your college ensemble and conducting class experience, your high school band or orchestra experience, etc. as the basis of your deliberation. This should be about one page long, single-spaced, with one-inch margins all around.

## *For Reference and Further Reading*

Abeles, Harold F.; Hoffer, Charles R.; and Klotman, Robert H. (1984). *Foundations of Music Education*. New York: Schirmer Books.

Abrahams, Frank and Head, Paul (1998). *Case Studies in Music Education*. Chicago: GIA Publications, Inc.

Bartner, Arthur Charles (1963). The Evolution and Development of the University and College Marching Band. Unpublished masters thesis. The University of Michigan.

Birge, Edward Bailey (1966). *History of Public School Music in the United States*. Reston, VA: Music Educators National Conference.

Boston, Bruce (1995). *With One Voice: A Report from the 1994 Summit on Music Education*. Reston, VA: Music Educators National Conference.

Britton, Allen P. (1958). "Music in Early American Public Education: A Historical Critique." In *Basic Concepts in Music Education*. Nelson B. Henry (Ed.). Chicago: The University of Chicago Press.

Britton, Allen P. (1961). Music education: an American specialty. In *One Hundred Years of Music in America*, Paul Henry Lang (Ed.). New York: Schirmer, Inc.

Britton, Allen P. (1991). American music education: is it better than we think? In *Basic Concepts in Music Education, II*, Richard J. Colwell (Ed.). Niwot, CO: University Press of Colorado.

Bryant, Carolyn (1975). *And the Band Played On* (1776-1976). Washington, DC: Smithsonian Institution Press.

Buttelman, Clifford V. (1962). *Will Earhart—A Steadfast Philosophy*. Washington, D.C.: Music Educators National Conference.

Choate, Robert A., (Ed.) (1968). *Documentary Report of the Tanglewood Symposium*. Washington, DC: Music Educators National Conference.

Colwell, Richard (1994). Thinking and walking backwards into the future. *Arts Education Policy Review*. *95/5* (May/June).

Covey, Stephen R. (1990). *The Seven Habits of Highly Effective People: Restoring the Character Ethic*. New York: Fireside

Csikszentmihalyi, Mihaly, and Robinson, Rick E. (1990). *The Art of Seeing*. Malibu, CA: J. Paul Getty Museum and the Getty Center for Education in the Arts.

Csikszentmihalyi, Mihaly, et al. (1993). *Talented Teenagers: The Roots of Success and Failure*. New York: Cambridge University Press.

Csikszentmihalyi, Mihaly (1995). Singing and the self: choral music as "active leisure." *Choral Journal*. (Feb.) (13-19).

Elliott, Charles (1990). Comments on music education. In *Artistic Intelligences—Implications for Education*, William J. Moody (Ed.). New York: Teachers College Press. pp. 140-144.

Elliott, David J., and Rao, Doreen (1990). Musical performance and music education. *Design for Arts in Education*. (May/June) (23-34).

Elliott, David J. (1995). *Music Matters: A New Philosophy of Music Education*. New York: Oxford University Press.

Fennell, Frederick (1954). *Time and the Winds*. Kenosha, WI: Leblanc Publications.

Fowler, Charles (1990). One nation, undercultured and underqualified. In *Artistic Intelligences: Implications for Education*, William J. Moody (Ed.). New York: Teachers College Press. pp. 159-169.

Fowler, Charles (1991). Finding the way to be basic: music education in the 1990s and beyond. In *Basic Concepts in Music Education*, *II* , Richard J. Colwell (Ed.). Niwot, Colorado: University Press of Colorado.

Forsythe, Jere L. (1987). The blind musicians and the elephant. In *Applications of research in Music Behavior* [[edited by Clifford K. Madsen and Carol A. Prickett]]. Tuscaloosa, AL: The University of Alabama Press. pp. 329-338.

Gardner, Howard (1990). Multiple intelligences: implications for art and creativity. In *Artistic Intelligences—Implications for Education*, William J. Moody (Ed.). New York: Teachers College Press. pp. 11-27.

Gardner, Howard (1991). *The Unschooled Mind: How Children Think and How Schools Should Teach*. New York: BasicBooks.

Gardner, Howard (1993). *Frames of Mind (2nd ed.)*. New York: BasicBooks.

Gardner, Howard (1993). *Multiple Intelligences: The Theory in Practice (2nd ed.)*. New York: BasicBooks.

Gardner, Howard (1995). Reflections on multiple intelligences: myths and messages. *Phi Delta Kappan*. (Sept., 200-209).

Ginott, Haim (1972). *Teacher and Child: A Book for Parents and Teachers*. New York: The Macmillan Company.

Goldman, Richard Franco (1961). Band music in America. *In One Hundred Years of Music in America*, Paul Henry Lang (Ed.). New York: Schirmer, Inc.

Goldman, Richard Franco (1962). *The Wind Band*. Boston, MA: Allyn and Bacon, Inc.

Gordon, Edwin (1971). *The Psychology of Music Teaching*. Englewood Cliffs, NJ: Prentice-Hall, Inc.

Gordon, Edwin (1988). *Learning Sequences in Music*. Chicago: G.I.A. Publications.

Green, Elizabeth A.H. (1966a). *Orchestral Bowings and Routines*. Ann Arbor: Campus Publishers.

Green, Elizabeth A. H. (1966b). *Teaching Stringed Instruments in Classes*. Englewood Cliffs, NJ: Prentice-Hall, Inc.

Hitchcock, H. Wiley (1969). *Music in the United States: A Historical Introduction*. Englewood Cliffs, NJ: Prentice-Hall, Inc.

Holz, Emil A. (1960). The national school band tournament of 1923 and its bands. Ph.D. Dissertation, University of Michigan.

Holz, Emil A. (1962). The school band contest of America (1923). *Journal of Research in Music Education*. 10 (Spring), pp. 3-12.

Holz, Emil A., and Jacobi, Roger E. (1966). *Teaching Band Instruments to Beginners*. Englewood Cliffs, NJ: Prentice-Hall, Inc.

Humphreys, Jere T. (1992). Instrumental music in American education: in service of many masters. In *The Ithaca Conference on American Music Education: Centennial Profiles*, Mark Fonder (Ed.). Ithaca, NY: Ithaca College. pp. 25-51.

Keene, James A. (1982). *A History of Music Education in the United States*. Hanover, NH: University Press of New England.

Langer, Suzanne K. (1953). *Feeling and Form*. New York: Scribner.

Langer, Suzanne K. (1957). *Philosophy In A New Key (3rd ed.)*. Cambridge, MA: Harvard University Press.

Lautzenheiser, Tim (1992). *The Art of Successful Teaching: A Blend of Content and Context*. Chicago: GIA Pub.

Leonhard, Charles and House, Robert W. (1972). *Foundations and Principles of Music Education (2nd ed.)*. New York: McGraw-Hill Book Company.

Maddy Joseph E. (2000, reprint from 1956). Early American school and college bands. *The Instrumentalist*. 54/10 (May) (86-87).

Maddy, J.E., and Giddings, T.P. (1928). *Instrumental Class Teaching—A Practical Teachers' Guide*. Cincinnati, OH: The Willis Music Company.

Manno, Bruno V. (1995). The new school wars: battles over outcome-based education. *Phi Delta Kappan*. (May, 720-726).

Mark, Michael L. (1992). American music education in the national context, 1892 to 1992. In *The Ithaca Conference on American Music Education: Centennial Profiles*, Mark Fonder (Ed.). Ithaca, NY: Ithaca College. pp. 1-23.

Mark, Michael L. and Gary, Charles L. (1999). *A History of American Music Education (2nd ed.)*. Reston, VA: MENC.

Metz, Donald (1980). *Teaching General Music in Grades 6-9*. Columbus, OH: Charles E. Merrill Publishing Co.

Moody, William J. (Ed.) (1990). *Artistic Intelligences—Implications for Education*. New York: Teachers College Press.

(The) National Commission on Excellence in Education (1983). *A Nation at Risk: The Imperative for Educational Reform*. U.S. Government Printing Office.

*Performance Standards for Music: Grades PreK-12 (1996)*. Reston, VA: Music Educators National Conference.

Reimer, Bennett (1970). *A Philosophy of Music Education*. Englewood Cliffs, NJ: Prentice-Hall, Inc.

Reimer, Bennett (1994). Is musical performance worth saving? *Arts Education Policy Review*. 95/3 (Jan./Feb.) (2-13).

Sizer, Theodore R. (1992). *Horace's School: Redesigning the American High School*. New York: Houghton Mifflin Co.

Stein, Jess (Ed.) (1988). *Random House College Dictionary, revised*. New York: Random House.

Stevenson, Robert Louis (1916). *Treasure Island*. New York: The MacMillan Co.

Suzuki, Shinichi (1996). *Nurtured By Love: The Classic Approach to Talent Education (Waltraud Suzuki, Trans.) (2nd ed.)*. Mattituck, NY: Amereon.

Tellstrom, A. Theodore (1971). *Music in American Education: Past and Present*. New York: Holt, Rinehart and Winston, Inc.

Thomson, John (1995). Teaching with goals, not answers: an interview with John Whitwell. *The Instrumentalist*. December, pp. 11-15.

Tindall, George Brown (1988). *America: A Narrative History (2nd ed.)*. New York: W.W. Norton & Company, Inc.

Walters, Darrel L, and Taggart, Cynthia Crump (ed.) (1989). *Readings in Music Learning Theory*. Chicago, GIA Publications, Inc.

Whitehill, Charles D. (1969). Sociological conditions which contributed to the growth of the school band movement in the United States. *Journal of Research in Music Education*. 27 (Spring), pp. 179-191.

Whitwell, David (1980). *A New History of Wind Music*. Evanston, IL: The Instrumentalist Co.

Whitwell, David (1993). *Music as a Language: A New Philosophy of Music Education*. Northridge, CA: WINDS.

# Final Comments

We have covered an enormous amount of information in this book. The goal has been to prepare you as thoroughly as possible to begin teaching and learning. It is impossible to anticipate every situation you will encounter when you begin teaching, but I hope you have gained enough skills, knowledge, and understanding to solve each new problem—and enough desire and enthusiasm to continue to learn new skills and techniques on your own.

Be a positive and enthusiastic teacher—your students will respond better and learn much more. Be a person who sets priorities and who schedules priorities—you will be a more effective teacher, spouse, and parent. Be a real leader—one who is able, and willing, to set a life example for your students. Work hard, keep it all in perspective, and enjoy making beautiful music with your students.

We live in an exciting and challenging time for education. It seems that *everything* is being evaluated and reformed. That constitutes opportunities for gifted and hard-working music teachers to make significant improvements for our students and our profession—just as the giants of our profession did in the early days of music in the schools.

Being a band or orchestra director is a job with enormous responsibilities and pressures, but also one that is very rewarding. You have a wonderful opportunity to present fine music to young people, and to use that music to help shape and mold their lives. I hope *you* enjoy it, and I hope you enable your *students* to enjoy it.

## On-line Resources

Professors may wish to visit the GIA Publications, Inc., website (www.giamusic.com/cooper) to view and download suggested course syllabi for use with this text. One syllabus is for a comprehensive

Instrumental Methods course, elementary through high school. You will also find a suggestion for a two-course sequence—an Elementary and Middle School Instrumental Methods course and a High School Instrumental Methods course.

I am also available to answer questions about the text. Please contact me at lynn.cooper@asbury.edu.

# Appendix A — Suggested Band Literature

## CONCERT & FESTIVAL LITERATURE

### *Grade 1*

| Title | Composer/Arranger | Publisher |
|---|---|---|
| African Folk Trilogy | Anne McGinty | Queenwood |
| African Sketches | James Curnow | Curnow |
| Ahrirang | Robert Garofalo & Garwood Whaley | Meredith |
| Air and Dance | John Kinyon | Alfred |
| Allegro and Dance | W.A. Mozart/John Cacavas | Presser |
| All Ye Young Sailors | Pierre La Plante | C. Fischer |
| American Frontier | Philip Gordon | Elkan-Vogel |
| Argonauts, The | Mike Hannickel | Curnow |
| Barn Dance Saturday Night | Pierre La Plante | C. Fischer |
| Capriccio | Franz Haydn/Robert Foster | Wingert-Jones |
| Chant for Percussion | Andrew Balent | Barnhouse |
| Charioteers, The | Mike Hannickel | Curnow |
| Chester | William Billings/Eric Osterling | Jenson |
| Country Wildflowers | Larry Daehn | Daehn |
| Crusaders' Hymn | Andrew Balent | C. Fischer |
| English Hunting Song | John Kinyon | Alfred |
| Festivo De Noel | Mike Hannickel | Curnow |
| Fields of Glory | Elliot Del Borgo | Curnow |
| Finale, from "Symphony No. 1" | Brahms/Timothy Johnson | Curnow |
| First Individualized Concert Collection | James Froseth | GIA |
| Hotaku Koi | Nancy Fairchild | C. Fischer |
| Hungarian Folkround | Robert Garofalo & Garwood Whaley | Meredith |
| Londonderry Air, A | John Kinyon | Alfred |
| Minuet and Country Dance | Mozart/Philip Gordon | Presser |
| Modal Overture | John Kinyon | Alfred |
| Music From The Great Hall | arr. by Katheryn Fenske | Daehn |
| New Alliance | James Hosay | Curnow |
| Nottingham Castle | Larry Daehn | Daehn |
| Of Honor and Glory | Carmine Pastore | Curnow |
| Prehistoric Suite, A | Paul Jennings | Jenson |
| Prelude and March | Bob Margolis | Manhattan Beach |
| Rondo Royale | Frank Erickson | Summit |
| Shaker Hymn, A | John O'Reilly | Alfred |
| Song and Dance | Dmitri Kabalevsky/John O'Reilly | Alfred |
| Sugar Creek Saga | James Curnow | Curnow |
| Suncatcher | James Curnow | Curnow |
| Theme and Variations | Timothy Broege | Manhattan Beach |
| Tuskegee Airmen | Mike Hannickel | Curnow |
| Two Minute Symphony, The | Bob Margolis | Manhattan Beach |

# Grade 2

| Title | Composer/Arranger | Publisher |
|---|---|---|
| Air for Band | Frank Erickson | Bourne |
| All Through The Night | Sammy Nestico | Kendor |
| American Hymn, An | Robert E. Foster | Wingert-Jones |
| Ancient Voices | Michael Sweeney | Hal Leonard |
| Andante and Allegro | A. Corelli/Philip Gordon | Etling |
| Arioso | Handel/John Kinyon | Studio PR |
| Ave Verum Corpus | W.A. Mozart/Barbara Buehlman | Ludwig |
| Ave Verum Corpus | W.A. Mozart/Timothy Johnson | Curnow |
| Bach Variants | James Curnow | Curnow |
| Ballad (Theme and Variations) | Vaclav Nelhybel | Presser |
| Balladair | Frank Erickson | Bourne |
| Benediction Chorales | Robert E. Foster | Wingert-Jones |
| Bist Du Bei Mir | J.S. Bach/Anne McGinty | Queenwood |
| Black Is The Color of My True Loves Hair | James Ployhar | Byron-Douglas |
| Bristol Bay Legend | Robert Sheldon | Barnhouse |
| British Isles Ballads | John Kinyon | Alfred |
| Buckwheat | Heskel Brisman | Presser |
| Canterbury Overture | Anne McGinty | Queenwood |
| Canticum | James Curnow | Hal Leonard |
| Canto | W. Francis McBeth | Southern |
| Canzone Antica | Stephen Bulla | Curnow |
| Caprice | William Himes | Kjos |
| Carpathian Sketches | Robert Jager | Belwin |
| Castlebrook Overture | Claude T. Smith | Jenson |
| Cavata | W. Francis McBeth | Southern |
| Chanson | John Kinyon | Warner Bros. |
| Chanteys | James Andrews | Shawnee |
| Chester | William Billings/Eric Osterling | Jenson |
| Childhood Hymn, A | David Holsinger | TRN |
| Chorale from Jupiter | Gustav Holst/James Curnow | Hal Leonard |
| Clair de Lune | Claude Debussy/Kenneth Henderson | Trigram |
| Clouds | Anne McGinty | Queenwood |
| Conquerors | Timothy Johnson | Curnow |
| Courtly Festival | Henry Purcell/Philip Gordon | Belwin |
| Crusaders Hymn | James Ployhar | Belwin/CPP |
| Devil Dance | John Kinyon | Alfred |
| Dorian Festival | Frank Erickson | Belwin |
| Early English Suite | W. Duncombe/Walter Finlayson | Boosey & Hawkes |
| Elizabethan Suite | Philip Gordon | Kalmus |
| Enconium | Anne McGinty | Hal Leonard |
| Fanfare, Pastorale and Serenade | Robert Starer | Marks |
| Fantasy On A Danish Theme | Albert O. Davis | Byron-Douglas |
| Festivity | John Kinyon | Alfred |
| Firebrook Prelude | James Curnow | Curnow |
| First Light On The Chesapeake | James Hosay | Curnow |
| Fitzwilliam Suite | Philip Gordon | Marks |
| For Children | Bela Bartok/Walter Finlayson | Boosey & Hawkes |
| From An 18th Century Album | Theldon Meyers | TRN |

| | | |
|---|---|---|
| From The Land of Fire and Ice | David Magnusson/Grant Hull | Wynn |
| George Washington Suite | Mike Hannickel | Curnow |
| Greenwillow Portrait | Mark William | Alfred |
| Highbridge Excursions | Mark Williams | Alfred |
| Hill Songs | James Andrews | Shawnee |
| Hundred Pipers, A | James Ployhar | C. Fischer |
| Hymn for Band, A | Hugh Stuart | Shawnee |
| In Dulci Jubilo | John Zdechlik | Kjos |
| Jefferson County Overture | John O'Reilly | Alfred |
| Jessamine Station Overture | James Curnow | Shawnee |
| Korean Folk Rhapsody | James Curnow | Hal Leonard |
| Legend of the Eagle | Anne McGinty | Hansen |
| Legend of Knife River | Stephen Bulla | Curnow |
| Lion of Lucerne, The | James Curnow | Jenson |
| Little Prelude | Walter Finlayson | Boosey & Hawkes |
| Little Suite for Band | Clare Grundman | Boosey & Hawkes |
| Londonderry Ballad | John Kinyon | Alfred |
| Meadowlands | W. Francis McBeth | Alfred |
| Miniature Chorale and Fugue | Charles Carter | Luverne |
| Montevista | Robert Smith | CPP/Belwin |
| Musette and March | J.S. Bach/John Kinyon | Studio PR/CPP |
| New Frontiers | Douglas Court | Curnow |
| Old Scottish Melody | Charles Wiley | TRN |
| Pavana and March | William Byrd/Philip Gordon | Presser |
| Poem | Fibich/Spinney | Byron-Douglas |
| Polyphonic Suite | Charles Carter | Ludwig |
| Portrait of A Clown | Frank Ticheli | Manhattan Beach |
| Prelude and Scherzo | James Curnow | Hal Leonard |
| Red Balloon, The | Anne McGinty | Queenwood |
| Rhythm Machine | Timothy Broege | Bourne |
| Sandcastle Sketches | Robert Sheldon | Barnhouse |
| Sandcastles | James Curnow | Curnow |
| Scenes from A Royal Tapestry | Stuart Johnson | R. Smith |
| Scenes of Russia | Elliot Del Borgo | Curnow |
| Scottish Tryptich, A | James Curnow | Curnow |
| Sea Song Trilogy | Anne McGinty | Queenwood |
| Set of Early English Airs | John Kinyon | Boosey & Hawkes |
| Shalom Chaverim | Timothy Johnson | Curnow |
| Shenandoah | James Ployhar | Byron-Douglas |
| Slavonic Folk Suite | Alfred Reed | Jenson |
| Snakes | Thomas Duffy | Ludwig |
| Song for Winds | John Edmondson | Hansen |
| Stars Asleep, the Break of Day, The | Bob Margolis | Manhattan Beach |
| Still Wie die Nacht | Carl Bohm/Charles Spinney | Byron-Douglas |
| Suite in Minor Mode | Kabalevsky/Siekman & Oliver | MCA |
| Swedish Melody | Earl Slocum | TRN |
| Taddington Square | James Curnow | Curnow |
| Tales of the Bay | James Hosay | Curnow |
| Tallis Prelude, A | Doug Akay | Queenwood |
| Thousand Hills Overture, A | Claude T. Smith | Jenson |
| Three English Folk Songs | John Edmondson | Barnhouse |
| Three Songs of Colonial America | Leroy Jackson | Warner Bros. |

| | | |
|---|---|---|
| Two Moods | Clare Grundman | Boosey & Hawkes |
| Ukranian Bell Carol | James Ployhar | Carl Fisher |
| Where The Rivers Meet | Douglas Court | Curnow |
| Wyndham Marziale | Paul Curnow | Curnow |
| Yorkshire Ballad | James Barnes | Southern |

## Grade 3

| Title | Composer/Arranger | Publisher |
|---|---|---|
| Adagio for Winds | Elliot Del Borgo | Shawnee |
| Alleluia | W.A. Mozart/Clifford Barnes | Ludwig |
| Allerseelen | Richard Strauss/Albert Oliver Davis | Ludwig |
| American Folk Rhapsody (No. 1-4) | Clare Grundman | Boosey & Hawkes |
| American River Songs | Pierre LaPlante | Daehn |
| An Occasional Suite | G.F. Handel/Eric Osterling | Ludwig |
| Arietta For Winds | Frank Erickson | Bourne |
| Armida Overture | Franz Joseph Haydn/Bowles | Barnhouse |
| As Summer Was Just Beginning | Larry Daehn | Daehn |
| As Torrents in Summer | Edward Elgar/Albert Oliver Davis | Ludwig |
| Australian Up-Country Tune | Percy A. Grainger/Glenn C. Bainum | G. Schirmer |
| Ave Maria | Anton Bruckner/Barbara Buelhman | Ludwig |
| Battaglia | W. Francis McBeth | Southern |
| Battle Pavanne, The | Tielman Susato/Bob Margolis | Manhattan Beach |
| Belle Que Tiens Ma Vie | Thoinot Arbeau/Bob Margolis | Manhattan Beach |
| Black Is the Color of My True Loves Hair | James Curnow | Jenson |
| Blue and the Gray, The | Clare Grundman | Boosey & Hawkes |
| Blue Ridge Overture | John Kinyon | Alfred |
| Bristol Bay Legend | Robert Sheldon | Barnhouse |
| Cambridge Overture | John Tatgenhorst | Barnhouse |
| Canterbury Chorale | Jan Van der Roost | de Haske |
| Canterbury Tales | James Curnow | Hal Leonard |
| Carnival of the Animals | C. Saint Saens/Mark Bender | Heritage Music Press |
| Chant and Jubilo | W. Francis McBeth | Southern |
| Chesford Portrait | James Swearingen | Barnhouse |
| Chorale | Vaclav Nelhybel | Belwin |
| Chorale Prelude: Be Thou My Vision | Jack Stamp | Kjos |
| Come, Sweet Death | J.S. Bach/Mark Hindsley | Hindsley |
| Court Festival | William Latham | Summy-Birchard |
| Courtly Airs and Dances | Ron Nelson | Ludwig |
| Crown of Thorns | Julie Giroux | Southern |
| Denbridge Way | James Swearingen | Barnhouse |
| Devonshire Overture | James Ployhar | Belwin |
| Die Nacht | R. Strauss/Albert Oliver Davis | Ludwig |
| English Masters Suite | Purcell, Croft, Laes/Philip Gordon | Belwin |
| English Suite | Clare Grundman | Boosey & Hawkes |
| Fa Una Canzona | Larry Daehn | Daehn |
| Fanfare, Ode and Festival | Bob Margolis | Manhattan Beach |
| Fanfare Prelude on "Lobe Den Herren" | James Curnow | Jenson |

| | | |
|---|---|---|
| Fanfare Prelude on "Lancashire" | James Curnow | Jenson |
| Fall River Overture | Robert Sheldon | Barnhouse |
| Fantasy for Band | Frank Erickson | Bourne |
| Fantasy on Amer. Sailing Songs | Clare Grundman | Boosey & Hawkes |
| Fantasy on "Sakura, Sakura" | Ray E. Cramer | TRN |
| Festivo | Vaclav Nelhybel | Belwin |
| Flourish For Wind Band | Ralph Vaughan Williams | Oxford |
| Folk Legend | Donald Hunsberger | Remick |
| Four Sketches | Bela Bartok/William Schaefer | Elkan-Vogel |
| Gathering of the Ranks at Hebron, The | David Holsinger | TRN |
| Hebrides Suite | Clare Grundman | Boosey & Hawkes |
| Hymn of Praise | Anton Bruckner/Philip Gordon | Carl Fischer |
| Hymn to Yerevan | Alan Hovhaness | Peters |
| If Thou Be Near | J.S. Bach/R.L. Moehlmann | Fox |
| If Thou Be Near | J.S. Bach/Alfred Reed | Barnhouse |
| In The Bleak Midwinter | Gustav Holst/Robert W. Smith | Belwin |
| Irish Rhapsody, An | Clare Grundman | Boosey & Hawkes |
| Irish Suite for Band | Charles Spinney | Byron Douglas/Belwin |
| Jesu, Joy of Man's Desiring | J.S. Bach/Erik Leidzen | Carl Fischer |
| Jesu, Joy of Man's Desiring | J.S. Bach/Alfred Reed | Barnhouse |
| Jesus, Jesus Rest Your Head | Tom Wallace | Arrangers' Publishing |
| Kentucky 1800 | Clare Grundman | Boosey & Hawkes |
| King Across The Water, The | Bruce Fraser | Brand |
| Komm Susser Tod | J.S. Bach/Erik Leidzen | Carl Fischer |
| Linden Lea | Ralph Vaughan Williams/John Stout | Boosey & Hawkes |
| Little English Suite | Clare Grundman | Boosey & Hawkes |
| Lone Star Celebration | James Curnow | Curnow |
| Lyric Overture | Frank Erickson | Summit/Belwin |
| Meditation and Festival | Jared Spears | Barnhouse |
| Mexican Folk Fantasy | Frank Erickson | Summy |
| Mini Suite | Morton Gould | Chappell |
| Mystery on Mena Mountain | Julie Giroux | Southern |
| Nathan Hale Trilogy | James Curnow | Hal Leonard |
| Nimrod | Edward Elgar/Alfred Reed | Belwin |
| Northern Legend | James Curnow | Hal Leonard |
| Olympus | Mike Hannickel | Curnow |
| On A Hymnsong of Lowell Mason | David Holsinger | TRN |
| On A Hymnsong of Philip Bliss | David Holsinger | TRN |
| Overture for Winds | Charles Carter | Bourne |
| Overture On A Minstrel Tune | Pierre LaPlante | Daehn |
| Plymouth Trilogy | Anthony Iannaccone | Ludwig |
| Polly Oliver | Thomas Root | Kjos |
| Praises | W. Francis McBeth | Southern |
| Prelude and Fugue in Bb Major | J.S. Bach/R.L. Moehlmann | Warner/MPH |
| Prelude to Act I from "La Traviata" | Guiseppi Verdi/Leonard Falcone | Kjos |
| Prospect | Pierre LaPlante | Bourne |
| Quintessence | James Curnow | Hal Leonard |
| Renaissance Fair, The | Bob Margolis | Manhattan Beach |

| | | |
|---|---|---|
| Rhapsody On American Shaped Note Melodies | James Curnow | Curnow |
| Rhenish Folk Festival | Albert Oliver Davis | Ludwig |
| Rhosymedre | Ralph Vaughan Williams/W. Beeler | Galaxy |
| Rhythm of The Winds | Frank Erickson | Belwin |
| Royal Coronation Dances | Bob Margolis | Manhattan Beach |
| Sarabande and Polka | Malcolm Arnold/John Paynter | C. Fischer |
| Scotch Folk Suite | Albert Oliver Davis | Ludwig |
| Shenandoah | Frank Ticheli | Manhattan Beach |
| Sinfonia VI | Timothy Broege | Manhattan Beach |
| Sleepers Awake | J.S. Bach/Alfred Reed | Barnhouse |
| Sonatina for Band | Frank Erickson | Belwin |
| Songs of Wales | Albert Oliver Davis | Ludwig |
| Southwinds | Douglas Court | Curnow |
| Spoon River Saga | James Curnow | Hal Leonard |
| Spring, from "The Seasons" | Antonio Vivaldi/John Cacavas | Presser |
| St. Anthony Divertimento | Franz Joseph Haydn/James Wilcox | G. Schirmer |
| Stargazing | Donald Erb | Merion |
| Suite des Symphonies No. 1 | J. Mauret/Schaefer | Franco Colombo |
| Suite from Bohemia | Vaclav Nelhybel | Kerby |
| Swords Against The Sea | James Hosay | Curnow |
| Symphonic Overture | Charles Carter | C. Fischer |
| Te Deum | Charles Gounod/Lloyd Conley | Columbia |
| Terpsichore Suite | Michael Praetorius/Conrad Ross | Ludwig |
| The Good Daughter Overture | Nicolo Piccini/Eric Osterling | Ludwig |
| They Led My Lord Away | Adoniram J. Gordon/Fred J. Allen | TRN |
| Three Ayres From Gloucester | Hugh Stuart | Shawnee |
| Three Chorale Preludes | William Latham | Summy-Birchard |
| Three Colonial Ballads | James Curnow | Hal Leonard |
| Three Pieces for American Band Set 2 | Timothy Broege | Bourne |
| Three Songs from Sussex | Hugh Stuart | Shawnee |
| Toccata for Band | Frank Erickson | Bourne |
| Tournament | Stephen Bulla | Curnow |
| Two Gaelic Folk Songs | Thomas Tyra | Barnhouse |
| Variation Overture | Clifton Williams | Ludwig |
| Variants on An Early American Hymn Tune | James Curnow | Jenson |
| Welsh Folk Song Suite | Albert Oliver Davis | Ludwig |
| Ye Banks & Braes O' Bonnie Doon | Percy A. Grainger | G. Schirmer |

# *Grade 4*

| Title | Composer/Arranger | Publisher |
|---|---|---|
| Amazing Grace | Frank Ticheli | Manhattan Beach |
| American Civil War Fantasy | Jerry Bilik | Southern |
| American Elegy, An | Frank Ticheli | Manhattan Beach |
| Ballad for Band | Morton Gould | Chappell |
| Battell, The | William Byrd/Gordon Jacob | Boosey & Hawkes |
| Blessed Are They | Johannes Brahms/Barbara Buelhman | Ludwig |
| Caccia and Chorale | Clifton Williams | Barnhouse |
| Cajun Folk Songs | Frank Ticheli | Manhattan Beach |
| Canadian Folk Song Rhapsody | James Curnow | Hal Leonard |

| | | |
|---|---|---|
| Canticle of the Creatures | James Curnow | Jenson |
| Cause for Celebration | William Himes | Curnow |
| Celestial Celebration | James Curnow | Jenson |
| Chorale and Alleluia | Howard Hanson | C. Fischer |
| Chorale and Shaker Dance | John Zdechlik | Kjos |
| Chorale Prelude: O Cool Is The Valley | Vincent Persichetti | Elkan-Vogel |
| Chorale Prelude: O God Unseen | Vincent Persichetti | Elkan-Vogel |
| Chorale Prelude: So Pure the Star | Vincent Persichetti | Elkan-Vogel |
| Chorale Prelude: Turn Not Thy Face | Vincent Persichetti | Elkan-Vogel |
| Color | Bob Margolis | Manhattan Beach |
| Copland Tribute, A | Aaron Copland/Clare Grundman | Boosey & Hawkes |
| Corsican Litany | Vaclav Nelhybel | Bourne |
| Credo | Fisher Tull | Boosey & Hawkes |
| Crystals | Thomas Duffy | Ludwig |
| Dedicatory Overture | Clifton Williams | Piedmont Music |
| Dragoons of Villars, The | Maillart/Barnes | Ludwig |
| Dramatic Prelude | Claude T. Smith | Wingert-Jones |
| Elegy | John Barnes Chance | Boosey & Hawkes |
| Elegy for a Young American | Ronald LoPresti | Presser |
| Elsa's Procession To the Cathedral | Richard Wagner/Lucien Cailliet | Warner |
| Emperata Overture | Claude T. Smith | Wingert-Jones |
| English Dances | Malcolm Arnold/Johnstone | Belwin |
| English Folk Song Suite | Ralph Vaughan Williams | Boosey & Hawkes |
| Epinicion | John Paulson | Kjos |
| Fanfare and Flourishes | James Curnow | Curnow |
| Fantasia In G Major | J.S. Bach/Goldman & Leist | Presser |
| Fantasia for Band | Vittorio Giannini | Franco Columbo |
| Fantasy On A Colonial Air | James Curnow | Hal Leonard |
| Festival Prelude, A | Alfred Reed | Marks/Belwin |
| Fiddle Tunes | James Curnow | Curnow |
| First Suite in E-flat | Gustav Holst | Boosey & Hawkes |
| Folk Dances | Dmitri Shostakovich/H.R. Reynolds | Fischer |
| Havendance | David Holsinger | TRN |
| Four Cornish Dances | Malcolm Arnold/Thad Marchiniak | G. Schirmer |
| Hounds of Spring, The | Alfred Reed | Belwin |
| Imperatrix | Alfred Reed | Marks |
| In Praise of Gentle Pioneers | David Holsinger | TRN |
| Intrada, Adoration and Praise | Claude T. Smith | Jenson |
| Irish Tune from County Derry | Percy A. Grainger/Mark Rogers | Southern |
| Italian In Algiers, Overture | Gioacchino Rossini/Lucien Cailliet | Sam Fox |
| Jubilant Overture, A | Alfred Reed | Barnhouse |
| Kaddish | W. Francis McBeth | Southern |
| Last Spring, The | Edvard Grieg/James Curnow | Curnow |
| Liturgical Music for Band, Op. 33 | Martin Mailman | Belwin |
| March and Procession of Bacchus | Leo Delibes/Erik Leidzen | C. Fischer |
| Masque | W. Francis McBeth | Southern |
| Merry Music | Frigyes Hidas | Edition Music Budapest |
| Morning Alleluias | Ron Nelson | Ludwig |

| | | |
|---|---|---|
| Nocturne, Op. 9, No. 2 | Alexander Scriabin/Alfred Reed | Marks |
| North Bridge Portrait | Stephen Bulla | Curnow |
| Original Suite, An | Gordon Jacob | Boosey & Hawkes |
| Overture On A Southern Hymn | Robert Palmer | Shawnee |
| Pageant | Vincent Persichetti | C. Fischer |
| Persis | James Hosay | Curnow |
| Prelude, Siciliano and Rondo | Malcolm Arnold/John Paynter | C. Fischer |
| Psalm for Band | Vincent Persichetti | Elkan-Vogel |
| Psalm 46 | John Zdechlik | Schmitt |
| Puszta | Jan Van der Roost | De Haske |
| Requiem | Fisher Tull | Southern |
| Royce Hall Suite | Healey Willan/Teague | AMP |
| Salvation is Created | Pavel Tschesnokoff/B. Houseknecht | Kjos |
| Sang! | Dana Wilson | Ludwig |
| Satiric Dances | Norman Dello Joio | G. Schirmer |
| Second Prelude | George Gershwin/John Krance | New World Music |
| Serenade for Band | Vincent Persichetti | Elkan-Vogel |
| Somersault | Hale Smith | Marks |
| Sussex Mummer's Christmas Carol | Percy Grainger/R.F. Goldman | Galaxy |
| Symphonic Suite | Clifton Williams | Summy-Birchard |
| Symphonic Triptych | James Curnow | Hal Leonard |
| Third Suite | Robert Jager | Volkwein |
| Toccata | Girolamo Frescobaldi/Earl Slocum | CPP-Belwin |
| Transylvania Fanfare | Warren Benson | Shawnee |
| Trauersinfonie | Richard Wagner/Erik Leidzen | AMP |
| Two Grainger Melodies | Percy Grainger/Joseph Kreines | Barnhouse |
| Variations On A Korean Folk Song | John Barnes Chance | Boosey & Hawkes |
| Variations on A Shaker Melody | Aaron Copland | Boosey & Hawkes |
| Walking Tune | Percy A. Grainger/Larry Daehn | Daehn |
| Watchman, Tell Us Of The Night | Mark Camphouse | Kjos |
| When Jesus Wept | William Schuman | Presser |
| Wycliff Variations | Paul Whear | Ludwig |

## Grade 5

| Title | Composer/Arranger | Publisher |
|---|---|---|
| After A Gentle Rain | Anthony Iannaccone | Shawnee |
| Alcotts, The | Charles Ives/Richard Thurston | AMP |
| Alleluia! Laudamus Te | Alfred Reed | Marks |
| Ambrosian Hymn Variants | Donald White | Ludwig |
| American Overture for Band | Joseph Wilcox Jenkins | Presser |
| American Salute | Morton Gould/Lang | Belwin |
| Armenian Dances, Part I | Alfred Reed | Fox |
| Armenian Dances, Part II | Alfred Reed | Barnhouse |
| Ballet Sacra | David Holsinger | TRN |
| Ballo Del Granduca | Sweelink/Walters | E. C. Schirmer |
| Beowulf, An Heroic Trilogy | W. Francis McBeth | Southern |
| Be Glad Then, America | William Schuman | Presser |
| Be Thou My Vision | David Gillingham | C. Alan |
| Blue Lake Overture | John Barnes Chance | Boosey & Hawkes |

| | | |
|---|---|---|
| Canzona | Peter Mennin | Fischer |
| Celebration Overture | Paul Creston | A. Templeton |
| Celebrations | John Zdechlik | Kjos |
| Chester Overture | William Schuman | Presser |
| Circuits | Cindy McTee | MMB |
| Culloden | Julie Giroux | Musica Propria |
| Divertimento for Band | Vincent Persichetti | Presser |
| Do Not Go Gentle Into That Good Night | Elliot Del Borgo | Shawnee |
| Fanfare and Allegro | Clifton Williams | Summy-Birchard |
| Fantasia in G | Timothy Mahr | Kjos |
| Festive Overture | Dmitri Shostakovich/Donald Hunsberger | MCA |
| Festivo | Edward Gregson | Novello |
| Firestorm | Stephen Bulla | Curnow |
| Five Miniatures | Joaquin Turina/John Krance | AMP |
| Four Colonial Country Dances | James Curnow | Curnow |
| Four Scottish Dances | Malcolm Arnold/John Paynter | Fischer |
| Gavorkna Fanfare | Jack Stamp | Kjos |
| George Washington Bridge | William Schuman | G. Schirmer |
| Immovable Do, The | Percy Grainger | G. Schirmer |
| Incantation and Dance | John Barnes Chance | Boosey & Hawkes |
| Jubilee | Michael Hennagin | Walton Music |
| La Belle Helene Overture | Offenbach/Laurence Odom | Kjos |
| Liturgical Dances | David Holsinger | Southern |
| Lonely Beach | James Barnes | Southern |
| Mannin Veen | Haydn Wood | Boosey & Hawkes |
| Masquerade for Band | Vincent Persichetti | Elkan-Vogel |
| Medieval Suite | Ron Nelson | Boosey & Hawkes |
| Melita | Thomas Knox | Ludwig |
| Molly On The Shore | Percy Grainger/Mark Rogers | Southern |
| Movement for Rosa, A | Mark Camphouse | TRN |
| Nabucco Overture | Giusseppi Verdi/Lucien Cailliet | Sam Fox |
| Occident et Orient | Camille Saint Saens/David Whitwell | WINDS |
| Of Sailors and Whales | W. Francis McBeth | Southern |
| Outdoor Overture, An | Aaron Copland | Boosey & Hawkes |
| Overture for Winds | Felix Mendelssohn/John Boyd | Ludwig |
| Overture to Candide | Leonard Bernstein/Walter Beeler | G. Schirmer |
| Prelude on Three Welsh Hymn Tunes | Ralph Vaughan Williams/J. Curnow | Jenson |
| Rejouissance | James Curnow | Jenson |
| Russian Christmas Music | Alfred Reed | Sam Fox |
| Scenes from "The Louvre" | Norman Dello Joio | Marks |
| Second Dawning, The | James Hosay | Curnow |
| Second Suite in F | Gustav Holst | Boosey & Hawkes |
| Serenade Romantic | Joseph Turrin | Curnow |
| Sinfonietta | James Curnow | Hal Leonard |
| Sketches on A Tudor Psalm | Fischer Tull | Boosey & Hawkes |
| Slava! | Leonard Bernstein | Boosey & Hawkes |
| Soaring Hawk, The | Timothy Mahr | Hal Leonard |
| Stormworks | Stephen Melillo | Melillo |
| Suite Francaise | Darius Milhaud | MCA |
| Suite of Old American Dances | Robert Russell Bennett | Chappell |
| Symphonic Dance #3, "Fiesta" | Clifton Williams | Fox |
| Symphony for Band | Morton Gould | G. Schirmer |
| Symphony No. 3, Finale | Gustav Mahler/ Reynolds | Shawnee |

| | | |
|---|---|---|
| Theme and Fantasia | Armand Russell | Educational |
| To Bind The Nation's Wounds | James Curnow | Curnow |
| Toccata and Fugue in D Minor | J.S. Bach/Erik Leidzen | Fischer |
| Toccata Marziale | Ralph Vaughan Williams | Boosey & Hawkes |
| Tribute | Mark Camphouse | TRN |
| Trittico | Vaclav Nelhybel | Franco Columbo |
| Variations on "America" | Charles Ives/William Rhoads | Presser |
| Where Never Lark or Eagle Flew | James Curnow | Hal Leonard |
| William Byrd Suite | Gordon Jacob | Boosey & Hawkes |

## Grade Six

| Title | Composer/Arranger | Publisher |
|---|---|---|
| Academic Festival Overture | Johannes Brahms/Mark Hindsley | Hindsley |
| Awayday | Adam Gorb | Maccenas |
| Blue Shades | Frank Ticheli | Manhattan Beach |
| Colas Breugnon Overture | Dmitri Kabalevsky/Walter Beeler | Shawnee |
| Colonial Song | Percy Grainger | Fischer or South- ern |
| Dance of the Jesters | Tschaikowsky/Ray Cramer | Curnow |
| El Salon Mexico | Aaron Copland/Mark Hindsley | Boosey & Hawkes |
| Emblems | Aaron Copland | G. Schirmer |
| Enigma Variations | Edward Elgar/Earl Slocum | Shawnee |
| Festival Variations | Claude T. Smith | Wingert-Jones |
| Fiesta Del Pacifico | Roger Nixon | Boosey & Hawkes |
| Hammersmith | Gustav Holst | Boosey & Hawkes |
| Heros, Lost and Fallen | David Gillingham | Hal Leonard |
| Hill Song No. 2 | Percy Grainger | TRN |
| In The Spring At The Time When Kings Go Off To War | David Holsinger | Southern |
| La Fiesta Mexicana | H. Owen Reed | Belwin |
| Leaves Are Falling, The | Warren Benson | Hal Leonard |
| Lincolnshire Posy | Percy Grainger/Fennell | Ludwig |
| Lochinvar | James Curnow | Curnow |
| Mutanza | James Curnow | Jenson |
| Passing Bell, The | Warren Benson | E.C. Schirmer |
| Pines of Rome, The | O. Respighi/Guy Duker | Belwin |
| Praetorius Variations | James Curnow | Curnow |
| Rocky Point Holiday | Ron Nelson | Boosey & Hawkes |
| Sinfonietta | Ingolf Dahl | Pro Art |
| Soundings | Cindy McTee | MMB |
| Symphony for Band | Jerry Bilik | RBC Publications |
| Symphony in Bb | Paul Hindemith | Schott |
| Symphony #1, "Lord of The Rings" | Johan de Meij | Amstel |
| Symphony No. 2 | John Barnes Chance | Boosey & Hawkes |
| Symphony No. 3 | Vittorio Giannini | Belwin |
| Symphony No. 6 for Band | Vincent Persichetti | Elkan-Vogel |
| Terpsichore | Bob Margolis | Manhattan Beach |
| Theme and Variations, Op. 43a | Arnold Schoenberg | G. Schirmer |
| Tunbridge Fair | Walter Piston | Boosey & Hawkes |
| Variants on A Medieval Tune | Norman Dello Joio | Marks |

# MARCH LITERATURE

## *Grade 1 & 2*

| Title | Composer/Arranger | Publisher |
|---|---|---|
| American Heritage March | John Edmondson/James Swearingen | Queenwood |
| Bonds of Unity March | Karl L. King | Barnhouse |
| Brandy Station March | John Edmondson | Hal Leonard |
| Bunker Hill March | John Edmondson | Queenwood |
| Concord March | Frank Erickson | Summit |
| Copper Creek March | John Edmondson | Queenwood |
| Eagle Crest March | Bruce Pearson | Kjos |
| Flying Tigers | John Edmondson | Queenwood |
| Hammerfest | James Ployhar | Byron-Douglas |
| Island Empire March | William Himes | Kjos |
| Kingsbury March | Chuck Elledge/Bruce Pearson | Kjos |
| Kitty Hawk March | John Edmondson | Queenwood |
| Lexington March | John Edmondson | Queenwood |
| March of the Irish Guard | James Ployhar | C. Fischer |
| March of the Scots Guards | Robert Foster | Wingert-Jones |
| Maxium Concert March | David Shaffer | Barnhouse |
| Mighty Mac | Lloyd Conley | Studio PR |
| Military Escort | Henry Fillmore | Fillmore |
| Military March | Ludwig van Beethoven/Robert Foster | Wingert-Jones |
| Omega March | John Edmondson | Queenwood |
| Regal March | Bruce Pearson & Chuck Elledge | Kjos |
| Sandy Bay March | Brian West | Yamaha |
| Turkish March | Ludwig von Beethoven/John Kinyon | Alfred |
| United Nations | Karl L. King | Barnhouse |
| Valley Forge March | John Edmondson | Queenwood |
| Westchester March | James Swearingen | Barnhouse |
| Winchester March | John Edmondson | Queenwood |
| Wyndham March | Bruce Pearson & Chuck Elledge | Kjos |

## *Grade 3*

| Title | Composer/Arranger | Publisher |
|---|---|---|
| Band of Gold | George Kenny | Barnhouse |
| Bandology | Eric Osterling | C. Fischer |
| Billboard March | John N. Klohr | C. Fischer |
| Block M March | Jerry H. Bilik | Mills |
| Brighton Beach | William Latham | Summy-Birchard |
| Burnished Brass | John Cacavas | C. Fischer |
| Corcoran Cadets, The | John Philip Sousa/Frederick Fennell | Ludwig |
| Emblem of Unity | J.J. Richards | Barnhouse |
| Footlifter, The | Henry Fillmore | Fillmore |
| Hosts of Freedom | Karl L. King | Barnhouse |
| Huntress, The | Karl L. King | Barnhouse |
| Journey to Centaurus | James Curnow | TRN |
| March Grandioso | Roland Seitz | Southern |
| Men of Ohio | Henry Fillmore | Fillmore |
| Nutmeggers | Eric Osterling | Bourne |

| | | |
|---|---|---|
| Orange Bowl | Henry Fillmore | Fillmore |
| Sea Songs | Ralph Vaughan Williams | Boosey & Hawkes |
| Tall Cedars | Eric Osterling | C. Fischer |
| Thundercrest | Eric Osterling | C. Fischer |
| Totem Pole | Eric Osterling | Bourne |
| Trombone King, The | Karl L. King | King |

## Grade 4

| Title | Composer/Arranger | Publisher |
|---|---|---|
| Americans We | Henry Fillmore/Frederick Fennell | C. Fischer |
| Amparito Roca | Jaime Texitor | Boosey & Hawkes |
| Army of the Nile | Kenneth J. Alford/Frederick Fennell | Boosey & Hawkes |
| Athletic Festival March | Serge/Prokofieff/R.F. Goldman | Leeds |
| Barnum and Bailey's Favorite | Karl L. King | Barnhouse |
| Billboard, The | John N. Klohr/Frederick Fennell | C. Fischer |
| Black Horse Troop, The | John Philip Sousa | John Church |
| British Eighth | Zo Elliott/Hilmar F. Luckhardt | C. Fischer |
| Chicago Tribune | W. Paris Chambers/John Boyd | Ludwig |
| Colonel Bogey March | Kenneth J. Alford | Boosey & Hawkes |
| Combination March | Scott Joplin/Schuller | Margun |
| Dam Busters, The | Eric Coates | Chappell |
| El Capitan | John Philip Sousa | John Church |
| Entry March of the Boyares | Johan Halvorsen/Frederick Fennell | Ludwig |
| Fairest of the Fair, The | John Philip Sousa | John Church |
| Free Lance, The | John Philip Sousa/William D. Revelli | Jenson |
| Glory of the Yankee Navy, The | John Philip Sousa/Frederick Fennell | Presser |
| His Honor | Henry Fillmore/Frederick Fennell | C. Fischer |
| Jubilee | Kenneth G. Whitcomb | Summy-Birchard |
| Kentucky Sunrise | Karl L. King/Robert E. Foster | Barnhouse |
| Knightsbridge March | Eric Coates/Paul Yoder | Chappell |
| L'Inglesina (The Little English Girl) | D. Delle Cese | Pagani |
| Lowlands March | Charles Wiley | TRN |
| Invictus | Karl L. King | King |
| Lassus Trombone | Henry Fillmore | Fillmore |
| Liberty Bell | John Philip Sousa | Kalmus |
| March, from "A Little Suite" | Malcolm Arnold/Peter A. Sumner | Patterson's |
| March of the Steel Men | Charles Belsterling/Harry L. Alford | Fillmore |
| Marche Lorraine | Louis Ganne/Fennell & Mahl | C. Fischer |
| Marche Militaire Francaise | Camille Saint-Saens/Godfrey | C. Fischer |
| March of the Belgian Paratroopers | Pierre Leemans/Charles A. Wiley | TRN |
| Minuteman | Robert Pearson | Templeton |
| Montmartre | Haydn Wood | Big Three |
| Moorside March | Gustav Holst | Boosey & Hawkes |
| National Emblem | E.E. Bagley/Frederick Fennell | C. Fischer |
| Old Comrades | Carl Teike/Laurendeau | C. Fischer |
| On The Mall | Edwin Franco Goldman | C. Fischer |
| Pathfinder of Panama | John Philip Sousa/Raymond Dvorak | John Church |
| Royal Welch Fusiliers, The | John Philip Sousa | Presser |
| Semper Fidelis | John Philip Sousa | C. Fischer |
| Silver Quill, The | Harpham & Nestico/Nestico | Volkwein |

| | | |
|---|---|---|
| Sinfonians, The | Clifton Williams | Marks |
| Slavic Farewell, A | Vasilij Agapkin/John R. Bourgeois | Wingert-Jones |
| Spirit of the Guard, The | James Curnow | Jenson |
| Them Basses | G. H. Huffine | Fillmore |
| Vanished Army, The | Kenneth Alford | Boosey & Hawkes |
| Vilabella | Kenneth Williams/Alfred Reed | Sam Fox |
| Washington Grays | C.S. Grafulla/G.H. Reeves | C. Fischer |
| Whip and Spur Galop | Thomas S. Allen/Ray E. Cramer | TRN |
| Zacatecas | Genero Codina/Richard E. Thurston | Southern |

## Grade 5 and 6

| Title | Composer/Arranger | Publisher |
|---|---|---|
| Boys of the Old Brigade, The | W. Paris Chambers/Claude T. Smith | Wingert-Jones |
| Bravura | Charles E. Duble | John Church |
| Children's March | Percy Grainger/Mark Rogers | Southern |
| Circus Bee, The | Henry Fillmore | C. Fischer |
| Commando March | Samuel Barber | G. Schirmer |
| Country Band March | Charles Ives/James Sinclair | Presser |
| Crown Imperial | William Walton/Duthoit | Boosey & Hawkes |
| Esprit de Corps, march | Robert Jager | Hal Leonard |
| Florentiner, The | Julius Fucik/Lake & Fennell | C. Fischer |
| George Washington Bicentennial | John Philip Sousa | Sam Fox |
| Golden Ear, The | Mariano San Miguel/Taylor | Powers |
| Hands Across The Sea | John Philip Sousa | John Church |
| Lads of Wamphrey | Percy Grainger | C. Fischer |
| March, Op. 99 | Sergei Prokofieff/Paul Yoder | MCA |
| March, from Symphonic Metamorphosis | Paul Hindemith/Keith Wilson | Schott |
| Pas Redouble | Camille Saint-Saens/Franckenpohl | Shawnee |
| Passo Doppio Sinfonico | Leonardo Marino/Nicholas Falcone | Southern |
| Pride of the Wolverines | John Philip Sousa/Frederick Fennell | Sam Fox |
| Purple Carnival, The | Harry L. Alford/Frank Erickson | G. Schirmer |
| Purple Pageant, The | Karl L. King/John Paynter | Barnhouse |
| Radetzky March | Johann Strauss Jr. | C. Fischer |
| Rifle Regiment March, The | John Philip Sousa | C. Fischer |
| Southerner, The | Russell Alexander/G.C. Bainum | Barnhouse |
| Stars and Stripes Forever | John Philip Sousa/Brion & Schissel | Barnhouse |
| Valdres | Johannes Hanssen/G.C. Bainum | Boosey & Hawkes |

# Appendix B—
# Suggested Orchestra Literature

## Grade 1

*(Note: all in this grade level for strings only)*

| Title | Composer/Arranger | Publisher |
|---|---|---|
| Apollo Suite | Merle Isaac | Highland/Etling |
| Cripple Creek | Siennicki | Highland/Etling |
| Dance of the Tumblers | Rimsky-Korsakov/Sandra Dackow | Ludwig |
| Dona Nobis Pacem | Elliott Del Borgo | Belwin-Mills |
| Frog In A Tree | Siennicki | Highland/Etling |
| Kathleen Album | James Brown | Galaxy |
| Little Classic Suite | Akers | C. Fischer |
| Little Fugue | Handel/Edmund Siennicki | Highland/Etling |
| Loch Lomond | Noah Klauss | Kendor |
| Sailor's Song | Grieg/Myers | Lake State |
| St. Anthony Chorale | Haydn/Sandra Dackow | Ludwig |
| Sinfonietta for Strings | Spinosa/Rusch | Kjos |
| Three Baroque Chorales | Philip Gordon | Kendor |
| Two by Two | Fred Hubbell | Highland/Etling |
| Two Pieces | Bartok/Robert Frost | Lake State |
| Two Tone Pictures | Philip Gordon | Skidmore |
| Ukrainian Folk Song | Sandra Dackow | Ludwig |
| Variations on A Ground | Shapiro | Kjos |
| Village Dance | Rameau/Gordon | Kendor |
| Wexford Circle | Elliott Del Borgo | Kendor |

## Grade 2

*(Note: all in this grade level for strings only)*

| Title | Composer/Arranger | Publisher |
|---|---|---|
| Air and Dance | M. Daniels | Kjos |
| Air and Pizzicato-Staccato | Arthur Frankenpohl | Kendor |
| American Folk Song Suite #2 | Merle Isaac | Highland/Etling |
| Andante and Allegro | Mozart/Isaac | Highland/Etling |
| Baroque Suite #1 | Merle Isaac | Highland/Etling |
| Bohemian Suite | Vaclav Nelhybel | Christopher |
| Belvedere Suite | Merle Isaac | Highland/Etling |
| Caprice for String Orchestra | Robert Frost | Southern |
| Czech Folk Song Suite | Merle Isaac | Highland/Etling |
| Chorale and March | Bach/Siennicki | Highland/Etling |
| Dance Suite for Strings | Maurice Whitney | Warner |
| Fumble Fingers | John Caponegro | Kendor |
| Gavotte | Lully/Isaac | Wynn |
| Handel Suite | Kreichbaum | Kjos |
| Hornpipe | Robert Frost | Southern |
| Little Bartok Suite, A | Bartok/Gordon | C. Fischer |
| Little Fugue | Handel/Edmund Siennicki | Highland/Etling |
| Minuet and Trio | Robert Frost | Kendor |
| Mock Morris Dance | Wesley Sontag | G. Schirmer |

| | | |
|---|---|---|
| Musette and Minuet | J.S. Bach/Siennicki | Ludwig |
| Petite Suite for Strings | Paul Whear | Ludwig |
| Petite Tango | C.B. Kriechbaum | Highland/Etling |
| Quinto-Quarto Suite | Merle Isaac | Highland/Etling |
| Set of Four, A | Wesley Sontag | Sam Fox |
| Slovakian Dances | Al Cechvala | Kendor |
| Symphony No. 14 (1st mvt.) | F. J. Haydn/P. Gordon | Kendor |
| Suite for Strings | Elliott Del Borgo | Kendor |
| Two Moods | Philip Gordon | Elkan-Vogel |
| Two Pieces | Bartok/Robert Frost | Lake State |
| Ukrainian Folk Songs | Sandra Dackow | Ludwig |
| Walking Basses | Merle Isaac | Highland/Etling |

# Grade 3

*(\* = for string orchestra)*

| Title | Composer/Arranger | Publisher |
|---|---|---|
| Adagio and Allegro | Corelli/J. Frederick Muller | Ludwig |
| Adagio Cantabile * | Beethoven/McLeod | Kendor |
| Air for Strings * | Norman Dello Joio | Marks |
| Air from "Peasant Cantata" | J.S. Bach/Philip Gordon | Kendor |
| Allegro | Stamitz/Edmund Siennicki | Highland/Etling |
| Andante, from Sym. in G Major | Haydn/Merle Isaac | Carl Fischer |
| Baroque Suite #1 * | J.S. Bach/Merle Isaac | Highland/Etling |
| Bratislava | J. Holesovsky | Presser |
| Catskill Legend | Paul Whear | Elkan-Vogel |
| Chorale Fantasy | William Presser | Highland/Etling |
| Concertino in G Major | Sammartini/J. Frederick Muller | Ludwig |
| Concerto Grosso, Op. 6, No. 1 * | G.F. Handel/Sandra Dackow | Ludwig |
| Dance of the Tumblers | Rimsky-Korsakov/Sandra Dackow | Ludwig |
| Dance Suite * | Mozart/Johnson | Kjos |
| Danse Macabre | Saint-Saëns/Merle Isaac | Carl Fischer |
| Divertimento in G Major | Haydn/Leroy Walter | Lydian |
| English Suite, An | H. Purcell/Scarmolin | Ludwig |
| Exultate Jubilate Alleluia | W. A. Mozart/Merle Isaac | Highland/Etling |
| Festique | M.L. Daniels | Ludwig |
| Fitzwilliam Suite | Philip Gordon | Marks |
| Gift, The | Hofeldt | Kjos |
| Good Daughter Overture, The | Piccini/Scarmolin | Ludwig |
| Grand March, from "Aida" | Verdi/Merle Isaac | Belwin-Mills |
| Hungarian Dance No. 4 * | Brahms/Merle Isaac | Highland/Etling |
| Hungarian Dance No. 6 | Brahms/Merle Isaac | Highland/Etling |
| Kamarinskaya | Glinka/Barnes | Tempo |
| Little Baroque Suite | Gordon | Carl Fischer |
| Little Bartok Suite, A | Bartok/Gordon | Carl Fischer |
| Lullaby | William Hofeldt | Kjos |
| Marcello Suite * | Marcello/Siennicki | Highland/Etling |
| March and Sonatina | W.A. Mozart/Merle Isaac | Highland/Etling |
| Minuetto and Country Dance * Isaac | Beethoven/Merle Highland/Etling | |
| Overture Russe | Merle Isaac | Carl Fischer |
| Passacaglia | Vaclav Nelhybel | Colombo |

| | | |
|---|---|---|
| Prelude and Polka | Arthur Frankenpohl | Shawnee Press |
| Prelude from Cantata 156 | J.S. Bach/Siennicki | Highland/Etling |
| Queen Anne Suite | J. Eccles/Gordon | Alfred |
| Rhosymedre | R. Vaughan Williams/Foster | Galaxy Music |
| Russian Chorale and Overture | Tschaikowsky/Merle Isaac | Carl Fischer |
| Serenade for String Orchestra * | Norman Leyden | Plymouth Music |
| Sinfonia | Scarlatti/Errante | Highland/Etling |
| Sinfonia in D * | J.C. Bach/Sandra Dackow | Ludwig |
| Sinfonia in D | Elliott Del Borgo | Highland/Etling |
| Sinfonia in D | David Heinichen | Wingert-Jones |
| Slavonic Dance No. 8 | Antonin Dvorak/Merle Isaac | Highland/Etling |
| Sleigh Ride | W.A. Mozart/Stone | Boosey & Hawkes |
| Suite for Strings * | Elliot Del Borgo | Kendor |
| Symphony in D Major | Sammartini/Scarmolin | Ludwig |
| Theme from the Moldau | Smetana/Robert Frost | Kendor |
| Three Bagatelles | Tommy J. Fry | Southern |
| Three Rustic Dances | von Weber/Gordon | Kendor |
| Yorkshire Ballad | James Barnes | Southern |

# Grade 4

*(\* = for string orchestra)*

| Title | Composer/Arranger | Publisher |
|---|---|---|
| Academic Festival Overture | J. Brahms/Mueller | Kjos |
| Ballet Parisien | Offenbach/Merle Isaac | Carl Fischer |
| Boyce Suite, A | Boyce/Benoy | Oxford |
| Brevard Sketches | Elliott Del Borgo | Kjos |
| Canon for Strings * | Pachelbel/Ades | Shawnee |
| Capriccio Italien | Tschaikowsky/Merle Isaac | Highland/Etling |
| Capriol Suite * | Warlock | Curwen |
| Chaconne in E Minor | Buxtehude/Whitney | Kjos |
| Divertimento for String Orchestra * | Joseph Baber | Oxford |
| Fantasia on "Greensleeves" | Vaughan Williams/Stone | Oxford |
| Farandole, from "L'Arlesienne Suite #2 | Bizet/Stone | Boosey & Hawkes |
| Fidelio Overture | Beethoven/Merle Isaac | Wynn |
| Finale, from Fifth Symphony | Beethoven/Woodhouse | Boosey & Hawkes |
| Great Gate of Kiev, The | Moussorgsky/Stone | Oxford |
| Hatikvah | Ovanin | Ludwig |
| Il Re Pastore | W.A. Mozart/Muller | Kjos |
| Iphegenia En Aulis | Gluck | Carl Fischer or Kalmus |
| Jesu, Joy of Man's Desiring | J.S. Bach/Roberts | Carl Fischer |
| Jubilee | Ron Nelson | Boosey & Hawkes |
| La Pinta Giardiniera | W. A. Mozart | Carl Fischer |
| Lancaster Overture | Paul Whear | Ludwig |
| March of the Boyars | Halvorsen/Merle Isaac | Highland/Etling |
| March to the Scaffold | H. Berlioz/Carter | Oxford |
| Mighty Fortress, A | Vaclav Nelhybel | Kerby |
| Movement for Orchestra | Vaclav Nelhybel | Colombo |
| Music for the Royal Fireworks | Handel/Stone | Novello |

| | | |
|---|---|---|
| Night in Mexico | Paul Creston | Shawnee |
| Ode to Freedom | Robert Washburn | Oxford |
| Overture, "Nabucco" | Verdi/Sandra Dackow | Ludwig |
| Overture, "Rienzi" | Wagner/Sandra Dackow | Ludwig |
| Overture and Allegro | Couperin/Milhaud | Elkan-Vogel |
| Overture in C Minor | Franz Schubert | Luck's |
| Overture in D Minor | Handel/Merle Isaac | Highland/Etling |
| Overture to "Samson" | Handel/Muller | Ludwig |
| Palladio | Karl Jenkins | Boosey & Hawkes |
| Pavane, Op. 50 | Faure/Gearhart | Shawnee |
| Petrouchka | Stravinsky/Merle Isaac | Belwin |
| Praeludium | J.S. Bach/Gearhart | Shawnee |
| Prelude | Shostakovich | Highland/Etling |
| Prelude, from "Holberg Suite" | *Grieg | Kalmus |
| Romeo and Juliet | Tschaikowsky/Muller | Kjos |
| Russian Sailors Dance | Gliere/Merle Isaac | Carl Fischer |
| Saint Lawrence Overture | Robert Washburn | Boosey & Hawkes |
| Serenade for Strings * | Robert Washburn | Oxford |
| Sheep May Safely Graze | J.S. Bach/L. Cailliet | Boosey & Hawkes |
| Shepherd's Hey | Grainger/Alshin | Alfred |
| Short Overture for Strings * | Jean Berger | Kjos |
| Sinfonia in Bb | J.S. Bach/Muller | Kjos |
| Slavonic Dance No. 3 | Dvorak/Merle Isaac | Highland/Etling |
| Slavonic Dance, Op. 46, No. 8 | Dvorak/Stone | Boosey & Hawkes |
| Suite for Strings * | Robert Washburn | Oxford |
| Suite from Tannhauser | R. Wagner/Merle Isaac | Highland/Etling |
| Symphony in D Major | Sammartini/Scarmolin | Ludwig |
| Symphony No. 2 (mvt. 1) | Borodin/Merle Isaac | Highland/Etling |
| Three Pieces for Orchestra | Robert Jager | Elkan-Vogel |
| Variations on A Theme/ | | |
| Thomas Tallis | Ralph Vaughan Williams | Luck's |
| Vocalise, Op. 34 | Rachmaninoff/Gearhart | Shawnee Press |
| William Bryd Suite | Gordon Jacob | Boosey & Hawkes |
| Youth Overture | Emma Lou Diemer | Belwin |

# Grade 5

*(\* = for string orchestra)*

| Title | Composer/Arranger | Publisher |
|---|---|---|
| Abduction from the Seraglio | Mozart/Merle Isaac | Belwin |
| Alceste, Overture | Gluck | Kalmus |
| Arioso, from Cantata No. 1568 | | J.S. Bach/Fry |
| Carl Fischer | | |
| Brook Green Suite * | Gustav Holst | G. Schirmer |
| Capriccio Espagnol | Rimsky-Korsakov | Boosey & Hawkes |
| Catskill Legend Overture | Paul Whear | Ludwig |
| Chaconne in E Minor * | Buxtehude/Hause | Shawnee |
| Choral Prelude, Sleepers Awake | | J.S. |
| Bach/Ormandy | Boosey & Hawkes | |
| Choreography * | Norman Dello Joio | Marks |
| Concerto Grosso, Op. 6, No. | | |
| 1 or 6 * | G.F. Handel | Schott |
| Dance Rhythms, Op. 58 | Riegger | Associated |

| | | |
|---|---|---|
| Danse Macabre, Op. 40 | Saint-Saens | Kalmus |
| Egmont Overture | Beethoven | Kalmus |
| Elegy | Robert Washburn | Boosey & Hawkes |
| Elsa's Procession, from | | |
| "Lohengrin" | Wagner/Campbell | Kalmus |
| Festival Prelude, A | Alfred Reed | Marks |
| Festival Overture | Robert Washburn | Oxford |
| Festive Overture | Dmitri Shostakovich | Kalmus |
| Francesca Da Rimini | Tschaikowsky/Muller | Kjos |
| Fugue in G Minor, "The | | |
| Little Fugue" | J.S. Bach/Cailliet | Carl Fischer |
| Galop, from "The Comedians" | Kabalevsky | Kalmus |
| Good Daughter Overture, The | Piccini/Scarmolin | Ludwig |
| Hoedown, from "Rodeo" | Aaron Copland | Boosey & Hawkes |
| Hungarian Dances | Brahms | Bourne |
| Intermezzo, from "Hary Janos | | |
| Suite" | Kodaly | Boosey & Hawkes |
| L'Arlessiene, Suite No. 2 | Bizet | Kalmus |
| Last Spring, The * | Grieg | Kalmus |
| Marche Militaire Francaise | Saint-Saens/Merle Isaac | Carl Fischer |
| Marche Slav | Tschaikowsky | Kalmus |
| Moorside Suite, A | Gustav Holst | Boosey & Hawkes |
| Outdoor Overture | Aaron Copland | Boosey & Hawkes |
| Overture to "The Impresario" | Mozart | Carl Fischer |
| Pelleas and Melisande | Faure | Kalmus |
| Polovetsian Dances | Borodin | Kalmus |
| Prelude in E Minor * | J.S. Bach/Stokowski | Kalmus |
| Preludio for String Orchestra * | Paul Whear | Ludwig |
| Psalm and Fugue * | Alan Hovhaness | C.F. Peters |
| Psalm for Strings * | Walter Hartley | Presser |
| Rosamunde Overture | Schubert/Moses | Carl Fischer |
| Rumanian Folk Dances | Bela Bartok | Boosey & Hawkes |
| St. Lawrence Overture | Washburn | Boosey & Hawkes |
| Symphony No. 5 | Tschaikowsky | Kalmus |
| Symphony No. 25 in G Minor, | | |
| K. 183 | Mozart/Matesky | Highland/Etling |
| Three Piece for Orchestra | Robert Jager | Elkan-Vogel |
| Titus Overture | Mozart/Isaac | Highland/Etling |
| Toccata | Frescobaldi/Kindler | Belwin |
| Variations On A Shaker | | |
| Melody | Aaron Copland | Boosey & Hawkes |
| Waltz, from "Billy The Kid" | Aaron Copland | Boosey & Hawkes |

## *Grade 6*

*( * = for string orchestra)*

| Title | Composer/Arranger | Publisher |
|---|---|---|
| Academic Festival Overture, | | |
| Op. 80 | Brahms | Kalmus |
| Adagio for Strings * | Samuel Barber | G. Schirmer |
| American Salute | Morton Gould | Belwin/CPP |
| Bacchanale, from "Samson & | | |
| Delilah" | Saint-Saens/Reibold | Sam Fox |
| Candide, Overture to | Bernstein | G. Schirmer |

| | | |
|---|---|---|
| Capriccio Italien | Tschaikowsky | Kalmus |
| Carnival Overture | Dvorak | Boosey & Hawkes |
| Colas Breugnon Overture | Kabalevsky | Kalmus |
| Concerto for Orchestra in D Minor | Handel/Ormandy | C. Fischer |
| Concerto Grosso, Op. 6, No. 8 * | Corelli/May | Schott |
| Die Fledermaus, Overture | Strauss | Kalmus or C.F. Peters |
| Die Meistersinger Overture | Richard Wagner | Kalmus |
| Don Giovanni, Overture to | Mozart | Boosey & Hawkes |
| Donna Diana Overture | Reznicek | Kalmus |
| Fidelio, Overture | Beethoven | Kalmus |
| Fingal's Cave ("The Hebrides") | Mendelssohn | C. Fischer or Kalmus |
| Holberg Suite * | Grieg | C.F. Peters |
| Hungarian March | Berlioz | Boosey & Hawkes |
| Impressario Overture, The | Mozart | Kalmus |
| Introit for Strings * | Vincent Persichetti | Elkan-Vogel |
| Les Preludes | Liszt | Kalmus |
| Little Suite for Strings * | Nielsen | Kalmus |
| Merry Wives of Windsor, Overture | Nicolai | Boosey & Hawkes |
| Nabucco, Overture | Verdi | Kalmus |
| Night On Bald Mountain, A | Moussorgsky/Sopkin | C. Fischer |
| Oberon, Overture to | Weber | Kalmus |
| Overture for Stings * | Gordon Jacob | Oxford |
| Polovetsian Dances | Borodin | Kalmus |
| Prometheus, Overture | Beethoven | Kalmus |
| Roman Carnival Overture | Berlioz | Kalmus |
| Roumanian Rhapsody No. 1 | Enesco | Kalmus |
| Russian Easter Overture | Rimsky-Korsakov | Kalmus |
| Russlan and Ludmilla Overture | Glinka | Bourne |
| Semiramide Overture | Rossini | Kalmus |
| Serenade, Op. 48 * | Tschaikowsky | Kalmus |
| Serenade for String Orchestra, Op. 20 * | Elgar | Kalmus |
| Soirees Musicales | Britten | Boosey & Hawkes |
| St. Paul Suite * | Gustav Holst | G. Schirmer |
| Suite for Strings * | Leos Janacek | International |
| Symphony No. 1 | Brahms | Kalmus |
| Symphony No. 2 | Vittorio Giannini | Chappell |
| Symphony No. 2 | Sibelius | Kalmus |
| Symphony No. 4 ("Italian") | Mendelssohn | Kalmus |
| Symphony No. 5 ("Reformation") | Mendelssohn | Kalmus |
| Symphony No. 6 ("Pastorale") | Beethoven | Kalmus |
| Symphony No. 9 ("New World") | Dvorak | Kalmus |
| Symphony No. 40 in G Minor | Mozart | C.F. Peters or Kalmus |
| Symphony No. 94 | Haydn | Boosey & Hawkes |
| Toccata and Fugue in D Minor | J.S. Bach/Cailliet | C. Fischer |
| Vocalise | Rachmaninoff | Boosey & Hawkes |

# Appendix C: Recommended Reading for Music Educators

Abeles, Harold; Hoffer, Charles; and Klotman, Robert (1984). *Foundations of Music Education.* New York: Schirmer Books.

Abrahams, Frank and Head, Paul (1998). *Case Studies in Music Education.* Chicago: GIA Publications, Inc.

Bennett, William (1992). *The De-Valuing of America.* New York: Summit Pub.

Blocher, Larry R. and Miles, Richard B. (1998). *Scheduling and Teaching Music.* Chicago: GIA Publications, Inc.

Bloom, Allan (1987). *The Closing of the American Mind.* New York: Simon and Schuster.

Boston, Bruce (1995). *With One Voice: A Report from the 1994 Summit on Music Education.* Reston, VA: Music Educators National Conference.

Casey, Joseph L. (1993). *Teaching Techniques and Insights for Instrumental Music Educators (rev.).* Chicago: GIA.

Colwell, Richard (1995). Will voluntary national standards fix the potholes of arts education? *Arts Education Policy Review,* 96/5 (May/June).

Covey, Stephen R. (1990). *The Seven Habits of Highly Effective People: Restoring the Character Ethic.* New York: Fireside

Covey, Stephen R. (1992). *Principle-Centered Leadership.* New York: Fireside.

Covey, Stephen R.; Merrill, A. Roger; Merrill, Rebecca R. (1994). *First Things First.* New York: Fireside.

Csikszentmihalyi, Mihaly, and Robinson, Rick E. (1990). *The Art of Seeing.* Malibu, CA: J. Paul Getty Museum and the Getty Center for Education in the Arts.

Csikszentmihalyi, Mihaly, et al. (1993). *Talented Teenagers: The Roots of Success and Failure.* New York: Cambridge University Press.

Eisner, Elliot W. (1982). *Cognition and the Curriculum.* New York: Longman.

Eisner, Elliot W. (1992). *The federal reform of schools: looking for the silver bullet.* Phi Delta Kappan, May, 722-723.

Eisner, Elliot W. (1995). *Standards for American schools: help or hindrance?* Phi Delta Kappan. June 1995 (758-764).

Elliott, David J. (1995). *Music Matters: A New Philosophy of Music Education.* New York: Oxford University Press.

Ellul, Jacques (1990). *The Technological Bluff.* Grand Rapids, MI: Wm. B. Eerdmans Publishing Co.

Fuchs, Peter P. (1969). *The Psychology of Conducting.* New York: MCA.

Gardner, Howard (1993). *Frames of Mind (2nd ed.).* New York: Basic Books.

Gardner, Howard (1993). *Multiple Intelligences: The Theory in Practice.* New York: Basic Books.

Gardner, Howard (1995). *Reflections on multiple intelligences: myths and messages.* Phi Delta Kappan. (Sept., 200-209).

Gardner, Howard (1991). *The Unschooled Mind: How Children Think and How Schools Should Teach.* New York: Basic Books.

Garofalo, Robert (1983). *Blueprint for Band.* Ft. Lauderdale, FL: Meredith Music Publishers.

Ginott, Haim (1972). *Teacher and Child: A Book for Parents and Teachers.* New York: The Macmillan Company.

Gordon, Edwin (1988). *Learning Sequences in Music.* Chicago: G.I.A. Publications.

Gordon, Edwin (1971). *The Psychology of Music Teaching.* Englewood Cliffs, NJ: Prentice-Hall.

Green, Elizabeth A.H. (1992). *The Modern Conductor (5th ed.).* Englewood Cliffs, NJ: Prentice-Hall.

Green, Elizabeth A.H. (1975). *The Conductor and His Score.* Englewood Cliffs, NJ: Prentice-Hall.

Green, Elizabeth A.H. (1987). *The Dynamic Orchestra.* Englewood Cliffs, NJ: Prentice-Hall.

Holz, Emil and Jacobi, Roger (1966). *Teaching Band Instruments to Beginners.* Englewood Cliffs, NJ: Prentice-Hall, Inc.

Keene, James A. (1982). *A History of Music Education in the United States.* Hanover, NH: University Press of New England.

Kohn, Alfie (1992). *No Contest: The Case Against Competition (revised ed.).* New York: Houghton Mifflin Co.

Kohn, Alfie (1993). *Punished by Rewards: The Trouble with Gold Stars, Incentive Plans, A's, Praise, and Other Bribes.* New York: Houghton Mifflin Co.

Lautzenheiser, Tim (1992). *The Art of Successful Teaching: A Blend of Content and Context.* Chicago: GIA Publications, Inc.

Lehman, Paul, ed. (1994). *The School Music Program: A New Vision.* Reston, VA: Music Educators National Conference.

Leonhard, Charles and House, Robert W. (1972). *Foundations and Principles of Music Education (2nd ed.).* New York: McGraw-Hill Book Company.

Lisk, Edward S. (1991). *The Creative Director: Alternative Rehearsal Techniques (3rd ed.).* Ft. Lauderdale, FL: Meredith Music Publishers.

Littrell, David and Racin, Laura R. (Eds.) (2002). *Teaching Music through Performance in Orchestra.* Chicago: GIA Publications, Inc.

Mark, Michael (1984). *Contemporary Music Education (2nd ed.).* New York: Schirmer Books.

Mark, Michael L. and Gary, Charles L. (1999). *A History of American Music Education (2nd ed.).* Reston, VA: MENC.

McBeth, W. Francis (1972). *Effective Performance of Band Music.* San Antonio, TX: Southern Music Co.

Miles, Richard B. and Blocher, Larry R. (1996). *Block Scheduling: Implications for Music Education.* Chicago: GIA Publications, Inc.

Miles, Richard (ed.) (1997). *Teaching Music through Performance in Band (Vol. 1).* Chicago: GIA Publications, Inc.

Miles, Richard (ed.) (1998). *Teaching Music through Performance in Band (Vol. 2).* Chicago: GIA Publications, Inc.

Miles, Richard (ed.) (2000). *Teaching Music through Performance in Band (Vol. 3).* Chicago: GIA Publications, Inc.

Miles, Richard and Dvorak, Thomas (eds.) (2001). *Teaching Music through Performance in Beginning Band.* Chicago: GIA Publications, Inc.

Moody, William J. (ed.) (1990). *Artistic Intelligences: Implications for Education.* New York: Teachers College Press.

(The) National Commission on Excellence in Education (1983). *A Nation At Risk: The Imperative for Educational Reform.* U.S. Government Printing Office.

*Opportunity-to-Learn Standard for Music Instruction (1994).* Reston, VA: Music Educators National Conference.

*Performance Standards for Music: Grades PreK-12 (1996).* Reston, VA: Music Educators National Conference.

Schleuter Stanley L. (1997). *A Sound Approach to Teaching Instrumentalist (2nd ed.).* New York: Schirmer Books.

Suzuki, Shinichi (1996). Nurtured By Love: *The Classic Approach to Talent Education* (Waltraud Suzuki, Trans.) *(2nd ed.).* Miami, FL: Summy-Birchard.

Walters, Darrel L, and Taggart, Cynthia Crump (ed.) (1989). *Readings in Music Learning Theory.* Chicago, GIA Publications, Inc.

Whitwell, David (1993). *Music as a Language: A New Philosophy of Music Education.* Northridge, CA: WINDS.

Williamson, John E. and Neidig, Kenneth L., ed. (1998). *Rehearsing the Band.* Cloudcroft, NM: Neidig Services.

# Appendix D: Internet Sites for Instrumental Music Educators

(Note: This is not an exhaustive list. Many sites have links to other sites.)

## *Composers and Publishers*

C. Alan Music Publications: http://www.c-alanpublications.com
Alfred Publishing Co., Inc.: www.alfred.com
Amstel Music (Netherlands): http://www.euronet.nl/~amsmusic/
Arrangers Publishing Company: http://www.ArrPubCo.com
Boosey & Hawkes publishers: http://www.ny.boosey.com
Derek Bourgeois (composer): http://www.tramuntana.demon.co.uk/
Carl Fischer Music Publisher: http://www.carlfischer.com
Curnow Music Press: http://www.despub.com/Curnow.htm#TOC
De Haske Music Publishers: http://www.dehaske.com
Julie Giroux: http://juliegiroux.www2.50megs.com
David Holsinger: http://www.davidrholsinger.com/music.htm
Hal Leonard Music: http://www.halleonard.com
Hindsley Transcriptions: http://www.hindsleytranscriptions.com
Honey Rock Publishing (percussion): http://www.bedford.net/honeyrock/Index.htm
Edwin F. Kalmus & Co., Inc.: http://www.kalmus-music.com/
GIA Publications: http://www.giamusic.com
Great Lake Music Enterprises, Inc. (recordings & publications): http://www.great-lakesmusic.com/index.html
Kendor Music, Inc.: http://www.kendormusic.com
Kjos Music Company: http://www.kjos.com
Ludwig Music Publishing Co.: http://www.ludwigmusic.com
Manhattan Beach Music: http://members.aol.com/mbmband/
Masters Music Publications, Inc.: http://www.masters-music.com
Meredith Music Publications: http://www.meredithmusic.com
MMB Music, Inc.:http://www.mmbmusic.com
MSB Publishing Co.: http://members.aol.com/MSBPUBCO/index.html
Musica Propria (features music of Julie Giroux): http://www.musicapropria.com
RBC Music Publishers, Inc.: http://www.rbcmusic.com
G. Schirmer, Inc. (includes a large links page): http://www.schirmer.com
Shawnee Press, Inc.: http://www.shawneepress.com
David E. Smith Publications (sacred instrumental music): http://www.despub.com
John Philip Sousa Home Page (lots of information): http://www.dws.org/sousa
Sousa site: http://www.dws.org/sousa/works.htm
Southern Music Co. (band & orchestra music): http://www.southernmusic.com
Stormworks (some free music!): http://www.stormworks.net
Theodore Presser Co.: http://www.presser.com/
Thompson Editions, Inc. (solo & chamber music, solo accompaniments): http://www.thompsonedition.com
TRN Music Publishers (free tapes): http://www.trnmusic.com
Wingert-Jones Music: http://www.wjmusic.com

## *Music Retailers*

Luck's Music Library (orchestral music): http://www.lucksmusic.com/index.html
Malecki Music, Inc.: http://www.maleckimusic.com
Mannerino's Sheet Music (Cincinnati, OH): http://www.mannerinos.com

Penders Music Co. (Denton, TX): http://www.penders.com
J.W. Pepper & Son, Inc.: http://www.jwpepper.com
Shattinger Music Co. (St. Louis, MO): http://shattingermusic.com

## Music Organizations

American Bandmasters Association: http://americanbandmasters.org
American Harp Society: http://www.harpsociety.org
American Music Conference (advocacy, etc.): http://www.amc-music.com
American School Band Directors Association: http://www.asbda.com
American String Teachers Association: http://www.astaweb.com/index.html
American Symphony Orchestra League: http://www.symphony.org
ASCAP: http://www.ascap.com
Association of Concert Bands: http://www.acbands.org
College Band Directors National Association: http://www.cbdna.org
Conductors Guild: http://www.conductorsguild.org
International Association for Jazz Education: http://www.iaje.org
International Clarinet Association: http://www.clarinet.org
International Double Reed Society: http://idrs.colorado.edu
International Horn Society: http://www.hornsociety.org
International Society of Bassists: http://www.ISBworldoffice.com
International Trombone Association: http://www.ita-web.org
International Trumpet Guild: http://www.trumpetguild.org
International Tuba and Euphonium Association: http://www.iteaonline.org
MENC—The National Association for Music Education: http://www.menc.org
The Midwest Clinic—An International Band and Orchestra Conference:
    http://www.midwestclinic.com
Music Publishers Association (a list of publishers and valuable information about copyright
    law): http://www.mpa.org
National Band Association: http://www.nationalbandassoc.org
National Flute Association Inc.: http://nfaonline.org
OrchList (orchestra links): http://www.artsinfo.com/artslists/orchlist/index.html
Percussive Arts Society: http://www.pas.org
Smithsonian Jazz: http://www.smithsonianjazz.org
Suzuki Association of the Americas, Inc.: http://www.suzukiassociation.org
Talent Education Research Institute: http://www.suzukimethod.or.jp/E_mthd121.html
The Viola Web Site: http://www.viola.com
Violin Society of America: http://www.vsa.to
World Association for Symphonic Bands and Ensembles: http://www.wasbe.org

## Performing Ensembles

American Military Band Links: http://www.imt.net/~tmbc/bandlink/index.html
Community Band and Orchestra Home Pages: http://www.boerger.org/c-
    m/commother.shtml
Dallas Wind Symphony: http://www.dws.org
Tokyo Kosei Wind Orchestra: http://www.tkwo.jp/indEnl.html
U.S. Air Force Band: http://www.bolling.af.mil/band
U.S. Army Band: http://www.army.mil/armyband
U.S. Marine Band: http://www.marineband.usmc.mil/
U.S. Navy Band: http://www.navyband.navy.mil

## *Resources*

About conductors (jokes): http://people.clemson.edu/~alevin/conduct/

BandChat Online (discussion): http://www.band-chat.org

Bandworld Magazine: http://bandworld.jeffnet.org/

Community Music Mailing List (with lots of links: http://www.boerger.org/c-m/

Gordon Institute for Music Learning: http://www.giml.org

Harvard Project Zero: http://www.pz.harvard.edu

The History of Music Education site: http://www.utc.edu/~wlee/

Indiana University School of Music Library (links): http://www.music.indiana.edu/music_resources

International Society for Music Education: http://www.isme.org/index.shtml

K-12 Resources for Music Educators:
   http://www.isd77.k12.mn.us/resources/staffpages/shirk/k12.music.html

Mark Custom Recording Services, Inc. (source of recordings):
   http://www.markcustom.com

Mozart Effect Resource Center: http://www.mozarteffect.com

Music Education Curriculum Links: http://www.howard.k12.md.us/connections/musick12.html#top

Music Education links (over 500): http://news.cbel.com/education_music

Music Education Madness Site (articles & information): http://www.musiceducationmadness.com/

Music Education Resource Links: http://www.cs.uop.edu~cpiper/musiced.html

Music Links: http://www2.coastalnet.com/~p8d3m8gt/musiclinks.html

Music Matters (David Elliott's homepage): http://www.utoronto.ca/musicmat/

Program notes for bands/wind ensembles:
   http://www.windband.org/foothill/pgm_note.htm

Research Perspectives In Music Education: http://music.arts.usf.edu/rpme.htm

Research Studies in Music Education: http://www.arts.uwa.edu.au/CIRCME/rsme/research.htm

Resources for Instrumental Music Educators (book/websites):
   http://www.bdsd.k12.wi.us/ms/boor/resproj.htm

School Band and Orchestra Magazine: http://www.sbomagazine.com/

University of Illinois Bands Resources List: http://www.bands.uiuc.edu/library/resources.asp

Walking Frog Records (Reference recordings for band works):
   http://www.walkingfrog.com

Wind Ensemble Repertoire list: http://www.geocities.com/Vienna/Opera/2716/

# Index